Blender
FOR
DUMMIES®

by Jason van Gumster

WILEY

Wiley Publishing, Inc.

Blender For Dummies®

Published by
Wiley Publishing, Inc.
111 River Street
Hoboken, NJ 07030-5774

www.wiley.com

Copyright © 2009 by Wiley Publishing, Inc., Indianapolis, Indiana

Published by Wiley Publishing, Inc., Indianapolis, Indiana

Published simultaneously in Canada

For general information on our other products and services, please contact our Customer Care Department within the U.S. at 877-762-2974, outside the U.S. at 317-572-3993, or fax 317-572-4002.

For technical support, please visit www.wiley.com/techsupport.

Wiley also publishes its books in a variety of electronic formats. Some content that appears in print may not be available in electronic books.

Library of Congress Control Number: 2008942698

ISBN: 978-0-470-40018-0

Manufactured in the United States of America

10 9 8 7 6 5 4

WILEY

About the Author

Jason van Gumster got into animation when he realized that he wanted to create movies . . . but that actors are generally intolerant of having pianos dropped on them. Using open source tools at nearly every step, Jason has produced animations and visual effects for television, film, and video games in his official capacity as a Production Monkey for Hand Turkey Studios, the company he helped start in 2005. A Blender user since 1998, Jason has given numerous live demonstrations and workshops on Blender internationally and his Advanced Blender Fluids training DVD from cmiVFX is recognized as one of the best learning resources for Blender's integrated fluid simulator. In January of 2008, Jason worked with the Blender Foundation to assemble the Blender Certification Review Board and lead the launch of the Blender Foundation Certified Trainer (BFCT) program. He also periodically writes for BlenderNation (www.blendernation.com), the primary news Web site for Blender users. Based in Richmond, Virginia, Jason can often be found in cafés and diners drawing, espousing the virtues of open source software, or catching confused looks from strangers as he contorts his body to better visualize a scene he's animating.

Dedication

To my friends and family, which I consider one and the same. You tolerate my eccentricity, encourage my success, and give me a swift kick to the pants when I'm completely full of it. I couldn't appreciate you more.

Author's Acknowledgments

My first thanks go to Blender's team of developers, lead by our "benevolent dictator," Ton Roosendaal. Without them, Blender would never exist in the state that it does today. Of course, equally deserving of gratitude is the overall Blender community, without which Blender would never have been made open source.

Thanks, also, to everyone at Wiley, particularly my acquisitions editor, Kyle Looper, and my project editor, Linda Morris. They are refined professionals, and I'm grateful for their ability to keep me on task and (mostly) on schedule. I'd also like to thank Bassam Kurdali for agreeing to work as the book's technical editor. He's one of the most knowledgeable and talented members of the Blender community, and I hate to think of how little sense this book would've made without his input.

I'd also like to give a quick thank-you to the first human who learned to filter water through coffee grounds. Without your precious discovery, I'm certain that not just this book, but many of my accomplishments would've never occurred.

And finally, I'd like to thank my fellow Hand Turkeys, Warren Belfield and Roberto Rubet. Not only are these guys talented artists and business partners, but they are definitely true friends whose feedback (and insults) I value greatly.

Publisher's Acknowledgments

We're proud of this book; please send us your comments through our online registration form located at http://dummies.custhelp.com. For other comments, please contact our Customer Care Department within the U.S. at 877-762-2974, outside the U.S. at 317-572-3993, or fax 317-572-4002.

Some of the people who helped bring this book to market include the following:

Acquisitions, Editorial, and Media Development

Project Editor: Linda Morris

Acquisitions Editor: Kyle Looper

Copy Editor: Linda Morris

Technical Editor: Bassam Kurdali

Editorial Manager: Jodi Jensen

Media Development Project Manager: Laura Moss-Hollister

Media Development Assistant Project Manager: Jenny Swisher

Media Development Assistant Producers: Angela Denny, Josh Frank, Shawn Patrick, and Kit Malone

Editorial Assistant: Amanda Foxworth

Sr. Editorial Assistant: Cherie Case

Cartoons: Rich Tennant (www.the5thwave.com)

Composition Services

Project Coordinator: Katherine Key

Layout and Graphics: Reuben W. Davis, Joyce Haughey, Melissa K. Jester, Sarah Phillipart, Christin Swinford, Ronald Terry

Proofreader: Broccoli Information Management

Indexer: Broccoli Information Management

Publishing and Editorial for Technology Dummies

Richard Swadley, Vice President and Executive Group Publisher

Andy Cummings, Vice President and Publisher

Mary Bednarek, Executive Acquisitions Director

Mary C. Corder, Editorial Director

Publishing for Consumer Dummies

Diane Graves Steele, Vice President and Publisher

Composition Services

Gerry Fahey, Vice President of Production Services

Debbie Stailey, Director of Composition Services

Contents at a Glance

Table of Contents

Introduction

$\mathcal{B}$lender: an awesome little 3D content creation suite that animates characters, surprises nay-sayers, simulates physics, and gives you foot massages if you've had a bad day! Okay, the last part is an exaggeration, but it's difficult to imagine a task in computer animation that Blender can't do. With it, you can create 3D models, animate those models, edit those animations into a movie, and even create video games with them. All this in a free program that's as small as a 9 MB download. Crazy!

Blender sits at a very unique position in the world of 3D computer graphics. It used to be that to get into 3D modeling and animation, you only had a few options and most of them were too expensive, too limiting, or – *ahem* – too illegal for people just trying to see what this whole 3D thing was all about. Blender circumvents all of that because it's free. And it's not just free as in, "This costs me zero dollars." It's truly free software that a world full of developers and users constantly contribute to, enhancing and improving it at a mind-boggling pace.

Of course, 3D computer graphics is a complex topic and all software of this type is dense with buttons, options, settings, and unique ways of working. Perhaps more than any other program like it, Blender carries a pretty heavy reputation for being difficult to understand. It's not typically viewed as software for beginners. But, if I've done my job right, this book will help simplify things. *Blender For Dummies* is not just a book on using Blender. Sure, I explain why things in Blender work in their peculiar Blenderish ways, but I also make it a point to explain core principles of 3D computer graphics as they are relevant. There's no use in being able to find a button if you're not really sure what it does or how it works. My hope is that with this combined knowledge, you can actually take advantage of Blender's unique traits to create your own high-quality 3D art as quickly and efficiently as possible. Perhaps you can even become as addicted to it as I am!

About This Book

Blender is an extremely complex program used for the even more complex task of producing high quality 3D models and animations. As such, there's no way I could cover every single feature and button in Blender within a mere 400 pages. For that, I recommend you refer to the very excellent online documentation available through Blender's Web site at `wiki.blender.org`.

The purpose of this book is to bring you up to speed on working in 3D space with Blender so you can start bringing your ideas to life as soon as possible. To that end, I focus on introducing you to the fundamental "Blender way" of working. Not only do I show you *how* something is done in Blender, but I often take the time to explain *why* things are done a certain way. This approach should hopefully put you on the fast track to making awesome work and also allow you to figure out new parts of Blender on your own when you come across them.

You'll notice throughout the book that I frequently make reference to the Blender community. Blender's user community is probably one if its most valuable assets, and I would be remiss to neglect bringing it up. Not only do many members of the community create great work, but they also write new code for Blender, write and edit documentation, and help each other improve. And understand that when I use the word "we" in reference to the community, I include you in that as well. As of right now, you are a Blenderhead: a fellow Blender user and therefore a member of our community.

It's worth mentioning here that Blender is a truly *cross-platform* program, running on Linux, Windows, Macintosh, and even variants of the Unix operating system. Fortunately, not much in Blender differs from one platform to another. However, for the few things that are different, I'll be sure to point them out for you.

Foolish Assumptions

This book is written for two sorts of beginners: people who are completely new to the world of 3D, and people who know a thing or two about 3D, but are completely new to Blender. That being the case, I tend to err on the side of explaining too much rather than too little. If you're someone who is already familiar with another program like 3DS Max, Maya, or Softimage, you can probably skip a number of these explanations. Likewise, if you're a complete newbie, you might notice that I occasionally compare a feature in Blender to one in another package. However, that is mostly for the benefit of these other users. I write so you can understand a concept without having to know any of these other programs.

I do, however, make the assumption that you have at least a basic understanding of your computer. You should know how to start programs, find files, and have a basic idea of the difference between a computer's processor and its hard drive. I assume you know how to use a mouse, and I *highly* recommend that you use a mouse with at least two buttons and a scroll wheel. You *can* use Blender with a one or two-button mouse, and I provide workarounds for the unfortunate souls in that grim state (*cough*Mac users*cough*), but it's certainly not ideal. Because Blender makes use of all your mouse buttons,

I make it a point to stipulate whether you need to left-click, right-click, or middle-click. And in case you didn't already know, the middle mouse button is accessed by pressing down on your mouse's scroll wheel.

Another assumption of sorts that I make is that you're working with Blender's default settings and theme. You are more than welcome to customize the settings for yourself, but if you do that, Blender might not behave exactly like I describe. In most instances, I do make it a point to mention what Blender's default behavior is, so you know what to expect, but I can't account for every different configuration that Blender allows you to have.

One last assumption that I make is that you can access the Internet from time to time. You don't need an Internet connection to use Blender, but there are a lot of resources online that definitely come in handy.

How This Book Is Organized

As with most books in the *For Dummies* series, *Blender For Dummies* is structured as a reference that you can refer back to over and over again. You should be able to go to the Table of Contents or the Index and jump straight to the topic you're interested in. Of course, if you're completely new to Blender and 3D, the chapters build upon one another so you can read from cover to cover.

Also, rather than give you tutorials that are only useful for creating one specific thing ("this is how you model a teacup" or "making the perfect tooth material"), I tend to lean towards more broad explanations of a tool's use and purpose. That said, I use certain specific examples because they tend to be fairly common tasks.

The book's chapters are grouped into relatively cohesive sections called Parts. Like the chapters, each part is meant to be modular and stand on its own, but is also structured in such a way that each one adds to the next. The following section describes the content of each part.

Part 1: Wrapping Your Brain around Blender

Not only is Blender complex, but it also has some pretty unique ways of approaching the problem of creating in three dimensions. This part is dedicated to melding your mind with the Blender way of thinking. If you've ever started up Blender and wondered, "Why in the world is it doing things *this* way?!" this part is well worth the read.

Part II: Creating Detailed 3D Scenes

Each chapter in this Part is dedicated to getting your work to look good, focusing on the skills of modeling, adding materials, and lighting your scenes. The techniques here are geared primarily toward creating static images, but nearly all of it is also relevant to getting animations to communicate clearly and be believable (not to mention, totally sweet to look at).

Part III: Get Animated!

Motion! Motion! Motion! Very few things in the world compare to the excellent feeling of bringing an inanimate object to life. It's hard work and can be very time-consuming, but the payoff of seeing a character move and watching people react to it is worth every little bit of toil you put into it. This Part shows you the basics of rigging and animating, as well as touching on getting Blender to do a little animating for you with simulated physics.

Part IV: Sharing Your Work with the World

You *could* sit in a room and create a mountain of awesome work just for yourself, but there's certainly something rewarding about putting your work out for the world to see. That's what this Part is all about. I walk you through the adventures of rendering out still images and animations so you ultimately have something worth sharing. This part also introduces the beautiful cheating that you can do with post production and video sequencing.

Part V: The Part of Tens

In a way, I really kind of wanted to write this entire book as a series of helpful lists that would help get you started in Blender, but that's not really the best structure for the entire thing. That said, I had a lot of fun writing this part. These chapters are geared to making sure your time with Blender is well-spent, so I cover troubleshooting and tips on improving your experience.

Icons Used in This Book

This icon calls out suggestions that help you work more effectively and save time.

These are things that I think you should try to keep in mind while working in Blender. Sometimes it's a random tidbit of information, but more often than not, it's something that you'll run into repeatedly and is therefore worth remembering.

Working in 3D can involve some pretty heavy technical information. You can usually work just fine without ever having to know these things, but if you do take the time to understand it, I bet you dollars to donuts that you'll be able to use Blender more effectively.

This icon doesn't show up often, but when it does, I definitely recommend that you pay attention. You won't blow up your computer if you overlook it, but you could lose work.

Conventions Used in This Book

As a Blender user, I absolutely love hotkeys, and I use them generously in examples throughout the book. Blender makes use of nearly every key on your keyboard, so some keys are a bit difficult to put in writing, particularly punctuation keys like the period (.) or tilde (~). When I suggest you press these keys, I do just as did in the last sentence: I spell the symbol and then put the actual symbol in parentheses.

I also make use of this cool little arrow (⇨) for indicating a sequence of steps. It could be a series of hotkeys to press or menu items to select or places to look in the Blender interface, but the consistent thing is that they are used for steps that you need to do sequentially.

Where to Go from Here

The easy answer here would be to say "Just dive on in!" but that's probably a bit too vague. As I mentioned before, this book is primarily intended as a reference. If you already know what you're looking for, flip over to the Table of Contents or Index and start soaking in the Blender goodness. For those of you who are just starting out, I suggest you merely turn a couple of pages, start at Chapter 1, and enjoy the ride. And even if you are the sort of person who knows exactly what you're looking for, take the time to read through other sections of the book. There are a bunch of valuable little bits of information that may help you work more effectively.

Regardless of how you read this book, though, my one hope is that you find it to be a valuable resource that makes you as addicted to Blender as I am.

Part I
Wrapping Your Brain Around Blender

The 5th Wave   By Rich Tennant

"I failed her in Algebra, but was impressed with the way she animated her equations to dance accross the screen, scream like hyenas, and then dissolve into a clip art image of the La Brea Tar Pits."

In this part . . .

Typically, when people first come into contact with Blender, they feel an incredible shock of "Ahhh! What is this crazy thing?!" The purpose of this part is to ease you into the Blender swimming pool so you can start to have fun with the rest of us. You get an idea of how Blender thinks and how to start taking advantage of the tools it provides you with. If you've got experience in another 3D program, these chapters explain some of the essential interface concepts that permeate nearly all tools and features in Blender.

Time to have some fun. Wheeeeeeee!

Chapter 1

Discovering Blender

*I*n the world of 3D modeling and animation software, programs are usually expensive: Like, really, really, thousands-of-dollars-and-maybe-an-arm expensive. And there are *some* valid reasons for that. Software companies spend millions of dollars and countless hours developing these programs. And the large production companies that buy these programs for their staff make enough money to afford the high cost.

But what about us? You and I, the little guys? We are the ambitious dreamers with big ideas, high motivation . . . and tight budgets. How can we bring our ideas to life and our stories to a screen, even if it is our own computer monitors? Granted, we could shell out that cash (and hopefully keep our arms) for the expensive programs that the pros use. But even then, animation is a highly collaborative art and it's difficult to produce anything in a reasonable amount of time without some help.

We need quality software and a strong community to work, grow, and evolve with. Fortunately, Blender can provide us with both of these things. This chapter is an introduction to Blender, its background, its interface, and its community.

Getting to Know Blender

Blender is a free and open source 3D modeling and animation suite. Yikes! What a mouthful, huh? Put simply, Blender is a computer graphics program that allows you to produce high quality still images and animations using three-dimensional geometry. If you've seen one of the recent animated feature films or watched a television show where they explain how they made an actor look like he's being chased by a giant monster even though he's really just standing in a big green room, you've seen what can be done with 3D computer graphics. In the right hands, Blender is capable of producing this kind of work. With a little patience and dedication, *your* hands can be the right hands.

One of the things that makes Blender different and special compared to other comparable 3D software is the fact that it is free and *open source*. This means that not only can you go to the Blender Web site (www.blender.org) and download the entire program right now without paying a dime, but the code that makes up the program, called the source, is also freely available for download. For most programs, the source code is a heavily guarded and highly protected secret that only certain people can see and modify (mostly programmers hired by the company that distributes the program). Because it's open source, anybody can see Blender's source code and make changes to it. The benefit of this is that, rather than having a small group of paid programmers work on the program, Blender can be improved by programmers all over the world!

Because of these strengths, Blender is an ideal program for small animation companies, freelance 3D artists, independent filmmakers, students beginning to learn about 3D computer graphics, and dedicated computer graphics hobbyists. Blender has a reputation for being difficult to understand for new users, but at the same time, it is also known for allowing experienced users to bring their ideas to life. Fortunately, helping you bridge that gap is the very reason this book exists.

Discovering Blender's History

The Blender we know and love today wasn't always free and open source. It's actually pretty unique in that it's one of the few software applications that was "liberated" from proprietary control by its user community.

Originally, Blender was written as an internal production tool for an award-winning Dutch animation company called NeoGeo, founded by Blender's original (and still lead) developer, Ton Roosendaal. In the late 1990s, NeoGeo started making copies of Blender available for download from their Web site. Slowly but surely, interest grew in this less-than-2MB program. In 1998, Ton spun off a new company, Not a Number (NaN), to try to market and sell Blender as a software product. NaN still distributed a free version of Blender, but also offered an advanced version with more features for a small fee. There was strength in this strategy and by the end of 2000, there were well over 250,000 Blender users worldwide.

Unfortunately, even though Blender was gaining in popularity, NaN was not making enough money to satisfy its investors, especially in the so-called "dot bomb" era that happened around that time. Because of this, in the early part of 2002, NaN shut its doors and stopped working on Blender.

Ironically, this is where the story starts to get exciting.

Even though NaN went under, Blender had developed quite a strong community by this time, and this community was eager to find a way to keep their beloved little program from becoming lost and abandoned. In July of 2002, Ton provided a way. Having established a non-profit called the Blender Foundation, he arranged a deal with the original NaN investors to run the "Free Blender" campaign. The terms of the deal were that, for a price of €100,000, the investors would agree to release Blender's source to the Blender Foundation for the purpose of making Blender open source. Initial estimations were that it would take as much as six months to raise the necessary funds. Amazingly, the community was able to raise that money in a mere *seven weeks*.

Because of the Blender community's passion and willingness to put its money where its metaphorical mouth is, Blender was released under the GNU General Public License on October 13, 2002. With the source in the community's hands, Blender had an avalanche of development and new features added to it in a very short time. We were even finally able to have Undo, a functionality that was conspicuously missing and highly desired since the initial releases of Blender by NeoGeo!

Six years later, the Blender community is larger and stronger than ever, and Blender itself is a powerful modern piece of software that competes with quality on par to similar software that costs thousands of dollars. Not too shabby. Figure 1-1 shows a screenshot of Blender from its early days compared to the Blender of today.

Figure 1-1:
Blender of
old (left)
versus
Blender of
today (right).

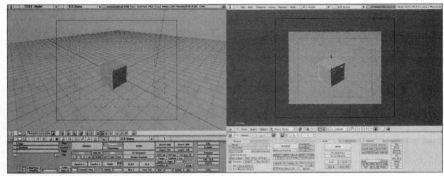

Making Open Movies and Games

One of the cool things about the programmers who write Blender is that many of them also use the program regularly. They're writing code not just because they're told to do it, but because they want to improve Blender for their own purposes. Part of this has to do with Blender's open-source nature, but quite a bit also has to do with the fact Blender was an in-house production tool, built for artists, based on their direct input, and often written by the artists themselves.

Seeking to get even more of this direct artist feedback, the Blender Foundation launched "Project Orange" in 2005. The purpose of the project was to create an animated short movie using open source tools, primarily Blender. A team of six members of the community were assembled in Amsterdam, in the Netherlands, to produce the movie. Roughly seven months later, *Elephants Dream* premiered and was released to the public as the first *open movie*, meaning not only that it was created using open-source tools, but all of the production files — 3D models, scenes, character rigs, and so on — were also released under a permissive and open Attribution Creative Commons license.

Due to the success of the Orange project, Ton established the Blender Institute in the summer of 2007 for the expressed purpose of having a permanent space to create open movie and game projects, as well as provide the service of training people in Blender. The first open project to come out of the Blender Institute was Project Peach, which, following the model of Orange, assembled a team of artists who produced a short comedic animation called *Big Buck Bunny*, which premiere in April 2008. Like *Elephants Dream*, all production files for the Peach project were released under an open license. Figure 1-2 shows an image from *Big Buck Bunny*.

Figure 1-2:
Big Buck
Bunny.

Not being inclined to rest on its laurels, the Blender Institute launched Project Apricot as the team creating *Big Buck Bunny* was wrapping up its production. Apricot was a project similar to Orange and Peach, but rather than create an animated movie, the goal here was to create a video game by combining Blender's strengths with the strength of the Crystal Space game engine. The result of this was *Yo Frankie!*, a game based on the "leader squirrel" character from the *Big Buck Bunny* project. The DVD containing this game shipped out in November 2008, containing playable levels in the Blender game engine as well as the Crystal Space engine. And of course, all of the content is freely available under a permissive Creative Commons license.

With the completion of each of these projects, the functionality and stability of Blender increased by a large degree. Orange brought improved animation tools, basic hair, and a node-based compositor. Peach provided enhanced particles for better hair and fur, optimizations for large scenes, improved rendering, and even better animation and rigging tools. Apricot revitalized Blender's internal game engine, which extended to better real-time visuals when modeling and animating in Blender. In fact, much of the content of this book wouldn't even exist without these projects. For example, Chapter 13 starts with using Blender's particle system to do exciting effects along with hair and fur. Half of Chapter 15's content is focused on the node compositor, a way of combining and enhancing still images and animations. In fact, nearly all of Part III is devoted to features that were enhanced or directly added for one of these three projects.

All of these projects continue to exhibit the strength of the Blender community. This is because each of them are financed in a large part by DVD pre-sales from users who understand that regardless of the project's final product, great improvements are the result and everyone benefits from that.

Joining the community

Congratulations! You're part of a community. As a Blender user, you're joining a very diverse group that spans all age ranges, ethnicities, professional backgrounds, and parts of the globe. We are a passionate bunch: proud of this little 3D program and more than willing to help others enjoy using it as much as we do. Have a look at Chapter 18 for a list of community resources that are invaluable, not only for discovering the intricacies of using Blender, but also for improving yourself as an artist. You can find innumerable opportunities for critique, training, discussion, and even collaboration with other artists, some of whom might also be Blender developers. I've made quite a few good friends and colleagues through the Blender community, both through the various community Web sites as well as by attending events like the annual Blender Conference. I go by the name "Fweeb" on these sites and I look forward to seeing you around!

Getting to Know the Interface

Probably one of the most daunting aspects of Blender for newcomers and long-time 3D professionals alike is its unique and somewhat peculiar interface. It's arguably the most controversial feature Blender has. In fact, merely calling it a "feature" might raise the blood pressure of some of you who tried using Blender in the past, but gave up in frustration when it did not behave as you expected. Figure 1-3 shows what you're presented with when you start Blender for the first time. It's been called everything from "brilliantly thought-out" to "thrown together by a pack of monkeys."

This book explains some of the design decisions in Blender's interface and ultimately allows you to be productive with it. Who knows, you might even start to like it and wonder why other programs don't work this way!

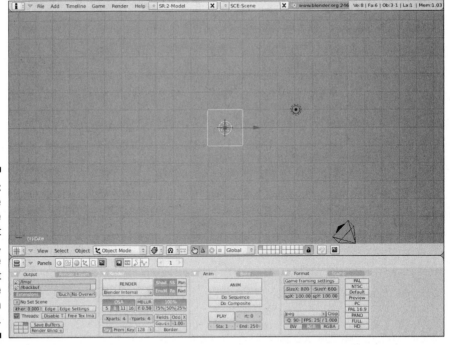

Figure 1-3:
The first time you start Blender, the entire world might seem like an alien planet.

Fast to use versus fast to learn

One of the key things to remember is that Blender was originally designed as an in-house tool for commercial production. Working in that industry (especially television production) requires very short turn-around times and extremely tight deadlines. For this reasons, 3D artists have to work very quickly to produce high quality work in a short period of time. Blender was built from the ground up to facilitate this need. And because artists worked side-by-side with the developers, they could tailor the whole program to match the way they worked.

The upside to this is that the program evolved with the artists and enabled them to successfully produce great work at a blazingly fast rate. The downside is that, as with most things that are customized, Blender became somewhat difficult to understand for people who had never been exposed to it before. This is what I mean when I say "fast to use versus fast to learn." You can be extremely productive with Blender after you understand how it thinks. However, your first few projects with Blender might be arduous. Of course, alleviating that potential pain is what this book is all about.

The Blender non-blocking interface

The first thing to understand about Blender's interface is the concept of a *non-blocking interface*. This means that windows in Blender never overlap one another and working in one window typically won't restrict you from working in any of the others. As an example, in most software, if you want to open a new file or save your project, a file browser dialog box pops up for you to do this. This is an overlapping window. Not only does it block things behind it from view, but it usually also prevents you from making any changes to your file. This isn't the case with Blender. In Blender, the file browser shows up in a window just like any other, and it makes perfect sense to be able to make a couple tweaks to your scene before hitting the save button. Figure 1-4 shows what this might look like.

At first, this way of working might seem to be really restrictive. How do you see different types of windows? Can you see them at the same time? Everything looks like it's nailed in place; is it even possible to change anything? Fortunately, all of these things are possible and you get the benefit of never having your view of one window obstructed by another. This is a great way to be able to see what's going on in your file at a glance.

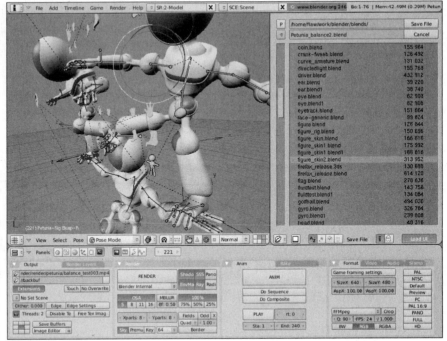

Figure 1-4:
Doing those
last couple
of tweaks
before
finally
saving.

The windows can all be modified and changed in the same way: Change the
size of windows by left-clicking the seam between windows and dragging it
to a new position. This increases the size of one window while reducing the
size of some of those that adjoin it. You can also add new windows by right-
clicking the seam and choosing Split Area from the menu that pops up. After
you do that, a line appears under your mouse cursor. Move your mouse to
where you would like to create a new seam and left-click to confirm. If you
decide you no longer wish to have this additional window, you can remove it
by right-clicking that seam and selecting Join Areas. This darkens the window
your mouse is in and draws an arrow to indicate which window you would
like to remove. Figure 1-5 shows the process of splitting an area to create a
new window and then removing that window by joining areas. When I work in
Blender, I find myself constantly changing the screen layout by splitting and
joining new windows as I need them.

When you right-click the seam between windows, you see a third option
that says No Header. Choosing this option removes the header bar from the
window your mouse cursor was in last. You can put the header back by right-
clicking the seam again and choosing Add Header. You can also change the
location of the header to either the top or bottom of the window it belongs
to. To do so, right-click the header bar and choose one of the three available
options: Top, Bottom, or No Header.

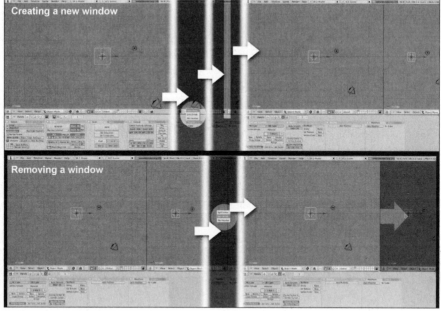

Creating a new window

Removing a window

Figure 1-5:
Creating a new window and then removing that window.

When working in Blender, you also occasionally need to maximize a window. This is particularly useful when you're working on a model or scene and you just want to get all of the other windows out of your way so you can use as much screen space as possible. To maximize any window, hover your mouse over that window and press Shift+Spacebar. You can toggle back to the tiled screen layout by pressing Shift+Spacebar again. These options are available in almost all window types by choosing View⇨Maximize/Tile Window from that window's header. The only exception to this is the Buttons window. In this window, the option is available by choosing Panels⇨Maximize/Tile Window.

You might notice that the hot keys next to these menu items are Ctrl+UpArrow for maximizing and Ctrl+DownArrow for tiling, rather than Shift+Spacebar. Those hotkeys also work, but I find that I don't have to move my left hand as much to hit Shift+Spacebar, so that's much more convenient for me.

This non-blocking window philosophy, combined with the fact that Blender's entire interface is written in a standardized programming library for graphics called OpenGL, is the precise reason that Blender looks the same, no matter where you run it. Whether you run it from Linux, Windows, a Mac, or even a cell phone, Blender looks and behaves like Blender. There's an additional benefit to being written in a 3D library like OpenGL: Many parts of Blender's interface allow you to zoom in on them. Try it! Place your mouse in the Buttons window (the bottom window) and hold Ctrl while scrolling your mouse wheel. You can make the panels in this window much larger or smaller than they are by default. Pretty cool!

So now you have a taste of how Blender thinks. That's not so bad, is it? Of course not! Of course, this little bit is just a start into the wild world that is Blender and it's interface. The next chapter goes into the interface in more detail and gets you started with editing objects in Blender.

Chapter 2

Understanding How Blender Thinks

In This Chapter

▶ Familiarizing yourself with Blender's windows

▶ Customizing Blender to fit the way you work

▶ Working in three-dimensional space

*I*t's time to get intimate with Blender. No, I don't mean you need to start placing scented candles around your computer. I mean this chapter's focus is a detailed introduction to Blender's interface and how you can start finding your way around in it. First of all, it's pretty important to have an understanding of the various types of windows that Blender has, and how to access them. These windows are the gateways and tools for creating whatever you want. And with the knowledge of what you can do with these windows, the next thing is actually building those creations. To do that, you need to understand how to work in a virtual three-dimensional space, and specifically, you need to understand how Blender handles that space. These topics are also covered in this chapter.

Looking at Window Types

Each Blender window can be changed to any window type. You can see what window types are available by left-clicking the button on the far left of that window's header. Figure 2-1 shows the menu that appears when you press this button.

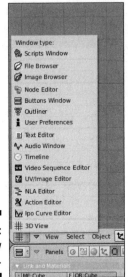

The window types available through this menu are as follows. Next to each of these types is the hotkey sequence to bring up the window type quickly:

- ✔ **Scripts Window:** Blender has a built-in scripting engine that uses the Python programming language. Scripts give Blender additional functionality and automate tedious tasks. This window is where you load these scripts, and in the case of some scripts, it's also where you interact with them.

- ✔ **File Browser:** This window allows you to look through the files on your computer.

- ✔ **Image Browser:** This window is much like the File Browser window, except it shows icons for folders and files, including thumbnails, or smaller-sized versions, of image files.

- ✔ **Node Editor (Shift+F3):** Blender has a Node Editor for materials as well as for compositing. This window is where you modify these node structures. See Chapters 7 and 15 for more on this.

- ✔ **Buttons Window (Shift+F7):** Nearly all of the different buttons for working on your scene reside in the panels of the Buttons Window. This window is covered in-depth later in this chapter in the section, "Understanding the Buttons Window."

- ✔ **Outliner (Shift+F9):** The Outliner gives a hierarchical view of all the objects in your scene and the ability to see how they are related to one another. It's also a quick way to select objects in a complex scene.

✔ **User Preferences:** Through the User Preferences window, you can customize how you interact with Blender.

✔ **Text Editor (Shift+F11):** Blender's integrated Text Editor is not only handy for keeping notes about your scenes and models, but it's also a convenient place to write and test your own Python scripts in Blender.

✔ **Audio Window:** The Audio Window displays the waveform for any audio file you load and relate it to the time and frame rate you specify for your project.

✔ **Timeline:** The Timeline window offers you a convenient way to quickly jump from one part of your animation to another.

✔ **Video Sequence Editor (Shift+F8):** Blender's Video Sequence Editor (VSE) is a lightweight video editor. It isn't as powerful as some of the programs created specifically for editing video, but it's quite effective for stringing a sequence of scenes together and doing basic effects, overlays, and transitions.

✔ **UV/Image Editor (Shift+F10):** With the UV/Image Editor, you can do basic image editing as well as edit the texture coordinates for your models. More on this in Chapter 7.

✔ **NLA Editor (Ctrl+Shift+F12):** NLA stands for *non-linear animation*. The editor in this window allows you to mix pre-animated actions on a single character (such as mixing a waving hand animation with a walking animation to have your character walk and wave her hand).

✔ **Action Editor (Shift+F12):** The Action Editor is where you create and adjust actions. Actions can be used to animate all of a character's movement in a scene, or they can be mixed together in the NLA Editor.

✔ **IPO Curve Editor (Shift+F6):** IPO is short for *InterPOlation*. Blender's IPO Curve Editor shows a graphical representation of an object's animatable attributes as they change over time.

✔ **3D View (Shift+F5):** This is arguably the most-used window in Blender. The 3D View shows you the three-dimensional view of your model or scene and allows you to modify it.

The only window type that is not available through this menu is the Data Browse window. You can access it by pressing Shift+F4. This window gives you a view of the raw database-like structure of all of the objects in your project file, called a *.blend file* (pronounced "dot-blend file"), because Blender project files all end with ".blend". It looks very similar to the File Browser window except it shows only the data in the file you're currently working on. Most Blender artists never need to use this window, but it's helpful for discovering what exactly is going on in your saved project file and for doing some technical maintenance on it. This window is more useful for Technical Directors than it is for regular 3D artists and animators.

Understanding the Buttons window

The Buttons window is probably the second-most used window in Blender. In it are a series of sub-windows, each with panels containing buttons dedicated to modifying specific parts of your scene. Below is a list of each type of sub-window:

- ✔ **Logic (F4):** This window is dedicated to Blender's integrated game engine. Chapter 12 touches on this topic briefly.

- ✔ **Script:** Some Blender scripts require you to enable options in this window. In particular, the left-clicking Enable Script Links button allows .blend files to use integrated scripts when first loaded.

- ✔ **Shading (F5):** The buttons in the Shading window allow you dramatically change the appearance of objects in your scene. Chapters 7 and 8 go into this window in much more detail.

- ✔ **Object (F7):** The Object sub-window allows you to make changes that affect an object as a whole. This is also where physics and particles buttons live. See Chapter 13 for more on these topics.

- ✔ **Editing (F9):** Buttons in the Editing sub-window change slightly depending on what sort of object you have selected, but their primary purpose is to make fundamental changes to the structure of an object.

- ✔ **Scene (F10):** Scene buttons determine what the final output of your scene will look like when you decide to render it to an image or video. The Scene buttons get covered more in-depth in Chapters 14 and 15.

If you have a background in another software package like 3DS Max or Maya, you may be more comfortable with a screen layout that lines the buttons panels vertically along one side of the screen. Fortunately, Blender and the Buttons window allows for this. To get a vertical Buttons view, follow these steps:

1. **Join the 3D view and the Buttons window by right-clicking the seam between the windows and choosing Join Areas. Left-click in the Buttons window to confirm the join.**

2. **Split a new area on the right of the screen by moving your mouse to the seam between the 3D view and the top header; right-click⇨Split Area.**

   Move the line until you like the position. Don't worry too much about location; you can always adjust it later.

3. **Change your new side window to the Buttons Window type by pressing Shift+F7 with your mouse in that window, or by selecting it from the Window type list.**

4. **Your buttons panels are still horizontally aligned. Fix this by right-clicking anywhere in the Buttons window except for its header and choosing Vertical from the Panel Alignment menu that pops up.**

Figure 2-2 shows this process.

One thing that may concern you is that this vertical Buttons window layout might obscure some of the available buttons in the header. In this case, there are two things you can do. The first thing you can do is left-click the downward-pointing triangle at the left of the header. This collapses the text menus from view so they're out of the way when you don't need them. If that still doesn't give you enough space, Blender has another trick up its sleeve: Middle-click the header and drag your mouse left and right. This moves the contents of the header left and right so you can bring those obscured buttons into view. This feature is very handy for people who work on small monitors.

Working with screens

"Cool!" you say, "I like this vertical layout. Is there a way for me save it so I don't have to change Blender's layout each time I load it?" As a matter of fact, there is! Actually, you can make a variety of layouts depending on the sort of work you're doing. In Blender, these workspace layouts are called *screens,* and, by default, Blender comes with five: Animation, Model, Material, Sequence, and Scripting. When you first load Blender, it puts you in the Model screen layout. You can cycle through these screens by pressing Ctrl+← and Ctrl+→. If you prefer to use a menu, you can use the one at the top of the window, as shown in Figure 2-3, and left-click the up/down arrows next to the name of the current screen.

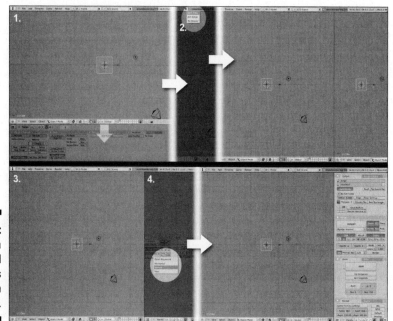

Figure 2-2: Creating a vertical buttons screen layout.

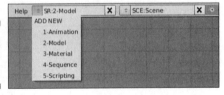

Figure 2-3:
The Screens
menu.

One thing worth mentioning here is that the "SR:" that appears before the screen name is not actually part of the name. It's just there to remind you that this menu is for screens. Any screen can be renamed by switching to that screen and left-clicking the screen's name. From here, you can rename it to anything.

Something to note, however, is that the default screens have numbers as part of their names (such as "1-Animation" and "3-Material"). This is done to keep those screens in that specific order. The screens, and therefore the order that they're cycled through when you press Ctrl+← or →, are arranged in alphabetical and numerical order, for fast and logical organization. Keep this in mind if you're creating a screen that you would like to appear in a specific place on the list.

To create a new screen, left-click the up/down arrow next to the current screen name in the header and choose Add New. This produces a new menu where you can choose to duplicate an existing screen or start with an empty one. From here, you can make the changes to your workspace layout, creating a vertical Button Window layout or a traditional "four-panel" layout with a separate 3D View window for top, front, side, and perspective views. When you are happy with changes you've made and you want to have these screens available each time you start Blender, save your settings by choosing File➪Save Default Settings or pressing Ctrl+U.

Before creating a new screen that you want to keep around for future use, first return to your default setup by selecting File➪New or pressing Ctrl+X. The reason for this is that when Blender saves your user settings, it saves them to a special .blend file that gets loaded each time it starts. So any models you have in the 3D View and any changes you make to other layouts are saved, too. Fortunately, if you've made a mistake, you can always return to the default setup by choosing File➪Load Factory Settings and recreate your custom layouts from there.

Setting user preferences

This section on user preferences is by no means comprehensive. The number of options available in Blender's User Preferences is mind-bogglingly large. My intent here is to introduce you to the most helpful and relevant options to get you working effectively. For specific details on every *single* button, see the online documentation available at www.blender.org.

Of course, the first question is, "Where exactly *are* the buttons for user preferences?" If you've used other programs, you might expect an Edit⇨Preferences option that pops up a new window with a bunch of options to play with. Don't go looking for that; You won't find it. Remember that Blender uses a philosophy of non-blocking windows. So, technically, the User Preferences window can exist anywhere. Just change the window type to User Preferences and *BAM!* All of the options are there for you.

Actually, though, there's an easier way. Left-click the seam between the 3D view and the topmost header and drag it down. The user preferences are conveniently tucked above the main menu. This is the fastest way to get to the preferences.

View & Controls

The first set of available options in Blender's user preferences relate to views and controls within the 3D window (shown in Figure 2-4). Moving from left to right, some of the more useful options are as follows:

Figure 2-4:
The View & Controls options in user preferences.

   ✔ **Object Info:** This option is on by default and toggles whether the name of the current frame number and active object are displayed in the lower left corner of a 3D View window.

   ✔ **View name:** Off by default, turning this option on places text in the upper left corner of a 3D View window to indicate the perspective from which you're viewing the scene (such as Top Perspective or Camera Perspective).

✔ **View rotation:** By default, Blender uses the Trackball setting. However, users who are familiar with other 3D programs might prefer the Turntable setting. The difference may seem subtle to a new user, but it can be very disorienting for people from other software packages who may be used to turntable orbit style.

✔ **Select with:** This option is somewhat mislabeled because it does more than change what you select with. It actually completely swaps what the left mouse button and right mouse button do in Blender. Default is Right Mouse. I cover this more later in this chapter in the section called "Selecting objects".

✔ **Emulate 3-Button Mouse:** Blender was designed to be used with a three-button mouse. However, not all computers have three-button mice, particularly Macintosh machines and some tablet PCs. Enabling this option helps these users compensate by using Alt+left-click to do what is normally done with the middle-click.

✔ **Invert Zoom:** Similar to the Trackball/Turntable option, some people are more comfortable scrolling forward to zoom out and back to zoom in. This gives users that option.

✔ **Smooth View:** Smooth View is probably one of the coolest "convenience options" added to Blender in recent history. By default, it's disabled by being set to zero. However, change that value to its maximum of 1000, go to your 3D View window, and choose View➪Camera. The 3D view smoothly animates the change from the default Top View to the Camera's perspective. Pretty slick, huh? The 1000 setting is a bit slow for my tastes: I prefer a setting around 250. Play with it on your own and see what works best for you.

Edit Methods

The next set of options is related to the act of editing objects. As shown in Figure 2-5, the most relevant options are as follows:

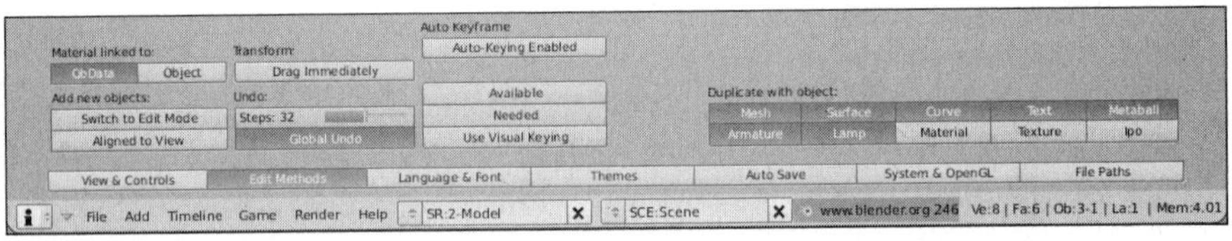

Figure 2-5:
The Edit
Methods
options in
user prefer-
ences.

✔ **Add New Objects:** The two options for adding new options are new to Blender as of version 2.46. Both are disabled by default. In this configuration, Blender behaves much like any other 3D program when adding new objects. New objects are added in Object mode and aligned with the global axis. Enabling both of these options makes Blender behave like it did prior to version 2.46.

✔ **Undo:** The options related to undo are pretty important. Here you can adjust how many steps of undo you have when working in Blender (default is 32), as well as toggle Global Undo on and off. Now, you may be wondering why in the world anyone would *ever* want to disable the ability to undo a mistake. The most common answer to this question is performance. Having undo enabled requires more memory from your computer and each level of undo requires a little bit more. Sometimes, when working with very complex scenes or models, an artist might disable undo so that all of the memory is dedicated to their current scene rather than the steps used to create it. This occurs most when artists work with Blender's multi-resolution sculpt tools (see Chapter 5).

Language & Font

The first time you load this set of options, you see only a single button that says International Fonts. However, when you click that button, you get a set of options like the ones in Figure 2-6. This section is most useful to non-English-speaking Blender users as it allows most menu items to be translated to their native language. However, there is one additional benefit for all Blender users. By turning on International Fonts, all text in the Blender interface can be displayed in any TrueType font you choose. Simply left-click the Select Font button and use the File Browser to track down the font you would like to use. Even if you just use the default font that's built into Blender, you should notice that the text is much cleaner and less jagged looking with this option enabled. Enabling this function causes your machine to take a slight performance hit, but it's usually barely noticeable on even the slowest of machines.

Figure 2-6:
The Language & Font options in user preferences.

Themes

Blender has quite a bit of flexibility in adjusting how it looks. This is all done through the Themes options, shown in Figure 2-7. By default, Blender ships with two themes: Default and Rounded. Almost all of the screenshots taken for this book are done using the Default theme. However, when I work in Blender, I use my own theme that I derived from the Rounded theme. It's a bit darker and easier on the eyes. This is particularly important if, like me, you're known for sitting behind the computer and working in Blender for 10-15 hour stretches. In situations like that, the less stress you can put on your eyes, the better. A copy of the theme I use is included on the DVD that comes with this book. Feel free to use it for your Blender sessions, or make your own! Everyone has their own tastes. In fact, one of the more popular Blender users, Pablo Vazquez (known as VenomGFX) uses a theme that's completely purple and pink!

Figure 2-7:
The Themes options in user preferences.

Auto Save

Before Blender had undo functionality, users relied heavily on its Auto Save features. These options, as shown in Figure 2-8, are a life-saver, even in the age of undo.

- ✔ **Save Versions:** Each time you manually save a file in Blender, it takes your last save and stores it as an earlier version. You may have created work in Blender before and noticed some .blend1 files in the same place you saved your .blend files. Those .blend1 files are the earlier version. This option allows you to determine how many of these earlier versions you'd like Blender to retain for you.

- ✔ **Auto Save Temp Files:** Enabled by default, this is Blender's auto save functionality. It saves a "hot backup" in your Temp directory (adjustable in the File Paths options; see below) every few minutes, as dictated by the Minutes field below this button. The Open Recent button closes the current file you're working on *without saving* and opens your most recent backup in the Temp directory.

- ✔ **Recent Files:** The number in this field tells Blender how many of your past files to remember when you go to File⇨Open Recent or press Ctrl+O.

✔ **Save Preview Images:** This option is turned off by default, but when enabled, it saves a small preview image of each texture and material in your project and embeds it into your .blend file. This way, you can use Blender's Image Browser to see materials and textures when you append or link from other files.

System & OpenGL

Whereas the View & Controls options dictate how you interact with Blender, the options in the System & OpenGL section, shown in Figure 2-9, tend to dictate more how Blender interacts with you. Many of the options here are geared toward optimizing for performance, and generally the defaults work well. Some of the more interesting options follow:

✔ **Solid OpenGL lights:** With these settings, you can adjust the standard lighting used in your 3D View window. Some Blender users set these colors to drastically different settings so they can have a good sense of each side of their model and more easily see some of the contours. You have the ability to turn on up to three lights. On each one, you can adjust the direction of the light by left-clicking and dragging on the sphere. You can adjust either of the two colors below (main color and highlight or *specularity* color, respectively) by left-clicking them and using the color picker that pops up.

✔ **Emulate Numpad:** This is a very handy option for laptop users. As you see in the next section, Blender makes use of the numeric keypad for quick access to top, front, side, and camera views in the 3D window. Unfortunately, most laptop users do not have an easily accessible numeric keypad on their keyboards. As a workaround for this, the Emulate Numpad option uses the number keys at the top of the keyboard to have the functionality that the corresponding numpad numbers have. This disables the normal layer-switching functionality that the number keys at the top of the keyboard have, but the ability to quickly change views tends to be more valuable to users than the ability to quickly change layers anyway.

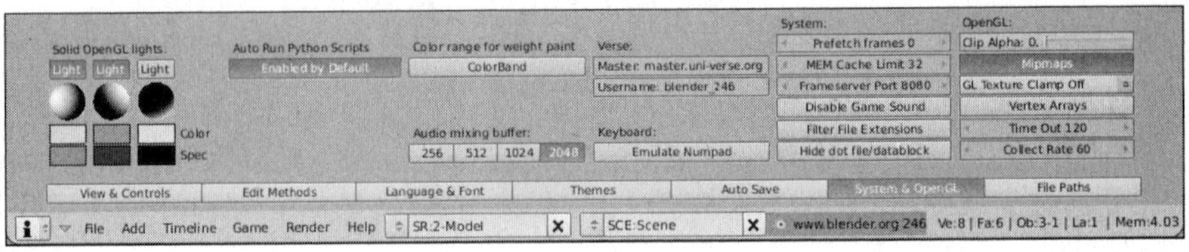

Figure 2-9:
The System
& OpenGL
options in
user pref-
erences.

File Paths

The File Paths options shown in Figure 2-10 show the default locations where Blender looks for or places certain files. Here you can indicate where your fonts are located, where you want to save your renders by default, and where to look for textures and sounds. However, probably the most important path in this section is the one for Temp. This is the location where Blender stores Auto Save files and it is also where it stores the notorious quit.blend file, which is great for recovering your last blender session. The default location for temporary files is /tmp/. Unfortunately for users of Microsoft's Windows operating system, this location does not make any sense and actually doesn't even exist. If you're using Windows, I *strongly* advise that you change this to "C:\Windows\Temp" or create a folder called tmp on your C:\ drive. Linux users may also want to change this location because some Linux distributions like Ubuntu automatically clear the /tmp directory on each boot.

Figure 2-10:
The File
Paths
options in
user pref-
erences.

Navigating in Three Dimensions

As I mentioned earlier in this chapter, the 3D view is probably the most used window type in all of Blender. It also has some of the most unique interface decisions of any 3D software program. The purpose of this section is to guide you to understanding how to wield this part of Blender like a virtual 3D ninja!

Alright, so perhaps I was a little over the top with the whole ninja thing, but hopefully this section will take you at least one or two steps closer to that goal.

Orbiting, panning, and zooming the 3D view

When trying to navigate a three-dimensional space through a two-dimensional screen like a computer monitor, you can't interact with that virtual 3D space exactly like you would in the real world, or as I like to call it, meatspace. The best way to visualize this is to imagine the 3D view as your eyes to this 3D world. But rather than think of yourself as moving through this environment, imagine that you have the ability to move this entire world around in front of you.

The most basic way of navigating this space is called *orbiting*. This is the rough equivalent of rotating the 3D world around a fixed point in space. In order to orbit in Blender, middle-click anywhere in the 3D view and drag your mouse cursor around.

Occasionally, you have the need to keep your orientation to the world, but you'll want to move it around so you can see a different part of the scene from the same angle. In Blender, this is called *panning*, and you do it by holding Shift while middle-clicking in the 3D View. Now when you drag your mouse cursor around, the world shifts around without changing the angle that you're viewing from.

The third way of navigating 3D space is when you want get closer to an object in your scene. Similar to working with a camera, this is called *zooming* the view. In Blender, there are two ways to zoom. The easiest method is by using your mouse's scroll wheel. By default, scrolling forward zooms in and scrolling back zooms out. However, this method doesn't always give you fine control and some people don't have a mouse with a scroll wheel. In these cases, you can zoom by holding Ctrl while middle-clicking in the 3D view. Now, when you drag your mouse cursor up or left, you zoom in, and when you drag your mouse cursor right or down, you zoom out.

Of course, if you happen to be working with a mouse that does not have a middle mouse button, Blender's default behavior is to emulate the middle mouse button by pressing Alt+left-click. So orbiting is Alt+left-click, panning is Shift+Alt+left-click, and zooming is done with Ctrl+Alt+left-click. Table 2-1 has a more organized way of showing this.

Table 2-1	Keyboard/Mouse Keys for Navigating 3D Space	
Navigation	*Three-Button Mouse*	*Emulated Three-Button Mouse*
Orbit	Middle-click	Alt+left-click
Pan	Shift+middle-click	Shift+Alt+left-click
Zoom	Ctrl+middle-click	Ctrl+Alt+middle-click

Changing views

Although using the mouse to work your way around the 3D space is the most common way to adjust how you view things, Blender has some menu items and hotkey sequences that help give you specific views much faster and more accurately than you can do alone with your mouse.

The View menu

On occasion, you want to know what a model looks like when it's viewed head-on from the front, side, or top. Blender has some convenient shortcuts for quickly switching to these views. The most obvious way is to use the View menu in the 3D view's header, as shown in Figure 2-11. This menu lets you choose the top, front, side, and user view, as well the view from any of the cameras you may have in your scene. You can also use this menu to switch between orthographic and perspective views. The *orthographic* view of a 3D scene is similar to how technical drawings and blueprints are done. If two objects are the same size, they always appear to be the same size, regardless of how far away from you they are. This view is ideal for getting sizes and proportions correct in your models, especially if they are based on blueprints or technical drawings. The *perspective* view is more akin to how we actually see things. That is, objects in the distance look smaller than objects that are near you.

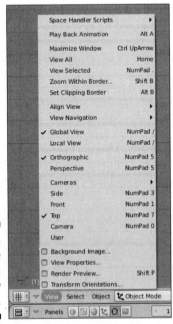

Figure 2-11:
The View
menu in the
3D View
window.

Behold the power of the numeric keypad!

The View menu is certainly helpful, but there's an even faster way to change your view: the numeric keypad. Each of the buttons on your keyboard's numeric keypad has an extremely fast way of changing your view in the 3D window. It also has some options that aren't available to you in the View menu. Figure 2-12 is an image of the numeric keypad with an indication of what each key does.

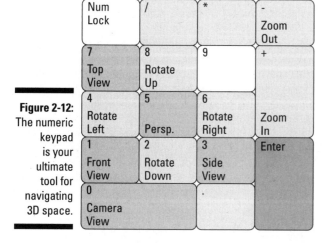

Figure 2-12:
The numeric keypad is your ultimate tool for navigating 3D space.

Notice that the hotkeys are arranged in a way that corresponds with how you would expect them to be. Top view is at the top of the keypad at Numpad 7. The front view is accessed at Numpad 1, and if you move to the right on the keypad, you can see the side view by pressing Numpad 3. Because it's the view you render from, the active camera is the most important and therefore gets the largest key at Numpad 0. Pressing Numpad 5 is a quick way to toggle between orthographic and perspective views. If you have View Name turned on in the Views & Controls section of the user preferences, it actively informs you about which view you are using. And having the very cool Smooth View option enabled definitely helps you keep from getting disoriented while working.

Here is where the numeric keypad shows its real power. You may have noticed that the View menu doesn't appear to give you the ability to see the bottom, back, or left-side view of your scene. With the numeric keypad, it's easy. To see the opposite side of the standard views, press Ctrl while hitting the corresponding Numpad key. For example, if you want to see the bottom view, press Ctrl+Numpad 7. Of course, say you *really* like the View menu, or you're one of the unfortunate souls who doesn't have a numeric keypad on your keyboard. Well, the good news is that Blender's developers thought ahead and actually did add this functionality to the View menu, and it works about the same way: Just hold Ctrl while picking your view, and you'll get the opposite side. Ctrl+View⇨Front gives you the back view of your scene.

Now, maybe you got a little bit excited and hit Ctrl+Numpad 0 to see what the opposite of the camera view is and had some unexpected results. This is because Ctrl+Numpad 0 does something slightly different. It actually allows you to treat any selectable object in Blender as a camera, with the view looking down the object's local Z-axis. If this doesn't make any sense to you, take a quick look at the beginning of Chapter 3 for more explanation on local and global coordinate systems. It may seem like a strange feature to have, but it can be really helpful for doing things like aiming lights and checking the line of sight of an object or a character.

Another cool thing you can do with Numpad 0 is to quickly snap the camera to your user view. For example, say you've been working on 3D model for a while from a certain angle and you want to see what the model looks like in a render from that specific angle. Rather than try to grab and rotate your camera to get close to this same angle, you can simply press Shift+Numpad 0 and the camera jumps directly to where you are viewing your model from. I find myself using this hotkey sequence quite a bit when I'm creating my models. Sometimes it's just easier to change your user view and snap your camera to it than it is to aim the camera how you want it.

The numeric keypad also gives the ability to navigate your scene like you might normally do with your mouse. This is done with the 8, 4, 6, and 2 keys on the keypad. Numpad 8 and Numpad 2 orbit the view forward and back, respectively, whereas Numpad 4 and Numpad 6 orbit it left and right. By default, Blender does these rotations in 15-degree increments, but you adjust this to be more fine or coarse in your user preferences under Views & Controls⇨Rotation Angle. This a nice way to get a quick turntable view of a scene, particularly if you have your View rotation set to Trackball in your user preferences. You can also pan the view by pressing Ctrl in combination with any of these buttons. For example, Ctrl+Numpad 4 and Ctrl+Numpad 6 pan the view left and right. You can even zoom the view by using the Numpad-plus and Numpad-minus keys.

There are two more very useful hotkeys on the numeric keypad: Numpad-slash (/) and Numpad-dot (.). They are somewhat more esoteric than the other keys, but they definitely come in handy. Of the three, I tend to use Numpad-slash the most. It toggles what Blender calls Local View. Basically, it hides everything in your scene except for the object or objects you have selected. It's really useful for temporarily isolating a single object or set of objects in a complex scene so that you can work on it without anything else getting in your way. The Numpad-dot hotkey also comes in handy when you want to focus on a specific part of your scene. It centers the objects you've selected in the 3D View for you. This is particularly useful if you've rotated or panned everything out of sight and you want to bring your selected objects back into view. If the image in Figure 2-12 doesn't quite work for you as a reference, Table 2-2 shows what each key does in a table-based format.

Table 2-2		Hotkeys on the Numeric Keypad			
Hotkey	*Result*	*Hotkey*	*Result*	*Hotkey*	*Result*
1	Front	Ctrl+1	Back	+	Zoom in
2	Orbit back	Ctrl+2	Pan down	-	Zoom out
3	Right side	Ctrl+3	Left side	/	Toggle local view
4	Orbit left	Ctrl+4	Pan left	.	View selected
5	Ortho/ Persp				
6	Orbit right	Ctrl+6	Pan right		
7	Top	Ctrl+7	Bottom		
8	Orbit for- ward	Ctrl+8	Pan up		
0	Camera view	Ctrl+0	Set active object as camera	Shift+0	Set user view as camera

One other key worth mentioning, although it's not exactly on the numeric keypad, is the Home key. Whereas using Numpad-dot brings your selected objects into view, pressing Home zooms your view back until all objects in your scene are visible in the 3D View. This is a very convenient key for getting an overall idea of what's going on in your scene.

Ways to See Your 3D Scene

Aside from changing the angle from which you view your 3D world, you may also want to change how the world is shown in the 3D view. This is called the *draw type* or *draw mode* for the view. By default, Blender starts in the Solid draw type. This shows your models as solid 3D objects, lit by the OpenGL lights you can set in Blender's user preferences under System & OpenGL. You can change the draw type by going to the 3D View's header and left-clicking the button that looks like a cube with little protrusions coming from its faces, as seen in Figure 2-13.

Figure 2-13:
3D View
draw types.

Clicking this button reveals the following possible draw types:

- ✔ **Textured:** The Textured draw type attempts to faithfully show you what your object will look like when textured and lit for the final render. It may differ a bit from what the final looks like, but it should give you a good idea to work from. Pressing Alt+Z quickly toggles between this draw type and the Solid draw type. If you have the a modern accelerated video card, you can enable GLSL shaders (Game⇨Blender GLSL Materials) and when you use image-based textures, the Textured draw type will be more accurate. More on this topic is in Chapter 8.

- ✔ **Shaded:** The Shaded draw type is similar to the default Solid draw type, except it uses the lights you actually have in the scene for lighting, rather than the OpenGL lights set in the user preferences. This setting is helpful for tweaking your lighting rig without constantly needing to rerender. Press Shift+Z to quickly toggle between the Shaded and Wireframe draw types.

- ✔ **Solid:** The default draw type that Blender starts with. Press Z to toggle between this draw type and Wireframe. This is usually the standard work mode for working in Blender. If you have an older video card, the Shaded and Textured draw types will perform much slower than this one.

- ✔ **Wireframe:** This draw type shows the objects in your scene as transparent line-drawings. This is a good quick way to get an idea of the structure of your models. And because it's a bunch of lines, Blender doesn't have to worry about shading and therefore doesn't tax your computer's processor as much. On older computers, Blender is a lot more responsive using the Wireframe draw type than the Solid, Shaded, or Textured draw types.

- ✔ **Bounding Box:** The Bounding Box draw type replaces your 3D object with a wireframe cube that shows how much space your object takes up in the 3D world. It's not as commonly used as the other draw types, but it does come in handy for quickly placing objects in a scene or detecting when two objects might collide.

Besides the menu in the 3D View's header and the various combinations of Z, Shift+Z, and Alt+Z for switching views, you can also press D anywhere in the 3D view to bring up a menu under your mouse that allows you to choose a draw type. You may also notice that if you have more than one 3D View window, they don't all have to have the same draw type. You can see the wireframe of your model in one window while adjusting the lighting in the Shaded draw type in another window.

Selecting objects

How you select objects is one of the most controversial design decisions in Blender's interface: In nearly every other program, you select things — be they text, 3D objects, files, or whatever — by left-clicking them. This is not the case in Blender. When you left-click in the 3D view, all it seems to do is move around some strange crosshair thing. That is Blender's 3D cursor. I talk more about that later, but in the meantime, you're probably thinking, "How in the world do I select anything?"

The answer is simple: You select objects in Blender by right-clicking them. Multiple objects are selected by Shift+right-clicking them.

Although this certainly seems strange, there is actually a reason for doing it this way. This design decision was not made at random or just to be different for the sake of being different. There are actually two reasons: one is philosophical and the other is practical. The first comes from how the mouse is used in Blender. In Blender, the left mouse button is intended to be used to perform or confirm an action. You left-click on buttons or menus and left-click to confirm the completion of an operation like moving, rotating, or scaling an object, and you use it to place the 3D cursor. Selecting an object doesn't really act upon it or change it. So right-click is used to select objects as well as cancel an operation before it's completed. It's a bit abstract, but as you work this way, it does actually begin to make sense.

The second reason is more practical: 3D modelers and animators are known for working at a computer for insanely long stretches of time. Repetitive stress injuries, or RSI, is a real concern. The more you can spread the work across the hand, the lower the chance of RSI. By making it so you're not doing every single operation with the left mouse button, Blender helps in this regard. Also, many 3D artists like to use a drawing tablet, rather than a mouse. Having right-click to select is actually really helpful for this type of interface.

Bottom line, the "right-click to select" paradigm really is a nice, efficient way of working in 3D space after you get used to it. However, if you try it out and still don't like it, Blender offers you the ability to swap left and right mouse button usage in the View & Controls section of the user preferences window. Do note, however, that this book is written with the default right-click behavior in mind, so remember that as you read other chapters.

Taking advantage of the 3D cursor

"Okay," you say, "I can handle the right-click-to-select thing. But what's with these crosshairs that move to where ever I left-click? It seems pretty useless."

That's the 3D cursor. It's a unique concept that I've only seen in Blender and it's anything but useless. The best way to understand it is to think about a word processor or text editor. When you add text or want to change something, it's usually done with or relative to the blinking cursor on the screen. Blender's 3D cursor serves pretty much the same purpose, but in three dimensions. When you add a new object, it's placed wherever the 3D cursor is located. When you rotate or scale an object, you can do it relative to the 3D cursor's location. And when you want to snap an object to a specific location, you do it with the 3D cursor.

In terms of adjusting your 3D View, you can use the 3D cursor as a quick way to recenter your view. To try this, place the 3D cursor anywhere in the 3D view by left-clicking. Now press C and watch as the View pans to put the cursor at the center of the window. This is similar to pressing Numpad-dot, except you don't have to select any objects. Another convenient hotkey sequence is Shift+C. This relocates the 3D cursor to the origin coordinates of the 3D environment and then brings all objects into view. This is like pressing Home with the added benefit of moving the cursor to the origin.

In Chapter 3, the topic of grabbing, scaling, and rotating objects is covered. Usually, you want to use Blender's default behavior of doing these operations relative to the median point of the selected objects. However, you can also perform any of these operations relative to the 3D cursor by pressing the period (.) key on your keyboard or selecting 3D Cursor from the Pivot menu in the 3D View's header, as shown in Figure 2-14. You can use this menu to switch back to the default behavior or press Shift+comma.

Figure 2-14:
The Pivot
menu in the
3D View
window.

The 3D cursor is also very useful for *snapping*, or moving to a specific point in space. For a better idea of what this means, hover your mouse over the 3D View window and press Shift+S. A menu like the one in Figure 2-15 appears.

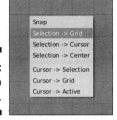

Figure 2-15:
The Snap
menu.

Through this menu, you can snap your selected object to a fixed coordinate on the grid in the 3D View, the location of the cursor, or to the center of the grid, also known as the *origin* of the scene. You also have the ability to snap the 3D cursor to the middle of multiple selected objects, a fixed location on the grid, or to the active object in the scene. This is a very effective way to move an object to a specific point in 3D space, and it's all thanks to the little 3D cursor.

Chapter 3

Getting Your Hands Dirty Working in Blender

In This Chapter

▶ Understanding coordinate system orientations

▶ Speeding up the process with hotkeys

▶ Making changes to 3D objects

*B*lender is built for speed, and its design heavily emphasizes working as quickly and efficiently as possible for extended periods of time. On more than one occasion, I've found myself working in Blender for 10-15 hours straight. Although, admittedly, part of this has to do with my own minor lunacy, the fact that I'm able to be that productive for that long is a testament to Blender's design. This chapter gets you started in taking full advantage of that power. This chapter covers the meat and potatoes of interacting with three-dimensional (3D) space in Blender, such as moving objects and editing polygons. If you've worked in other 3D programs, chances are good that a number of Blender concepts will seem particularly alien to you. To quote Yoda, "You must unlearn what you have learned" in your journey to become a Blender Jedi. If you've never worked in 3D, you probably have an advantage over a trained professional who's used to a different workflow. Hooray for starting fresh!

In addition to having an emphasis on efficiency, Blender is designed to allow you to work for as long as possible while incurring the least amount of repetitive stress. For this reason, relatively few operations in Blender require you to hold down a key. Typically, you press a key to begin the operation and confirm its completion by left-clicking with your mouse or pressing Enter. To cancel the operation, right-click, or press Esc.

Grabbing, Scaling, and Rotating

The three basic object operations in a 3D scene are the transformations known (by mathematicians) as translation, scale, and orientation. People who speak Blenderese use the terms *grab, scale,* and *rotate,* respectively. Other programs might also use the term *move* in place of grab or *size* in place of *scale.* You can use these three operations to place any object in 3D space at any arbitrary size and with any arbitrary orientation. Also, because Blender tries to maintain consistency throughout its interface, you can use these transform operations in more than just the 3D view. For instance, the same grab and scale operations work when you want to edit keyframes and motion curves in the IPO, short for interpolation, window! How's that for convenient?

Differentiating between Coordinate Systems

Before you bound headlong into applying transformations, such as rotation and scaling, to your objects, you need to understand how coordinate systems work in 3D space. All coordinate systems in Blender are based on a grid consisting of three axes: X, Y, and Z. The X-axis typically represents side-to-side movement, whereas the Y-axis represent front-to-back and the Z-axis goes from top to bottom. This is referred to as the *Cartesian grid.* The *origin,* or center, of this grid is at the (0,0,0) coordinate. The difference in the systems lies in the way this grid is oriented relative to a selected 3D object. Figure 3-1 shows the Coordinate System Orientation menu in the 3D view header when you left-click it.

Figure 3-1:
The
Coordinate
System
Orientation
menu.

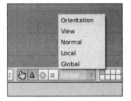

As the figure shows, there are four orientations to choose from: *View,* *Normal, Local,* and *Global.* Working in of these coordinate systems gives you absolute control of how your object lives in 3D space. Depending on how you would like to transform your object, one orientation might be more appropriate than the others.

This list describes details of the four possible orientations:

- ✔ **View:** The orientation from the perspective of the window. The View orientation appears relative to how you're looking at the 3D View window. Regardless of how you move around in a scene, you're always looking down the Z-axis of the View coordinate system. The Y-axis is always vertical, and the X-axis is always horizontal in this orientation.

- ✔ **Normal:** The orientation that's perpendicular to some arbitrary plane. When working with just objects, this description doesn't really apply, so the Normal axis is exactly the same as the Local axis. When you begin editing meshes, though, it makes more sense because you have *normals* to work with. Blender also uses the Normal orientation for the local coordinate system of bones when working with Armatures for animation. Chapter 4 covers editing meshes in more detail and Chapter 11 covers working with Armatures depth.

- ✔ **Local:** The orientation of the object relative to its initial location and orientation. In addition to the Global orientation, each 3D object in Blender has a local coordinate system. The origin of this system isn't the same as the Global origin. Instead, this coordinate system is relative to the center point of your object. The *center point* is represented by the pink dot that's usually located at the center of your 3D object.

- ✔ **Global:** The orientation of Blender's base grid that you see in the 3D View. In many ways, this is the primary orientation to which everything else relates. When you first start Blender, you're in Top view, looking down the Z-axis. The Y-axis is marked in green, moving along the front-to-back line, and the X-axis is in red, along the side-to-side line. The origin is located directly at the center of the grid. For example, moving in the negative X direction moves the object to the left, if you're looking from Top view.

All these coordinate system explanations can be (please forgive the pun) disorienting. An easy way to visualize this concept is to imagine that your body represents the Global coordinate system and this book is a 3D object oriented in space. If you hold the book out in front of you and straighten your arms, you move the book away from you. It's moving in the positive Y direction, both globally and locally. Now, if you twist the book to the right a few degrees and do the same thing, it still moves in the positive Y direction globally. However, in its local axis, the book is moving in both a positive Y direction and a negative X direction. To move it in just the positive local Y direction, you move the book in the direction in which its spine is pointing.

To relate this concept to the View orientation, assume that your eyes are the View axis. If you look straight ahead and move the book up and down, you're translating it along the View orientation's Y-axis. For a clear reference, Figure 3-2 shows the difference between the coordinate systems.

Figure 3-2:
The Global,
Local, View,
and Normal
coordinate
orientations.

The last object you select is the *active* object. If you're using the Local or Normal orientations and select multiple objects, the transform operations happen relative to the active object's orientation. (In Chapter 2, I show you how to select multiple objects at the same time.)

Transforming an Object by Using the 3D Manipulator

In Blender's default configuration, the 3D *manipulator* is activated and viewable at the center of your selected object. You can use the manipulator to transform any object in a 3D scene. When Blender first starts, the manipulator is in Translate (Grab) mode, which you can determine in two ways:

- ✔ The manipulator itself looks like a set of colored axes located at the center of the selected object.
- ✔ The button with the red triangle on it (refer to Figure 3-1) is depressed to indicate that the manipulator is in Translate mode. By default, the manipulator is oriented to align with the Global axis.

In all coordinate system orientations under Blender, blue represents the Z-axis, green the Y, and red the X.

Switching manipulator modes

As you might expect, translation isn't the only transform operation available to you with the manipulator. Refer to Figure 3-1. The button with the green circle on it activates Rotation manipulator mode, and the button with the blue square activates Scale mode. Press the Rotation Mode button to see the change in the look of the 3D manipulator. In this mode, the manipulator is a set of circles around the object's center, with the proper color representing each axis. Pressing the Scale Mode button for the manipulator changes it to look much like it does in Translate mode, except that you see a small cube, rather than an arrow, at the end of each axis.

The 3D manipulator should be familiar to you if you've used other programs, where the corresponding tool might be called a *widget* or a *gizmo*. However, the Blender manipulator also does something else: It lets you activate multiple modes at the same time. Hold down Shift while pressing the appropriate button to activate a manipulator. You can then make any combination of transform modes active simultaneously. Many Blender users find this capability particularly helpful for animation, where there are situations that require quick access to translation and rotation but not necessarily to adjust the object's scale. Figure 3-3 shows the three separate modes of the manipulator as well as the "combo" manipulator.

Figure 3-3:
The
Translate,
Rotate,
Scale, and
Combo
manipulator
modes.

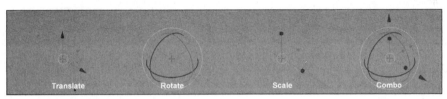

Using the manipulator

To translate a selected object with the manipulator, follow these steps:

1. **Make sure that Translate mode is active by left-clicking the Translate manipulator mode button in the 3D View's header.**

2. **Left-click the manipulator arrow that points in the direction you want to move the object.**

   For instance, to move an object along the X-axis, left-click the red arrow on the manipulator.

3. **To confirm the placement of the object, left-click again or press Enter.**

   To cancel the operation, right-click or press Esc.

For quick adjustments, left-click-and-drag an arrow. When you release the mouse button, the placement is confirmed.

In all transform operations, the same controls listed above are available in the Blender multifunction buttons. Move in fixed increments by holding down the Ctrl key. Hold down the Shift key while transforming an object to make adjustments on a finer scale. Hold down the Ctrl+Shift key combo while transforming to make adjustments in smaller fixed increments.

This fixed-increment control is similar to the basic *snapping to the grid* found in other 2D and 3D applications. Blender also offers the ability to snap your selected object to other objects in your scene. To turn this on, press the icon shaped like a magnet in the 3D View's header, as shown in Figure 3-4. After it's activated, you have a choice of snap modes: *Closest*, *Center*, *Median*, and *Active*. The way snapping works, you first select what you want to transform. Then you activate one of the various transform operations (Grab, Scale, Rotate). While transforming, hold down Ctrl. As your mouse cursor comes near a vertex in another mesh, a small circle appears around that vertex. When this happens, your selection snaps according to the behavior dictated by the snap mode you've chosen.

Figure 3-4:
The Snap
Target
Mode
button.

The different available types of Snap Target Modes that Blender provides you are as follows:

- **Active**: In Object mode, the last thing that you select is considered the *active object*. In Blender's default theme, it's a bit difficult to distinguish from your other selected items, but active selections are a lighter color than your other selected objects. When using Active snap mode, your active selection is what snaps to your target vertex.

- **Median**: Median snap mode operates similar to Center snapping. In fact, for two-dimensional meshes such as planes and symmetrical objects, Median snapping is almost always identical to the results of Center snap mode. However, when working in three dimensions and asymmetric meshes, the calculated median and calculated center are not always the same.

- **Center**: In Center snap mode, Blender calculates the true center of your selection and snaps that to your target vertex.

- **Closest**: In this snap mode, the vertex in your selection that is nearest to your target vertex is the one that snaps to it.

Snapping modes work in both Object mode as well as Edit mode. For more information on Edit mode, see Chapter 4.

You can observe the changes made to your object in real time by looking in the 3D View window's header as you transform it. Figure 3-5 shows how the header explicitly indicates how much you're changing the object in each axis.

Figure 3-5:
You can
view
changes
in the
3D View
window's
header.

Notice also the white circle around the origin of the Translate manipulator in Figure 3-3. To translate a selected object in the X and Y axis of the View orientation, left-click this circle. This convenient shortcut prevents you from having to continually switch orientation modes for the manipulator.

Suppose that you don't want to move the object in the direction of just one axis. Instead, you prefer the freedom to move the object in the plane created by two axes, such as the XY, XZ, or YZ planes. Just Shift+left-click on the axis that's perpendicular to the plane in which you want to move. This is the axis that's "normal to the plane," as defined earlier in the chapter. For example, assuming that you want to scale the object in the XY plane, Shift+left-click the Z-axis cube of the Scale manipulator.

I use this technique a lot when modeling furniture and buildings. I can quickly scale along a plane a cube that has the proper depth, to create a tabletop or a wall. Figure 3-6 illustrates this concept.

Transform operations are consistent across all manipulator modes in Blender, so you can apply any of these methods of interacting with the Translate manipulator in the Rotate and Scale manipulator modes. The only exception is that Shift+left-clicking an axis on the Rotate manipulator operates just like simply left-clicking the axis: It doesn't make sense to try to simultaneously rotate around two axes with any form of control. And don't forget that you aren't limited to working in just the Global coordinate system. You can choose any of the other three orientations from the Coordinate System Orientation menu and the 3D manipulator adjusts to fit that axis.

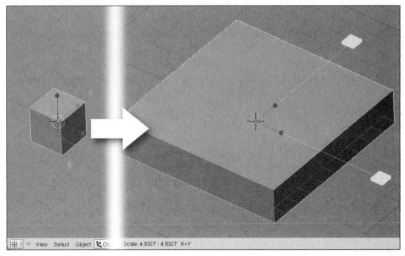

Figure 3-6:
Building a
tabletop out
of a cube.

Saving Time by Using Hotkeys

Now, many professional Blender users find that the manipulator obstructs their view too much when working, so they disable it outright. To do this, go to the 3D View's header near the manipulator mode buttons and press the button with the white pointing hand on it (refer to Figure 3-1 if you need to refresh your memory). You can also do this by pressing Ctrl+spacebar and selecting Enable/Disable. But wait, with the manipulator gone, how do I transform my objects? I'm glad you asked. It is time to introduce you to one of the most powerful features of Blender: hotkeys.

Part of the beauty of Blender's hotkeys are that they take a lot of pressure off of your mouse hand and shorten the distance of mouse-based operations. For example, the Ctrl+spacebar combination that you used to disable the manipulator also gives you the option to directly select which mode you want to enable for the manipulator. Because the menu pops up right beneath your mouse, you don't have to travel all the way to the 3D View window's header each time you want to switch modes. It's especially helpful if you've removed the header from your 3D view or the manipulator mode buttons are somehow obstructed. The accumulation of little time-saving actions like these makes using hotkeys so powerful.

G, S, and R: Transforming with hotkeys

Nearly every piece of major functionality in Blender can be accessed with hotkeys. Transforms are no exception. Remember that I said *translate* in Blenderese is called *grab*? Use the following steps to Grab/Translate your object:

1. **Select the object you want to move by right-clicking it.**

2. **Press G.**

    Congratulations! You're translating your object.

3. **And just like with the 3D manipulator, confirm the translation by left-clicking or pressing Enter.**

    Cancel by right-clicking or pressing Esc.

To rotate your object, press R. Scale it by pressing S. See a pattern here? The majority of Blender hotkeys are easy to remember. Most of them just use the first letter from the operation in question. And just like when using the manipulator, the familiar Ctrl, Shift, and Ctrl+Shift keypresses for fixed increments and fine adjustments still apply here.

Hotkeys and coordinate systems

By default, your transformations all happen in the View coordinate system. This means that no matter how you're viewing the scene, you're working in the XY-plane of the window. Suppose, however, you want to grab your object and move it in the Global Z-axis. You use a sequence of keypresses to do this action. Use the following steps to grab an object and move it to the Global Z-axis:

1. **With your object selected, press G.**

    This puts you in Grab/Translate mode.

2. **Now, without canceling this operation, press Z.**

    A blue line should appear that indicates the Global Z-axis. Your object is locked to move only along that line. If you press Y, your object moves only along the Global Y-axis and pressing X locks it to the Global X-axis.

Pretty neat, huh? This works with rotating and scaling as well (for example, R⇨Z rotates around the Global Z-axis and S⇨X scales along the Global X-axis).

What about the Local axis? That's just one more keypress in the sequence. Follow these steps to grab an object and move it along its Local Y-axis:

1. **Act like you are going to translate the object in the Global Y-axis by pressing G⇨Y.**

2. **Then press Y a second time.**

    This gets you translating in the Local Y-axis. Pressing Y a third time brings you back into moving in the default View coordinate system.

TIP

Again, this works with scaling and rotation as well. Keying the sequence R⇨ X⇨X rotates around the local X-axis and S⇨Z⇨Z scales along the local Z-axis.

One of the more powerful features of the 3D manipulator is the ability to work in a plane rather than just one axis. This, too, can be done with hotkeys using the same logic used in the manipulator. Use Shift plus the letter of the axis that's perpendicular to the plane you want to move in. For instance, to scale your object in the Global XY-plane, press S⇨Shift+Z. For the Local XY plane, press S⇨Shift+Z⇨Shift+Z. This same methodology also works for the Grab operation (though, like with the manipulator, not for the Rotate operation). Table 3-1 shows most of the useful hotkey sequences for transforming your objects.

Table 3-1	Useful Hotkey Sequences for Transformations		
Grab	*Scale*	*Rotate*	*Orientation*
G	S	R	View
G⇨Z	S⇨Z	R⇨Z	Global Z-axis
G⇨Y	S⇨Y	R⇨Y	Global Y-axis
G⇨X	S⇨X	R⇨X	Global X-axis
G⇨Z⇨Z	S⇨Z⇨Z	R⇨Z⇨Z	Local Z-axis
G⇨Y⇨Y	S⇨Y⇨Y	R⇨Y⇨Y	Local Y-axis
G⇨X⇨X	S⇨X⇨X	R⇨X⇨X	Local X-axis
G⇨Shift+Z	S⇨Shift+Z	N/A	Global XY-plane
G⇨Shift+Y	S⇨Shift+Y	N/A	Global XZ-plane
G⇨Shift+X	S⇨Shift+X	N/A	Global YZ-plane
G⇨Shift+Z⇨ Shift+Z	S⇨Shift+Z⇨ Shift+Z	N/A	Local XY-plane
G⇨Shift+Y⇨ Shift+Y	S⇨Shift+Y⇨ Shift+Y	N/A	Local XZ-plane
G⇨Shift+X⇨ Shift+X	S⇨Shift+X⇨ Shift+X	N/A	Local YZ-plane

There is one other, potentially faster, way to lock your transformations to a particular axis: using the middle mouse button. Assume you want to grab your object and translate it along the global X-axis. Select the object and press G, as if you would do any translation. Now use your mouse to move the object in the general direction of the X-axis. As you do this, middle-click and release. Your object should automatically lock to the global X-axis. Blender makes a guess based on the direction you're moving the object in and, when you middle-click, it locks your object to that axis. And of course, this also works with the other transform operations on any of the global axes.

An even faster way to constrain to axes involves using the middle mouse button. As an example, select an object and Grab (G) it. Now move your mouse in roughly the direction of the X-axis and then middle-click. A red line should appear through your object's centerpoint and the object should be locked to moving along that line, constraining you to that axis. The same thing works in both the Y- and Z-axes. For an even more interactive way of doing this, hold down your middle mouse button while you're Grabbing. All three axes will appear and your object will lock to one of them as you bring your mouse closer to them. I absolutely *love* this feature.

To get a good idea of just how much Blender makes use of the keyboard, have a look at the HotKey and MouseAction Reference in the Help menu (Help⇨ HotKey and MouseAction Reference). This is a comprehensive list of all of the hotkeys that Blender uses. It's a great reference and is even searchable if you happen to forget a hotkey or, say, five. (It's okay, there are a lot of hotkeys. Even veteran Blender users occasionally forget a few every now and then.)

Using gestures to work faster

In the previous section, you saw how Blender uses your mouse movement to work with you and work faster by guessing your intent. This isn't the only way Blender uses mouse movement to enhance your workflow. Blender also supports gestures. If you've used the Opera Web browser or Apple's iPhone, you may already be familiar with some of the power of gestures. In essence, gestures rely on your making a movement with your mouse that Blender interprets as a command. To perform a gesture, left-click and drag your mouse, drawing a line. Blender's primary gestures are for transformations, and Figure 3-7 illustrates them. They're also listed as follows:

- **Grab/Translate:** Draw a straight line.
- **Rotate:** Draw a curved line.
- **Scale:** Draw a V-shaped line.

Figure 3-7:
Mouse move-
ments for
Blender's
gestures.

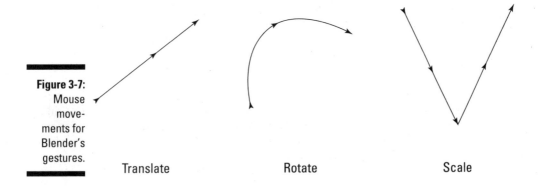

Translate   Rotate   Scale

Gestures are particularly useful for Blender users who work with a drawing tablet, PDA, or tablet PC. The pen-like interface of these devices makes it very convenient to draw these shapes and work very quickly. Of course, even for those of us who work with a mouse or trackball, gestures can be quite handy.

Numerical input

Not only can you use hotkeys to activate the various transform modes, but you can also use the keyboard to explicitly input exactly how much you would like your object to be transformed. You do this by simply typing in the number of units you want to change after you activate the transform mode. As an example, suppose you want to rotate your object 32 degrees around the Global X-axis. To do this, press R⇨X⇨32 and confirm by pressing Enter. Translate your object -26.4 units along its Local Y-axis by pressing G⇨Y⇨Y⇨-26.4⇨Enter. This can be a very quick and effective means of flipping or mirroring an object because mirroring is just scaling by –1 along a particular axis. For instance, to flip an object along the Global Z-axis, press S⇨Z⇨–1⇨Enter. For consistency, these numerical input operations are also available when using the 3D manipulator.

The Transform Properties floating window

One other way to explicitly translate, scale, and rotate your object is through the Transform Properties floating window. Although Blender's interface is primarily designed to be non-blocking, it does allow a few floating windows. Transform Properties is one of them. To activate this window, go to Object⇨Transform Properties in the 3D View window's header or press N. The Transform Properties window floats over the 3D View and allows you to explicitly enter numerical values for Location, Scale, and Rotation. Close the Transform Properties window by left-clicking the X in its upper left corner or by pressing N a second time.

One thing to be careful of here is to note that, when in Object mode, the values in the Transform Properties window do not change depending on which coordinate system you've selected. Location is always in the Global orientation, whereas Rotation and Scale are always in Local.

Chapter 4

Working in Edit Mode and Object Mode

In This Chapter

▶ Making changes to your 3D objects

▶ Adding new objects to a scene

▶ Saving, opening, and appending .blend files

*W*hen working on a scene in Blender, your life revolves around repeatedly selecting objects, transforming them, editing them, and relating them to one another. You shift from dealing with your model in Object mode to doing refinements in Edit mode. And this is not only the process for modeling, but also for most of the other heavy tasks performed in Blender. Therefore, the skills you pick up in this chapter can be reused in parts of Blender that have nothing to do with modeling objects in 3D. Just as many of the transform operations work in windows other than the 3D View, many of the concepts here transfer nicely to other parts of Blender. Even if you don't know how to do something, chances are good that if you think like Blender thinks, you'll be able to guess.

Making Changes Using Edit Mode

Moving primitive objects around is fun and all, but you're interested in getting in there and completely changing these objects to match your vision. You want to do 3D modeling. Well, you're in the right place for that. This section introduces you to Edit mode, a concept that's deeply embedded throughout Blender for editing objects. Even though this section is focused mostly on polygon modeling, also called *mesh editing*, most of the same principles apply for editing curves, surfaces, armatures, and even text. Remember, when you understand how Blender thinks, it's much easier to figure out unknown parts of the program.

Distinguishing between Object mode and Edit mode

In Chapter 3, everything you did was in what's called Object mode. As its name indicates, this is where you work with whole objects. However, it isn't very useful for actually changing the structure of your object. For example, right-click the cube in the default scene to select it. You know that you can turn it into a more rectangular shape by scaling it in one of the axes. But what if you want to turn the cube into a pyramid? To do that, you need to modify the actual components that make up the cube. You do this by entering Edit mode.

You can get to Edit mode in one of two ways: with the mouse or with a hotkey. To use the mouse method, left-click the Object Mode button in the 3D View's header. From the pop-up menu that appears, shown in Figure 4-1, select Edit Mode. Now, if you're working with an object other than a mesh, such as an armature, the contents of this menu may vary slightly to relate more to that object. However, with the exception of Empties, all objects have an Edit mode.

Figure 4-1:
The Object
Mode
button.

Of course, Blender also has a hotkey to enter Edit mode. Actually, technically speaking, the hotkey toggles you between Object mode and Edit mode. Press Tab to switch between modes. This is the preferred way to switch between modes in Blender and it's used so frequently that Blender users often use tab as a verb and say they're *tabbing into* Edit mode or Object mode. It's something you come across fairly often in Blender user forums and in some of Blender's online documentation.

Selecting vertices, edges, and faces

After you tab into Edit mode, notice that the cube changes color and that points form at each of the cube's corners. Each of these points is a *vertex*. The line that forms between two vertices is an *edge*. A *face* in Blender is a polygon that has been formed by three or four connecting edges.

Faces in Blender are limited to only three-sided and four-sided polygons, often referred to as *tris* (pronounced like *tries*) and *quads*. Other programs have something called an *n-gon* that can have virtually a limitless number of sides. Blender developers are working on building this feature into Blender and have made great progress. However, at this time, only some development versions of Blender have n-gon functionality. The current release is still limited to tris and quads. This isn't a completely horrible situation, however. A lot can still be done with just three- and four-sided faces. In fact, most detailed character models are made completely with quads, and all 3D geometry is reduced to triangles when it gets to your computer hardware.

For polygon editing, there are actually three different types of Edit modes: Vertex Select, Edge Select, and Face Select. By default, the first time you Tab into Edit mode, you are in Vertex Select mode. You can tell this for two reasons. First of all, you can see the individual vertices in the mesh. Secondly, as Figure 4-2 shows, three new buttons show up in the 3D View's header when you are in Edit mode. The button on the left with the four dots on it is selected, indicating that you are in Vertex Select mode.

Figure 4-2:
The Edit
mode Select
buttons.

To the right of the Vertex Select button is a button with a diagonal line in it. Click this button to activate Edge Select mode. When you do this, notice that the vertices are no longer visible on your mesh. Depressing the last button in this block, which has a triangle shape on it, activates Face Select mode. When Face Select mode is active, vertices are not visible and each polygon in your mesh has a square dot in the center of it.

Now, you might be looking at these buttons and noticing that they're blocked together, kind of like the 3D manipulator buttons. Does this mean that, like with the manipulator, you can simultaneously activate multiple modes? Absolutely! Simply Shift+left-click the Select mode buttons to get this function. Some Blender modelers like to have Vertex Select and Edge Select modes active at the same time to speed up their workflow. This gives them immediate control at the vertex and edge level, and faces can be easily selected with one or two extra clicks. Figure 4-3 shows the default cube in each of the select modes as well as a Combo Select mode.

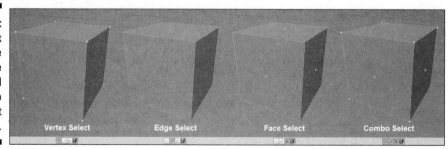

Figure 4-3:
Vertex
Select, Edge
Select, Face
Select, and
Combo
Select
modes.

Of course, the various select modes can also be accessed with a hotkey sequence. While you are in Edit mode, if you press Ctrl+Tab, you are presented with a menu that lets you switch between modes. This menu does not let you set multiple modes, so if you want to do that, you still have to use the buttons in the 3D View's header.

Also, by default the first time you Tab into Edit mode, all vertices/edges/faces are selected. Selecting things in Edit mode works just like selecting anywhere else. Right-click on any vertex to select it. Multiple vertices can be selected and deselected by Shift+right-clicking on them. Large groups of vertices can be selected using the Border Select tool (press B) or Brush Select (press B⇨B). In Border and Brush Select, left-click and drag to add to your selection. Middle-click and drag to subtract from your selection and right-click or press Esc to exit Border or Brush Select. Blender also has a Lasso Select functionality. To use it, Ctrl+left-click and drag around the vertices you wish to select. Anything within the selection region is added to your selection. And, of course, all of these selection tools work in Edge and Face Select modes. Figure 4-4 shows what the various selection tools look like when in use.

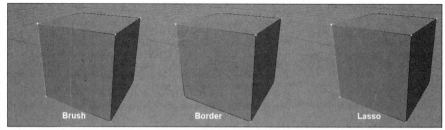

Figure 4-4:
Brush
Select,
Border
Select,
and Lasso
Select.

If you want to select everything (in Object mode, all objects; and in Edit mode, all vertices in the active object) you can do so by pressing A. The A hotkey is a toggle, so anything previously selected when you press A will be deselected. However, if nothing is previously selected, pressing A selects everything. Using this hotkey, you'll find yourself pressing A until you have either everything or nothing selected.

Another handy way to select things in Edit mode is by selecting linked vertices. *Linked vertices* are a set of vertices within a mesh that are connected by edges. In order to understand this better, go through the following steps:

1. **Right-click to select your default cube in Blender and tab into Edit mode.**

   All of the vertices should be selected. If they are not, press A until they are.

2. **With all of the vertices selected, press Shift+D or spacebar⇨Edit⇨ Duplicate to duplicate your selection.**

   When you do this, Blender creates a copy of your selection and automatically switches to Grab mode.

3. **When you duplicate anything, Blender automatically Grabs the duplicate, allowing you to move it. So just use your mouse pointer to move your new cube off the original and confirm your placement by left-clicking or pressing Enter.**

4. **Notice that none of the vertices in the original cube are selected.**

   Each cube represents a set of linked vertices. So what if you want to select all of the vertices in that cube too? Sure, you could use the Border, Brush, or Lasso Select tools mentioned above, but on complex meshes, this could get cumbersome. Instead, place your mouse pointer near any vertex in the original cube and press L. Blam! All of the vertices in both of your cubes should now be selected.

Of course, the natural next question is, "How do I deselect linked vertices?" That's just as easy. Place your mouse cursor near any vertex on the duplicate cube you created and press Shift+L. This deselects all of the vertices connected to the one near your mouse pointer. I've found myself using L and Shift+L pretty heavily when trying to place teeth in a mouth I've modeled. These are *very* handy hotkeys.

Quite a few more selection options are available to you when working with meshes. These selection methods are described in detail in Chapter 5.

While you are in edit mode, you are can only work with the object at hand. You cannot select and manipulate other objects while you're in Edit mode.

If you are using Blender's default settings, you might notice that you can see through your model and even select vertices, edges, and faces on the back side of the model, regardless of whether you are using the Solid or Wireframe Viewport Shading settings (toggle between the two by pressing Z). On complex models, this can get confusing and you can find yourself making selections on the back of your model that you don't want. To get around this, click the Occlude Background Geometry button. It's the button with the cube icon at the right end of the Selection Modes block in the 3D View's header. (Refer to Figure 4-2 if you need a refresher.) Click this button to hide the vertices, edges, and faces on the back of your model. This is often referred to as *backface culling* and it is incredibly useful when you're working with complex models.

Blender's #1 modeling tool: Extrude

Besides the transform operations, the most commonly used modeling tool in Blender is the Extrude function. In the physical world, *extrusion* is a process whereby some material is pushed through a shaped hole of some sort. When you were a kid, did you ever cut out a shape in cardboard and force clay or mud or Play-Doh through it? If so, you were extruding. If not, you certainly missed out on a good solid five to ten minutes of fun.

In 3D, extrusion follows a similar concept, except you don't have to create the hole to extrude through. Instead, that shape is determined by your selection and you can extend that selection in any direction. Use the following steps to extrude:

1. **Select the object you want to edit by right-clicking it.**

2. **Tab into Edit mode.**

3. **Select the vertices, edges, or faces you wish to extrude.**

   Do this using any of the selection methods listed in the previous section.

4. **Press E to extrude your selection.**

After you extrude your selection, Blender automatically puts you into Grab mode, constraining the extrusion along its normal. There are advantages and disadvantages to this. The advantages are that you have all the transform functionality, such as axis-locking, snapping, and numerical input immediately available to you. The disadvantage is that, because of this "autograb" behavior, if you cancel the operation by right-clicking or pressing Esc, the newly extruded vertices, edges, or faces are still there, just located in exactly the same place as the vertices, edges, or faces that they originated from.

For this reason, if you cancel an extrude operation, it's always a good idea to make sure your duplicate vertices, often called *doubles*, are no longer there. A quick way to check is to press G after you've canceled your extrusion. If it looks like you're extruding again, you have doubles. You can get rid of doubles in a variety of ways:

- ✔ If you still have the doubles selected, delete them by pressing X or Del and choosing Vertices from the pop-up menu.

- ✔ If the canceled extrusion operation was the last thing you did, undo it by pressing Ctrl+Z.

- ✔ If you are unsure whether you have doubles from previous canceled extrusions, Blender has a special Remove Doubles function. Follow these steps to use it:

1. **In Edit Mode, select all by choosing Select⇨Select/Deselect All from the 3D View's header or pressing A until all vertices are selected.**

   Blender's Select All function is a toggle that selects everything or nothing, depending on whether anything is already selected.

2. **Press W⇨Remove Doubles and Blender removes all doubles from your mesh.**

   This option can be found in Mesh⇨Vertices⇨Remove Doubles in the 3D View's header, as well as the toolbox (spacebar⇨Edit⇨Vertices⇨Remove Doubles).

Depending on what you've selected, you may have a few options available to you when extruding. If you have one vertex or a set of vertices that have no connecting edges between them, you have no options. However, if you have edges selected, you are presented with a pop-up that lets you choose between extruding Only Vertices or Only Edges. If you have faces selected, you are presented with four options: Only Vertices, Only Edges, Individual Faces, or Region. Table 4-1 gives a more detailed description of each option.

Table 4-1		Extrusion Options
Option	*Selection Type*	*Description*
Only Vertices	Vertices, Edges, Faces	Extrudes the selected vertices relative to the View Orientation, creating edges between the new vertices and the ones they originated from.
Only Edges	Edges, Faces	Extrudes the selected edges relative to the View Orientation, creating faces between the new edges and the ones they originated from.
Individual Faces	Multiple Faces	Extrudes the selected faces relative to the View Orientation, creating faces between the new faces and the ones they originated from. Note that the new faces are not directly connected together. That is a *region* extrusion.
Region	Single or Multiple Faces	Extrudes the selected faces as a single unit in the direction normal to the selection, creating faces between the new region and the one it originated from.

Note that these options also depend on your selection mode. As you might expect, if you're in Edge Select mode, then you won't see options pertaining to vertices. And if you're in Face Select mode, then options for both edges and vertices will not be visible.

Now, when you're modeling, the most common type of extrusion you want is related to what you've selected. For instance, if you want to extrude an edge, you select that edge, or if you select a group of faces, chances are good that you want to extrude that as a region. As expected, Blender has shortcuts for these common modeling tasks. To perform a quick extrusion, use the following steps:

1. **Select your object and Tab into Edit mode.**

2. **Select the vertices, edges, or faces you wish to extrude.**

3. **Ctrl+left-click where you would like the extrusion to end.**

   This automatically decides what kind of extrusion you want and extrudes your selection right where you would like. Working this way is particularly useful for doing a series of multiple extrusions, one right after the other. You often do this when roughing out a shape by "drawing" with vertices or edges.

Although Ctrl+left-clicking for quick extrusion is convenient for creating rough models to start with, there are certainly workflow benefits to extruding with the E key. The biggest benefit is the quick access to your other transform tools. To illustrate this, use the following steps to model a skyscraper from a single plane:

1. **Open Blender and tab into Edit mode on the default cube.**

2. **Press Numpad 3 to change to Side View.**

3. **Translate everything by one unit in the positive Z direction (G⇨Z⇨1⇨ Enter).**

4. **Middle-click and drag in the 3D view so you can get a good view of the top face of the cube.**

5. **Switch to Face Select mode (Ctrl+Tab⇨Faces).**

6. **Right-click to select the top-most face of the cube and delete it by pressing X⇨Vertices.**

7. **Perform a multi-subdivide with two cuts (W⇨Subdivide Multi⇨2⇨ Enter).**

8. **Switch to Edge Select mode (Ctrl+Tab⇨Edges).**

9. **Select the edges that form the corners of the plane.**

   Using regular right-clicking, Brush Select (B⇨B), or Lasso Select (Ctrl+left-click and drag) works best for this.

10. **Extrude these edges and scale them by 1.1 in the XY-plane (E⇨S⇨ Shift+Z⇨1.1⇨Enter).**

11. **Select all (A⇨A).**

12. **Extrude the region along the global Z-axis (E⇨Region).**

    By default, your extrusion is locked along the direction of the region's normal. Fortunately, because of the way you are working, that normal coincides with the global Z-axis. The height of this level can be whatever you like. I extruded mine by 3 units.

13. **With the region still selected, extrude again, but scale the region by 0.9 in the XY-plane (E⇨Region⇨S⇨Shift+Z⇨0.9⇨Enter).**

14. **Translate this new region along the Z-axis by 0.1 units (G⇨Z⇨0.1⇨ Enter).**

15. **Perform steps 12-14 as many times as you would like to get the sky-scraper to your desired height.**

    I gave mine three layers.

16. **On your last extruded region, scale the selection in the XY-plane to a generally pyramid-shaped peak (S⇨Shift+Z).**

17. **Tab back into Object mode and behold the awesome beauty of your skyscraper!**

    Figure 4-5 shows an illustration of the major steps in this process.

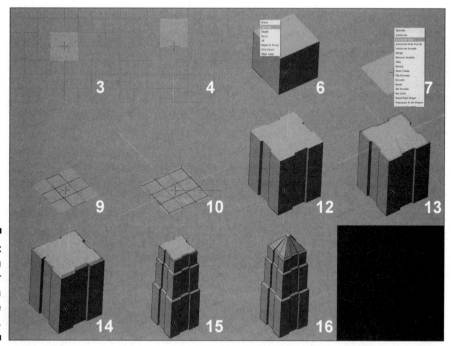

Figure 4-5: Modeling a skyscraper from a single plane.

Going through this process, notice how immediately after executing the extrude operation, you could scale the extrusion to create insets and outsets to grow your building from. Using extrusion with your transform tools in this manner gives you an immense amount of speed and flexibility when modeling.

Modeling organically with the Proportional Edit tool

Often, when you are modeling organic objects or objects with smoothly curved surfaces, such as characters, creatures, or sports cars, you may find yourself pushing and pulling a bunch of vertices to obtain that smooth surface. There's an easier way to do this using Blender's *Proportional Edit Tool* (PET). If you come from another 3D package, you might recognize this as being similar to the "soft select" feature. You activate PET by left-clicking the PET button, which looks like two concentric circles in the 3D View's header, in Edit mode and selecting On. The hotkey for this operation is O. Now when you perform a transform operation, a circle appears around your selection. Any vertices that are within this circle are influenced by your transformation with a gradual falloff. You can adjust the influence of the PET by scrolling your mouse wheel or pressing Alt+Numpad-plus and Alt+Numpad-minus. Additionally, you can control how gradual the falloff is by left-clicking the button with the curve icon next to the PET button in the 3D view's header or by cycling through the options by pressing Shift+O. You have the following options:

✔ **Smooth Falloff:** This is the default falloff for PET — it offers a nice smooth transition from your selected vertices to those outside of the PET's influence.

✔ **Sphere Falloff:** Sphere Falloff works as expected, with the falloff following a general spherical shape from your selection. It does not have a particularly smooth transition to vertices outside the PET's influence.

✔ **Root Falloff:** Root Falloff is similar to Sphere Falloff, but it has a slightly sharper, more parabolic shape. Like the Sphere Falloff, the transition to outside vertices can be rather abrupt.

✔ **Sharp Falloff:** This falloff setting is similar to Smooth Falloff in that it offers a nice transition to the vertices outside the PET's influence; however, the drop from your selected vertices to the outside vertices is much less gradual. This is useful for generating creases and the appearance of seams in your models.

✔ **Linear Falloff:** Linear Falloff has a "straight line" transition from your selected vertices to the vertices outside of the PET's influence. This setting is pretty useful for creating corners and pyramid-like shapes on your mesh.

✔ **Random Falloff:** This falloff setting is not used very often, but it can be very helpful for giving your models a natural, randomized feel. Of course, things can get a touch out of hand, but this setting certainly has its uses.

✔ **Constant Falloff:** With Constant Falloff, any vertices that are within the PET's influence range are transformed right with the selected vertices with an abrupt drop to outside vertices.

There is one more useful option in PET. On complex meshes, you may want to use PET on one set of vertices that are connected to one another, but not to other nearby vertices in the same mesh. For example, say you've modeled a character and her hand is at her side near her leg, and you would like to smoothly edit her hand and pull it away from the leg without having to gradually adjust the vertices of the arm. PET is the perfect tool for this job. However, when you try to use it, some of the leg vertices are within the PET's influence and you end up moving those unintentionally. Wouldn't it be great if the PET could understand that you only want to move the hand? Well, I have good news: It can! Click the PET button in the 3D view header and select Connected or press Alt+O. The Connected option for PET only adjusts vertices that are connected to each other within its influence area. Neat, huh?

Adding to a Scene

There's got to be more to life than that plain default cube, right? Indeed, there is. Blender offers a whole slew of *primitives*, or basic objects, to build from.

Anytime you add a new object in Blender, the center of that object is located wherever you've placed the 3D cursor.

Getting to know the toolbox that lives in your spacebar

Anytime you want to add a new object in Blender, you want to use the toolbox. To access the toolbox, hover your mouse in the 3D view and press spacebar. Directly beneath your mouse, a menu pops up with the following options:

- ✔ **Add:** This is where all Blender's primitives live. These primitives include modeling objects like meshes, curves, and meta-objects as well as special primitives such as cameras, lights, and armatures.

- ✔ **Edit:** This menu item gives you a variety of editing options, depending on the context of what you're doing. In Object mode, not many options are available to you other than creating duplicates and entering Edit mode.

- ✔ **Select:** The Select menu provides you with different selection options. In Object mode, the most commonly used functions are Select/Deselect All and Inverse. In Edit mode, depending on the type of object you are editing, there are quite a few more options.

- **Transform:** Nearly all of the transform options discussed in the previous section are available to you in this menu.

- **Object:** This menu has object-level operations, including copying, linking, parenting, and moving layers. In Edit mode, the menu changes to operations that are specific to the type of object you are editing.

- **View:** Options related to the 3D view live in this menu. Functions include changing the view angle, adjusting the viewport shading mode, and playing back animations.

- **Render:** From this menu, you have options for generating the final output, or render, of your 3D scene from the perspective of your camera. You can also enable the Render Preview floating window, which renders according to the viewport orientation, rather than the camera.

The toolbox gives you access to the majority of Blender's functions. It is actually possible to complete most tasks right from the toolbox menu. Of course, this isn't as fast or efficient as making use of all of Blender's hotkeys, but it's good to know it's possible, particularly for users who work using a Tablet PC or PDA.

You may notice that for pop-up menus like the toolbox, Blender places the last menu option you choose directly under your mouse cursor. This is a workflow feature to help increase your speed. The idea is that you often want to do the same task multiple times in a row. Blender makes it easier by shortening the distance you have to move your mouse with each function.

Adding objects

To add a new object to your scene, press spacebar⇨Add and choose the type of primitive you want to put into the scene. You have the following choices:

- **Mesh:** Meshes are polygon-based objects made up of vertices, edges, and faces. They are the most common type of modeling object used in Blender.

- **Curve:** Curves are objects made up of curved or straight lines that are manipulated with a set of *control points*. Control points are similar to vertices, but they can be edited in a couple of ways that vertices can't. Blender has two basic forms of curves, Bèzier curves and NURBS (Non-Uniform Relational B-Spline) curves. You can also use curves as paths to control other objects.

- **Surface:** A surface is similar to a mesh, but rather than being made up of vertices, edges, and faces, surfaces in Blender are defined by a set of NURBS curves and their control points.

✔ **Meta:** Meta objects are unique primitives with the cool ability to kind of melt into one another and create a larger structure. They are handy for a variety of effects that involve blobby masses such as clouds or water, as well as quick rough clay-like models.

✔ **Text:** The text object allows you to bring type into your 3D scene and manipulate it like other 3D objects.

✔ **Empty:** The unsung hero of Blender objects. Empties do not show up in finished renders: Their primary purpose is merely to serve as a reference position, size, and orientation in 3D space. This basic purpose, however, allows them to work as very powerful controls.

✔ **Group:** A group is a set of objects you define as being related to each other in some way. The objects in a group do not have to be the same type and are handy for organization as well as appending sets of objects from external files.

✔ **Camera:** Like real-world cameras, camera objects define the location and perspective from which you are rendering your scene.

✔ **Lamp:** Lamp objects are necessary for lighting your scene. Just like in the physical world, if you don't have any light, you don't see anything.

✔ **Armature:** Armature objects are skeleton-like structures that consist of linked bones. The bones in an armature can be used to deform other objects and are particularly useful for creating the puppet-like controls necessary for character animation.

✔ **Lattice:** Like armature objects, lattices are used to deform other objects. They are often used in modeling and animation to squash, stretch, and twist models in a non-permanent way. Lately lattices are used less and less in Blender because users have gained the ability to deform objects with curves and meshes.

By default, when you add a new object in Blender, its local orientation is aligned to the global axes. This default behavior is new to Blender as of version 2.46. In prior versions of Blender, new objects were added with their local orientation aligned to the view orientation. Blender also used to automatically set newly added objects in Edit mode. One way is not really any better than the other, and it depends mostly on your personal preference. The latter method is a bit faster while the former is somewhat less disorienting. You can test out the old behavior by looking in Edit Methods under Blender's Preferences and clicking the appropriate buttons on the left side. Figure 4-6 illustrates the difference between inserting a new object aligned to the global axes versus inserting a new object aligned to the view orientation.

Note that the preceding paragraph only makes sense if you are adding primitives in Object mode. Blender allows you to add new primitives in Edit mode as long as they are of the same type as the object you are editing. And because you are adding to an already existing object, the new primitive is aligned to view and the object's orientation won't change.

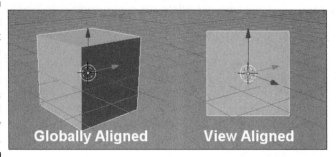

Figure 4-6:
New object
aligned to
global
orientation
versus
aligned
to view
orientation.

Globally Aligned   **View Aligned**

If you want to add a new primitive aligned to the global orientation while in Edit mode, add your object from the top view (Numpad 7). Figure 4-7 shows how primitives added in Edit mode are aligned to view.

When adding new objects, be aware of whether you are in Object mode or Edit mode. If you add while in Edit mode, then your addition options are limited to the type of object you're editing. Also, your new object's data is joined with the object you're editing. If you don't want this to happen, then make sure you Tab back to Object mode before adding anything new.

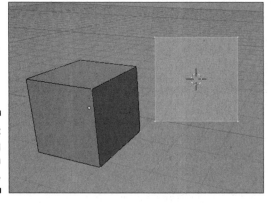

Figure 4-7:
Adding
primitives in
Edit mode.

Meet Suzanne, the Blender monkey

Many 3D modeling and animation suites have a generic semi-complex primitive that is used for test renders, benchmarks, and examples that necessitate something a little more complex than a cube or sphere. Most of these other programs use famous Utah teapot as their test model. In Blender, you have something a little more interesting and unique. Blender has a monkey head that's affectionately referred to as "Suzanne," a reference to the ape in two of Kevin Smith's films: *Jay and Silent Bob Strike Back* and *Mallrats* (close to the end). Add Suzanne to your scene by pressing spacebar⇨Add⇨Mesh⇨Monkey. If you look through the Blender community's forums and many of Blender's release documentation, you see Suzanne and references to her all over the place. In fact, the annual awards festival at the Blender Conference in Amsterdam is called the Suzanne Awards. Figure 4-8 shows a test render featuring Suzanne.

Figure 4-8:
Suzanne!

Joining and separating objects

In the course of creating models for your scenes, you may have a need to join or separate objects. You might have to do this if you accidentally add a new primitive while you are still in Edit mode. Of course, you could simply undo, tab into Object mode, and re-add your primitive, but why act like you made a mistake and go through all those extra steps? There's another way. Notice that when you add a new primitive while in Edit mode, all of the elements of your new primitive are selected and nothing from your original object is selected. If only there was a command that would let you break this primitive away from this object and into an object of its own. Fortunately, there is. Press P⇨Selected, and your new primitive is separated into its own object. You can also access this function in the toolbox (spacebar⇨Edit⇨Vertices⇨S eparate) as well as the 3D view's header (Mesh⇨Vertices⇨Separate).

Tab back into Object mode and right-click your new object to select it. Notice that its center is located in the same place as its original object's center. To put the center of your new object at its actual center, press spacebar⇨Transform⇨ Center New. This checks the size of your object and calculates where its true center is. Then Blender places the object's center at that location. You can also specify that the object's center be placed wherever your 3D cursor is located by pressing spacebar⇨Transform⇨Center Cursor. A third option is similar to Center New, but it moves the object's content rather than the center point. Do this by pressing spacebar⇨Transform⇨ObData to Center. There are also buttons for placing the center of an object in the Mesh panel of the Editing Button window (F9). Figure 4-9 shows a screenshot of this panel.

Figure 4-9:
The Mesh
panel in
the Editing
Buttons
window.

As expected, you can also join two objects of the same type into a single object. To do this, you need to first select multiple objects. In Object mode, you can use the Border Select or Lasso Select tools, or you can simply Shift+right-click objects to add to your selection. The last object you select is considered your *Active Object* and is the object that the others join into. With your objects selected, press Ctrl+J to join them.

You can only join objects that are of the same type. That is, you can join two mesh objects, but you can't join a mesh object with a curve object. Using parenting or groups might be more appropriate for that.

Creating duplicates and links

Earlier in this chapter, while working with linked vertices in Edit mode, you saw an example that involved duplicating your selected vertices using Shift+D (or spacebar➪Edit➪Duplicate). As you might expect, this operation also works in Object mode. This duplication method is great if you intend on taking an existing object and using it as a starting point to model another, more individualized, object by tweaking it in Edit mode. However, suppose you want your duplicated object to be identical to the original in Edit mode. And wouldn't it be nice if, when you do go into Edit mode, your changes happen to the original *as well as* all of the duplicates? For something like that, you want to use the power of *linked duplicates*. Linked duplicates are objects that share the same internal data. This is similar to what other programs call *instance copies*. The process to create a linked duplicate is pretty straightforward:

1. **Select the object you wish to duplicate by right-clicking it.**

2. **With the object selected, press Alt+D or spacebar➪Edit➪Duplicate Linked.**

3. **From here, the behavior is just like regular duplication.**

   The object is automatically in Grab mode. You can place it with your mouse and confirm it by left-clicking it or by pressing Enter.

In a few ways you can verify that this is, in fact, a linked duplicate. The easiest way would be to tab into Edit mode on the original object or any of the duplicates. When you do this, all of the linked objects appear to go into Edit mode and any changes you make here automatically update all the other objects immediately. Figure 4-10 shows three linked duplicates of Suzanne being simultaneously modified in Edit mode.

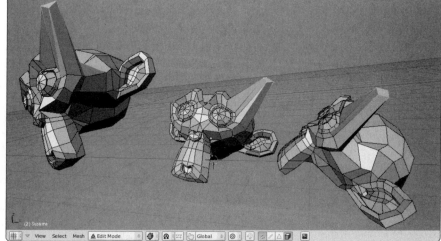

Figure 4-10:
Editing
duplicated
Suzannes!

A second way to verify their linked status is to look in the Editing buttons in your Buttons window by pressing F9. In the Link and Materials panel that appears, look at the text field at the top right. This is the Object Name field. It should read *OB* and the name of your object as listed in the bottom left corner of the 3D View. To the left of this field is the Datablock Name field. If there is a number to the right of the name (and to the left of a button with an F on it), that is the number of objects linked to this data. In other words, this is the count of your linked duplicates. Figure 4-11 shows how this panel looks when one of the Suzannes in the previous figure is selected.

Figure 4-11:
Three
objects are
sharing this
datablock.

One other way to see how duplicates are linked is with the Oops Schematic in the Outliner window. Use the following steps to split open an Outliner window with the Oops Schematic:

1. **Right-click the seam between the 3D View and the Buttons windows and select Split Area.**

2. **Place the split line so you create a new, somewhat narrower window.**

3. **In this new window, change the window type to Outliner by pressing Shift+F9 with your mouse pointer in the window or by left-clicking the left-most button in the window's header and selecting Outliner.**

4. **By default, Blender puts you in the Outliner view of the Outliner window. To change this, choose View↷Show Oops Schematic from the Outliner's header.**

The Oops Schematic gives you an overview of all of the little bits of data in your scene, called *datablocks*, including objects, materials, and mesh data. With it, you can see how the datablocks relate to one another. Figure 4-12 shows the Oops Schematic for the above scene involving the three linked duplicates of Suzanne.

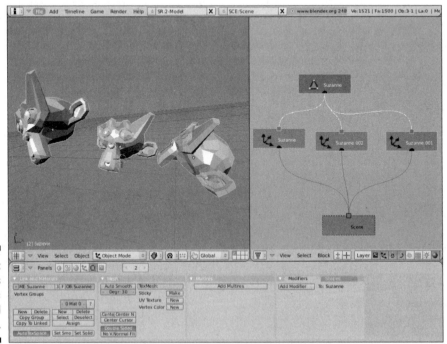

Figure 4-12:
An Oops Schematic of linked Suzannes.

Blender can do this because of the way Blender's .blend files are structured. Basically, it's like a database with various datablocks linked to one another. In programmer-speak, each datablock is called an *object*. The Oops Schematic is one of the easiest ways to visualize this. In fact, OOPS is actually an acronym for *Object-Oriented Programming System*. The real power comes in allowing multiple objects to share each other. For example, you can have objects share materials, mesh data, animation curves, actions, and even particle systems. And different scenes can even share objects! Taking advantage of this feature not only reduces the size of your .blend files, but it can also seriously reduce the amount of redundant work you have to do.

So say you've been using Blender for a while without knowing about linked duplicates and your .blend file is rife with redundant mesh data. Is there way to get rid of those regular duplicates and make them linked duplicates? Of course there is! Follow these steps:

1. **Select all of the objects that you would like to have share the same data.**

   You can do this with any of the selection tools available to you (Border, Brush, Lasso, and Shift+right-click). Note that all of the objects must be of the same type, hence you can't have a mesh object and a curve object share the same data.

2. **With each of your desired duplicates selected, Shift+right-click the object with the data you would like to share to make it an active object.**

3. **Press Ctrl+L or spacebar⇨Object⇨Make Links to bring up the Make Links pop-up. The third option from the top is the one you want.**

   If you are working with meshes, this option says Mesh Data; if you're working with curves, it says Curve Data, and so on.

Figure 4-13 shows the above process using a bunch of cubes and a Suzanne object.

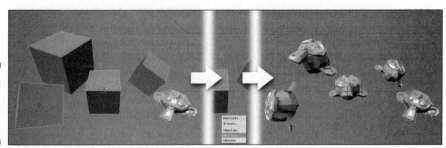

Figure 4-13:
Linking
cubes to
Suzanne.

You probably noticed that the Make Links popup had some other interesting options. Below is a description of what each one does:

- ✔ **To Scene...:** If you have multiple scenes in your .blend file, you can make those scenes share the same objects. Left-clicking this option brings up another menu with all of the scenes in the file. By choosing a scene, the object or objects that you selected have a linked duplicate(s) created in that scene.

- ✔ **Object Ipo:** This relates directly to animation. *Ipo* is short for "interpolation" and it's the Blenderese term for the curves that describe the motion of an animated object. Chapter 9 has more information on Ipos if you're not already familiar with them. Choosing this option causes all of your selected objects to share the same motion curves as the active object.

- ✔ **Mesh/Curve/Lamp/and so on Data:** This option is the one you used in the example above. It links the internal data — be it a mesh, a curve, a lamp, or nearly any other object — of the selected objects to the internal data of the active object. Again, note that for this to work, all the selected objects must be of the same type. This is the only option where that is important.

- ✔ **Materials:** Choosing this option causes all of the selected objects to share the same material settings. For more information on materials, have a look at Chapter 7.

Of course, if there's a way to create links and duplicates, it's logical (and correct) to think that there would be some way to convert a linked duplicate into an object with its own, non-shared datablocks. In Blender, this is called giving that datablock a single user. The reason for the *single user* terminology goes back to how these datablocks are tied together. From the perspective of the datablock, each object that's connected to it is considered a user. Glance back at Figure 4-12. Each Cube object is a user of the Suzanne datablock. By choosing to "Make Single User," you are effectively telling Blender to duplicate that datablock and make sure it only connects to a single object. To do this, select the object you would like to make a single user and then press U. This brings up a menu with the following options:

- ✔ **Object:** Use this option when you have an object that is linked to multiple scenes and you would like to make changes to it that only appear in the specific scene that you are currently working on.

- ✔ **Object & ObData:** For cases like the preceding example with the linked Suzanne meshes where you have a linked duplicate that you would like to edit independently of the other meshes, choose this option. Doing so effectively converts a linked duplicate into a regular duplicate.

✔ **Object & ODdata & Materials+Tex:** If you have an object that is not only sharing internal object data with others, but also sharing material settings, choose this option and both of those datablocks are duplicated and singly linked to your selected object. Using this option is a pretty good way to make sure that your selected object isn't sharing with any other objects.

✔ **Materials+Tex:** In cases where you no longer wish to share materials between objects, choosing this option makes sure your selected object has its own material settings independent of all the other objects.

✔ **Ipos:** This is the inverse of the Make Links⇨Object Ipos. If your selected object is sharing animation curves with any other objects, choosing this option makes sure it has curves of its own.

There is one other way to make object data a single user. Refer back to Figure 4-11. In that figure, the number 3 is highlighted, showing that three objects share that particular datablock. If you left-click that number, a confirmation box pops up, asking you if it is okay to make that a single user. Left-click again or press Enter to confirm. This little button shows up in many places throughout the Blender interface. The datablocks that it operates on vary with context (for example, seeing this button in the Materials buttons means it's working on a material datablock; seeing it in the Ipo Curve Editor means it's working on Ipos, and so on), but it always means the same thing: Create a datablock like this one that has only the selected object as its user.

Discovering parents, children, and groups

Working in 3D, you may encounter many situations where you will want a set of objects to behave like a single organizational group. Now, if the objects are all of the same type, you could join them into a single object, but even with the L and Shift+L linked selection operations in Edit mode, this can get unwieldy. And it would require you to tab into Edit mode each time you want to work with an individual item. That's not very efficient and it doesn't give you the flexibility of working with different kinds of objects as a single unit. The better way to do it is with parent-child relationships or with groups.

Creating parent-child relationships between objects, or *parenting* in Blenderese, organizes the objects hierarchically. This means that an object can have any number of children, but no object can have more than a single parent:

1. **To make an object a parent, first select the objects you wish to be children.**

   They do not have to be of the same type.

2. **Make your last selection (the active object) the object that you wish to become the parent.**

3. **After you've done this, press Ctrl+P or spacebar⇨Object⇨Parent⇨Make Parent.**

   After you confirm the operation left-clicking or pressing Enter, Blender adds a dotted line from the center point of each child object to the center point of the parent. Now when you select just the parent object and perform a transform operation on it, it affects each of the children. However, if you select a child object and transform it, none of the other children or the parent object are influenced.

Parenting is a great way to organize a set of objects that have a clear hierarchy. For example, say you've modeled a dinner table and the chairs to go around it. Now you would like to place that table and chairs in a room, but the room is scaled much smaller than the table and chairs. Rather than select, scale, grab, and move each object into place, you can parent each of the chairs to the table. After you've done that, you can just select and transform the table. When you do so, all of the chairs transform right along with it, as if they were a single object! Woohoo! Figure 4-14 illustrates this example.

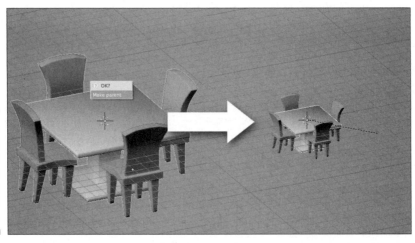

Figure 4-14:
Parenting some chairs to a table and placing them in a room.

To clear a parent relationship, the process is only a click and a hotkey:

1. **Select the child object that you wish to remove from the hierarchy.**

2. **Press Alt+P to clear the parent relationship. This brings up a pop-up menu with three options:**

- **Clear Parent:** This removes the parent-child relationship between your selected object and its parent. If the parent object was transformed after the parenting took place, the cleared child snaps back to the position, scale, and rotation that it was in before it was parented.

- **Clear and Keep Transformation (Clear Track):** This option behaves the same as Clear Parent, except any transformations that were made while the selected object was a child are applied. This means that the cleared child does **not** snap back to its original pre-parented state.

- **Clear Parent Inverse:** This option is a bit tricky to understand. It actually does not remove the link between the selected child object and its parent. Instead, it basically clears the parent's transformation from the child. This is handy for situations where you've transformed an object before parenting it and you want it to relate to the parent as if it had not been transformed prior to parenting. To be honest, I don't use this option very often, but it's certainly good to have around when you need it.

Of course, under some circumstances, parenting doesn't make sense to use for organizing a set of objects. A good example of this would be a lighting setup that you would like to adjust and reuse. Sure, you could rationalize that perhaps the key light is the most important light and therefore should be the parent, but that's a bit of a stretch and it doesn't make much sense in more complex setups.

For cases like these, Blender's *grouping* feature is ideal. To create a group, select all of the objects you wish to include in the group and press Ctrl+G⇨Add to New Group. When you do this, all of the objects in the group share a green selection outline instead of the default pink. This is to indicate that the object is a member of at least one group. That is another example of how grouping and parenting differ. Whereas an object can only have one parent, it can be a member of any number of groups. Now, when you press Ctrl+G, you have a number of options:

- **Add to Existing Group:** This option only appears if there are already other groups in existence. When you choose this option, a second menu pops up with a list of existing groups. The selected object is added to the one you pick.

- **Add to Active Objects Groups:** This option only appears if there are already other groups in existence. Use this option similar to how you would create a parent.

    1. Select the objects to be added to the group.

2. Select an active object that is already the member of one or more groups.

3. Press Ctrl+G⇨Add to Active Objects Groups. When you do this, each of your selected objects are included in all of the same groups that the active object is in. This is quite a time-saving shortcut.

✔ **Add to New Group:** This option is always available and creates a new group, adding your selected objects to it.

✔ **Remove from Group:** This option only appears if there are already groups in existence. Choosing this option pops up a second menu that allows you to choose from which group you would like to remove your selected objects.

✔ **Remove from All Groups:** This option is always available and choosing it removes the selected objects from any groups they may be a member of. Note that removing all objects from all groups does not delete those groups while your Blender session is still active.

Furthermore, you might notice that groups have names. Press F7 to show the Object buttons in the Buttons window. In the first panel, Object and Links, there is a list of groups that the selected object belongs to. Left-click any group name to change it to something more relevant to that group's organization. Clicking the X next to the group name removes the selected object from that group. The set of layer buttons under the group name have a special application for larger, more complex projects that involve linking groups between .blend files. Basically, if some objects in your group are on a layer that is not enabled in these buttons, then those objects will not be visible when the group is linked to another file.

When you're using parenting and groups, you gain the ability to rapidly select your objects according to their groupings. To do this, press Shift+G. This brings up a pop-up menu with a variety of options:

✔ **Children:** If you have a parent object selected, choosing this option adds all of that object's children to the list of selected objects.

✔ **Immediate Children:** Similar to selecting all children, accepting this option traverses down the hierarchy by one step only. Children of children are not added to the selection.

✔ **Parent:** If the object you've selected has a parent object, that parent is added to the selection.

✔ **Siblings (Shared Parent):** This option is useful for selecting all of the children of a single parent. Note that it does not select the parent object, nor does it select any children that these sibling objects may have.

✔ **Objects of Same Type:** This is useful for making very broad selections. Use this when you want to select all lamps or all meshes or armatures in a scene. It bases its selection on the type of object you currently have selected.

✔ **Objects on Shared Layers:** Use this option to select objects that live on the same layers. Note that if an object is on multiple layers, any of the objects that share any layer with your selected object are added to the selection.

✔ **Objects in Same Group:** This option adds to the selection any object that is in the same group as your selected object. If the selected object belongs to more than one group, a secondary pop-up menu displays each of the group names for you to choose from.

✔ **Object Hooks:** If you've added hooks, which are objects that control selected vertices or control points in an object, this option selects them. More information on hooks can be found in Chapter 10.

✔ **Object PassIndex:** Similar to layers, objects may have a PassIndex value that is useful for compositing and post-production work in Blender. Choosing this option selects any objects that share the active object's PassIndex value. More information on PassIndex can be found in Chapter 14.

Saving, opening, and appending

Quite possibly the most important feature in any piece of software is the ability to save and open files. This was especially true for early versions of Blender, which lacked any sort of undo function. Blender users learned very quickly to save early, save often, and save multiple versions of their project files. One of the benefits of all of this is that Blender reads and writes its files *very* quickly, even for complex scenes, so you very rarely ever have to wait more than a second or two to get to work or save your work.

To save to a file, choose File⇨Save As from the main header or use the F2 hotkey. One strange thing that you might notice is that Blender does not bring up the familiar Save dialog box that Windows, Mac, or Linux uses. This is for two reasons. First and foremost, such a dialog box violates Blenders non-blocking interface concept (see Chapter 2 for more on this). More importantly, though, the Blender file browser has some neat Blender-specific features that aren't available in the default OS save boxes. Not only that, but this way, you can be guaranteed that no matter what kind of computer you use, Blender always looks and behaves the same on each platform.

Take a look at the File Browser shown in Figure 4-15. The topmost text field is the current path on your hard drive to the folder/directory you are currently viewing. If you type in a word at the end of this text field, Blender creates a new folder at that location with the name you typed. To the left of this text field is a button with a P on it. Clicking this button takes you up the directory structure on your hard drive. Beneath this button is a small button with up/down arrow icons on it. Clicking this button gives you a list of commonly used folders in which you can save your file. On Windows-based machines, this button also displays drive letters if you have multiple hard drives. To the right of this button is the text field for the actual name of your file. In this field, type your project's name. Pressing Enter or clicking the Save File button in the upper right corner saves the file for you. Below this is a list of the files in the current folder. If you aren't familiar with Linux and Unix, the first two items in this list might seem odd to you. The first is a single dot (.). Left-clicking this refreshes the list. This is good for checking to see if new files have been added to the current folder. The next item is a double-dot (..). Left-clicking this is just like clicking the P button at the top of the File Browser. Figure 4-15 shows the Blender File Browser window and labels the various buttons in it.

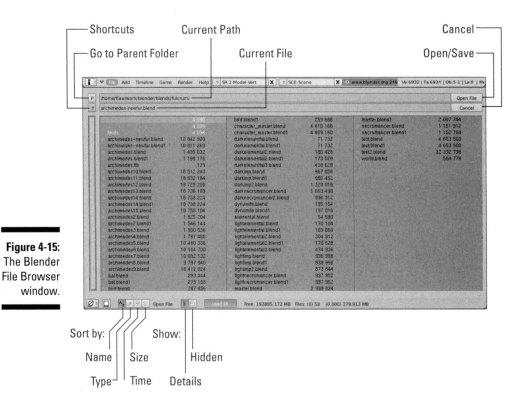

Figure 4-15:
The Blender File Browser window.

After you save your .blend file once, saving gets much quicker. To do a fast save while you are working, you can choose File➪Save from the main header or, even faster, press Ctrl+W and confirm the overwrite by left-clicking or pressing Enter. On larger projects, however, you may not want to continually overwrite the same file. In those cases, it's often more favorable to save progressive versions of your project as you work on it. You could do this by opening the File Browser and typing a new name for each version. However, that's slow and we don't like slow. Often, when people save versions of a project file, they usually append a number to the end of the filename (for example, file1.blend, file2.blend, file3.blend, and so on). Blender knows this and aims to help you out. The ultra-fast way to do this is with the following hotkey sequence: F2⇨+⇨Enter. Pressing + while in the File Browser automatically appends that number to your filename for you. And if the file already has a number, it increments it by one. And for logical consistency, pressing – decrements that value. How's that for speedy?

Opening a .blend file is a straightforward task. Choose File⇨ Open from the main header or press F1. This loads up the File Browser window again and allows you to choose which file you would like to load. To load it, left-click the filename and click the Open File button in the upper right corner. If you have a large monitor and you don't want to move your mouse that far or you're just interested in speedy shortcuts, you can quickly select and open a file by middle-clicking it.

Now, what if you have a model of a really excellent character saved in one .blend file and you'd like to bring it into a scene that you've been working on in another .blend file? Wouldn't it be convenient if you could bring that character in and not have to remodel it from scratch? Of course it would! This is precisely what Blender's Append feature is for. To append an item, choose File⇨Append from the main header or press Shift+F1. This again opens the File Browser window, but now when you click on a .blend file, you can actually drill down into its structure. With this, you can select any datablock in the file and bring it as well as anything it's linked to into your project. This means that if you select an object, you append that object, its object data (mesh, curve, and so on), any materials and textures it may have, and any Ipo curves linked to it. If you want to append just a material or texture, you can do that, too!

One thing to pay attention to when appending are two buttons at the bottom of the File Browser window, as highlighted in Figure 4-16: Append and Link.

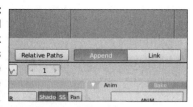

Of the two, Append is the default behavior. When this button is active, any datablock that you append from another .blend file is completely copied into the current .blend file. From here, you can make custom changes to either file and neither has any influence on the other. However, if the Link button is active, the datablock is not actually copied into the current .blend. Instead, a reference is made that points to the datablock in the original file. I like to call this a *linked appendage*. The advantage of this is that any changes you make to the original file are automatically updated in the file that links to it. This is really quite handy in large projects where you have a variety of models, materials, and other resources that you would like to use over and over again. One of the complications of linked appendages, however, is that the linking file can't make any changes to the object that it links to. The only exception to this rule is groups.

When a group is made to a linked appendage, the linking file creates an empty and binds the group reference to that as kind of a child. With this scheme, you can successfully transform and even animate your linked object. If you don't use groups and you want to modify an object appended with a link, your only option would be to make that appended object local to the current file. You do this by selecting the appended object and pressing L➪Selected Objects. You may also choose Selected Objects and Data or choose All to completely confirm that you are no longer linked to that other file. Of course, this increases the size of your .blend file and removes the collaborative benefit of working with linked appendages.

The moral of this story: If you are appending with links, it's probably in your best interest to create a group in the original file and create a linked appendage to that from the new one. This is the primary way that things are done on medium-to-large animation projects.

Part II
Creating Detailed 3D Scenes

The 5th Wave   By Rich Tennant

It started out as a wrap-around porch, but then Stuart took a one-day class on 3D modeling with Blender, and, well, it just sort of "took shape"...

In this part . . .

People don't start using a 3D computer graphics program to play with its interface. They use it because they want to create something awesome. That whole process starts with creating models. There are models for characters, settings, props, and even text and logos. The chapters in this part show you how to create meshes, curves, surfaces, and text objects in Blender. These are the building blocks used in CG to create incredible visuals.

In addition to modeling, lighting and materials can easily make or break a scene. To that effect, this part also shows how to set up lights effectively and how to use Blender's material system to get the models you create to look their best.

Chapter 5

Creating Anything You Can Imagine with Meshes

In This Chapter

▶ Working with vertices

▶ Using modifiers such as Mirror, Subsurf, and Array

▶ Sculpting meshes to have extremely high detail

*P*olygon-based meshes are at the core of nearly every computer-generated 3D animation from video games to television commercials to feature-length films. Computers typically handle meshes more quickly than other types of 3D objects like NURBS or metaballs, and meshes are generally a lot easier to control. In fact, when it comes down to it, even NURBS and metaballs are converted to a mesh of triangles — a process called *tesselation* — when the computer hardware processes them.

For these reasons, meshes are the primary foundation for most of Blender's functionality. Whether you're building a small scene, creating a character for animation, or simulating water pouring into a sink, you'll ultimately be working with meshes. Working with meshes can get a bit daunting if you're not careful, because you have to control each vertex that makes up your mesh. The more complex the mesh, the more vertices you have to keep track of. Chapter 4 gives you a lot of the basics for working with meshes in Edit mode, but in this chapter, you are exposed to a bunch of the handy features Blender has that help you work with complex meshes without drowning in crazy vertex soup.

When working with meshes or any other type of 3D object in Blender, it's often helpful to work from reference images. If you have a separate monitor, it can be helpful to have references displayed on it. However, you can also load an image into the background of any orthographic 3D View by choosing View⇨Background Image and left-click the Use Background Image button in the floating window that appears. The Load button allows you to pick any image from your hard drive. People who model faces like to split the 3D View, showing the front view on one side and the side view on the other. With reference photos of the same size in the proper window, it makes the process of modeling very speedy.

Pushing Vertices

A *mesh* consists of a set of vertices that are connected by edges. Edges connect to each other to form either three- or four-sided faces. (Chapter 4 covers this in more detail, along with how to work with each of these mesh building blocks.) When you tab into Edit mode on a mesh, you can manipulate that mesh's vertices (or edges or faces) with the same basic Grab (G), Rotate (R), and Scale (S) tools that work on all objects, as well as the very handy Extrude (E) function. These actions form the basis for 3D modeling, so much so that some modelers like to refer to themselves as *vert pushers* because sometimes it feels like all they do is move little points around on a screen until things look right.

Of course, there's more to modeling than that. You actually have a choice between two primary methodologies when it comes to modeling: *box modeling* and *point-for-point modeling*. The differences between the two are outlined below:

- **Box modeling:** As its name indicates, *box modeling* starts with a rough shape — typically a box or cube. By adding edges and moving them around, the artist forms that rough shape into the desired model. Bit by bit, you refine the model, adding more and more detail with each pass. This technique tends to appeal to people with a background in sculpture because the processes are very similar. If you need to add more to the mesh outside of the initial box shape, you select a set of edges or faces and extrude them out or pull them out. If you need to bring part of the mesh in from the initial box shape, you select those edges or faces and either extrude inward or just pull them in. This is a great way to get started in modeling, but you run a danger of ending up with really blocky models if you aren't careful about how you move your edges around.

- **Point-for-point modeling:** Point-for-point modeling consists of deliberately placing each and every vertex that comprises the model and creating the edges and faces that connect these vertices. It's actually not as bad as it sounds. You can think about it like drawing in three dimensions. And as you might expect, this technique appeals to people who come from a drawing background (or control freaks like me!). The advantage of this method is that you can control the final look of your model and you're less inclined to end up with a boxy shape. However, some beginner modelers fall into the trap of getting too detailed too quickly with this technique, so you have to be careful.

Figure 5-1 shows the basic steps in creating a rough human head using box modeling techniques versus using a point-for-point method.

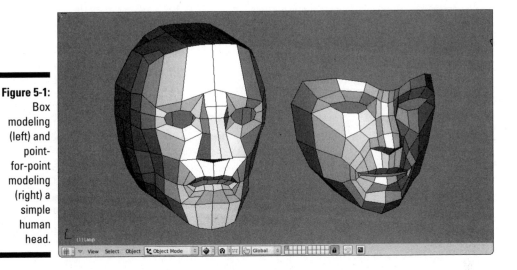

Figure 5-1:
Box
modeling
(left) and
point-
for-point
modeling
(right) a
simple
human
head.

Although many modelers have a preference for one methodology over the other, most agree that each method has its advantages and often modelers take a hybrid approach. They may use a point-for-point technique to rough out the model and then make refinements by box modeling. With the advent of 3D sculpting, which is covered later in this chapter, this way of working has gotten even more popular.

Working with Loops and Rings

Regardless of whether you're box modeling or point-for-point modeling, understanding the concepts of *loops* and *rings* definitely makes your life as a modeler a lot less crazy. Generally speaking, an *edge loop* is a series of edges that connect to form a path where the first and last edges connect to each other. This is the ideal case; I like to call it a "good" edge loop. Of course, this raises the question, "What's a 'bad' edge loop?" Well, calling them "bad" isn't really accurate because you can't always avoid them, but bad edge loops are a path of edges that don't connect the first and last loop.

To get a better understanding of this, open Blender and add a UV Sphere (spacebar⇨Add⇨Mesh⇨UV Sphere) with the default settings for rings, seg-ments, and radii. Tab into Edit mode on the sphere and Alt+right-click one of the horizontal edges on the sphere. Doing this selects an edge loop that goes all the way around the sphere, as shown in the left image of Figure 5-2. This is what I call a good edge loop. Press A to deselect all and now Alt+right-click a vertical edge. Notice that doing this selects a path of vertices that terminates at the top and bottom *poles*, or junctions of the sphere, as shown in the right image of Figure 5-2. That's the other sort of edge loop.

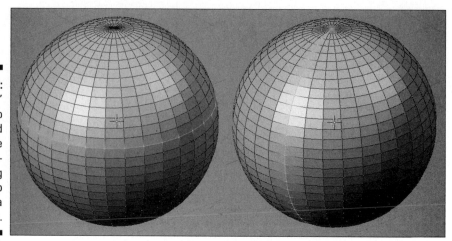

Figure 5-2:
A "good"
edge loop
(left) around
a sphere
and a non-
looping
edge loop
(right) on a
sphere.

The vertical loop doesn't go all the way around because, technically speaking, edge loops rely on *four-point poles*, or a vertex that's at the junction of four edges. Imagine that following an edge loop is like driving through a city. The four-point pole would be like a four-way stop, where you have the option of going left, right, or straight. Well, to properly follow the loop, you would keep traveling straight. However, if you come up to a fork in the road (a three-point pole) or a five-way (or more) intersection, you can't necessarily "just go straight" and be sure that you're following the loop. Therefore, the loop terminates at that intersection. That's why the horizontal edge loop in Figure 5-2, which is made up entirely of four-point poles, connects to itself whereas the vertical loop stops at the top and bottom of the sphere, where all of the edges converge to a single junction.

In addition to edge loops, you can also have face loops. A *face loop* consists of the faces between two parallel edge loops. Figure 5-3 shows horizontal and vertical face loops on a UV Sphere. In Blender, you can select face loops when you are in Face Select mode (in Edit mode, press Ctrl+Tab⇨Faces) the same way you select edge loops in Vertex Select or Edge Select modes: Alt+right-click a face in the direction of the loop you'd like to select. For example, going back the UV Sphere, to select a horizontal face loop, Alt+right-click the left or right side of one of the faces in that loop. To select a vertical face loop, Alt+right click the top or bottom of the face.

In some Linux window managers, the Alt key manipulates windows, which supersedes Blender's control of it and prevents you from doing a loop select. Most of these window managers allow you to remap that ability to another key (like the Super or Windows key). However, if you use a window manager that doesn't offer that remapping ability, or you just don't feel like remapping that key, you can still select loops by using Shift+Alt+right-click. This key combination allows you to select multiple loops, but if you have no vertices, edges, or faces selected, it behaves just like Alt+right-click.

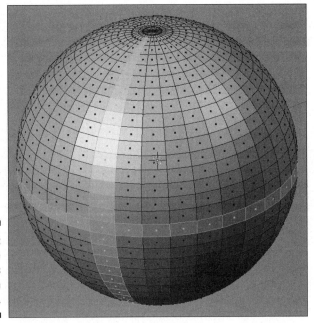

Figure 5-3:
Some
face loops
selected on
a sphere.

Now, say that rather than wanting to select an edge loop or a face loop, you would like to select just the edges that bridge between two parallel edge loops, as seen in Figure 5-4. These edges form an *edge ring*. You can only do this from Edge Select mode (in Edit mode, press Ctrl+Tab⇨Edges). When you're in Edge Select mode, you can select an edge ring by using Ctrl+Alt+right-click. Trying to use this hotkey sequence in Vertex Select or Face Select mode just selects a face loop.

Being able to select loops for selecting groups of vertices in an orderly fashion can be a huge benefit and timesaver for modeling. Say you're modeling a bumper car and you have the shape of the car down, but no bumper. You can quickly create this bumper by selecting a face loop around the bottom of the car and extruding that region in the XY plane. (Tab to Edit mode⇨Ctrl+Tab⇨ Faces⇨Alt+right-click the face loop⇨E⇨Region⇨S⇨Shift+Z⇨left-click to confirm placement.) When creating organic models like humans or faces, using edge loops effectively to control your *topology*, or the layout of the vertices, makes the life of a character rigger and animator a lot easier (more on this in the sidebar called "The importance of good topology" later in this chapter).

The ability to select loops and rings is nice, but the ability to create new loops is even more helpful when you want to add detail to a model. You do this with what's called a *loopcut*. You can find this function in the Edge Specials menu (Ctrl+E⇨Loopcut). Alternatively, you can simply press Ctrl+R to access it directly. Regardless of how you choose to enable it, notice that when you run your mouse cursor over your model, a pink/purple line is drawn on the mesh, indicating where you might want to add your edge loop. After you decide where you want to cut, left-click to confirm. Doing so creates the edge loop and automatically enables the Edge Slide function on that loop. With Edge Slide, you can move your mouse around and your loop travels along the surface of the mesh, allowing you to place it precisely where you want it to go when you left-click. If you ever want to use Edge Slide without creating a new loop, select the edge loop (or portion of an edge loop) that you want to slide and press Ctrl+E⇨Edge Slide.

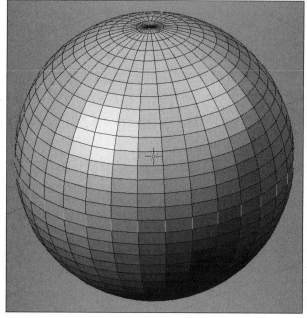

Figure 5-4:
An edge
ring
selected
on a UV
sphere.

When doing a loopcut, you can actually do multiple parallel loop cuts at the same time. When you activate the loopcut tool (Ctrl+R or Ctrl+E⇨Loopcut), scroll your mouse wheel and you'll be able to add multiple loops all at the same time. You can also explicitly enter a number to add a large number of loops all at once. Note that if you add multiple loops at the same time, Blender doesn't go into the Edge Slide functionality because it doesn't make sense to slide multiple parallel edges.

You can make cuts other than loopcuts. They are accessible with the Knife tool when you press K while in Edit mode. Doing so presents you with four options:

✔ **Loop Cut (CTRL+R):** This is the loopcut tool as described above.

✔ **Knife (Exact):** Creates connected vertices exactly where the line from the Knife tool intersects selected edges.

✔ **Knife (Midpoints):** Creates connected vertices located at the midpoints of the edges that the Knife tool intersects. When I use the Knife, I tend to use this feature the most.

✔ **Knife (Multicut):** This is the same as the midpoints option, but it creates based on the number of cuts you specify. All new vertices are spaced equally along the edges that the Knife tool's line intersects.

Unlike the loopcut, the Knife tool works only on the vertices that are currently selected. Of course, it's also helpful to see the actual edges that you're cutting through. To do that, I recommend switching to wireframe view or turning off the Occlude Background Geometry button. To use the knife tool, follow these steps:

1. **Select the edges you wish to cut.**

2. **Orient the 3D view so you can see all of your selected edges.**

3. **Press K and choose the type of knife cut you'd like to make.**

4. **Draw a line to indicate where the cuts should be.**

   You can draw the line in two ways. You can left-click+drag your mouse cursor in the 3D View to draw line that way, or you can just left-click without dragging. If you do it the latter way, Blender draws a straight line between each place you click. If you decide you don't want to cut, you can cancel at any time by right-clicking or pressing Esc.

5. **After you've drawn your cut line, confirm it by pressing Enter.**

   With that, your selected edges that intersect your cut line should have additional vertices.

With the knife tool, you must select the edges you wish to cut before using it.

Simplifying Your Life as a Modeler with Modifiers

As I stated earlier in the chapter, working with meshes can get complicated when you have complex models consisting of lots and lots of vertices. Keeping track of these vertices and making changes to your model can quickly become a very daunting and tedious task, even with the ability to use loops and rings. You can quickly run into problems if you have a symmetrical model where the left side is supposed to be identical to the right, or if you need more vertices to make your model appear smoother. In times like these, you really want the computer to take on some of this tedious additional work so you can focus on the creative parts.

Fortunately, Blender actually has something that does just that. They're called modifiers. Despite their rather generic-sounding name, *modifiers* are an extremely powerful way to save you time and frustration by letting the computer assume the responsibility for "grunt work" like adding smoothing vertices or making your model symmetric for you. Another benefit of modifiers is that they're *non-destructive*, meaning that you can freely add and remove modifiers to and from your object. As long as you don't "apply" the modifier, it won't actually make any permanent changes to the object itself. You can always return to the original, unmodified mesh.

The modifiers for mesh can be accessed in the Editing buttons (F9) on the last panel, called Modifiers. Left-click the Add Modifier button to see a list of the modifiers that are available. Figure 5-5 shows the Modifier panel with the list of available modifiers for meshes.

Figure 5-5:
All of the modifiers you can use on mesh objects.

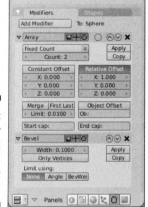

Because of space constraints, I can't give an extensive description on every modifier in the list, but I cover some of the most frequently used modifiers. That said, all of Blender's modifiers share some of the same controls between them. Have a gander at Figure 5-6. It shows the Modifier panel with two modifiers applied, Array and Bevel.

Figure 5-6:
The Array and Bevel modifiers in the Modifier panel.

The first thing to notice is that the modifiers are stacked one below the other. This stacking is by design, and what's more, the order in which the modifiers appear in the stack is important. This is because one modifier feeds into the next one. So the second modifier, Bevel in this case, doesn't operate on the original mesh data. It actually operates on the "new" mesh data provided by the first modifier, Array, in this example.

The stacking order for modifiers is a little bit counter-intuitive if you think about it in terms of layers, where one builds on top of another. Blender's modifier stack does not work like that. Instead, it would be better to think of Blender's modifier stack as a snowball rolling down a hill. Each modifier you hit on the way down the hill adds something or changes something about your snowball, modifying it more and more as it comes to the base of the hill. The top-most modifier is the first modifier and operates on the original mesh data. The modifier immediately below it works on the data that comes from the first modifier, and so on down the line.

In the previous example, the object is first made into an array. Then, the mesh that is created by the Array modifier has its edges beveled so that they're not as sharp-cornered. Now, you can change the stacking order by using the up/down arrow buttons on the right side of each modifier block. Left-clicking the up-arrow raises a modifier in the stack (bringing it closer to being first), whereas the down-arrow lowers it. Left-click the X to the right of these buttons to remove the modifier altogether. The downward triangle that's to the left of each modifier's name collapses and expands that modifier block when you left-click it. This is useful for hiding a modifier's controls after you've decided upon the settings you want to use.

To the right of the names of each modifier are three buttons. From left to right, these buttons control whether the modifier is enabled for rendering, viewing in Object mode, and viewing in Edit mode. You may be wondering why you would ever want to disable a modifier after you've added it to the stack, rather than just removing it and adding it back in later. The main reason for this is that many of the modifiers have an extensive set of options available to them. You may want to see how your object renders with and without the modifier to decide whether you want to use it. You may want to edit your original mesh without seeing any of the changes made by the modifier. If you have a slow computer, you want to have the modifier enabled only when rendering so you can still work effectively without your computer choking on all the data coming from Blender. Those buttons next to each name are for situations like these.

Some modifiers, like Array, have an additional little circle-shaped button in the space after the enable/disable buttons. It's not labeled with an icon or anything, but its tooltip says Apply Modifier to Editing Cage During Edit Mode. This means that not only are the effects of the modifier visible in Edit mode, but you can also select and perform limited changes to the geometry created by the modifier.

Only two more buttons are common among all modifiers. They are the Apply and Copy buttons on the right side of each modifier block in the stack. Left-clicking the Apply button takes the changes made by the modifier and directly applies them to the original object. Doing this actually creates the additional vertices and edges in the original mesh to make it match the results done by the modifier, and then removes the modifier from the stack. I said before that modifiers were non-destructive, meaning that they don't permanently change the original object, but the Apply button is the one exception.

The Apply button only works if the modifier is the first (top) modifier in the stack.

The Copy button creates a duplicate version of the modifier and adds it to the stack in the same position as the modifier you're duplicating, essentially forcing the original one further down the stack. You probably won't be using this function very often, but it's really useful when you need to double up a modifier, like if you want to bevel twice to get a more rounded edge than a single bevel operation can get you.

Doing half the work (and still looking good!) with the Mirror modifier

When I was first learning how to draw the human face, I used to have all sorts of problems because I'd draw half the face and then realize that I still needed to do just about the exact same thing all over again on the other side of the face. I found it tedious and difficult to try and match the first half of my drawing. Without fail, the first couple of hundred times I did it, something would always be off. An eye would be too large, an ear would be too high, and so on. I'm embarrassed to say that it actually took me quite a long time to get drawings that didn't look like Sloth from *The Goonies*. (Some of my co-workers might argue that some of my drawings still look that way!)

Fortunately, as a 3D computer artist, you don't have to go through all that. You can have the computer do the work for you. In Blender, you do this with the Mirror modifier (F9➪Modifiers➪Add Modifier➪Mirror). Figure 5-7 shows the buttons and options available for this modifier.

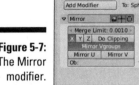

Figure 5-7:
The Mirror
modifier.

The Mirror modifier basically makes a copy of all the mesh data in your object and flips it along its local X, Y, or Z axis, or any combination of those axes. The Mirror modifier also has the cool feature of merging vertices along the center seam of the object, so it looks like one unified piece. You can adjust how close vertices have to be to this seam in order to be merged by changing the Merge Limit value.

The X, Y, and Z buttons dictate which axis or axes your object is mirrored across. For most situations, the default setting of just the local X axis is all you really need. I nearly always enable the Do Clipping button. This button takes the vertices that have been merged — as dictated by the Merge Limit value — and locks them to the mirror axis. This is a great feature when you're working on vehicles or characters where you don't want to accidentally tear a hole along the center of your model while you're tweaking its shape with the Proportional Edit Tool (tab to Edit mode⇨O). Of course, if you have to pull a vertex away from the center line, you can temporarily disable this button.

The next large button is Mirror Vgroups. Vgroups stands for *vertex groups*. Vertices in a mesh can be assigned to arbitrary groups that you can designate in the Link and Materials panel of the Editing buttons, as shown in Figure 5-8.

Figure 5-8: Vertex groups are created with the Link and Materials panel of the Editing buttons.

The actual process of creating vertex groups and assigning individual vertices to a group is covered more in-depth in Chapter 11. However, the most basic way to create a vertex group is to press the New button under Vertex Groups in the Link and Materials panel while in Edit mode. This makes a new vertex group named Group. Now select some vertices in your mesh and press the Assign button back in the Link and Materials panel. Congratulations! You've created a vertex group.

Now, the effect of the Mirror Vgroups button doesn't make itself apparent until you apply the Mirror modifier. Here's how it works: Say you've selected some vertices and assigned them to a group named Group.R, indicating that

it's the group for some vertices on the right-hand side. Say you've also created another group called Group.L for the corresponding vertices on the left-
hand side, but because you have not yet applied the Mirror modifier, there's
no way to assign vertices to this group. Well, if you have the Mirror Vgroups
button activated when you apply the Mirror modifier, the newly created
real vertices on the left side that correspond with the Group.R vertices are
automatically assigned to Group.L. This effect propagates to other modifiers
which are based on vertex group names, such as Armatures.

Referring back to Figure 5-7, the Mirror U and Mirror V buttons on the Mirror
modifier do the same kind of thing that the Mirror Vgroups button does, but
they refer to texture coordinates, or *UV coordinates*. (There's more on UV
coordinates in Chapter 8.) The simplest explanation, though, is that UV coordinates allow you to take a flat image and map it to a three-dimensional surface. Enabling these buttons on the modifier mirrors the texture coordinates
in the UV Image Editor and can possibly cut your texture unwrapping time
in half. Also, unlike the Mirror Vgroups button, you don't have to apply the
modifier to take advantage of the Mirror U or Mirror V features. To see the
results of what these buttons do, when you have a texture loaded and your
model unwrapped, bring up the View Properties floating window in the UV
Image Editor (View⇨View Properties) and left-click the Final Shadow button.
Hooray for non-destructive modifiers!

The last option in the Mirror modifier is the text field at the bottom that says
Ob. By default, the Mirror modifier uses the object's center point as the basis
for what to mirror. However, by typing in the name of any other object in this
field, you can use that object's center as the point to mirror. With this, you
can use an Empty as a kind of dynamic center point. That allows you to do
fun things like animate a cartoon character splitting in half to get around an
obstacle (literally!) and joining back together on the other side.

Blender's text fields have *tab completion*, so you can type the first few letters
of an object's name, press Tab, and, if the name is unique, Blender fills in the
rest of the name for you.

Smoothing things out with the Subsurf modifier

Another commonly used modifier, especially for organic models, is Subsurf.
Subsurf is short for *subdivision surfaces*. If you have a background in another
3D modeling program, you might know them as *sub-ds* or *subdivs*. If you're
not familiar with subdivision surfaces, the concept goes something like this:
Blender takes the faces on a given mesh and subdivides them with a number
of cuts that you arbitrarily decide upon (usually one to three cuts, or *levels of
subdivision*). Now, when the faces are subdivided, Blender moves the edges
of these faces closer together, trying to get a smooth transition from one

face to the next. The end effect is that a cube with a Subsurf modifier begins looking more and more like a ball with each additional level of subdivision, as shown in Figure 5-9.

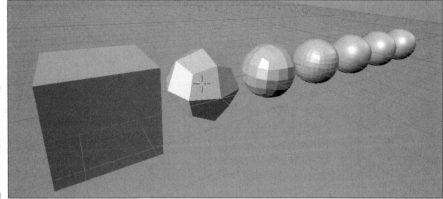

Figure 5-9:
A cube with increasing levels of subdivision from 1 to 6.

Now, the really cool thing about subdivision surfaces is that because they're implemented as a modifier, you get the smooth benefit of additional geometry without the headache of actually having to edit all of those extra vertices. In the preceding cube example, even at a subdivision level of six, if you Tab into edit mode, you control that form with just the eight vertices that make up the original cube. This is a very powerful way of working and nearly all high-end 3D animations use subdivision surfaces for just this reason. You have the smooth organic curves of dense geometry with the much more manageable control of a less dense, or *low poly* mesh, referred to as a *cage*.

For a better idea of the kind of results you can get with the Subsurf modifier, I'm going to break out Suzanne and apply it to her with the following steps:

1. **Add a Monkey mesh (spacebar⇨Add⇨Mesh⇨Monkey).**

   Ooh! Ooh! Ooh!

2. **Set smooth rendering on the monkey (F9⇨Link and Materials⇨Set Smooth).**

   At this point, Suzanne is pretty standard. She looks smoother than the faceted look she had when first added, but she's still blocky looking.

3. **Add a Subsurf modifier to the monkey (F9⇨Modifiers⇨Add Modifier⇨Subsurf or use the Ctrl+1 hotkey combo).**

   Now *that's* Suzanne! Instantly, she looks a lot more natural and organic, even despite her inherently cartoony proportions. Feel free to increase the Levels number in the Subsurf modifier to see how much smoother Suzanne can be.

4. **Tab into Edit mode and notice that the original mesh serves as the control cage for the subdivided mesh.**

   Editing the cage with Grab (G), Rotate (R), Scale (S), and Extrude (E) directly influences the appearance of the modified mesh within the cage.

Figure 5-10 shows the results of each of these steps.

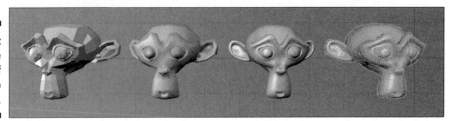

Figure 5-10: Adding the Subsurf modifier to Suzanne.

As powerful as the Subsurf modifier is, only a limited number of options come with it in the modifier stack. Figure 5-11 shows the Subsurf modifier block as it appears in the Modifiers panel. The first option is a drop-down menu that gives you the choice between Catmull-Clark subdivision or Simple subdivision. The former is the default and behaves just like I've described previously. The latter works more like doing W⇨Subdivide multiple times in Edit mode. It gives you more vertices in your meshes, referred to as geometry, but not the same kind of organic smoothness that the Catmull-Clark method provides. The simple subdivision method is good for some situations though, so it's nice that the option is available to you.

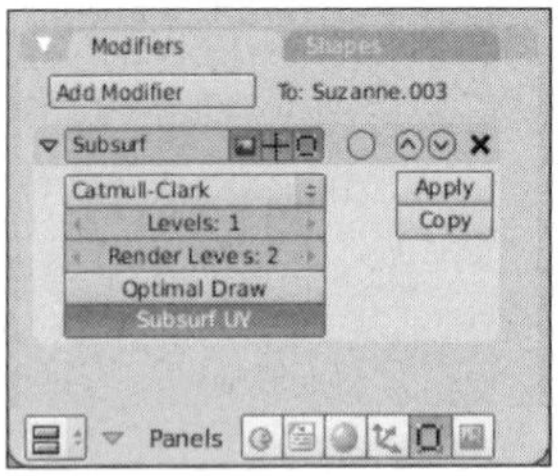

Figure 5-11: The Subsurf modifier.

The next button down is the Levels option, which allows you to set the level of subdivision that you see on your model in the 3D View. It can be set to a whole number from 1 to 6. Because I like to keep my 3D view fast and responsive, I tend to keep this down at 1. Occasionally, I push it up to 2 or 3 to get a quick idea of what it might look like in the final output, but I always bring it back down to 1. Beneath the Levels option is a similar button for Render

Levels. When you create the final output of your scene or animation, Blender uses this level of subdivision for your model, regardless of which level you set for the 3D view. It has the same range that Levels does, but typically this is set to a higher value because you usually want smoother, higher-quality models in your final render. Don't go too crazy with setting this value. On most of my work, which can get pretty detailed, I rarely ever use a setting higher than 3.

The Optimal Draw button is something I typically like to leave turned on all the time. It hides the extra edges that are created by the modifier when you view the model in wireframe view. On a complex scene, hiding the edges can definitely help you make sense of things when working in wireframe. Figure 5-12 shows the difference Optimal Draw makes on a Suzanne model with three levels of subdivision.

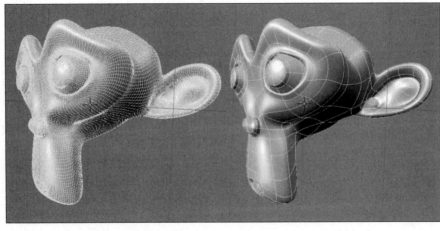

Figure 5-12:
Using
Optimal
Draw on
a mesh
with three
levels of
subdivision.

When working with the Subsurf modifier, I typically like to have this option on, along with the Apply Modifier to Cage button, otherwise known as "that circle-shaped button next to the modifier name." Everyone's different, though, so play with it on your own and see what works best for you.

Use the Subsurf UV button for texturing. Like the Mirror U and Mirror V buttons in the Mirror modifier, enabling this button adds the additional geometry to your UV map without requiring you to apply the modifier. Again, this can be quite a helpful timesaver when you're setting up your model for texturing. Also like the Mirror U and Mirror V options, you can see the results of the Subsurf UV button by enabling the Final Shadow button in the UV Image Editor (Shift+F10⇨View⇨View Properties⇨Final Shadow).

Using the power of Arrays

One of the coolest and most-fun-to-play-with modifiers in Blender is the Array modifier. In its simplest application, this modifier duplicates the mesh a specified number of times and places those duplicates in line evenly spaced apart. Have a model of a chair and need to put lines of chairs in a room to make it look like a meeting hall? Using a couple of Array modifiers together is a great way to do just that! Figure 5-13 is a screenshot of Blender being used to create that sort of scene.

You're not limited to using just one Array modifier on your object. The effect in Figure 5-13 was achieved by using two Array modifiers stacked together, one for the first row of chairs going across the room and the second to create multiple copies of that first row. Using multiple arrays in a row is an excellent way to build a complex scene with just one object.

Blender's Array modifier is loaded with all kinds of cool functions that can be used in lots of interesting ways. Some ways facilitate our desire to be lazy by making the computer do as much of the repetitive, tedious tasks for us as possible. (For example, it can be used to model a staircase or a chain-link fence or a wall of bricks.) However, you could also use it to do some really incredible abstract animations or specialized tentacles or even rows of dancing robots!

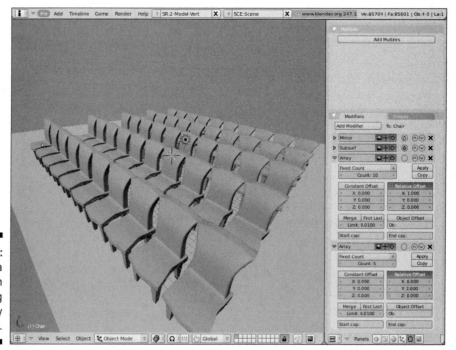

Figure 5-13:
Filling a room with chairs using the Array modifier.

The bulk of the power in the Array modifier lies in how it handles *offsets*, or the distances apart that the duplicates are set relative to one another. As shown in Figure 5-14, the Array modifier offers three different sorts of offsets, all of which can be used at the same time.

Figure 5-14:
The Array
modifier.

> ✔ **Constant Offset:** This offset adds a fixed distance to each duplicated object in the array, in Blender units. So setting the X value beneath this button to -5.0 shifts each of the duplicates five units in the negative X direction. The same behavior happens in the Y and Z axes when you set the values for those offsets as well.

> ✔ **Relative Offset:** Think of the Relative Offset like a multiplication factor, based on the width, height, and depth of the object. So no matter how large or small the object is, if you set the Z value to 1.0, for example, each duplicated object in the array is stacked directly on top of the one below it. This type of offset is the one that's used by default when you first add the Array modifier.

> ✔ **Object Offset:** The Object Offset is my personal favorite offset because of its incredible versatility. It takes the position of any object you name in the Ob: field — I prefer to use Empties for this — and uses its relative distance from the mesh you've added to Array as the offset. But that's just the start of it! Using this offset also takes into account the rotation and scale of the object you enter. So if you have an Empty that's one Blender unit away from your object, scaled to twice its original size and rotated 15 degrees on the Y axis, each subsequent duplicate is scaled twice as large as the previous and rotated an additional 15 degrees. Now you can make a spiral staircase like the one in Figure 5-15. And if you felt inclined to create a staircase where the stairs can be collapsed into each other and hidden, it's a simple as animating the offset object!

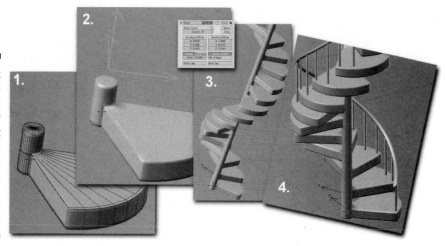

Figure 5-15:
1) Model the step. 2) Add an Empty for Object Offset and rotate in Z. 3) Add the Array modifier. 4) Make it pretty.

You also have a lot of control over how many duplicates the Array modifier creates. This is controlled with the Length Fit drop-down menu at the top of the Array modifier block. By default, the Length Fit setting is Fixed Count and you explicitly enter the number of duplicates in the Count field below it. That isn't your only option, however. You actually have three:

✔ **Fixed Count:** As described above, this lets you explicitly enter the exact number of duplicates you would like to create, up to 1000.

✔ **Fixed Length:** This creates the proper count of duplicate objects to fit in the distance that you define. Bear in mind that this length is not exactly in Blender units. It uses the local coordinate system of the object that you're making an array of, so the length you choose is multiplied by the scale of that original object as shown in the Transform Properties floating window (N).

✔ **Fit to Curve Length:** If you choose this option, you can enter the name of a curve object in the Ob field below it. When you do this, Blender calculates the length of that curve and uses that as the length to fill in with duplicated objects. Using this option together with a Curve modifier is a nice quick-n-dirty way of creating a linked metal chain like the one shown in Figure 5-16.

Another cool feature in the Array modifier is the ability to merge the vertices in one duplicate that are near the vertices in another. With the Merge button enabled and some fine adjustment to the Limit value, you can make your model look like a single unified piece, rather than being composed of individual duplicates. I've used this feature to model rope, train tracks, and stair rails, for example. The First Last button toggles to determine if the vertices in the last duplicated instance are allowed to merge with the nearby vertices in the first object of the array. Use this with Object Offset and you can create a closed loop out of your duplicates, all merged together.

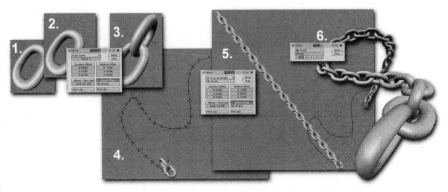

Figure 5-16:
Creating
a chain
using the Fit
Length to
Curve option
in the Array
modifier
along with
a Curve
modifier.

Say you're using the Array modifier to create a handrail for your spiral staircase and you don't want the handrail to simply stop at the beginning and end. Instead, you'd like the end of the handrail to have ornamental caps. You could model something and try to place it by hand, but this could get problematic if you have to make changes or animate the handrail in the future. (Hey, this is computer graphics. Handrails that move and are animated make *complete* sense!) So another way to handle this is to use the Start cap and End cap fields in the Array modifier. After you've modeled what you want the cap to look like, you can type the name of that object in these fields and it will be placed at the beginning and the end of the array, respectively. Pretty slick, huh?

Sculpting Multi-Resolution Meshes

Over the years, as computers have gotten more powerful and more capable of handling dense high poly models with millions of vertices, computer graphics artists have wanted more and more control over the vertices in their meshes. Using a Subsurf modifier is great for adding geometry to make models look more organic, but what if you're modeling a monster and you want to model a scar in his face? You have to apply the modifier to have access and control over those additional vertices. And even though the computer may be able to handle having them there, a million vertices is a lot for you to try to control and keep track of, even with all of the various selection methods and the Proportional Edit tool. This is exactly why Blender has *multi-resolution meshes* and *Sculpt mode*.

Multi-resolution, or *multires* for short, meshes address the problem of having to apply the Subsurf modifier before you can directly control the vertices that it creates. With a multires mesh, you can freely move between a level 1 subdivision and a level 6 subdivision, just like with the Subsurf modifier. However, the difference is that you can directly control the vertices of the level 6 subdivision just as easily as the level 1 subdivision using Blender's

Sculpt mode. And changes made at either level can be seen at the other one. (To varying levels of detail, depending on the level you're looking at. If you make a very fine detail change in level 6, it may not be readily apparent at level 1.) Figure 5-17 shows what the Multires panel looks like before and after you add Multires to your model.

Figure 5-17:
The Multires panel in the Editing buttons before (left) and after (right), adding Multires and a couple levels of subdivision.

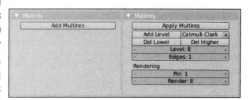

Turning a mesh into a multires mesh is as simple as left-clicking the Add Multires button in the Multires panel and then left-clicking the Add Level button for each level of subdivision that you would like to add to your mesh. Unlike with the Subsurf modifier, you don't have exactly six levels of subdivision to switch between. In Multires, the number can be as low as zero and as high as your computer's processor and memory can handle. And before adding a level, you have the option of choosing Catmull-Clark Subdivision or Simple Subdivision, like you can with the Subsurf modifier. The only difference here is that you cannot freely change between subdivision types on a given level with Multires. After you left-click the Add Level button, your choice is made.

If you have a Subsurf modifier on your mesh, I recommend applying it to your mesh or removing it from the modifier stack before adding Multires. Because Multires uses the same process to create subdivision levels, you don't need to have both active at the same time.

After you have a level added, you have some additional options available. The first two buttons that appear are Del Lower and Del Higher. Clicking these buttons removes all subdivision levels less than or greater than the level you are currently in, respectively. So if you have five levels of subdivision and you're at level 4, clicking Del Lower effectively kills levels 1 through 3. When these levels are removed, the current level — in this example, level 4 — becomes the new level 1. Del Higher works in a similar fashion.

The next field down, Level, lets you set which subdivision level you're currently looking at from the levels that you've added to your mesh. Below that is the Edges field. The Edges field allows you to set which level's edges you would like Blender to show in the 3D view. Setting it to 1 gives you an effect that's similar to Optimal Draw on the Subsurf modifier. Higher values progressively show more and more edges. Some 3D modelers who use sculpting tools like to overlay the model's wireframe on the mesh (F7⇨Draw⇨Draw Extra⇨Wire) as they work so they can have an idea of how their topology looks (see the sidebar "The importance of good topology" elsewhere in the chapter for more).

In the bottom right of this area are two fields associated with rendering. The Pin value determines which level of subdivision you want the modifier stack to work on when you render. By default, this is set to level 1. Increasing this value means that more vertices get seen by the modifier stack and can therefore *substantially* increase your render time, so do so carefully — or at least with the knowledge that you may have time to go out for a long meal and a nap while Blender renders your model. The Render value tells Blender which subdivision level you would like to have rendered. By default, this is set to your highest level. If you're rendering a test preview, you can speed things up by reducing this value.

Currently, multires meshes are created and managed in the Multires panel of the Editing buttons (F9). In future versions of Blender, the plan is to make Multires work like any other modifier, so some features may vary slightly if you're using a version of Blender newer than version 2.47.

Now, if you try to tab into Edit mode on a multires mesh, you may be faced with so many vertices that it's not easy or even useful to select and edit just one vertex or a few of them. Sculpt mode helps you manage all of these additional vertices created by Multires. It treats your mesh very much like a solid piece of clay. You have a variety of "sculpt brushes" that help you shape and form your mesh to look exactly how you want. Activate Sculpt mode from the Mode menu in the header of the 3D view, as shown in Figure 5-18. When you're in Sculpt mode, three additional tabs show up in the Editing buttons along with the Multires panel: Sculpt, Brush, and Texture.

Figure 5-18:
Going into
Sculpt
mode.

If you have a drawing tablet like the ones manufactured by Wacom, Sculpt mode takes advantage of the pressure sensitivity that a tablet offers. You can adjust the sensitivity and size of the tablet by going to Sculpt➪Input Settings in the 3D View window's header after you enter Sculpt mode.

Sculpt panel

Figure 5-19 shows the contents of the Sculpt panel. This is the primary panel for working in Sculpt mode. In fact, if you have the Transform Properties floating window (N) up in 3D view, when you switch to Sculpt mode, its content changes to match what's in this panel so you have quick access to it within the 3D view. The buttons in this panel can be broken down into three sections: brush types, brush controls, and axis-related controls.

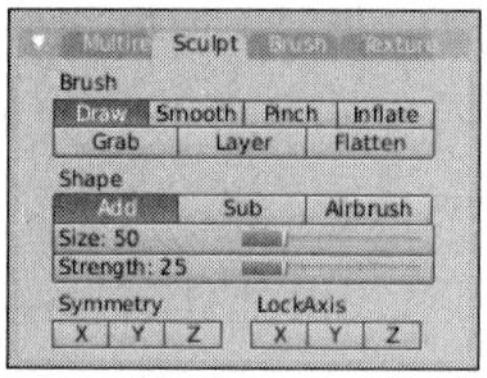

Figure 5-19:
The Sculpt
panel.

Brush types

Sculpt mode offers you seven different types of brushes to work with, each one modifying your mesh in a very specific way. All brushes work by left-clicking with the brush cursor over the mesh and dragging the cursor around the 3D View. If you're using a drawing tablet, this is a very natural way to work. Below are brief descriptions of each sculpt brush:

- ✔ **Draw (D):** The Draw brush basically pulls the surface of your mesh outward (or inward, if you enable the Sub button). By default, the brush works with an even fall-off, so the raised areas you draw tend to flow smoothly back into the rest of the mesh.

- ✔ **Smooth (S):** If you have jagged parts of your mesh or there are undesirable surface irregularities created while sculpting, using the Smooth brush cleans up those bumpy parts and makes the surface of your mesh, well, smoother.

- ✔ **Pinch (P):** If you enable the Pinch brush, vertices are pulled toward the center of your brush cursor as you move it over the mesh. This is a great way to add ridges and creases to a model.

- ✔ **Inflate (I):** The Inflate brush works a lot like the Draw brush. However, rather than move vertices more or less uniformly from the meshes surface, when you run the Inflate brush over your mesh, vertices move along their own local normals. This brush is good for fattening parts of a model.

✔ **Grab (G):** When you left-click and drag your mouse cursor on a mesh with the Grab brush activated, the vertices that are within the brush cursor's circle are moved to wherever you drag your mouse to. This is like selecting a bunch of vertices in Edit mode and pressing G.

✔ **Layer (L):** The Layer brush is like the Draw brush with a maximum height that it pulls the vertices, basically creating a raised mesa on the surface of your mesh.

✔ **Flatten (T):** In some ways, this brush does the opposite of the Draw brush. Where the Draw brush pulls vertices away from the surface of a mesh, the Flatten brush lowers vertices to try and get them to be as flat or *planar* as possible. If you're sculpting a landscape and you decide to remove a hill, this is the brush you want to use.

Brush controls

The next section of buttons, under the heading of Shape, actually control how the sculpt brushes influence your mesh. The first two buttons, Add and Sub, are only available for the Draw, Pinch, Inflate, and Layer buttons. Add is the default behavior described previously. If you enable Sub, it does the inverse. For instance, with Sub enabled, the Pinch brush pushes vertices away from the center of the brush cursor instead of pulling them in. Also, note that regardless of whether you've enabled Add or Sub, pressing Shift while using the brush does the opposite behavior. For example, if you're using the Draw brush with Add enabled, the normal behavior creates a small hill wherever you move your mouse cursor. If you press Shift+left-click and drag, you sculpt a small valley instead. Alternatively, you can toggle between Add and Sub by pressing V.

By default, if you left-click and hold your left mouse button down without moving the mouse, the Sculpt tool doesn't do a whole lot. It performs the brush's operation once and then waits for you to move your mouse. Suppose you prefer that the brush keep operating for as long as you hold down the left mouse button, regardless of whether you actually move the mouse. Enabling the Airbrush button (A) gives you just that ability. So if part of your mesh is an incredibly jaggy mess, you can switch to the Smooth brush (S), enable Airbrush (A), left-click on the jagged area, and hold down that left mouse button until the jaggies are gone.

The Size and Strength sliders control the size and strength of the brush you're currently using. There are hotkeys for changing these values while in the 3D view so you don't have to bring up this panel. To change brush size, press F, move your mouse until the brush cursor is the desired size, and left-click to confirm. To adjust the brush strength, press Shift+F and move your mouse to the center of the circle that pops up to increase the strength or away from the center to decrease the strength. When you're at the strength you want, left-click to confirm.

Axis-related controls

The next two blocks of buttons control how the sculpt brushes modify your mesh relative to the object's local axes. For example, if you left-click the X button under Symmetry, anything you do on the left side of the mesh automatically also happens on the right side of the mesh. This is an excellent timesaver for doing involved tasks like sculpting faces.

Likewise, the X, Y, and Z buttons under the LockAxis label constrain a vertex's movement in that axis. For instance, if you decide that you only want the Draw brush to move vertices in the Z direction, you would left-click the X and Y buttons under LockAxis to keep vertices under your brush cursor from moving in those directions.

The importance of good topology

If you listen to modelers talk or if you visit some of the Web forums where 3D modelers hang out, you'll hear the words *topology* and *edge flow* pretty often. These concepts are very important for a modeler, particularly if your model is destined to be animated. These terms refer to how the vertices and edges of your mesh lay out across its surface. When using subdivision surfaces to create organic models such as people, animals, and even plants, keep a few key guidelines in mind:

✔ **Use quads:** Try to avoid triangles whenever possible. Four-sided polygons look better when subdivided and they also tend to deform more cleanly when an armature is used to animate them.

✔ **Minimize poles that don't have four edges:** Remember that a pole is where multiple edges join at a single vertex. The UV Sphere mesh has two large poles at its top and bottom. Poles are harder to avoid than triangles, but you should do what you can to minimize their use because they can terminate edge loops (making the "bad" edge loops I described earlier in this chapter) and they don't deform as nicely as four-edged poles. If you are forced to use a pole like this, try to put it in a place on the mesh that won't deform a lot when it's animated.

✔ **Holes such as mouths and eye sockets should be encircled by concentric edge loops:** This is particularly important for character models that may be animated. Having concentric edge loops like this makes it easier to deform and animate these highly expressive parts of the face.

✔ **Edges should follow anatomy:** Following the flow of anatomy — particularly musculature — is important because doing so yields cleaner, more natural deformations. Arms don't pinch when you bend them; the crease from the side of the nose flows around the mouth. Following these little rules really makes the lives of riggers and animators much easier (and it helps make the final animation look better).

Brush panel

The Brush panel gives you control over how your sculpting brushes behave. By default, a curve controls how the intensity of the brush rolls off to the edges of the brush cursor. You can disable this control in favor of a more linear fall-off by left-clicking the Curve button, or you can edit the curve in the graph to the right to have more customized intensity fall-off. Figure 5-20 shows the contents of the Brush panel.

Figure 5-20:
The Brush panel for sculpting.

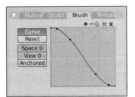

Texture panel

In the Texture panel, you have a set of eight texture channels, in addition to the Default, that you can use as brushes. So any texture that you can load or create in the Texture buttons (F6) can be used as a brush when you sculpt. This is an excellent way to get more details added to your mesh while sculpting. One button that you may want to use when you've loaded a texture into this panel is the Rake button. When this button is enabled, the texture is rotated as you sculpt to match the motion of the brush. This helps you avoid creating unnatural patterns from your textures when you sculpt. Figure 5-21 shows the contents of the Texture panel.

Figure 5-21:
The Texture panel for sculpting.

Sculpting with a high level of subdivisions can be taxing on your computer, using a *lot* of memory to store all of those additional vertices. If you use too many levels of subdivision, your computer may run out of memory and Blender could lock up or crash. In an effort to prevent this and give themselves more vertices to play with, many 3D modelers who use Blender's Multires go to the User Preferences under Edit Methods to disable Global

Undo and turn down the number of Undo Steps from the default value of 32 down to 0. This removes the safety net of undo, but it can often improve Blender's performance while sculpting.

Table 5-1 gives you a quick reference for the hotkeys used in Sculpt mode.

Table 5-1	Hotkeys for Sculpt Mode	
Description	*Hotkey*	*Menu Access*
Draw Brush	D	Sculpt⇨Draw
Smooth Brush	S	Sculpt⇨Smooth
Pinch Brush	P	Sculpt⇨Pinch
Inflate Brush	I	Sculpt⇨Inflate
Grab Brush	G	Sculpt⇨Grab
Layer Brush	L	Sculpt⇨Layer
Flatten Brush	T	Sculpt⇨Flatten
Toggle Add/Sub	V or Shift+left-click	Sculpt⇨Add
Airbrush	A	Sculpt⇨Airbrush
X Symmetry	X	Sculpt⇨X Symmetry
Y Symmetry	Y	Sculpt⇨Y Symmetry
Z Symmetry	Z	Sculpt⇨Z Symmetry
Rotate Brush	Ctrl+F	Sculpt⇨Rotate Brush
Brush Strength	Shift+F	Sculpt⇨Strengthen Brush
Brush Size	F	Sculpt⇨Scale Brush
Hide mesh outside of selection box	Shift+Ctrl+left-click	N/A
Hide mesh within selection box	Shift+Ctrl+right-click	N/A
Unhide All	Alt+H	N/A
Increase multires level	Page Up	N/A
Decrease multires level	Page Down	N/A

Chapter 6

Using Blender's Non-Mesh Primitives

. . . .

In This Chapter

▶ Working with curve objects and NURBS surfaces

▶ Understanding the benefits of meta objects

▶ Using text in Blender

. . . .

Although polygon-based meshes tend to be the bread and butter of modelers in Blender, they aren't the only types of objects that are available to you for creating things in 3D space. Blender also has curves, surfaces, meta objects, and text objects. These objects tend to have somewhat more specialized purposes than meshes, but when you need what they provide, they're extremely useful.

Curves and surfaces are nearly as general-purpose as meshes, but they're particularly handy for anything that needs to have a smooth, non-faceted look. They're also important for models that require mathematical precision and accuracy in their appearance. Meta objects are great at creating organic shapes that merge into one another, such as simple fluids. You can also use them to make a roughly sculpted model from basic elements if you don't want to work in Sculpt mode. Text objects are exactly what they sound like: You use them to add text to a scene and manipulate that text in all three dimensions. This chapter tells you more about working with all of these types of objects.

Using Curves and Surfaces

So, what's the biggest difference between curves and surfaces when compared to meshes? *Math!* Okay, I'm sorry. That was mean of me; I know that math can be a four-letter word for many artists. Don't worry, you won't have to do any math here. What I mean to say is that curves and surfaces can be described to the computer with a mathematical function. Meshes, on the other hand, are described with all of the individual vertices that they're composed of. This means that, in terms of the computer, curves and surfaces have two advantages:

✔ **They are very precise.** When you get down to it, the best that a mesh can be is an approximation of a real object. It can look really, really good, but it's not exact. Because curves are defined by math, they are exactly the correct shape. This is why designers and engineers like them. In fact, they're used as the reference for creating real objects. (So real objects are actually approximations of the curve design!)

✔ **They take up less memory.** Because the shape is mathematically defined, the computer can save that shape by saving the math, rather than saving all of the individual points. This means that complicated curves and surfaces usually take up quite a bit less space than the same shape made with meshes.

Of course, there are some caveats to these advantages. For one, curves and surfaces can sometimes be more difficult to control. Since curves and surfaces don't really have vertices for you to directly manipulate; you have to use *control points*. Depending on the type of curve, control points can sit directly on the shape, or float somewhere off of the surface as part of a control *cage*.

Another thing to bear in mind is that even though curves and surfaces are perfect mathematical descriptions of a shape, the computer is actually an imperfect way of displaying those perfect shapes. At the beginning of Chapter 5, I mentioned that all 3D geometry is eventually *tessellated*, or turned into a mesh of triangles, when the computer processes it. This means that even though curves and surfaces can take less memory on a computer, displaying them smoothly may actually take more time for the computer to process. To speed things up, you can tell the computer to use a rougher tessellation with fewer triangles. This means that what you see in Blender is an approximation of that perfect curve or surface shape. Do you find yourself thinking, "But hey, I thought curves were supposed to be perfect mathematical descriptions of a shape. What gives with these facets?" Well, the curve *is* perfect. It's just hard for the computer to show it to you directly.

But despite these minor disadvantages, using curves and surfaces is a really smart move in quite a few cases. For example, most designers like to use curves for company logos because curves can scale in print to any size without looking jagged or *aliased* around its edges. What this means to you as a 3D artist is that you can import the curves of a logo design and give the logo some depth, dimension, and perhaps even some animation. Speaking of animation, curves have quite a few handy uses there as well. For instance, you can use a curve to define a path for an object to move along. Curves are also used in Blenders Ipo Curve Editor to graph and control the changes to an object's properties over time. For modeling purposes, curves are great for pipes, wires, and ornate organic shapes. Figure 6-1 shows a park bench. I used only curves to model its sides.

Figure 6-1:
With the
exception of
the slats for
the seat and
back, this
entire park
bench was
modeled
with curves.

A set of curves used to define a shape in three dimensions is a *surface*. In some ways, curve surfaces are very similar to the subdivision surfaces on meshes that have the Subsurf modifier because they both have a control cage that defines the final shape that's created. The difference is that the curve surface has space and precision benefits that meshes don't have. Also, surfaces are a little bit easier to add textures to because you don't have to go through the additional step of *unwrapping*, or flattening the surface so a two-dimension texture can be applied to it. When you use a surface, you get that unwrapping for free because it's already done for you.

For these reasons — especially the precision — architects, industrial designers, and engineers prefer to work with surfaces on their models. Just about everything in your house was designed by someone. That includes your water faucet, your coffee maker, your television, your car, and even the house itself. If it was manufactured within the last 20 years, chances are good that it was designed on a computer and visualized with surfaces. Also, before the advent of subdivision surfaces on meshes, early characters for computer animations were modeled using curve surfaces because they were better at achieving organic shapes. Of course, if you're seen using curves to build a character these days, you might be viewed as a bit of masochist . . . especially if you try to do it in Blender. I go into why a little bit later in this chapter.

Understanding the different types of curves

In Blender, you can add curves by using Spacebar⇨Add⇨Curves and choosing the type of curve you'd like to use from the menu that appears. As shown in Figure 6-2, you can use two main kinds of curves: *Bézier curves* and *NURBS curves* (the Path curve is a specific type of Bézier curve). Bézier curves are generally used more for text and logos. By default, they only work in two dimensions, but you can get them to work in all three if you need to. You can tell you're using a Bézier curve because if you Tab into Edit mode to look at it, each control point has a pair of handles that can be used to give additional control over the curve's shape.

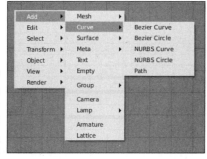

Figure 6-2:
The Add⇨
Curves
menu.

NURBS stands for *Non-Uniform Relational B-Spline*. The control points in NURBS curves don't have handles like Bézier curves do. In fact, by default, NURBS control points don't normally even touch the curve shape itself. Instead, the control points are *weighted* to influence the shape of the curve. Control points with higher weights attract the curve closer to them. Figure 6-3 shows the same curve shape made with Bézier curves and with NURBS curves.

Figure 6-3:
An arbitrary
shape
created
with Bézier
curves (left)
and NURBS
curves
(right).

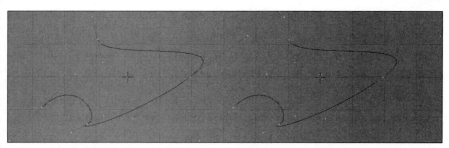

One thing to keep in mind is that although curves can work in three dimensions and can even create three-dimensional shapes like the park bench in Figure 6-1, they cannot be extruded to create a surface. If you want to create a surface, you need to actually navigate to the Surfaces menu (Spacebar⇨ Add⇨Surfaces) as shown in Figure 6-4. Notice that NURBS Curve and NURBS Circle are also options on this menu. Be aware, however, that these types of NURBS are treated differently than the NURBS curves available in the Curves menu. In fact, Blender doesn't even allow you to perform a Join (Ctrl+J) between NURBS curves and NURBS surface curves. It's a bit inconvenient, I know, but the situations where you'd actually want to do something like that are rare enough that you don't need to worry about it that much.

Figure 6-4:
The Add⇨
Surfaces
menu.

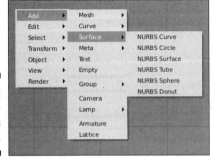

Working with curves

Surprisingly few specialized controls are specific to curves. Grab (G), Rotate (R), and Scale (S) work as expected and, like with meshes, you can Extrude a selected control point in Edit mode by either pressing E or Ctrl+left-clicking where you would like to extrude to. Joining separate curves in Edit mode can be done by selecting the end control points on each curve and pressing F, like making a face with meshes.

One place this doesn't work, however, is if the two control points you select are on the same curve. For something like that, you're probably wanting to close the curve, or, in Blenderese, you want to make the curve *cyclic*. To do this, press C while in Edit mode. Figure 6-5 shows a cyclic (closed) and non-cyclic (open) Bézier curve.

If you make a 2D curve cyclic, it creates a flat plane in the shape of your curve. And putting one cyclic curve within the borders of another actually creates a hole in that plane. However, this does not work with 3D curves because they aren't planar. In those situations, you want to use a surface.

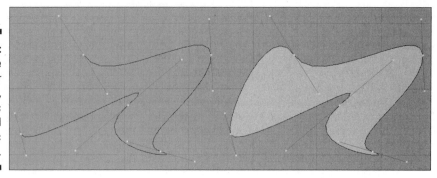

Curves are initially set to work only in two dimensions by default. It can be any arbitrary two-dimensional plane you want, but the control points are constrained to the curve object's local XY plane. To allow the curve to work in three dimensions, go to the Curve and Surface panel in the Editing buttons (F9), as shown in Figure 6-6, and left-click the 3D button. When you enable 3D on the curve, you might notice that in Edit mode, the curve now has little arrows spaced along it. These arrows indicate the direction of the curve. All curves have direction, even cyclic ones. Normally this isn't all that important except for when you are using the curve as a path. In that situation, the direction of the curve is the direction that the animated object is traveling along the curve. Switching the direction of the curve can be done by going to Curve⇨Segment⇨Switch Directions or pressing W⇨Switch Directions. To hide these arrows, reduce the NSize value in the Curve Tools1 panel, also shown in Figure 6-6.

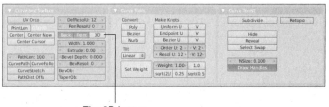

The 3D button

The buttons in the Curve and Surface panel are relevant to all curves, regardless of type. Some of the most important ones are in the right-hand column of buttons. First up are the DefResolU and RenResolU values. These values define the resolution of the curve. Remember that Blender only shows you an approximation of the real curve. Increasing the resolution here makes the curve look more like the curve defined by the math, at the cost of more processor time. That's why there are two resolution values. DefResolU is the default resolution and it's what you see in the 3D View. RenResolU is the resolution that Blender uses when you render. By default, this is set to zero, which means Blender uses whatever value that is in DefResolU.

With the exceptions of the 3D button – which I've already covered – and Width, the rest of the buttons in this column pertain to extruding and beveling your curve objects. Width is pretty interesting because it allows you to offset the curve from the control points. This is most apparent (and helpful) on cyclic curves. Values less than one are inset from the control points, whereas values greater than one are outset. (This is a quick way to put an outline on a logo or text because Blender does not have a stroke function for curves as do Inkscape or Adobe Illustrator.)

The Extrude value is probably the quickest way to give some depth to a curve, especially a 2D curve. However, you don't want to confuse this with the extrude capability you get by pressing E. This value affects the entire curve in Object mode, rather than just the selected control points in Edit mode. On a cyclic 2D curve, the flat planar shape that gets created extends out in the local Z direction of the curve object, with the caps drawn on it. And you can even control whether Blender draws the front or back cap by enabling or disabling the Front and Back buttons on the Curve and Surface panel. If you extrude a non-cyclic curve, you end up with something that looks more like a ribbon going along the shape of the curve. This is also what happens when you increase the extrude value on a 3D curve. Figure 6-7 shows some of the different effects you can get with an extruded curve.

Figure 6-7:
Some of the different things you can do with an extruded curve.

Of course, one of the drawbacks to extruding a curve is that you get a really sharp edge at the corners of the extrusion. Depending on what you're creating, harsh edges tend to look "too perfect" and unnatural. Fortunately, we have Bevel to take care of that for us. To give an extruded curve more natural corners, simply increase the Bevel Depth value. You may notice that when you do this, the bevel is really kind of simple: just a cut across the corner. Say you want that to be even smoother. You can make that happen by increasing the BevResol value. Like the DefResolU and RenResolU values, this value increases the resolution of part of the curve. In this case, it's the resolution of the bevel. Increasing the BevResol value makes a smoother, more curved bevel. This works on both cyclic and non-cyclic curves.

But say you want something more ornate, kind of like the molding or trim you'd find around the doorway on a house. For that, you want to use a *BevOb*, or Bevel Object. This basically means that you're going to use the shape of one curve to define the bevel on another. To get a better idea of what I'm talking about, use the following steps:

1. **Create a Bézier circle (Spacebar⇨Add⇨Curves⇨Bézier Circle).**

   Scale up nice and large with S so you can see what's going on.

2. **Extrude the circle by increasing the Extrude value in the Curve and Surface panel of the Editing buttons (F9).**

   The circle doesn't have to be excessively thick, just enough to give it some form of depth.

3. **Create a Bézier curve (spacebar⇨Add⇨Curves⇨Bézier Curve).**

   Tab into Edit mode and edit this curve a bit to get the bevel shape that you want. Keep the curve non-cyclic for now. When you're done editing, tab back out to Object mode.

4. **Select your Bézier circle and, in the BevOb field of the Curve and Surface panel in the Editing buttons, type in the name of your Bézier curve.**

   If you didn't rename it, it's probably called something like Curve or Curve.001. After you confirm this by pressing Enter, the corners of your Bézier circle are beveled with the shape defined by your Bézier curve. Now for fun, follow the next step.

5. **Go back and make the BevOb curve cyclic.**

   Doing so actually removes the front and back planes from the extrusion. You're left with a curve shape that follows the main Bézier circle's path. For extra kicks, select the Bézier circle and Tab into Edit mode. Select any control point and press Alt+S to shrink or fatten the beveled shape around that control point. Slick, huh?

When you use a BevOb, you're essentially handing control of the curve's shape over to the BevOb object. That being the case, after you do it changing the values for Extrude, Bevel Depth, and BevResol has no effect on the curve for as long as you have the BevOb there.

Figure 6-8 shows the results of these steps.

If you're using a curve to model anything roughly cylindrical in shape such as a pipe or a tube, there's actually no need to use a BevOb curve. It's a bit of a hidden function, but you can get the same effect by beveling the curve. I know that sounds odd (how do you bevel something that doesn't have any corners?), but trust me, it works. You do it by disabling both the Front and Back buttons in the Curve and Surface panel and then increasing the Bevel Depth. Increasing the BevResol value makes the cross-section more circular. Hooray! One less BevOb object to hide!

In the preceding example, I showed you that Alt+S can be used on individual control points to shrink or fatten the thickness of the extrusion. However, perhaps you would like to have more control than that along the length of the curve. This is where you would use the *TaperOb* field. Like the BevOb field, the TaperOb field uses one curve to define the shape of another. In this case, you're controlling the thickness along the length of the curve, and it works in very much the same way: Create a separate curve that dictates the taper shape and then type the name of that curve in the TaperOb field of the curve you'd like to control. Figure 6-9 shows how a TaperOb can give you complete control of a curve's shape along its length.

I prefer to create my BevOb and TaperOb curves in the Top view (Numpad 7) along the X-axis. This way, I have a good frame of reference of where the center line of the curve is. That's important because BevObs use the center line to define the front and back of a curve's extrusion. And you can think of TaperObs as a kind of profile that revolves around its local X-axis. Bringing your control points to the center line makes the tapered curve come to a point, whereas moving them away from the center line increases the thickness there.

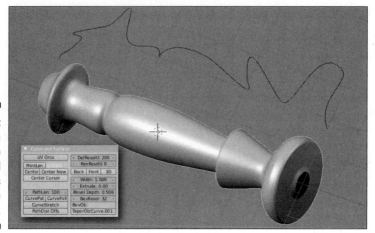

One other thing that you can control on curves is the *tilt* of the control points. In other programs, this might be called the *twist* property. To get a good idea of what you can do with tilt, try the following steps:

1. **Create a Bézier Curve (Spacebar⇨Add⇨Curves⇨Bézier Curve) and tab into Edit mode.**

2. **Make the curve cyclic (C).**

   You may also want to select (right-click) the handles and rotate (R) them so there's a cleaner arc.

3. **Enable 3D on the curve (F9⇨Curve and Surface⇨3D).**

4. **Select one of the handles and press T.**

   When you do this, move your mouse cursor around the point in a clockwise fashion. While you do that, watch how the Tilt value in the 3D view's header changes.

5. **Confirm completion (left-click or Enter).**

   If you increase the Extrude and Bevel Depth values, you should now have something that looks a bit like Figure 6-10.

Editing Bézier curves

The most defining aspect of Bézier curves are the handles on their control points. Handles on Bézier curves are always tangential to the curve and come in one of four varieties in Blender:

✔ **Aligned (H – toggles with Free):** Aligned handles are always in a straight line and they display in a pinkish color. If you grab (G) and move one handle on a control point, the other moves in the opposite direction to balance it out. You can, however have aligned handles of differing lengths.

✔ **Free (H – toggles with Aligned):** Free handles are sometimes referred to as "broken" handles. They display in black and don't necessarily have to be in a straight line. They are best suited for giving you sharp points that smoothly flow to the next control point.

✔ **Auto (Shift+H):** These handles are set by Blender to give you the smoothest possible result in the shape of your curve. They show up in yellow and generally form a straight line with equal lengths on either side. If you try to edit an Auto handle, it immediately reverts to an aligned handle.

✔ **Vector (V):** Vector handles are broken like free handles, but they point directly to the next control point. This makes the shape of the curve an exactly straight line from one control point to the next. Editing the handles on a vector control point turns it into a free handle.

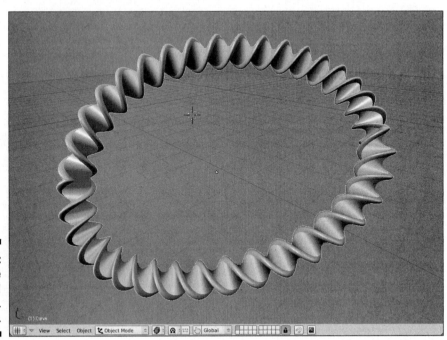

Figure 6-10:
Fun with the
tilt function!
Mmmm...
twisty.

Figure 6-11 shows four curves with the same exact control points, but with different types of handles. And, yes, you can mix handle types in a single curve. It's actually quite handy when you need a figure to be smooth in some parts and pointy in others.

Editing NURBS curves and surfaces

NURBS are a different kind of beast in terms of controls. They have control points, but NURBS curves are conspicuously without handles. Now, remember that Blender treats a NURBS curve differently than a NURBS surface curve. With that in mind, though, whether you're dealing with a curve or a surface curve, the following things generally apply to all NURBS:

✔ **Each control point has a weight.** The weight, which is a value between 0 and 1, influences how much that control point influences the curve. In Blender, you set the weight with the buttons at the bottom of the Curve Tools panel (see Figure 6-6 for reference). You can explicitly type the weight in the Weight field, or left-click one of the buttons near it to give it a preset value. After you decide the weight you want, left-click the Set Weight button. The value in the Weight field is applied to all selected control points.

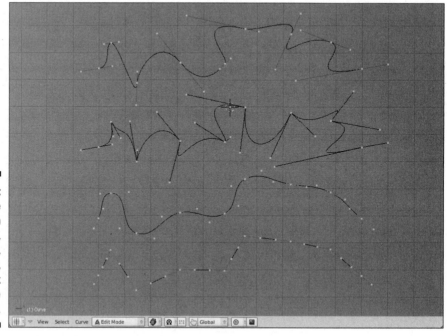

Figure 6-11:
The same curve with aligned, free, auto, vector, and a mix of curve handles.

✔ **NURBS have knots.** In math terms, *knots* are vectors that describe how the resulting curve is influenced by the control points. In Blender, you have three settings that you can assign to knots from the Curve Tools panel: Uniform, Endpoint, and Bézier. By default, NURBS are assigned uniform knots. You can tell this because the curve does not go all the way to the end control points. Those control points' weights are factored in with all of the others. Endpoint knots, in contrast, bring the curve all the way to the last control points, regardless of weight. Bézier knots treat the control points like they are free handles on a Bézier curve. Every three control points act like the center and two handles on a Bézier curve's control points.

✔ **NURBS have an order.** An *order* is another math thing. What it really means, though, is that the lower the order, the more the curve directly follows the lines between control points. And the higher the order, the smoother and more fluid the curve is as it passes the control points. The values for order can also be changed in the Curve Tools panel.

Figure 6-12 shows the influences that curve weights, knot types, and order can have on a NURBS curve.

Figure 6-12: Decreasing curve weights on a control point, differences between the three knot types, and increasing the order of a curve.

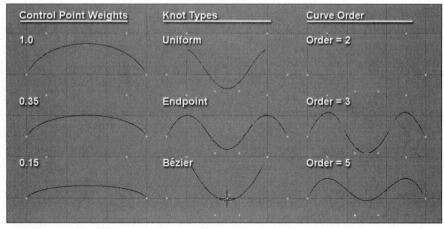

After you set the weight of a control point or a knot type, you can always set it to another value. However, there's currently no easy way to find out what weight each control point has or what type of knot the curve is using (although the latter is pretty easy to guess visually). So keep in mind that on a complex NURBS object, you might lose track of your weights.

You might notice in the Curve Tools panel that the knot, order, and resolution controls can each be independently set for a U or a V value. If you're dealing with just a curve, the U direction is all you need to worry about. However, a NURBS surface works in two directions: U and V. If you add a NURBS Surface (Spacebar⇨Add⇨Surfaces⇨NURBS Surface), you can visually tell the difference between the U segments, which are pinkish, and the V segments, which are yellow.

One of the really cool things that you can do easily with NURBS surfaces that's difficult to do with other types of surfaces is a process called *lofting*. (Other programs might call it *skinning*, but because that term actually means something else for rigging, I use *lofting* here.) Basically, lofting is the process of using a series of NURBS surface curves with the *same number of control points* as a series of profiles to define a shape. The cool thing about doing it in Blender is that after you have the profiles in place, it's as simple as selecting all control points (A) and pressing (F). The classic use for this is modeling the hull of a boat, as you see in the following steps and Figure 6-13:

1. **Add a NURBS surface curve (Spacebar⇨Add⇨Surfaces⇨NURBS Curve) and tab into Edit mode.**

2. **Select All and Rotate -90 degrees around the X-axis (A⇨R⇨X⇨-90).**

   This forms the bottom of your boat.

3. **Model a cross-section of the boat's hull. Add more control points using Extrude (E or Ctrl+left-click) and move them around with Grab (G). When doing this, it would be a good idea to press C and make the curve cyclic.**

   Try to keep the cross section as planar as possible. I like to work on this from the front view (Numpad 1).

4. **Select all control points in your cross section and duplicate it along the Y-axis (A⇨Shift+D⇨Y).**

5. **Make adjustments to the new cross section to suit your tastes, but *do not add any control points*.**

   Lofting requires that each cross-section has the exact same number of control points. If you add or remove control points from a cross-section, it doesn't work.

6. **Repeat steps 4 and 5 until you're satisfied.**

7. **Select All and press F.**

   Congratulations! You've made a canoe!

A quick note on paths

You might be begrudging the fact that I glazed over the fact that you can add a Path curve (Spacebar⇨Add⇨Curves⇨Path). The reason for this is that just about any curve can be turned into a path. By default, when you add a path, it's really a shortcut for adding a NURBS curve with two buttons enabled in the Curve and Surface panel: 3D and CurvePath. The important

one here is CurvePath. By enabling this button, Blender understands that this curve is a path and can be used to control the movement of an animated object. To make any NURBS or Bézier curve into a path, all you have to do is left-click this button. I get more into the use of paths as animation controls in Chapter 10.

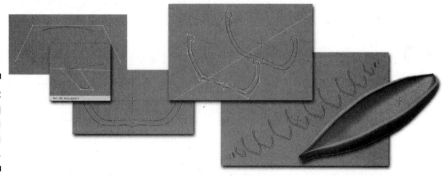

Figure 6-13:
Using lofting to create a the hull of a boat.

Understanding the strengths and limitations of Blender's surfaces

When compared to other tools that work with NURBS surface, Blender admittedly falls short in some functions. You can extrude surface endpoints, do lofting, and even *spin* surface curves (sometimes called *lathing* in other programs) to create bowl or cup shapes. However, that's about it. Blender currently doesn't have the functionality to do a ton of other cool things that can be done with NURBS surfaces, such as using one curve to trim the length of another or project the shape of one curve onto the surface of another. These are things that you cannot currently do with Blender's NURBS surfaces.

However, there's actually hope. It's been slow coming, but there's recently been more progress on the integration of better NURBS tools within Blender. If you're curious about this, do a Web search for "Blender and Nurbana" to see how progress is coming. If all goes well, the next version of Blender should show marked improvement. Ultimately, NURBS may even be able to use a large quantity of the modifiers that we enjoy using on meshes.

Using Meta Objects

Meta objects are cool little 3D surfaces that have been part of computer graphics for a long time. Sometimes they are referred to as *blobbies*. The principle behind them is pretty simple: Imagine that you have two droplets of water and you begin moving these two droplets closer and closer to each other. Eventually, the two droplets are going to merge and become a single, larger droplet. That's basically how meta objects work, except you have complete control over when the droplets merge, how much they merge, and you can re-separate them again if you'd like. You can also do something that's more difficult in the real world: You can subtract one droplet from the other, rather than add them together into a merged object. They're a ton of fun to play with and there are some pretty neat applications for them. Figure 6-14 shows two metaballs being merged.

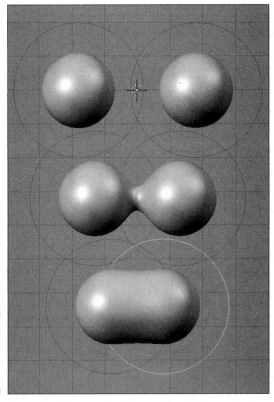

Figure 6-14:
Merging
two meta-
balls.

Meta-wha?

Meta objects are a bit like curves and NURBS in that their entire existence is defined by math. However, unlike NURBS or even meshes, you cannot control the surface of a meta object directly with control points or vertices. Instead, the shape of their surface is defined by a combination of the object's underlying structure – a point, a line, a plane, a sphere, or a cube – and its proximity to other meta objects. There are five meta object primitives:

- ✔ **Metaball:** The surface in this primitive is based on the points that are all the same distance from a single center point. This means that you can move and scale a metaball uniformly, but you cannot scale it in just one direction.

- ✔ **Metatube:** Whereas the basis for a metaball is a single point, the basis for a metatube is the line between two points. This means that you can scale the surface uniformly, like a metaball, but you can also scale it in its local X-axis, referred to as *dx*.

- ✔ **Metaplane:** The metaplane's underlying structure is, as you may have guessed, a plane. This means you have both the local X (dx) and the local Y (dy) axis for scaling, as well as scaling uniformly.

- ✔ **Metaellipsoid:** At first glance, you might mistake this meta object for a metaball. However, instead of being based on a single point, this object is based on a sphere. So if you keep the local X, Y, and Z dimensions equal, it behaves just like a metaball. However, you also have the flexibility to allow you to scale in any of the three individual axes.

- ✔ **Metacube:** The metacube is like the metaellipse in that it's also based on a three-dimensional structure. In the metacube's case, it's a cube rather than a sphere.

One of the coolest things about meta objects is that you can change from one primitive to another on the fly using the MetaBall Tools panel in the Editing buttons (F9). Figure 6-15 shows each of the primitives along with the default settings for them in the MetaBall Tools panel.

The MetaBall Tools panel appears when you tab into Edit mode on a meta object. The panel always displays the Stiffness value for the selected object. This value controls the influence that the selected meta object has on other meta objects. It's indicated visually in the 3D View with a green ring around the meta object's center point. You can adjust the Stiffness value here in the panel or, if you select the green ring (right-click), you can Scale (S) to adjust the Stiffness visually. By right-clicking the pinkish ring outside of that green ring, you can select the actual individual meta object.

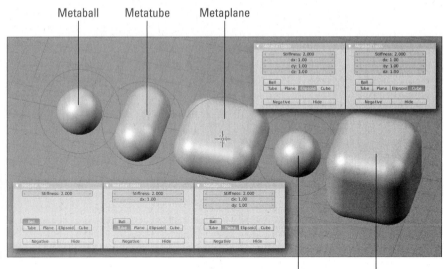

Metaball   Metatube   Metaplane

Metaellipsoid   Metacube

Figure 6-15:
The five
meta object
primitives.

And depending on the type of meta object primitive you're using, other values of dx, dy, and dz may appear in the MetaBall Tools panel. You can adjust these values here or in 3D View by using the S⇨X, S⇨Y, and S⇨Z hotkey sequences. At the bottom of the panel are buttons to either hide the selected meta object or give it a negative influence, subtracting it from the positive, and therefore visible, meta objects.

When you Tab back out to Object mode, you can move your combined meta object (a meta-meta object?) as a single unit. Note, however, that even though you've grouped these meta objects into a single Blender object, they don't live in a vacuum. If you have two complex Blender objects made up of metas, bringing the two of them together actually causes them to merge. Just something you may want to keep in mind and take advantage of in the future.

As a single Blender object, though, there are a few more things that you can control using the MetaBall panel, shown in Figure 6-16. This panel is always available to meta objects, whether in Object mode or Edit mode, and it normally sits to the right of the Link and Materials panel.

Figure 6-16:
The
MetaBall
panel.

The first two values in the MetaBall panel are Wiresize and Rendersize. Wiresize controls how dense the generated mesh is for the meta object in the 3D view. Lower values are a finer mesh, whereas higher values result in much more of an approximation. The Rendersize value does the same thing, except it only has an effect at render time. The reason for this is that meta objects can get really complex quickly and, because they're generated entirely by math, these complex combinations of meta objects tend to use a lot of computer processing power. Working at a larger wiresize in the 3D view helps keep your computer responsive while you work, whereas a finer Rendersize value keeps things pretty on output.

The Threshold value is an overall control for how much influence the metas in a single Blender object have over each other. This value has a range from zero to five, but in order for a meta object to be visible, it's individual Stiffness value must be greater than the Threshold value.

Below Threshold are four buttons that control how the meta objects get updated and displayed in the 3D View:

- **Always:** The slowest and most accurate setting. This is the default. Every change you make in the 3D View happens instantly (or as fast as your computer can handle it).

- **Half Res:** Enabling this button reduces the resolution of the meta object as you move or edit it to increase the responsiveness of the 3D View. As soon as you finish transforming the meta object, it displays in full resolution again.

- **Fast:** As the name implies, this is nearly the fastest setting. When you enable this button, Blender hides the meta objects when you perform a transform and then re-evaluates the surface when you finish. It works very nicely, but the downside is that you don't get the nice visual feedback that Always and Half Res give you.

- **Never:** This is certainly the fastest update method. Basically, if you try to edit a meta object, it hides everything and never updates in the 3D View. Although this may not seem useful at first, if you decide to bind your meta object to a particle system as a way of faking fluids, turning this setting on definitely increases performance in the 3D View.

What meta objects are useful for

Alright, so what in the world can you actually use meta objects to make? There are actually two answers to this question: all sorts of things, and not much. The reason for this seemingly paradoxical answer is that meta objects *can* be used to do quick, rough prototype models and they *can* also be used with a particle system to generate simple fluid simulations. However, with the advent of advanced modeling tools like multi-res sculpting and subdivision surfaces, meta objects don't get used as often for prototyping. And with more advanced fluid simulation and rendering technology, meta objects are also used less for those applications as well.

That said, even though meta objects are used *less* for these purposes, that doesn't mean that they're never used. In fact, not too long ago, I used a set of metaballs with a glowing halo material to animate the life force being forcefully pulled out of a guy. I mean, I could probably have used a particle system or fluid simulator to do it, but using metaballs was actually faster to set up and I had more direct control over where everything was placed on the screen. So don't count meta objects out just yet. There's still some life in these little suckers. Besides, they're still fun to play with!

Adding Text

Over the years, working with text in Blender has come a long, long way. As you might expect, the way you work with text in Blender has quite a few differences from what you might expect of word processing software like OpenOffice.org or Microsoft Word. What you might not expect is that Blender's text objects share a few features in common with desktop publishing programs like Adobe InDesign or QuarkXPress. In fact, one Blender developer even went so far as to create his own version of Blender specifically geared toward desktop publishing. If you're interested in finding out more about it, do a Web search for DTPBlender.

Blender's text objects are really a specialized type of curve object. This means that nearly all of the options I already described for the Curve and Surface panel in the Editing buttons also apply to text. For example, you can quickly bring text objects into the third dimension using the Extrude, Bevel, and even the BevOb and TaperOb fields. Figure 6-17 shows an example of the interesting things you can do with a single text object in Blender.

Adding and editing text

You add a text object in Blender the same way you would add any other object: with the toolbox. Press Spacebar⇨Add⇨Text and a text object is placed at the location of your 3D cursor with the default content of the word *Text*. To edit the text, you tab into Edit mode. After you're in Edit mode, the controls begin to feel a bit more like a word processor, although not exactly. For instance, you can't use your mouse cursor to highlight text, but if you press Shift+left arrow and shift+right arrow, depending on where the text cursor is located, you can highlight text this way.

Figure 6-17:
Taking
advantage
of the
curve-based
nature of
Blender text
objects.

Shift+Ctrl+left/right arrow highlights whole words at a time. Backspace deletes text and pressing Enter gives you a new line.

In addition to that, there are formatting controls in the Font panel of the Editing buttons, as shown in Figure 6-18. Two of the coolest buttons here are the Insert Text and Lorem buttons. If you already have a bunch of text created and don't feel like re-typing all of it in Blender, left-click Insert Text and use the File Browser to find the text file you want to load. After you do, the content of whatever is in that text file is added from the location of the text cursor. The Lorem button generates filler text in the form of Latin gibberish, also known as *lorem ipsum* text. Publishing layout designers use lorem ipsum a lot for defining layout when the actual content is not yet known. I've used this for adding placeholder credits when I didn't know everyone's names and titles.

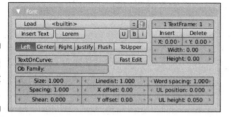

Figure 6-18:
The Font
panel.

When you're in Edit mode, notice that pressing Tab doesn't indent your text like you might expect because it's already assigned to getting you back out to Object mode. If you really, really need to use a Tab character, you have to import that from another file or use the third-to-last character in the first row of the Char panel (more on this in the next section, "Changing fonts").

Below the Insert Text and Lorem buttons is a block of alignment buttons to help you align your text relative to the center point of the text object. You have the following options:

- ✔ **Left:** Aligns text to the left. The text object's center serves as the left-hand guide for the text.

- ✔ **Center:** All text is centered around the text object's center point.

- ✔ **Right:** Aligns text to the right. The text object's center serves as the right-hand guide for the text.

- ✔ **Justify:** Aligns text both on the left and on the right. If the line is not long enough, Blender adds spacing, or *kerning*, between individual characters to fill the space. This option requires the use of text frames. (See the next section, "Working with text frames," for more details.

- ✔ **Flush:** This works similar to the way Justify does, but with two exceptions. First, if the line is the end of a paragraph, it doesn't force the text to align both sides. And second, Flush uses word spacing rather than kerning to get lines to align properly. Like Justify, this option requires the use of text frames.

- ✔ **ToUpper:** This really isn't an alignment button, but it's in the grouping, so it's worth covering here. Left-clicking this button toggles the characters in your text object between all uppercase letters and all lowercase letters.

Working with text frames

An important thing to notice is that both the Flush and the Justify options require the use of something called *text frames*. The Left, Center, and Right align options all work relative to the location of the text object's center. If you want to align your text on both the left and the right side, you need more than one reference point. Text frames are a way of doing this for you, but with a couple of additional benefits as well. Basically, they're a rectangular shape that defines where the text in your text object lives. Text frames are similar to the *frames* you might use in desktop publishing programs. They're also one of those things that you normally don't see in 3D software.

To work with text frames, you use the block of buttons on the upper right corner of the Font panel. The first button should read "1 TextFrame: 1". This means that you have one text frame in your text object and that's the one you're currently working on. If you left-click the Insert button, the field changes to say "2 TextFrame: 2," meaning you're on the second of two text frames. To go back to the first text frame, left-click the arrow on the left of the TextFrame field or left-click the center of it and type **1** for the value. You can delete the current text frame by left-clicking the Delete button. Of course, having a text frame doesn't mean much if you don't define its size and location. That's what the buttons at the bottom of the block are for. The X and Y fields determine where the top left corner of the text frame is located, whereas the Width and Height fields define its size in Blender units. As you adjust these values while in Edit mode, you should see a dashed rectangle in the 3D View.

Now, the cool thing about text frames is that if you have more than one defined, the text can overflow from one text frame into the other. This is an excellent way to get very fine control over the placement of your text. You can even do newspaper-style multi-column text this way, as shown in Figure 6-19.

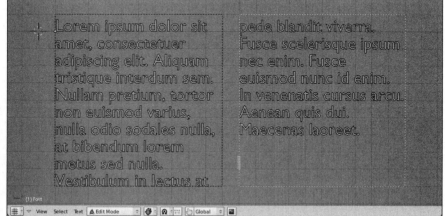

Figure 6-19:
Using text frames to get multi-column text layouts.

If you're working with a lot of text, you might find that Blender might not perform as speedily as you would like while editing. If you left-click the Fast Edit button in the Font panel, Blender uses just the outline to the text in the 3D View while in Edit mode. This gives Blender a bit of a performance boost so you're not waiting for characters to show up seconds after you finish typing them.

Controlling text appearance

The block of buttons at the bottom of the Font panel control how the text appears in the selected text object. Descriptions of each follow:

- ✔ **Size:** Font size on a scale from zero to ten. Adjusting this value should adjust the font size as dictated by the font. This is generally a better way to change the size of your text rather than simply scaling the text object.

- ✔ **Linedist:** Line distance, also referred to as *leading*. This value defines the distance between lines of text in your text object and it also has a range from zero to ten.

- ✔ **Word spacing:** Globally defines the space between words in your text object. This field has a range from zero to ten.

- ✔ **Spacing:** The global distance between all characters in your text object, also known as *tracking*. Like the previous fields, it has a range from zero to ten.

- ✔ **Shear:** A quick and dirty way to fake italics on a font. Values between 0 and 1 tilt characters to the right, whereas values between -1 and 0 tilt them all to the left.

- ✔ **X offset:** Offsets the text object to the left or right of its default position. Values less than zero shift it left, whereas values greater than zero shift it right.

- ✔ **Y offset:** Offsets the text object up or down from its default position. Values less than zero shift it down, whereas values greater than zero shift up.

- ✔ **UL position:** Determines the position of the underline, if enabled (Ctrl+U on highlighted text). This value has a range from -0.2 to 0.8.

- ✔ **UL height:** Controls the thickness of the actual underline, if enabled (Ctrl+U on highlighted text). You can set this value between 0.01 and 0.5.

If you're familiar with typography, you may notice two things right off the bat. First, the terms used here are not the standard typography terminology, and second, the values are not in your typical percentage, point, pica, or pixel sizes. There are two primary reasons for this. First, Blender is a 3D program intended for 3D artists, many of whom may not be familiar with typography terms and sizes. The second reason dovetails with that, but it's a bit more on the practical side. Blender text objects are 3D objects that can be just about any size in virtual 3D space. Sizes like points, pixels, and picas don't really mean anything in 3D because there's not a frame of reference, like the physical size of a printed piece of paper.

Changing fonts

Another thing that's different about Blender's text objects is the way it handles fonts. If you're used to other programs, you might expect there to be a drop-down menu that lists all of the fonts installed on your computer with a nice preview of each. Unfortunately, Blender does not currently have that ability. Instead, what you need to do is left-click the Load button and track down the actual font file for the typeface that you would like to use. Below are the standard places you might find fonts on Windows, Mac, and Linux machines:

- ✔ **Windows:** C:\Windows\Fonts

- ✔ **Mac OS:** /System/Library/Fonts or /Library/Fonts

- ✔ **Linux:** /usr/share/fonts

After you load a font into your .blend file, it's available for you to use whenever you want it from the font drop-down list. You always have Blender's built-in font available as well. Also, notice the button next to the drop-down with the icon that looks like a present. Left-clicking this button packs the font into your .blend file. This way, if you take your .blend file to a different computer that doesn't have the font you need, it's not a problem because it's packed in. If the font is already packed, left-clicking this button unpacks it to your computer's hard drive.

Now you would think that after you have a font loaded, you should be good to go, right? Well, not quite. See, Blender's buttons for bold and italics are kind of unique. They actually load a separate font altogether. The typical use for this would be to load the bold and italics versions of the main font you loaded. However, that's not a complete requirement. You can actually use an entirely different font altogether here. Because technically you can't arbitrarily change fonts in the middle of a text object, this is a good way to get around that. Just make your bold or italics font the other font you want to use! Figure 6-20 shows this in action. The way you assign a font to either bold, italics, or even both is pretty straightforward:

1. **Left-click either the B or i button on the Font panel (or both).**

   By default, the <built-in> font is chosen for this.

2. **Left-click the Load button to choose the font you would rather use.**

3. **After you confirm, you should be set to go.**

   That's it!

Figure 6-20:
Using the
bold and
italics fonts
to use
widely
different
fonts in a
single text
object.

You may find that while you're typing, you need certain special characters like the copyright symbol or the upside-down question mark for sentences written in Spanish. For these situations, you have three options:

- ✔ If the special character is common, you may find it in Text⇨Special Characters.

- ✔ You can memorize the hotkey combination for various commonly used special characters as listed in Blender's online documentation.

- ✔ If the character is rare or just not in the menu, you can find it using the box in the Char panel of the Editing buttons (F9). The Char panel has a grid that displays all of the characters in the font that Blender recognizes.

Another unique feature that Blender's text objects have is the ability to use any other Blender object as a font character. So if you want to use Suzanne the monkey every time the uppercase S character is used, you can actually do that. If you want to model letters with meta objects and spell something with them, like in Figure 6-21, you can! It's all done with the Ob Family field in the Font panel. Just use the following steps:

1. **Type the name of your font "family" in Ob Family.**

   This can be any name you'd like. I like to end it with a dot so I can differentiate my characters later. For example, you may use "MetaLetter." (ending in the period) in this case.

2. **Model a character you wish to use.**

   In this example, I'm using meta objects, so I would use Spacebar⇨Add⇨Meta⇨Metaball as my starting point and work from there.

3. **Name this object with the family name plus the character it will represent.**

   In this case, if you modeled an uppercase W, you would call it "MetaLetter.W." A lowercase W would be "MetaLetter.w." Now you see why we used the dot at the end of the family name in step 1. It helps keep things organized.

4. **Repeat steps 2 and 3 for each character you need.**

5. **Select (right-click) your text object and turn on Dupliverts (F7⇨Anim settings⇨Dupliverts).**

6. **Adjust size and spacing to fit. And *poof*! You've got metaletters!**

   Now to finish, move the original font text to another layer so it's out of the way of your metaletters.

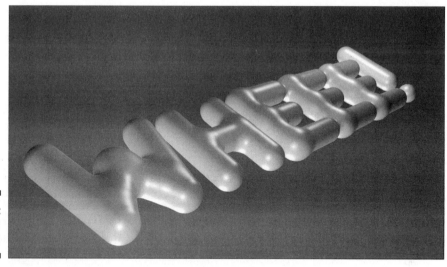

Figure 6-21:
Wheeeee!
Metaletters!

Deforming text with a curve

One of the other really powerful things you can do with Blender's text objects is to have the text flow along the length of a curve. This way, you can get text that arcs over a doorway or wraps around a bowl or just looks all kinds of funky. The key to this feature is the TextOnCurve field in the Font panel. To see how this works, use the steps in the following example:

1. **Create a text object (Spacebar⇨Add⇨Text).**

   Feel free to populate it with whatever content you would like.

2. **Create a curve to dictate the text shape
   (Spacebar⇨Add⇨Curve⇨Bézier Curve).**

   This example uses a Bézier curve, but a NURBS curve works fine as well. Also, I like to make my curve with the same center point location as my text object. Granted, that's just my preference, but it works nicely for keeping everything easily manageable.

3. **Select (right-click) the text object and type the name of the control curve in the TextOnCurve field.**

   Blam! The text should now follow the arc of the curve. If you select (right-click) the curve and tab into Edit mode, any change you make to it updates your text object live.

Figure 6-22 shows 3D text along a curve.

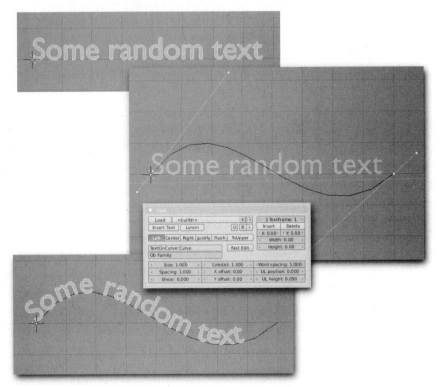

Figure 6-22:
Text on a
curve.

One thing to note is that you should keep your curve as a 2D curve. Because the text is technically a special type of 2D curve, trying to get it to deform along a 3D curve won't work. For that, you're going to need to convert the text into a mesh, as described in the next section.

Converting to curves and meshes

Of course, while Blender's text objects are pretty powerful, curves and meshes just do some things better. Fortunately, you don't have to model your type unless you really, really want to. Instead, you can convert your text object into a curve or a mesh by pressing Alt+C and choosing Curve, Curve (Single Filling Group), or Mesh. If you're curious as to some specific cases why you'd want to do this, here are a few:

✔ Custom editing the characters for a logo or a specific shape (convert to a curve).

✔ You need to share your .blend file, but the license of your font prevents you from legally packing it into the .blend (convert to a curve).

✔ Getting extruded text to follow a 3D curve (convert to a mesh).

✔ Rigging the letters to be animated with an armature (convert to a mesh).

✔ Using the letters as obstacles in a fluid simulation (convert to a mesh).

✔ Using the letters to generate a particle system (convert to a mesh).

Using Alt+C also works on curve objects, surfaces, and meta objects to convert them to meshes. Just be aware that most of these conversions are permanent. You can't go back on them without using the undo function.

Chapter 7

Changing that Boring Gray Default Material

. . . .

In This Chapter

▶ Understanding how Blender handles materials

▶ Taking advantage of Vertex painting

. . . .

As you work on your models in Blender, you're eventually going to get tired of that plastic gray material that all Blender objects have by default. Nothing against neutral colors – or plastic, for that matter – but we live in a vibrantly colorful world and you may occasionally want to use these colors in your 3D scenes. To do this, you use materials and textures. Blender's way of adding materials and textures to an object is in some ways one of the most confusing parts of the program, and it can be a pretty big challenge to wrap your brain around the full functionality of it.

This chapter is intended to give you the skills to know enough to be dangerous with Blender's materials. Hopefully, with a little practice, you can become lethal. Well, *lethal* might be the wrong word: I don't think I've ever heard of anyone killed by excessively sharp specular highlights. (Don't worry if you don't get the joke right now. After you finish this chapter, you'll realize how horrible a pun this is.)

Playing with Materials

The easiest way to change the look of an object is to adjust its material. The controls for this are in the Shading buttons (F5). The Shading buttons actually have five subcontexts, accessible by the buttons in its header, as shown by Figure 7-1. For now, I'm most interested in the Material button, which is accessed with the second subcontext button: the one with a red sphere as its icon.

Understanding how light reflects

To understand materials, it helps if you have an idea of how human sight works. This is because most *rendering engines*, or the code that converts your virtual 3D environment into a 2D picture, use this as the basic model for how they work. It goes something like this: In order to see, you need to have light. The light comes from one or more sources and bounces off of any object within its range. When the light hits these objects, they influence the direction that the light bounces and how much of the incoming light is absorbed versus reflected. When you look around, you are seeing light that is bounced off of these objects and into your eyes.

Most rendering engines, Blender's included, use a simplified version of this scenario. The biggest difference can be summed up in the following sentence: *Unless otherwise stipulated, light only bounces once.* If you've ever

been in a professional photographer's studio, you might notice that they often have their flash aimed away from their subject and into an umbrella-shaped reflector that bounces light back to whatever they're shooting. The light from the flash has at least two bounces to get to the camera's lens; once off of the umbrella and once off of the subject. Because this is more than one bounce, you can't set up something like this in Blender and expect it to work. Instead, you need to directly light your scenes, and your materials themselves control that one bounce the light has off of them and into the 3D camera.

Exceptions to this do, of course, exist, as do ways to cheat around them. I get into some of them later on in this chapter and in the next, particularly when talking about raytracing.

Figure 7-1:
The subcontext buttons for the Shading buttons: Lamp, Material, Texture, Radiosity, and World.

By default, all newly added objects in Blender share a gray, plastic-like material. The settings for this gray material on the default cube objects is shown in Figure 7-2. There are five blocks of panels visible:

✔ **Preview:** The Preview panel displays an image of the material on a variety of preset objects: a plane, a sphere, a cube, Suzanne's head, hair strands, and a sphere on a sky background.

✔ **Links and Pipeline:** This panel creates new material datablocks and controls how they link to objects in the scene. This panel also dictates how the material is noticed by Blender's internal renderer.

✔ **Material:** Set in this panel are broad, high-level controls for the active material, including color, transparency, and some basic rendering properties, that affect the material colors.

✔ **Shaders:** The Shaders panel has a little bit finer-grained control over the material than the Material panel does, dictating the specific ways that colors appear and react to light on the objects in the scene.

✔ **Texture:** Materials are not limited to solid, flat colors on objects. You can get finer control by using textures. This panel ties up to 10 textures to a given material.

Figure 7-2:
The
Material
buttons.

Of these panels, the Links and Pipeline panel gives you the most high level control over the material, defining which material gets assigned to the selected object and how the renderer recognizes the material. On the first line of buttons are datablock control buttons that link your material to the current selection. It functions the same as the datablock control buttons in the Link and Materials panel of the Editing buttons (F9), as explained in Chapter 4. From left to right, here is a description of what each button does:

✔ The up/down button on the left gives you the ability to add a new material or load an existing one that you've already created.

✔ The Datablock Name field allows you to give your material a custom name. To do this, left-click in the field and type the name you want to use.

✔ If your material is linked to more than one object, it has a numbered button next to it, representing the number of objects using this material. Left-clicking this button creates a copy of the material that is used only by the current active object.

✔ The X button disconnects the material datablock from the active object.

✔ The button with the icon that looks like a little car automatically creates a name for the material when you left-click it. The name is based on the current color of the material. Using a car icon may seem odd here, but if you don't think of it as a car, but an *auto*mobile, it begins to make sense. (Yes, it's kind of a goofy pun, but that's what it means.)

✔ The F button creates a "fake user" for the material datablock so it won't be deleted even though it may have no links to any objects in your scene.

To the right of the datablock control buttons is a Nodes button. This activates the advanced node-based material editor. Because that's a more advanced topic, look to Blender's online documentation for more information.

The next line of buttons is a pretty unique set of controls. Using them requires recalling information about how .blend files are structured. This is detailed in Chapter 4, but basically Blender objects are separate from the low level mesh, curve, surface, and so on, data. The objects link to this data. Now, here's how this relates to materials. By default, Blender's materials link to the low level datablock. You can verify this by noticing that the ME button in the Links and Pipeline panel is enabled. The left image in Figure 7-3 shows a screenshot from the Oops Schematic that illustrates this relationship. However, you also have the option of linking the material to the object as well, as shown in the right-hand screenshot of Figure 7-3. In fact, the middle image shows that the material can actually link to both the mesh as well as the object.

Figure 7-3:
The Oops
Schematic
showing
a material
linked to a
mesh, both
a mesh and
its object,
and just an
object.

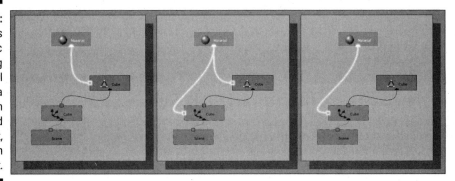

Why is having the ability to link a material to either the mesh or the object a useful option? Well, say you have bunch of objects that are linked duplicates, sharing the same mesh information. If the material is linked to the mesh, all of your linked duplicates have the exact same material. If you want to have different a material for each duplicate, this structure won't work. However, if you link the material to the object datablock rather than the mesh datablock, things work the way you want. Figure 7-4 shows a set of linked duplicate Suzanne heads, each with a different material thanks to the ability to change where the material datablock links to.

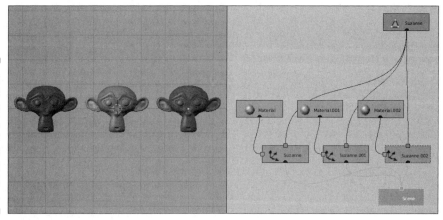

Figure 7-4:
Linked
duplicates
of Suzanne,
except they
don't share
the same
material
datablock.

Changing colors

The quickest and easiest way to customize the material on your object is to change its color. This is done at the bottom of the Material panel. There are three different types of colors you can set:

✔ **Diffuse:** The first color block, labeled *Col*. This is the main color of the object, or the primary hue that the material reflects to the camera.

✔ **Specular:** One of the cool things about working in computer graphics is that you have a say over things that you don't normally control in the real world. The Specular color, or *Spec*, is one of those things. By adjusting this color, you actually control the color of the highlights on the material.

✔ **Mirror:** Another material type of color that computer graphics gives you the ability to control is the Mirror color. If you turn on reflections for a material, the reflections in the object are tinted with the color you set here.

"Great, great, great . . . so how do I actually change the color?" I'm glad you asked. The simplest way to do this is to left-click on the color block next to the type of color you want to set. When you do this, Blender's color picker pops up. Figure 7-5 shows what the color picker looks like.

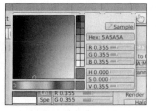

Figure 7-5:
Blender's
color picker.

The color picker is similar to what you might find in other graphics applications. Left-click anywhere in the large gradient square to choose the color you wish to use. By default, this square is all in the red hue. To change which hue you want to work in, left-click in the color spectrum below this large gradient to the color you want. The color picker also gives you the chance to use and set color presets with the set of swatches to the left of the gradient square. Left-clicking any one of these swatches automatically changes to that color. If you have a custom color that you would like to store, you can Ctrl+left-click a swatch to set it there. That color is saved in the swatch until you shut down Blender.

Another cool feature that the color picker gives you is a sampler. Left-click the Sample button in the upper right corner of the color picker and your mouse pointer changes to a color dropper. The next place you left-click is sampled for color, making it your selected color. The cool thing is that you can sample any color in Blender's interface, including the buttons and icons, if you want to.

When it comes to setting colors for materials, more often than not, I keep my spec and Mirror colors set to white. For the Mirror color, this can be particularly helpful if you want to have non-tinted reflections. The only exception to this is that, on occasion, it makes more sense to set the specular color to a value that is slightly lighter than the diffuse color. No hard-and-fast rule tells you when to go one way and when to go another in terms of the specular color. It's really a matter of experience and changing to what looks right in your final render.

Adjusting shader values

Ah, computer graphics: You have nearly complete control over how your materials look. Part of this control is how the diffuse and specular colors are dispersed across the surface of the object. You control both of these attributes independently with shader types. A *shader type* is a computer algorithm that defines how the color reacts in the material, and it's usually named after the computer scientist or mathematician who came up with it. So although the names may seem weird or arbitrary, the good news is that they're pretty universal from one piece of 3D software to another.

As you might guess, your shaders are set and controlled in the Shaders panel of the Material buttons (F5). To change your diffuse shader type, left-click the drop-down button at the upper left of the panel. By default, it's set to the Lambert shader, but you have the following options:

> ✔ **Lambert:** This is a good general purpose shader. The only adjustable setting for this shader is Ref, or reflection. This controls how much light the material reflects. The default setting of 0.8 means that the material reflects 80% of the light and absorbs 20%.

✔ **Oren-Nayar:** The Oren-Nayar shader is similar to the Lambert shader, although it has an additional roughness setting that takes into account the imperfections that the surface of an object may have. This gives you a material that reacts to light in a slightly more realistic way.

✔ **Toon:** In sharp contrast to the previous two shaders, the Toon shader does not aim to be realistic. Instead, it tries to reproduce the hard-edged *cel shading* that's often seen in traditional hand-drawn animation. By adjusting the Size and Smooth settings in addition to the Ref, you can control the number of discrete colors that the shader uses.

✔ **Minnaert:** This shader is pretty slick. By default, it's set up to behave just like the standard Lambert shader. However, if you adjust its Dark value to a number less than one, the edges of the object with this material get lighter. Setting Dark to values greater than one darkens the parts of the object that point to the viewer. This is a great way fake a backlight on an object or give it a somewhat velvety look. I also like to use this shader for shiny metals.

✔ **Fresnel:** Pronounced "FRAY-nel", this shader is also a nice one to use for metals and glassy materials. It's like the Minnaert shader, except instead of working relative to the viewer, it works relative to the light source. Higher Fresnel values darken parts that point toward the light source and this multiplies by the Fac, or factor value.

Figure 7-6 shows Suzanne shaded with each of the different diffuse shaders. For simplicity, the specular value has been reduced to zero in this figure.

Figure 7-6:
Suzanne
with
Lambert,
Oren-Nayar,
Toon,
Minnaert,
and Fresnel
shaders.

With the control of the diffuse shader, you also have control over the way the specular highlight appears on your materials. You change this by left-clicking the drop-down menu below the Diffuse Shader button. All specular shaders share a Spec value that controls the intensity of the specular highlights. Higher values make the highlights brighter; lower values make them dimmer and can reduce the specularity altogether. As with the diffuse shaders, you have a choice of algorithms that control how the specular highlight appears. These choices are listed below:

✔ **CookTorr (Cook-Torrance):** The Cook-Torrance shader is Blender's default specular shader. In addition to the spec value, it also has a setting to control hardness. Higher hardness values make the highlight smaller and more compact, whereas lower values spread the highlight over more of the object's surface. This shader is good for shiny plastic materials.

✔ **Phong:** This shader is nearly identical to the Cook-Torrance shader, although not quite as optimized. The edge of the specular highlight with this shader is a bit softer, making it a bit nicer for less shiny plastics and organic materials.

✔ **Blinn:** The Blinn shader is a more refined shader that is generally more accurate than the Cook-Torrance or Phong shaders. In addition to the Spec and Hard values, this shader also has a Refr, or refraction setting. Now, this refraction isn't quite like you might expect. What you really need to remember is that the Refr value controls the softness of the highlight. It's sort of a finer intensity control that Spec can give you. This shader works well with the Oren-Nayar diffuse shader for getting physically accurate materials that behave more like materials in the real world.

✔ **Toon:** Like the Toon diffuse shader, the Toon specular shader breaks the specular highlight into discrete bands of lightness to recreate the look of traditional cartoon coloring.

✔ **WardIso:** I like to use the WardIso, short for "Ward Isotropic" shader along with the Minnaert and Fresnel diffuse shaders for metallic or shiny plastic materials. The rms, or root-mean-square, value is a mathematic variable in the shader algorithm which controls the sharpness of the highlight's edge. Lower values are sharper and higher values are more dispersed.

Figure 7-7 shows Suzanne with the default Lambert diffuse shader and each of the different specular shaders.

Figure 7-7:
Suzanne
with Cook-
Torrance,
Phong,
Blinn,
Toon, and
WardIso
specular
shaders.

Reflection and transparency

In the "Changing colors," section earlier in this chapter, I wrote about the Mirror color setting. If you tried adjusting that color there, you might have noticed that not much changed. This is because you did not have any sort of reflection enabled to provide the mirroring. In order to enable mirroring, you need to go to the Mirror Transp panel in the Material buttons (F5), as shown in Figure 7-8. All of the Mirror settings are in the left column of this panel. Activate reflections by left-clicking the Ray Mirror button and increase the RayMir value using the slider directly beneath it.

Figure 7-8: The Mirror Transp panel.

An important thing to know about doing reflections this way is that it uses something called *raytracing*. In order to create accurate reflections, Blender's renderer follows, or traces, a ray of light as it bounces off of objects and into the camera. And to make sure it's accurate, the renderer follows thousands of these rays. This accuracy, of course, comes at the expense of using more processing power from your computer and may lengthen the rendering process. Figure 7-9 shows an example image with high reflectivity.

In order to properly see any raytraced results in your render, make sure that the Ray button is enabled in the Render panel of the Scene buttons (F10).

Ray Mirror is also one of those exceptions to the "light only bounces once" rule. In order to get a reflection, it has to have at least two bounces. The light comes from the light source, bounces off of one object, and then off of your reflective object before it reaches the camera. You can actually define how many bounces the renderer recognizes by adjusting the Depth value in the Ray Mirror column. Of course, the higher the Depth value, the more bounces that Blender has to trace and therefore the longer your renders might take.

Figure 7-9:
An example
image with
high levels
of raytraced
reflectivity.

In addition to reflectivity, you can also control an object's transparency. Like with 2D computer graphics, the main control for a 3D material's transparency is its *alpha* value. The alpha value in Blender runs on a scale from zero, for completely transparent, to one, for completely opaque. You adjust this value with the slider at the bottom of the Material panel, labeled "A". Now, you might notice that when you reduce the alpha value to make your material more transparent, the preview panel does not show the result that you might expect. Rather than showing the checkerboard pattern that's behind the preview object, a white-to-blue gradient shows up. What this means is that as you reduce the alpha value, the more your object's material is replaced with your scene's sky color. The sky color is set in the World buttons (F8). Chapter 9 covers setting the sky color and other World settings in greater detail.

Now, getting the object's material to show the sky color rather than what's actually behind it doesn't initially seem useful, but it's actually a really quick way to create a material that can make an object behave as a three-dimensional mask. Of course, you may not want a mask and instead you want to see the actual 3D environment through your object. The quickest and easiest way to get this to happen is to enable the ZTransp button in the Links and Pipeline panel. Doing so instantly makes the checkerboard background in the preview panel show up through the preview object.

Z-transparency is a quick way to get the rest of your scene's environment to show up through your object, but if you're trying to re-create glass, you might realize that things don't look quite right. With real glass, the transparent material actually bends the light, warping what you see through it. This is how a magnifying glass works. Regular Z-transparency cannot easily recreate this effect. In order to get that, you should use raytraced transparency instead.

You can activate raytraced transparency by left-clicking the Ray Transp button in the Mirror Transp panel. When you enable this button, notice two things. First, note that doing so automatically disables the ZTransp button. You can't have both of these settings active at the same time. The other thing to notice is that initially, it doesn't look like much changed by enabling Ray Transp. This is because the index of refraction, or IOR, value is set to 1.00. The *index of refraction* is the degree that the material bends light. A value of 1.00 means that the material has the same IOR as the air around it and therefore doesn't bend light as it passes through it. However, increasing the IOR warps the checkerboard pattern seen through the object. Now, the cool thing about the IOR value is that it actually matches the physical IOR values of real-world materials. This means you could look up the IOR value of a specific material, like glass or jade, on a table online or in a physics book and use it to get an accurately transparent material. Figure 7-10 shows the difference in results that you get with straight alpha transparency, Z-transparency, and raytraced transparency.

Figure 7-10:
From left to right, alpha transparency, z-transparency, and raytraced transparency with an alpha value of 0.5.

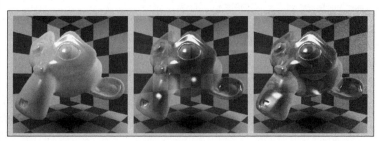

When it comes to the raytracing settings, both Ray Mirror and Ray Transp have a few values in common. The first ones you might notice are the Fresnel and Fac (for factor) sliders. The Fresnel setting adjusts an effect that's similar to the Fresnel diffuse shader, but with a specific influence on reflectivity and transparency. For reflectivity, rather than decreasing the material's color value in the direction of the light source like the Fresnel diffuse shader, increasing this value reduces the reflectivity relative to the camera.

For transparency, it's a bit different. It's also relative to the camera view, but rather than clouding out the transparency in that direction, it actually increases the transparency, reducing the color in the direction of the camera. Another interesting thing about the Fresnel setting for raytraced transparency is that it actually works on Z-transparency also. Keeping this in mind means you can take advantage of the Fresnel effect without having to fake it with color ramps.

Raytraced transparency versus Z-transparency

For simplicity, you might have the temptation to just use raytraced transparency all the time. If you need the flat transparency of Z-transparency, you can just set the IOR to 1.00 and let it rock. However, for the sake of your computer's CPU, this is a mistake. Z-transparency nearly always takes less processing power than raytraced transparency. This means that when you go to render, the more raytracing that your scene has, the longer your render typically takes. If you're working on an animation, you want to have your render times for each frame as low as possible. So the ideal thing to do is to use raytracing sparingly and know when it's the most to your advantage to use it. Here is a short list that shows where using raytraced transparency is best suited:

✔ Physically accurate materials for glass, fluids, and transparent plastics.

✔ Translucent materials that blur or obscure what you see through them, like sandblasted glass.

✔ Materials that are transparent up to a certain depth and translucent to opaque beyond that, like cloudy water or some minerals like imperfect crystals.

In short, you want to use raytracing where it's critical that you get a physically accurate material that refracts light. For nearly every other case, it's in your best interest to use Z-transparency. In fact, with enough work, you can usually even fake translucent materials with some clever material settings and Z-transparency. Another reason you may want to use Z-transparency is because, unlike raytraced transparency, it doesn't have a depth limitation. If you have a series of five objects with the same transparent material, using Z-transparency shows all of the objects through each other, whereas raytraced transparency only shows as many objects as its Depth value allows.

Another common setting between these raytraced effects is the Gloss value. The default value of 1.00 makes the material perfectly reflective and transparent. Reducing this value on either side blurs the reflection or makes the material more translucent than transparent. When changing the glossiness, you might notice that the blurry reflection looks dirty or pixelated. This is because of the way glossiness is done in Blender. The glossiness is approximated based on the Samples value, which is located beneath the Gloss slider for both raytraced reflection and raytraced transparency. Increasing the number of samples makes the glossiness appear more accurate, at the expense of longer render times. Figure 7-11 shows some of the cool effects you can get by varying the Gloss value.

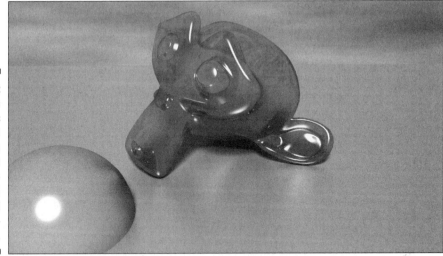

Figure 7-11:
Playing with
the gloss
value on an
object with
raytraced
reflec-
tions and
raytraced
transpar-
ency.

Assigning multiple materials to different parts of a mesh

Using the same material across an entire object is great for objects that are the same uniform material, but what if you wanted to have multiple different materials on the same object? For that sort of situation, you want to use material indices. Basically, you create a *material index* by defining a set of object subcomponents — faces in meshes, individual characters in text, and control points in curves and surfaces — and assigning them to a material. You create material indices in the Link and Materials panel of the Editing buttons (F9). To get a good idea of how this works, assume you want to model a beach ball and give it the classic primary-colored panels. Use the following steps:

1. **Add a UV sphere mesh (Spacebar⇨Add⇨Mesh⇨UVsphere).**

   Use 12 segments, 12 rings, and a radius of 1.00. You may also add a Subsurf modifier (Alt+1) and set the faces to render as smooth (F9⇨Links and Materials⇨Set Smooth).

2. **Tab into Edit mode and switch to Face Select mode (Tab⇨Ctrl+Tab⇨Faces).**

3. **Add a new material index (F9⇨Link and Materials⇨New).**

   Make sure the New button that you left-click is in the right column under the button that says "0 Mat 0." Left-clicking New adds a swatch next to this button and changes it to say "1 Mat 1," meaning your object has one material and you are on the first.

4. **Change the color to white by left-clicking the newly added swatch and choosing white with the color picker.**

   This makes the entire ball white. All of the faces are currently assigned to this material index.

5. **Use face loop select to select two adjacent vertical face loops (Alt+right-click and Shift+Alt+right-click).**

6. **Add another new material index (F9⇨Link and Materials⇨New).**

   This changes the material index value to "2 Mat 2," meaning that there are two material indices and you are working on the second one. Left-clicking on the left arrow in this button sends you back to "2 Mat 1," or the first material index of two. Left-clicking the right arrow takes you back to the second index.

7. **Change the color to blue by left-clicking the swatch and choosing blue with the color picker.**

   After you change the color of this swatch, you might expect the faces that you have selected to automatically change to match this color. That's not quite how it works: Even though you have these faces selected, they're still assigned to the first material index. Use the next step to remedy that situation.

8. **Assign the selected faces to the current material index (F9⇨Link and Materials⇨Assign).**

   The moment you left-click the Assign button, the selected faces should all change to the blue color you picked in the last step.

9. **Using the process in steps 5 through 8, work your way around the sphere, creating and assigning colors for the other panels.**

   If you create a beach ball like the one in Figure 7-12, you should end up with four material indices, one for each color on the ball.

Figure 7-12:
Creating a beach ball with a UV sphere and four material indices.

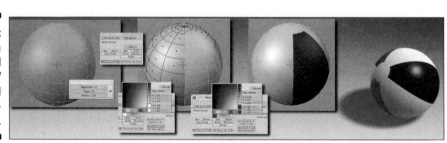

Material indices aren't limited to be used only by meshes. You can also use them on curves, surfaces, and text objects. The process is similar to meshes, with one main exception. Meshes, as shown in the previous example, allow you to assign individual faces to different material indices. This is not the case with curves, surfaces, and text objects, which assign material indices to discrete closed entities. So individual text characters and curves can be assigned to a material index. However, you can't set the material index of an individual control point or a portion of a text character. Figure 7-13 shows material indices working on a curve, surface, and text object.

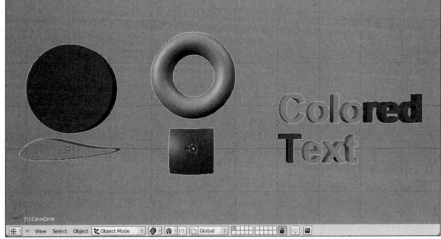

Figure 7-13: Material indices on curves, surfaces, and text objects.

Coloring Vertices with Vertex Paint

One of the downsides to material indices is the fact that although they make it easy to define multiple colors and materials on a single mesh, there's a very distinct line between materials. The color of one material does not smoothly transition into the next. For instance, if you want to create a car with a paint job that's light blue near the ground that smoothly transitions to a bright yellow on its roof and hood, you could not effectively do this with material indices. However, with *vertex colors*, it's completely doable. This technique only works on mesh objects, but it's also a very effective way of quickly coloring a mesh without the hard-edged lines that material indices give you.

The way it works is pretty simple. You assign each vertex in your mesh a specific color. If the vertices that form a face have different colors, there's a gradient going from each vertex to the others, where the color is most intense at the vertex and more blended with other colors the farther away it gets. Figure 7-14 shows an example with a plane using black for the bottom left vertex, gray for the upper left vertex, and white for both of the vertices on the right hand side. Notice how the color tries to smoothly blend in the face created by the vertices.

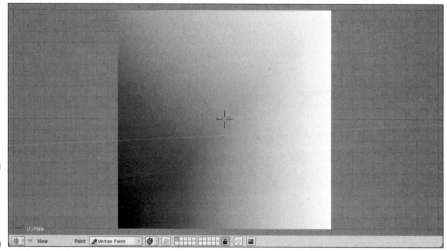

Of course, trying to go in and explicitly set the color for each and every vertex in a mesh can get really tedious on complex meshes. To alleviate this problem, Blender has a Vertex Paint mode. You activate Vertex Paint mode by selecting (right-clicking) the mesh object that you would like to paint in the 3D View and then pressing V. Your mouse cursor changes to look like a paint brush and a new panel appears in the Editing buttons (F9) called Paint. The Paint panel is shown in Figure 7-15.

Figure 7-15:
The Paint
panel for
Vertex Paint
mode.

The largest function of the Paint panel is setting the color you want to use and controlling how that color is applied to the selected object. You can choose the color you want by adjusting the RGB sliders or left-clicking the color swatch and choosing the color you want with the color picker that pops up. Also, if you have the Transform Properties floating panel (N) visible in the 3D View when you switch to Vertex Paint mode, you may notice that it changes to a floating color picker panel. This is pretty helpful for quickly switching colors without going back down to the Buttons window. Figure 7-16 shows the Paint Properties floating panel in the 3D view, which has this color picker.

Figure 7-16:
The Paint
Properties
floating
panel in the
3D view.

Another cool little shortcut is that while you're in Vertex Paint mode, right-clicking automatically samples the color under your mouse cursor and sets the paint color to that value. This is a pretty slick feature when you're painting with a set of defined colors on your mesh. No need to go to the color picker or the Paint panel, just right-click over the color that you've used before and get back to painting.

After you pick the color you want to use, left-click and drag your mouse over vertices in the 3D View, and those vertices take on the color you've defined. To get an idea of where the vertices that you're painting actually exist on your mesh, you may want to have Blender overlay the object's wireframe in the 3D view. To do this, navigate to the Draw panel in the Object buttons (F7) and left-click the Wire button in the block of buttons under the Draw Extra heading. When you do this, Blender adds the wireframe over the surface of the object, making it much clearer where each of the vertices of the mesh lie.

By default, the base vertex color for an object is a flat white. If you would rather start with a different base color, left-click the SetVCol button in the Paint panel. Doing that sets all the vertices in your mesh to have the color you have defined in the swatch above the button.

The column of buttons along the right side of the Paint panel controls how the paint color is applied to the vertices. The default setting of Mix simply blends the defined color with the color that the vertex already has assigned, according to whatever value is set by the Opacity slider. Enabling the Add, Sub, or Mul buttons takes the current color respectively and adds, subtracts, or multiplies that with the current vertex color under the brush in the 3D view. The Blur button is the only paint setting that doesn't use the selected color. It uses the vertices that are within the radius defined by the Size slider and attempts to mix their colors, effectively blurring them. The Lighter and Darker buttons take the value of the color you've chosen and use that to control how much influence it has on the already existing colors. So if you have your color set to full white, painting with Darker enabled won't change the vertex colors at all. But using that color to paint with Lighter enabled makes it appear everywhere you work.

If you're familiar with Sculpt mode, as discussed in Chapter 5, you may be tempted to try to adjust the size of your brush by using the F hotkey. Unfortunately, this is a bit of an inconsistency between Blender's painting modes and Sculpt mode. In the painting modes like Vertex Paint, Texture Paint (Chapter 8), and Weight Paint (Chapter 11), pressing F enables a sub-context in the paint mode that allows you to define a painting mask with the faces of the mesh. The other way to enable the painting mask is to left-click the button in the 3D view's header with an icon of a triangle overlaying a square, as shown in Figure 7-17.

Figure 7-17:
Enabling
the Painting
Mask
button.

When you enable the painting mask, you can select faces of your mesh by right-clicking. After you do that, these faces are the only ones that are affected by your painting. This is an excellent way of isolating a portion of your mesh for custom painting without changing the color of the faces around that area. By using a painting mask, you can actually get the hard-edged color changes that you get with material indices, should you want such a thing.

One of the downsides of vertex colors is that the amount of detail you can paint is limited to the number of vertices in your mesh. So it used to be that if you want to have more detail with vertex painting, you have to subdivide the mesh multiple times to create more vertices to be painted. Using the Subsurf modifier wouldn't be enough simply because the additional vertices created by that modifier are implicit and there's no direct access to them. However, with the advent of multi-resolution meshes, as covered in Chapter 5, the situation is different. You can use the multi-resolution workflow outlined in that chapter to get more vertices and therefore greater detail in your vertex painting. Figure 7-18 shows a version of Suzanne and a ball, both colored and painted using vertex colors and multi-resolution meshes.

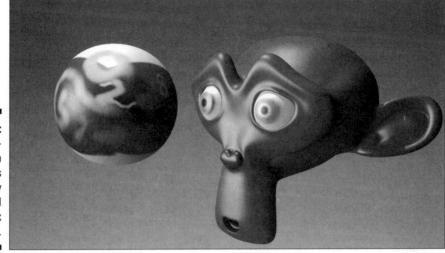

Figure 7-18:
Using multi-resolution meshes for highly detailed vertex painting.

In order to have your vertex colors appear in your render, you need to enable the VCol Paint button in the Material panel of the Material buttons. Refer back to Figure 7-2 if you need a refresher on where this button is located.

Chapter 8

Giving Models Texture

● ●

In This Chapter

▶ Using procedural textures

▶ Unwrapping a mesh to use image-based textures

● ●

*T*his chapter serves as a good pairing with Chapter 7. In that chapter, I wrote about adjusting the materials on your objects, but that was in broad strokes. That chapter covered how light reacts with the surface of your material so you could deal with the object's color, how that color spreads across the surface of the object, and how the specular highlights on that object behave. Of course, these are all broad strokes. If you want a more controlled way of adjusting the look of your object, then using material settings alone won't get you there. You could use Vertex paint, but if you're working on a model that you intend to animate, this causes you to have many extraneous vertices just for color. Those vertices end up slowing down the processes of rigging, animating, and even rendering. Also, you may want to have material changes that are independent of the edge flow and topology of your mesh.

For those sorts of scenarios, you're going to want to use textures. Generally speaking, a *texture* is a kind of image that you stretch or tile over the surface of your object to give it more detail without adding more vertices. Not only can textures influence the color of your object, but they can allow you to make additional adjustments, such as stipulating the specularity of some specific parts of the model. For instance, on a human face skin tends to be shinier across the nose and forehead, and a reduced specularity exists around the eyes. With textures, you can control these sorts of things. And the purpose of this chapter is to show you how you can apply that control.

Adding Textures

You can add and edit textures to a material using the Texture buttons (F6), as shown in Figure 8-1.

Figure 8-1:
The Texture
buttons.

Like the Material buttons, the Texture buttons have a Preview panel that displays the texture as you work on it. By default, the display in the Preview panel is completely black because the initial texture type is None. You can change this in the Texture panel with the drop-down list button on the right side of the panel. The left side of the panel is similar to the Texture panel in the Material buttons, and for good reason. These are the same ten texture channels that your material has available. The difference, though, is that with the Texture buttons, you can actually control what goes into these channels. Left-click any channel button to choose the channel that you want to work on. The channels that have textures in them display the name of the texture in the channel button. You can customize the name of the texture by left-clicking the name field at the top of the panel. This name field is part of a set of datablock control buttons that work just like the ones used in the Links and Pipeline panel of the Material buttons or the Object and Links panel of the Object buttons. As a quick refresher, here's what each button in the block does:

- ✔ The up/down button on the left gives you the ability to add a new texture or load an existing one.

- ✔ The X button disconnects the texture datablock from the channel.

- ✔ The button with the *auto*mobile icon *auto*matically creates a texture name based on the texture type.

- ✔ The F button creates a fake user for the texture datablock so that datablock won't be deleted even though it may have no links to any material's texture channels.

Using Procedural Textures

You can use basically two kinds of textures in Blender: image-based textures and *procedural textures*. Unlike image-based textures, where you explicitly create and load an image as a texture, procedural textures are created in software with a specific pattern algorithm. The advantage of procedural textures is that you can quickly add a level of detail to your objects without worrying about cleaning up seams from tiling errors or unwrapping the mesh. The software handles all of this for you. Of course, procedurals can be a bit more difficult to control than image-based textures. For instance, if you have a character with dark circles under his eyes, getting those circles to only show up where you want can be pretty tough, maybe even impossible. So the ideal use for procedural textures is as broad strokes where you don't need fine placement control. They're great for creating a foundation or a base to start with, such as providing the rough texture an orange rind's surface.

Blender has 11 procedural texture types that you can work with, accessible through the Texture Type drop-down list menu in the Texture panel of the Texture buttons (F6). In addition to these procedurals, you can also choose PlugIn, Image, or None as textures. All of the available texture types are shown in Figure 8-2.

Figure 8-2:
The available textures you can use that are built into Blender.

With only a couple of exceptions, when you select a texture type that you wish to use, a third panel appears in the Texture buttons. The options from one texture type to another vary, but with the exception of Voronoi, Noise, Blend, and EnvMap, all of the procedural textures share an option called *Noise Basis*. The Noise Basis is a specific type of pseudorandom pattern that influences the appearance of a procedural texture. There are two controls for the Noise Basis option that are always located at the bottom of the newly created panel: a Noise Basis drop-down menu and a Nabla value. The Nabla value offer some more advanced control of the sharpness or smoothness of the texture when it's applied to the material, but the Noise Basis offers an immense amount of flexibility in controlling a procedural texture's appearance. Left-clicking this drop-down menu list box displays the options shown in Figure 8-3.

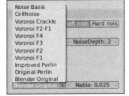

Figure 8-3:
Noise Basis types.

The types of Noise Basis can be roughly broken down into three different kinds of noise:

- **CellNoise:** A blocky, pixelated type of noise.

- **Voronoi family:** These noise types, including Crackle, F2-F1, F4, F3, F2, and F1 are all roughly based on the same algorithm. One of the primary attributes of Voronoi noise is a somewhat distinct partitioning throughout the texture with generally straight lines. This is most apparent in the Voronoi Crackle noise basis. These noise types are good for hammered metal, scales, veins, and that dry desert floor look.

- **Cloudy noise:** *Cloudy* is my own terminology, but it includes the Improved Perlin, Original Perlin, and Blender Original Noise Basis types. These types of noise tend to have more organic feel to them and work well for generic bump textures and clouds or mist.

The next few sections go into rough detail on each type of procedural texture.

Distorted Noise

The Distorted Noise texture is pretty slick. Actually, strike that; this type of texture is best suited to very rough, complex surfaces. The way it works is pretty cool, though. You use one procedural noise texture, specified by the Distortion Noise menu, to distort and influence the texture of your noise basis. With this, you can get some really unique textures. Figure 8-4 shows the Texture buttons for controlling a Distorted Noise texture.

Figure 8-4:
Texture buttons with a Distorted Noise texture.

Voronoi

The Voronoi procedural texture does not have a Noise Basis. This is because it's a more detailed control over the same algorithm that is used for the Voronoi Noise Basis options. It may be helpful to think of those basis options as presets, whereas this texture gives you full control over what you can do with the Voronoi texture. It's a pretty versatile texture, too. You can use it to create scales, veins, stained glass, textured metals, or colorful mosaics. Figure 8-5 shows the Voronoi Texture buttons.

Figure 8-5:
Texture
buttons with
a Voronoi
texture.

Musgrave

This procedural texture is extremely flexible and very well suited for organic materials. You can use it for rock cracks, generic noise, clouds, and even as a mask for rust patterns. As a matter of fact, with enough tweaking, you could probably get a Musgrave texture to look like nearly any other procedural texture. Of course, the trade-off is that it takes a bit longer to render than most of the other textures. Figure 8-6 shows the Texture buttons for controlling a Musgrave texture.

Figure 8-6:
Texture
buttons with
a Musgrave
texture.

Noise

This is the simplest procedural texture in Blender (well, the None texture type is probably simpler, but it's not very useful). This texture has no controls: It's simply raw noise. That means that you'll never get the same results twice using this texture. Each time you render, the noise pattern is different. This might be annoying if you're looking to do a bump map. However, if you're looking to have "white noise" on a TV screen, this texture is perfect. As Figure 8-7 shows, the Noise texture has absolutely no controls.

Figure 8-7:
Texture
buttons with
a Noise
texture.

Blend

The Blend texture is one of the unsung heroes in Blender's procedural texture arsenals. It may seem like a simple gradient, but with the right mapping, it's really quite versatile. I've used Blend textures for mixing two other textures together, creating simple toon-like outlines for meshes, and for adjusting the color along the length of hair strands. The real power of the Blend texture can be seen when you use it with a colorband that you define in the Colors panel of the Texture buttons. Figure 8-8 shows the Texture buttons for controlling a Blend texture.

Figure 8-8:
Texture buttons with a Blend texture.

Behold the power of the colorband!

One of the really powerful and under-recognized tools in Blender is the *colorband*. It's basically a gradient editor, and its interface is used in procedural textures, ramp materials, the material node editor, and even the node compositor. For materials, you can enable the colorband in the Ramps tab of the material buttons. For procedural textures, it appears in the Color tab. It's a great way to adjust the color of the stripes in the Wood texture or determine which colors you want to use for your Blend texture. You can even use the colorband with a ramp shader to have a more controlled custom toon coloring than you can get with the diffuse or specular Toon shaders. It works much like gradient editors in other programs. By default, it starts with a color positioned at either end of the colorband bar and the color smoothly transitions from one side to the other. The color can be any value in the RGB spectrum, and you also can control its transparency with the alpha value.

To change a color, first select it by either left-clicking its position in the colorband or adjusting the value in the Cur field. Color positions count up from left to right, starting at zero. So with the default arrangement, the transparent black color on the left is 0 and the cyan color on the right is 1. After you have selected the color, you can change its value by using the RGB and A sliders, or you can left-click the swatch and use the color picker that pops up. To move the color position, you can left-click and drag it along the colorband, or you can adjust the Pos, or Position value after you've selected it.

To add a new color position, left-click the Add button. This creates a 50% gray color at the halfway point in the color band. Any position may be deleted by selecting it and left-clicking the Del button.

It may not seem like much, but mastering the colorband and knowing when to use it makes your workflow for adding materials and textures much faster.

Magic

At first glance, the Magic texture may seem to be completely useless — or at the very least, too weird to be useful. However, I've managed to find quite a few cool uses for this eccentric little texture. If you treat it as a bump map, it works well for creating a knit texture for blankets and other types of cloth. If you stretch the texture with your mapping settings, you can use it to recreate the thin filmy look that occurs when oil mixes with water. And, of course, you can use it to make a wacky wild-colored shirt. Figure 8-9 shows the controls for the Magic texture.

Figure 8-9: Texture buttons with a Magic texture.

Wood

The Wood texture is a bit of a misnomer. Sure, you *can* use it to create textures that are pretty close to what you see on cut planks of wood. However, it's a lot more versatile than that. You can use the wood texture to create nearly any sort of striped texture. I've actually even used it to fake the look of mini-blinds in a window. Figure 8-10 shows the Wood Texture button controls.

Figure 8-10: Texture buttons with a Wood texture.

Stucci

Stucci is a nice organic texture that's most useful for creating bump maps. It's great for industrial and architectural materials like stucco, concrete, and asphalt. It's also handy if you just want to give your object's surface a little variety and roughen it up a bit. In Figure 8-11 are the buttons for controlling the options of the Stucci texture.

Figure 8-11:
Texture
buttons with
a Stucci
texture.

Marble

This texture has a lot of similarities with the Wood texture; however, as Figure 8-12 shows, it's a lot more turbulent. You can use it for creating the look of polished marble, but the turbulent nature of the texture also lends itself nicely to be used as a fire texture and, to a lesser extent, the small ripples you get in ponds, lakes, and smaller pools of water.

Figure 8-12:
Texture
buttons with
a Marble
texture.

Clouds

The Clouds texture is a good general purpose texture. You can treat it as a go-to texture for general bumps, smoke, and clouds. Figure 8-13 shows the Texture buttons for controlling a Clouds texture.

Figure 8-13:
Texture
buttons with
a Cloud
texture.

EnvMap

EnvMap is short for *environment map*. It's a way of using a texture to fake reflections on your object. It works by taking the position of a given object and rendering an image in six directions around that object: up, down, left, right, forward, and back. These images are then mapped to the surface of your object. So, this isn't exactly a procedural texture in the traditional sense, but because the environment images are taken automatically, I'll say it's part procedural and part image-based.

Environment maps aren't as accurate as using raytraced reflection, but they can be quite a bit faster. So if you need a generically reflective surface that doesn't need to be accurate, environment maps are a handy tool that keep your render times short. One thing to note about the EnvMap panel, as shown in Figure 8-14, is the Ob field. By default, this field is set to be the object that you intend on mapping the texture to. However, sometimes you can get a better reflective effect by using the location of a different object, such as an empty. This is particularly true when applying an environment map to an irregular surface.

Figure 8-14:
Texture
buttons with
an EnvMap
texture.

When using environment maps, make sure you do two things. First, enable the Refl button in the Map To panel of the Material buttons (F5). Secondly, enable the EnvMap button in the Render panel of the Render buttons (F10). Unless you do both of these things, your environment map won't work properly.

Understanding Texture Mapping

After you've created your texture, be it procedural or image-based, you're going to have to relate that texture to your material and, by extension, the surface of your object. This is done with a process called *mapping*, which basically consists of relating a location on a texture to a location on the surface of an object. Mapping controls are located in the panels of the last block of the Material buttons (F5). Specifically, I'm referring to the Map Input and Map To panels, as shown in Figure 8-15.

Figure 8-15:
The Texture,
Map Input,
and Map To
panels in
the Material
buttons.

Figure 8-15:
The Texture,
Map Input,
and Map To
panels in
the Material
buttons.

The Map Input panel controls how the texture is mapped to the object, defining how the texture coordinates are projected on it. The most important buttons are the block of mapping options at the top of this panel. The following list explains the type of mapping that each button represents:

✔ **Glob (Global coordinates):** Choosing this option uses the scene's coordinates to define the texture space. So if you have an animated object with a texture mapped this way, the texture will seem to be locked in place as the object moves across it. It's a kind of strange effect, but it's a helpful effect in a few situations, such as faking shadows on a moving character.

✔ **Object:** This is a neat option, allowing you to use a different object's location as a means of placing a texture on your object. To tell Blender which object you want to use for this, type its name in the Ob field. For example, you could load an image texture of a logo and place that logo on a model of a car by using the location, size, and orientation of an empty.

✔ **UV:** UV coordinates are probably the most precise way of mapping a texture to an object. NURBS surfaces have UV coordinates by default. For meshes, however, getting UV coordinates requires you to go through a process called *unwrapping*. To understand this process, think about a globe and a map of the world. The map of the world uses the latitude and longitude lines to relate a point on the three-dimensional surface of the globe to the two-dimensional surface of the map. In essence, the world map is an unwrapped texture on the globe, whereas the latitude and longitude lines are the UVs. More on unwrapping in the next section, "Unwrapping a Mesh."

✔ **Orco (Original coordinates):** This is the default setting and should work fine for most situations, especially when you are using procedural coordinates.

✔ **Stick (Sticky or Camera coordinates):** Sticky coordinates are a way of getting a somewhat precise mapping based on the location and orientation of the camera. You position your camera at some location, pointing toward your object. In the Editing buttons (F9), within the Mesh panel, left-click the Make button next to the word Sticky. This creates a mapping on the mesh based on the camera's current position. And now, unlike Global or Window coordinates, when you animate the object or the camera, the texture won't move. It stays stuck to the object.

✔ **Strand:** This option is not visible by default. It only appears when your object has a particle system with the Strand render option enabled. When that happens, this button takes the place of the Stick button. As the name indicates, it's intended specifically for particle strands. When activated, the texture is mapped along the length of the strand.

✔ **Win (Window coordinates):** This option is similar to the Global coordinates option, but rather than use the scene's global coordinates, it uses the coordinates from the finished render window. In other words, it uses the camera's coordinates. But unlike Sticky coordinates, which use the camera's coordinates just once, this option always uses them. So if the object is animated, the texture is not stuck to it. It remains in place.

✔ **Nor (Normal coordinates):** Enabling this button causes the texture to be mapped according to the normal vectors along the surface of the object. This is helpful for effects that require textures to react to the viewing angle of the camera.

✔ **Refl (Reflection coordinates):** The reflection option uses the direction of a reflection vector to map your texture to the object. Basically, you want to use this option with an environment map texture (EnvMap) to get fake reflections when you don't need the accuracy of raytracing.

✔ **Stress:** Stress maps are a pretty cool option that's intended for use with dynamic or simulated geometry. The stress value is the difference between the location of an original texture coordinate and location of the coordinate when rendered. As an example, say you have a character with stretchy arms. You could use stress mapping as a mask to make the arms more translucent the more they stretch.

✔ **Tangent:** In some ways, this option is similar to Normal coordinates. However, rather than use the surface normal, it uses an optional tangent vector to map the texture coordinates. Notice that I wrote "optional" tangent vector. By default, there is no tangent vector on the material, so enabling this button by itself won't do much to it. However, if you left-click the Tangent V button at the top right of the Shaders panel, you have a tangent vector for your texture to work with.

In addition to these map inputs, you can also control what's called the *texture projection*. This, along with the map input, controls how the texture is applied to the mesh for everything except UV textures. Because UV textures explicitly map a texture coordinate to a coordinate on the surface of your object, changing projection doesn't have an effect on anything. Blender has four different types of projection:

✔ **Flat:** This type of projection is the easiest to visualize. Imagine you have your texture loaded in a slide projector. When you point it at a wall, you get the best results. However, if you point it at a curved or uneven surface, you get a little bit of distortion. This is basically what happens with Flat projection.

✔ **Cube:** Cube projection uses the same idea as flat projection, but rather than having just one projector, imagine you have one pointing at the front, left, and top of your object (and shining through to the other side). The texture appears on all six sides of the cube. Of course, when you try to project on a more curved surface, you still get some seams and distortion.

✔ **Tube:** Tube projection is where the slide projector metaphor kind of stops making sense. Imagine that you have the unique ability to project on a curved surface without the distortion. This, of course, is pretty close to impossible in the real world, but pretty trivial in computer graphics. Using Tube projection is ideal for putting labels on bottles or applying other sorts of textures to tubular objects.

✔ **Sphere:** Spherical projection is best suited for spherical objects like planets and balls, and it's also the "cleanest" way to apply a texture to an arbitrary three-dimensional surface because it usually doesn't leave any noticeable seams as does Cube projection.

Figure 8-16 shows a set of primitive objects with Flat, Cube, Tube, and Sphere projection.

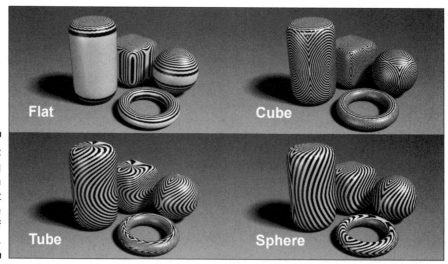

Figure 8-16:
Projecting
textures in
different
ways on the
same set of
3D objects.

Along the right side of the Map Input panel are fields that give you finer control over how your texture is positioned on your object. The ofsX, ofsY, and ofsZ values define an offset in the X, Y, and Z directions, respectively. And the sizeX, sizeY, and sizeZ values scale the texture in each of those directions. The grid of Xs, Ys, and Zs at the bottom left of this panel allow you to reorder the axes of the texture, letting you flip it around to try and get the best fit.

The offset and size values are not relative to the global or local coordinates in the 3D View. They're actually relative to the texture image itself. The X and Y values are horizontal and vertical whereas the Z value is a depth value into the texture. The Z values don't have a lot of influence unless the texture is a procedural texture with a Noise Basis.

Not only do you control how a texture is mapped to an object, but you also control how that texture affects the material. The controls for this are in the first two rows of buttons of the Map To panel.

Some of these Map To buttons are simple toggles. Left-clicking them once turns them on and left-clicking them a second time turns them off. However, most of them are *three-state* buttons. This means that the first left-click enables the option, but the second left-click changes the text in the button to yellow, indicating that the texture's effect on the material is inverted. A third left-click on the button disables it.

You can use any combination of the following options:

- **Col (Color — toggle):** Affects the material's diffuse color.
- **Nor (Normal — three-state):** Influences the direction of the surface normals on the material. Enabling this button enables bump mapping. It can give your object much more detail without the computational slowdown of additional geometry.
- **Csp (Specular Color — toggle):** Affects the material's specular color.
- **Cmir (Mirror Color — toggle):** Affects the material's mirror color.
- **Ref (Reflection — three-state):** Influences the reflection value in the material's diffuse shader.
- **Spec (Specularity — three-state):** Influences the specularity in the material's specular shader.
- **Amb (Ambience — three-state):** Affects the amount of ambient light the material gets.
- **Hard (Specular Hardness — three-state):** Affects the specular hardness values for the specular shaders that support it.
- **RayMir (Raytraced Reflection — three-state):** Influences the amount of raytraced reflection that the material has.
- **Alpha (three-state):** Controls the transparency and opacity of the material.
- **Emit (three-state):** Affects the material's emit value for radiosity.
- **TransLu (Tranlucency — three-state):** Affects the amount of translucency in the material.

↙ **Disp (Displacement – three-state):** This option is similar to the Nor option, except that it actually moves the geometry of the object based on the texture map. Whereas bump mapping only makes it *look* like geometry is added and moved around by tricking out the surface normal, displacement actually moves it around. The downside to Blender's displacement is that you have to have the vertices already in place to move around. It won't create them for you on the fly. You can get around this a bit by using the Subsurf modifier, but creating your additional vertices with that definitely increases your render times.

Unwrapping a Mesh

In the previous section, I mentioned that the most precise type of mapping you can use is UV mapping. Not only is UV mapping precise, but it also allows you to take advantage of a couple of other features in Blender, such as Texture Paint mode and texture baking. With NURBS surfaces, you get UV coordinates "for free" as part of their structure. However, Blender is predominantly a mesh editor, and in order to get proper UV coordinates on your mesh objects, you must put them through a process known as *unwrapping*. You unwrap a mesh in Blender by selecting all vertices (A) and pressing U while in Edit mode (Tab). Of course, pressing U brings up a menu with a variety of options to choose from, as shown in Figure 8-17.

Figure 8-17:
The UV Calculation unwrapping menu.

However, despite this variety of options, unless your mesh is simple or a special case, you should use the first menu item, Unwrap. Blender has very powerful unwrapping tools, but to take full advantage of them, you need to first define some seams. Remember that you're basically trying to flatten 3D surface to a 2D plane. In order to do so, you need to tell Blender where it can start pulling the mesh apart. This is a *seam*. If you were unwrapping a globe, you might choose the prime meridian as your seam. I like to think about it like a stuffed animal, such as a teddy bear. The seam is where the bear is stitched together from flat pieces of cloth. To add a seam to your mesh, use the following steps:

1. **Tab into Edit mode and switch to Edge Select mode (Tab⇨Ctrl+Tab⇨ Edges).**

   You could also do this from Vertex Select mode, but I find that it's easier in Edge Select.

2. **Select the series of edges you want to make into a seam (right-click⇨ Shift+right-click).**

   Using an edge loop selection (Alt+right-click) can really be helpful here. Everyone has their own tastes when it comes to defining seams, but a good rule of thumb is to put them on parts of the mesh that are easier to hide.

3. **Use the Edge Specials menu to make the seam (Ctrl+E⇨Make Seam).**

   Seams on your mesh are highlighted in orange. If you mistakenly make a seam with the wrong edges, you can remove the seam by selecting those edges (right-click) and pressing Ctrl+E⇨Clear Seam.

With your seams defined, you're ready to unwrap your mesh. In order to see what you're doing, though, there are a couple changes you should make to your screen layout. First, you should probably change the drawtype of your 3D View to Textured (Alt+Z). Then split off a new window and change it to be a UV/Image Editor window (Shift+F10). Your layout should look something like what is shown in Figure 8-18.

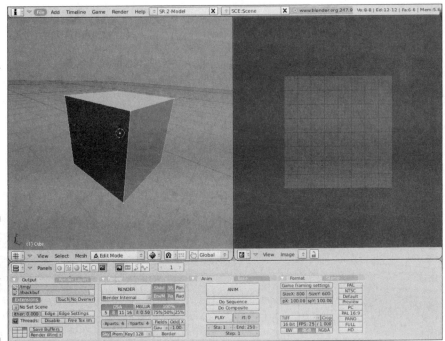

Figure 8-18: A typical screen layout for UV unwrapping and editing.

The next thing you need is an image to map to your mesh. It's common practice when unwrapping to use something called a *test grid*. This is basically an image with a colored checkerboard pattern. It's helpful for trying to figure out where the texture is stretched on your mesh. To add a test grid, go to the UV/Image Editor window and choose Image➪New or press Alt+N. When you do this, a set of buttons like the ones in Figure 8-19 are shown. Name the image something sensible, like "Test Grid" and left-click the UV Test Grid button. Leave the other settings at their defaults for now. Next, left-click OK. After you do this, the test grid image appears in the UV/Image Editor window.

Figure 8-19:
The New Image buttons for adding a test grid image.

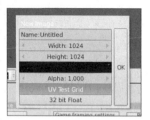

 It's possible to unwrap your mesh without going through the process of adding a test grid, but I find that it's helpful to have the grid up there so you have a frame of reference to work from when unwrapping.

 Also, you should note the size of the test grid image. The most obvious thing is that it's square. When you create the image, you have the option of making it non-square, but UV texturing is optimized for square images, so it's in your best interest to keep it that way. Another tip that helps performance when working with UV textures is to make your texture size a *power of two*. (In other words, a number that you get by continually multiplying 2 by itself.) The default size is 1024 pixels square. That's 2^{10}, or 2 multiplied by itself 10 times. The next larger size would be 2048 pixels and the next size down would be 512 pixels.

Alrighty, *now* you're ready to unwrap your mesh. You should still be in Edit mode on your mesh. If you aren't, tab back on in. From here, unwrapping is pretty simple:

1. **Select all vertices (A).**

   Remember that the A key is a toggle, so you may have to hit it twice to get everything selected.

2. **Unwrap the mesh (U➪Unwrap).**

   Poof! Your mesh is now unwrapped! If you used a Suzanne to practice unwrapping, you may have something that looks like Figure 8-20.

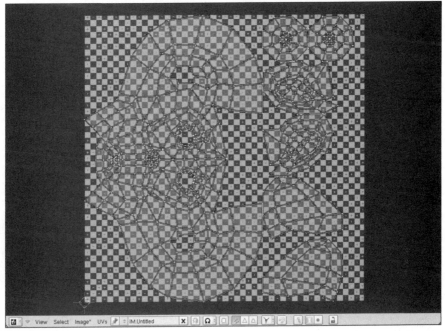

Figure 8-20:
An
unwrapped
Suzanne
head.

From here, you can edit your UV layout to arrange the pieces in a logical fashion and minimize *stretching*. You can tell a texture is stretched with your test grid. If any of the squares on the checkerboard look distorted or grotesquely non-square-shaped, stretching has taken place. If you don't see the test grid texture on your monkey, make sure you're in the Textured Draw Type (Alt+Z). The controls in the UV/Image Editor are very similar to working in the 3D View. The Grab (G), Rotate (R), and Scale (S) hotkeys all work as expected, as well as the various selection tools like Border select (B), Brush select (B⇨B), and Edge Loop Selection (Alt+right-click). There's even a cursor to help with snapping and providing a frame of reference for rotation and scaling.

If you're trying to fix stretching, you might notice that moving some vertices in your UV layout to fix stretching in one place distorts and causes stretching in another part. To help with this, Blender offers you two very helpful features: vertex pinning (P) and Live Unwrap Transform (UVs⇨Live Unwrap Transform). They actually work together. The workflow goes something like this:

1. **In the UV/Image Editor, select the vertices that you want to define as "control vertices" (right-click⇨Shift+right-click).**

    These are usually the vertices at the top and bottom of the center line and some corner vertices. I tend to prefer using vertices that are on the seam, but sometimes it's helpful to use internal vertices.

2. **Pin these selected vertices (P).**

When you do this, the vertices should appear larger and a bright red color. If you ever want to unpin a vertex, select it (right-click) and press Alt+P.

3. **Turn on Live Unwrap Transform (UVs⯈Live Unwrap Transform).**

   If there's a checkmark to the left of this menu item, you know it's currently enabled.

4. **Select one or more pinned vertices and move them around (right-click⯈G).**

   As you edit these pinned vertices, all of the other vertices in the UV layout automatically shift and adjust to compensate for this movement and help reduce stretching.

When using pinned vertices and Live Unwrap Transform, selecting and moving unpinned vertices isn't normally going to be very helpful. This is because the moment you select and move a pinned vertex, any manual changes you've made to unpinned vertices are obliterated.

You can actually see the changes you make in the UV/Image Editor in real time if you left-click the "lock" button in the header of the UV/Image Editor window. It's the last button, the one with a little lock icon in it.

Figure 8-21 shows the unwrapped Suzanne head from before, after a bit of editing and adjustment.

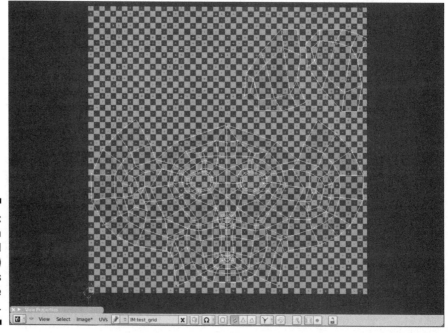

Figure 8-21:
An unwrapped and (mostly) stretchless Suzanne head.

Painting Textures Directly on a Mesh

So now you have an unwrapped mesh so the texture doesn't stretch on it. Woohoo! But say that, for some crazy reason, you don't want your object to have a checkerboard as a texture and you want to actually use this UV layout to paint a texture for your mesh. There are actually two ways to handle this: Paint directly on the mesh from within Blender, or export the UV layout to paint in an external program like The GIMP or Photoshop. I actually prefer to use a combination of these methods. I normally paint directly on the mesh in Blender to rough out the color scheme and perhaps create some bump and specularity maps. Then I export that image along with an image of the UV layout to get more detailed painting done in an external program.

After you have an unwrapped mesh, the starting point for all of this is Blender's Texture Paint mode. Activate it by left-clicking the mode button in the 3D view's header, as show in Figure 8-22.

Figure 8-22: Choosing Texture Paint mode from the mode button on the 3D view's header.

From here, things are pretty similar to Vertex Paint mode, with a few exceptions. The Transform Properties floating panel becomes a Paint Properties floating panel with a color picker and a Paint panel appears in the Editing buttons (F9), but the content of that panel is pretty different from the Paint panel that you have with Vertex Paint. The most striking difference is that you actually have a Brush datablock with definable attributes. With the Add New button at the bottom, you can actually define a texture for your brush, so you're not just painting flat colors. You define the brush texture in the Texture buttons (F6) like you set up any other texture. This gives your painting quite a bit more flexibility.

When you're in Texture Paint mode, start painting directly on your mesh by left-clicking and dragging your mouse cursor on it. If you have a test grid image already loaded on the image, you will begin painting directly on this image. In fact, if you still have the UV/Image Editor window open, you can watch the test grid image get updated as you paint your mesh. And actually, you can paint directly on the UV image itself by enabling painting

(Image⇨Texture Painting). With Texture Painting enabled in the UV/Image editor, you can also press C and an Image Paint floating panel appears with the same buttons that are available in the Paint panel of the Editing buttons.

Because of this, when I paint textures in Blender, I like to have my screen laid out like Figure 8-23 shows. I have the 3D View and UV/Image Editor windows both in Texture Paint mode, whereas my Buttons window shows the Texture buttons (F6) for editing brush textures. It's a pretty effective way to get work done.

Figure 8-23:
A good screen layout for texture painting directly on your mesh.

Of course, despite the cool things that you can do with Blender's Texture Paint mode, there are some things that you're better off doing in full-blown 2D graphics program like The GIMP or Photoshop. To work on your image in another program, you need to save the texture you've already painted as an external image. You should also export your UV layout as an image so you have a frame of reference to work from while painting. To save your painted texture, go to the UV/Image Editor and choose Image⇨Save As. This brings up a File Browser window that allows you to save the image to your hard drive in any format you like. I prefer to use PNG because it has small file sizes and lossless compression.

With your image saved, the next thing you probably want is your UV layout. To export this, you need to run a script. You access it from the UV/Image Editor window while in Edit mode (Tab). Navigate to UVs⇨Scripts⇨Save UV Face Layout. A button box pops up with some options, as shown in Figure 8-24.

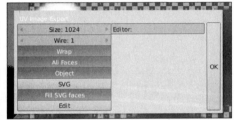

Figure 8-24:
Options for exporting your UV layout.

For now, leave all of these values at their defaults, with the exception of Size. For size, you want to use the same size that your texture image is. By default, the value is 512, but if your texture image is 1024x1024, like the default test grid is, you should change this value to 1024. When you left-click the OK button, a File Browser window appears, allowing you to save your UV layout to your hard drive as a Targa image. With the UV layout exported, you can load both of these images (the saved texture and the exported UV layout) as layers in your image editing program and proceed to paint the exact texture you want to use on your mesh. You may even paint separate textures for bump maps or specularity maps.

Baking Texture Maps from Your Mesh

There's another benefit that unwrapping your mesh gets you: *render baking*. Render baking is creating a flat texture for your mesh that's based on what it looks like when you render it. What good is that? Well, it's really useful to people who wish to create models for use in video games. Because everything in a game has to run in real time, models can't usually have a lot of complicated lighting or highly detailed meshes with millions of vertices. To get around this, you can fake some of these effects by using a texture. And rather than paint on shadows and detail by hand, you can let the computer do the work and use a high resolution render instead.

Although this technique is used a lot in video games, it's also helpful when creating models that will be animated for film or television. If you can create a model that looks really detailed, but still has a relatively low vertex count, your rendering and animating process goes faster. Another use is for texture painters. Sometimes it's helpful to have an ambient occlusion or shadow texture as a frame of reference to start painting a more detailed texture.

Alright, so how do you create these textures? Well, the magic all happens in the Bake panel of the Render buttons (F10). This panel is shown in Figure 8-25.

Figure 8-25:
The Bake
panel in the
Render
buttons.

As the figure shows, you have six different kinds of images that you can bake out:

- **Full Render:** This is the whole mess — textures, vertex colors, shadows, ambient occlusion, specular highlights — the works.

- **Ambient Occl:** Ambient occlusion, or AO, is an approximated form of *global illumination*, or the effect that happens from light bouncing off of everything. If you have AO enabled in the World buttons (F8), the results of it can be baked by enabling this button.

- **Shadow:** Any shadows that fall on this object are baked out as a texture.

- **Normals:** A normal map is similar to a bump map, but instead of just using a grayscale image to define height, normal maps can get even more detailed by using a full color image to define height as well as direction. Artists who like to use Sculpt mode bake the normals from their sculpted mesh to a low-resolution version of the mesh to get details on the model without the additional geometry.

- **Textures:** This option takes all of the textures you've applied to the mesh, both image-based and procedural, and flattens them out to a single texture.

- **Displacement:** Baking displacement is similar to baking normals. The difference is that normal maps just redirect surface normals to provide the illusion of more geometry, whereas a displacement map can actually be used to move geometry around and create real depth on the surface of the object. Using displacement maps in Blender can be computationally expensive. However, a few third-party rendering engines have a nice way of handling displacement maps without the need to heavily subdivide your mesh.

After you have an unwrapped mesh, the steps to bake a new texture are pretty straightforward. Create a new image in the UV/Image Editor (Alt+N) at the size you want the texture to be and just choose the type of texture that you'd like to bake out from the Bake panel. After you've done that, left-click the Bake button and wait for the texture to be generated.

would a book on Blender be without some full-color images in it?

be black and white, yes, but it would also be a bit lacking in showing how to use Blender, not to mention ool art that's been created with it. Have a look through here and enjoy the full-color glory!

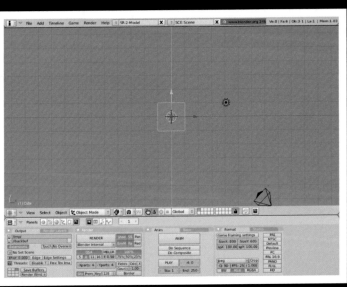

Blender's default theme. The first time you start Blender, this is what you see. Seems pretty simple, doesn't it?

A frame from *Big Buck Bunny*, the Peach open movie project from the Blender Institute.

blender game engine - ¿pfrankie.org

Keyboard reference for the hotkeys on the numeric keypad.

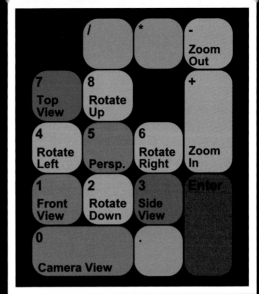

Screenshot of a highly involved node compositing network. Image courtesy of Daniel Salazar, a Costa Rican Blender user, also known as ZanQdo in the Blender community.

An architectural visualization scene from ZanQdo.

A fun character created by VenomGFX called "Frakas Dream," a bit of a play off of the first open movie project, *Elephants Dream*.

These two images are from the 2007 Suzanne awards. They feature Petunia, a robotic counterpart for Suzanne. The compositing for the video and the design and creation was done by Dolf Veenvliet, known as macouno in the Blender community.

Andy Goralcyzk, known simply as @ndy in the Blender community, is a much-celebrated and very talented Blender artist from Germany. This image is a character from a recent DVD tutorial he produced for the Blender Institute.

the pilgrim, the grey toad and the golden heart

A color version of Figure 9-1, showing some of the different dramatic effects you can achieve by simply changing the lighting.

A rather surreal image from the technical editor for this book, Bassam Kurdali, also known as slikdigit. Bassam is a Massachusetts-based Blender artist who spends quite a bit of his time traveling the world and helping studios create incredible animations with Blender.

This image is actually a piece of concept art from one of Bassam's personal animation productions, *Tube*.

Claudio Andaur, known as malefico, is an incredible Argentinean Blender artist who has achieved quite a bit of success with his two animation studios in Buenos Aires. He created this image as part of an article for the online Blender magazine, BlenderArt.

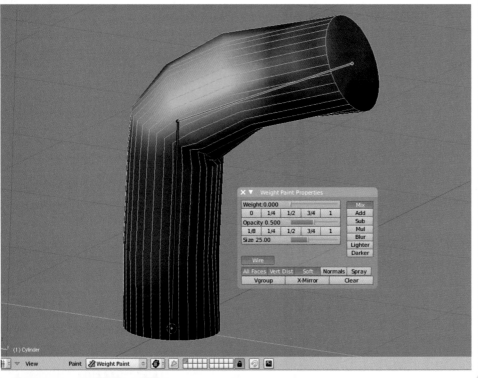

A color version of Figure 11-18. This shows how the default coloring works when weight-painting. Think about it like a thermal graph. Red is hot and the highest weight, whereas blue is cold and therefore represents no weight at all.

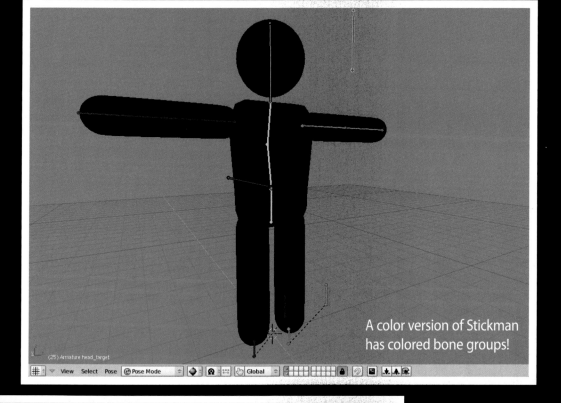

A color version of Stickman has colored bone groups!

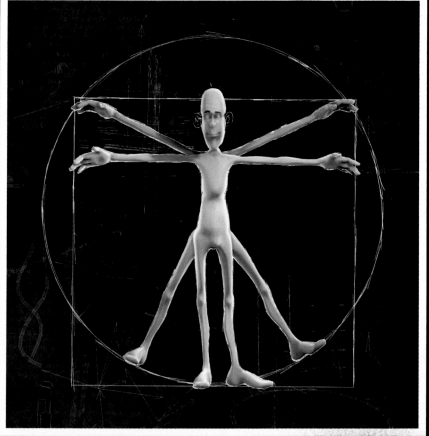

Meet Mancandy, created by Bassam. Yes, Mancandy has a very strange name (short for *The Manchurian Candidate),* but he's one of the baseline character rigs that Blender animators can use to practice their craft. He is included on the CD-ROM that accompanies this book.

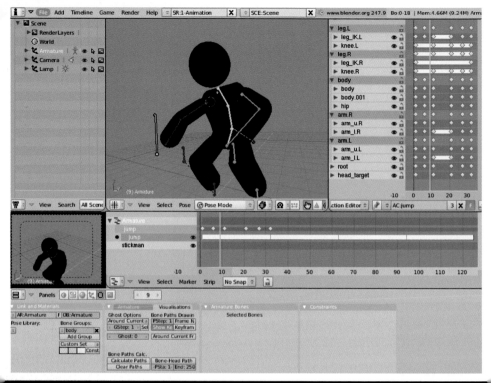

or version of Figure 12-12. This is a modified version of the standard Animation screen
s with Blender. In this example, the Ipo Curve Editor has been changed to an Action E
ow and the Timeline window has been changed to an NLA Editor.

2005
BLENDERO3D
JEAN SÉBASTIEN GUILLEMETTE

Ecks often collaborates with Jonathan Williamson, or mr_bomb, to create incredible scenes in Blender. Whereas Ecks focuses on hard body modeling, as shown on the left, mr_bomb's specialty is organic modeling, as exhibited in the image at the bottom right.

B-Bot

Jean-Sébastien Guillemette

An image produced by Andy Goralcyzk, called Moonman.

Sam Brubaker (known as Rocketman in the Blender community) uses Blender to create his Web comic, *Us the Robots*. These two images are from that comic. Laugh!

A pair of images from Mike Pan, or mpan3, out of Vancouver, Canada. Mike is perhaps best known for the insanely cool images and animations that he's created with Blender's fluid simulator, as shown in this figure.

That said, if you want to use a high resolution sculpt as the basis for a normal map on a lower-res mesh, you need to do a couple of extra steps to get it to work properly. The workflow goes something like this:

1. **Model your object using multires and Sculpt mode.**

   When you're done sculpting, you should have a few levels of multires.

2. **Duplicate your object, but don't move it from its current location (Shift+D⇨right-click).**

   It may be helpful to move this copy to another layer to temporarily get it out of your way (M⇨Alt+1).

3. **Select the original object and unwrap it at its lowest multires level.**

   It doesn't have to be the absolute lowest level, but it should be the level that you intend on rendering and animating with.

4. **Add a new image in the UV/Image Editor (Alt+N).**

   This image should be the size of the texture you want to bake to.

5. **Select (right-click) the duplicated, high-resolution version of your object and then add the low-resolution version to the selection (Shift+right-click).**

   This makes the low-resolution version of the mesh your active object.

6. **In the Bake panel of the Editing buttons (F9), left-click the Selected to Active button.**

   This tells Blender that you want to take the detail of the high-resolution mesh and bake it as a texture for the low-resolution mesh.

7. **Choose Normals as the type of texture you'd like to bake.**

   When you do this, a drop-down menu button appears on the left side of the panel. The options in this menu let you define the *Normal Space* that you would like to bake. The one you want to choose is Tangent.

8. **Left-click Bake.**

   When you're done, you can save your freshly baked normal map to a file on your hard drive. Done!

Using UV Textures

After you have a bunch of UV textures created, either from painting them yourself or by baking them from the mesh, you need a way to bring them back into Blender. This is where Image textures in your Texture buttons (F6) come in. Figure 8-26 shows the Texture buttons with image textures on two different channels, one for a color map and another for a bump map.

The process for adding an Image texture is pretty similar to adding any of the procedural textures:

1. **Choose Image from the Texture Type drop-down list in the Texture panel.**

2. **In the Image panel, left-click the Load button.**

   This opens a File Browser window where you can find the image you want to load as a texture.

3. **With the image loaded, left-click the Clip button in the Map Image panel.**

   This isn't a critical step, but it's something I like to do. Basically, it prevents the image from tiling. Because this is a UV texture, I don't need it to tile.

4. **Bring up the Material buttons (F5) and left-click the UV button in the Map Input panel.**

   This tells the material to use your UV layout for texture coordinates to properly place the texture. Even if the image isn't the original one you painted in Texture Paint mode, as long as you painted the texture using the UV layout as your reference, it should perfectly match your mesh.

5. **In the Map To panel, choose the material attributes you want the texture to influence.**

   If the texture is just a color map, left-click the Col button. If it's a bump map, left-click the Nor button, and so on.

6. **Repeat steps 1–5 for each texture channel that you want add a UV image texture to.**

Chapter 9

Lighting and Environment

In This Chapter

▶ Taking advantage of different types of lights in Blender

▶ Setting up effective lighting

▶ Changing the look of your scene with background images, colors, and ambient occlusion

*I*n terms of getting the work you've created in Blender out to a finalized still image or animation, having your scene's environment and lighting set up properly is incredibly important. It goes along hand-in-hand with setting up materials on your object (covered in Chapter 7) as well as the rendering process (covered in Chapter 14). Without light, the camera — and by extension, the renderer — can't see a thing. You could create the most awesome 3D model or animation in the world, but if it's poorly lit, it won't look good.

This chapter covers the types of lights available to you in Blender and details some of the best practices to use them in your scenes. In addition to lighting details, I go into setting up the environment in your scene with the settings in the World buttons. In many ways, these things are what give your scenes that final polish that make them look good.

Lighting a Scene

Lighting has an incredible amount of power to convey your scene to the viewer. Harsh, stark lighting can give you a dramatic "film noir" look. Low-angle lights with long shadows can give you a creepy horror movie feeling, whereas brighter high-angle lights can make things look like they are taking place during a beautiful summer day. Or, you can use a bluish light that projects a hard noise cloud texture and make your scene feel like it's happening under water.

Equally important is setting up your environment. Depending on how you set it up, you can achieve a variety of looks. You can set your scene in an infinitely large white space, commonly known as "the white void" in film and television. Or, you can set your environment to place your scene outside during the day or somewhere on the moon. When you combine good lighting and a few tricks, you can make your scene take place just about anywhere. Figure 9-1 shows a pretty simple scene with a few different environment and lighting schemes to illustrate this point.

Figure 9-1: Different lighting configurations can drastically affect the look of a scene.

Before I get too deep into how all of this is done in Blender, you should understand some standard lighting setups and terminology. The cool thing is that most of this information isn't limited to use in 3D computer graphics, but it's actually pretty standard in professional film, video, and still photography. In fact, quite a few photographers and directors like to use 3D graphics to test out lighting setups before arriving on set for shooting. (And you thought you were just making pretty pictures on a computer screen! Ha!) One of the most common ways to arrange lights is called *three-point lighting*. As the name implies, it involves the use of three different sets of lights. It's a common studio setup for interviews and it's the starting point for nearly all other lighting arrangements. Figure 9-2 shows a top-down illustration of a typical three-point lighting setup.

Setting up a three-point lighting scheme starts with placing your subject at the center of the scene and aiming your camera at that subject. Then you set up your main light, the *key light*. This is usually the most powerful light in the scene. It's where your main shadows come from as well as your brightest highlights. Typically, you want to set this light just to the left or just to the right of your camera and you usually want it to be higher than your subject. This is to ensure that the shadows fall naturally and you don't get that creepy flashlight-under-the-chin look that your friends used for telling scary stories around the campfire.

Figure 9-2:
A typical
three-point
lighting
setup.

After your key light is established, the next light you want to place is the *fill light*. The purpose of the fill light is to brighten up the dark parts of your subject. See, the key is great for putting shadows on your subject, but without any other light, the shadows are stark black and they obscure your subject. Unless you're aiming for a dramatic lighting effect, this is not what you normally want. The fill light tends to be less powerful than the key, but you want it to have a wider, more diffuse throw. The *throw* is the radius of space that the light reaches. For instance, a flashlight has a narrow throw, whereas fluorescent lights throw light wider. You want this wide throw on your fill because it reduces the amount of highlight generated by this light. You don't want highlights from your fill to compete with the highlights from your key. As far as placement goes, you normally want to place your fill on the opposite side of the camera from the key and roughly at the same height as your subject.

Here's a good way to figure out a good place to position your fill light. Draw an imaginary line from your key light to your subject. Now, with your subject as the pivot point, rotate that line 90 degrees. When you do that, the line points right where you should place the fill.

The last light in a three-point lighting configuration is the *back light* or *rim light*. This light shines at the back of your subject, creating a small edge of light around the profile. That sliver of light helps separate your subject from the background and serves as the nice little bit of polish that often separates a mediocre lighting setup from a really good one. Now, I've sat through long discussions about the best way to position a back light (yes, my friends are nerds, too). Some people like to make it directly opposite from the key light. This works well, but sometimes the light rim competes with the key's high-lights. Other people prefer placing it opposite to the camera. This, too, is a good way to go, but if the subject moves, you risk the possibility of blinding the audience. And yet another group of people recommend placing the back light opposite to the fill. This can create a nice rim of light that complements the key, but it can also look a bit unnatural.

As you can see, everything is a trade-off when it comes to lighting. And don't even get me started on whether the back light should be above or below the subject! In fact, the only really consistent thing that people agree on is that the light should generally point toward the subject. So the bottom line is that the best course of action is to play around with your back light and see for yourself where you get the best results. As for the power and throw of the back light, you typically want to use a back light that is less powerful than your key so things appear natural. The throw can vary because the high-lights are all on the opposite side of your subject. I personally like to keep it narrow, but a wide throw can work nicely for large scenes.

That's basic three-point lighting for you. It works well in computer graphics as well as the "real world" and it's the starting point for most other lighting configurations. Lower the angle of your key to make your subject creepy. Remove or reduce the power of your fill and back lights to get more dramatic shadows. Place your key behind your subject to get a mysterious or romantic silhouette. Add additional lights pointing away from your subject to light the rest of the environment. And that's just the tip of the iceberg!

Knowing when to use which type of lamp

After you're familiar with the basic principles of three-point lighting, you can use the knowledge to light your scenes in Blender. To add a new light, use spacebar➪Add➪Lamp and you see the menus shown in Figure 9-3.

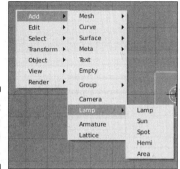

Figure 9-3:
Adding a
lamp in the
3D View.

The Lamp menu offers you the following types of lights to choose from:

✔ **Lamp:** This is often referred to as a *point light* or an *omni light*, meaning that the light is located at a single point in space and emanates in all directions from that point. The default scene when you first load Blender has a single light of this type in it. This is a good general purpose light, but I prefer to use it as secondary illumination or as a fill light.

✔ **Sun:** The Sun lamp represents a single universal light that comes from a single direction. Because of this, the location of the Sun lamp in your scene doesn't really matter, just the orientation. This type of light is the only one that affects the look of the sky and is well suited as a key light for scenes set outdoors.

✔ **Spot:** In many ways, the Spot is the workhorse of CG lighting. It works quite a bit like a flashlight or a theater spotlight and, of all the light types, it gives you the most control over the nature of the shadows and where light lands. Because of this control, spots are fantastic key lights.

✔ **Hemi:** A Hemi lamp is very similar to the Sun lamp in that it doesn't matter where you place the lamp in your scene. It's orientation is the most important aspect of it. However, because it's treated as a full hemisphere of light around the scene, lighting from a Hemi tends to be softer and flatter than the Sun. Hemis are also the only Blender light that cannot cast shadows. I like using them for fills and back lights. They're also handy for outdoor lighting.

✔ **Area:** Area lights are powerful lights that behave similar to Spots; however, the shadows tend to be softer and more accurate because they're based on having a grid of lights to work with. Because of this, they work well for key lights, but because they tend to take more time to process, you should use them sparingly.

Figure 9-4 shows what each light type looks like in the 3D view.

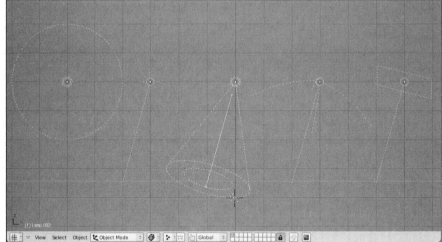

Figure 9-4:
From left to right, Lamp, Sun, Spot, Hemi, and Area lights.

Universal lamp options

When you've chosen a type of lamp and added it to the scene, the controls to modify these lamps are in the Lamp buttons, which are a subcontext of the Shading buttons. Pressing F5 with a Lamp selected automatically brings up the Lamp buttons. With a couple of exceptions, all of the lamps share a few of the same controls and panels in this window. Figure 9-5 highlights the options that are universal for nearly all lights.

Figure 9-5:
Panels and options available for all lamp types.

One of the really cool things about Blender's lamps is that you can instantly change lamp types whenever you want. Simply right-click the lamp you want to work with and choose the type of lamp you would like it be in the Preview panel. This is a great feature for quickly sorting out the type of light you want to use. You can test out different lighting schemes without having to clutter the scene with a bunch of extraneous lights that you have to move to other layers or hide.

The Energy value and RGB sliders control the strength and color of the lamp. I rarely set the Energy to a value greater than 1.0, but when you need it, it's handy to have the option. And of course, if you'd rather not use the RGB sliders, you can left-click the color swatch beneath them and use Blender's color picker.

The Dist value is visible for all light types, but it only really has any meaning for the Lamp, Spot, and Area lights. The value is in Blender units and, if an object is farther away from the light than that distance, it receives no light. For each of the light types, there's an indicator that defines the range of this value. For the Area light, it's a line pointing in the direction that the light is facing. For the Spot, it's the length of the cone. For the Lamp, there is no indicator on by default, but if you left-click the Sphere button in the Lamp panel, a dashed circle appears to indicate the distance of the Lamp's throw.

Be careful when enabling the Sphere button on the Lamp. It subtly changes how the light works. With Sphere enabled, light coming from the Lamp starts to weaken, or *attenuate*, starting at the light's location, so by the time it gets to the Dist value, no light is available. However, if you have Sphere disabled, that attenuation doesn't start until you actually reach that Dist value, so you have a farther throw. Having Sphere enabled makes the light behave more like it would in the real world (or, as I like to say, meatspace), but it's often more convenient to keep it disabled.

With the exception of the Hemi light, each light has the option of using raytracing to cast shadows. This is enabled in the Shadow and Spot panel by left-clicking the Ray Shadow button and is the default behavior for new lights. Know, however, that using raytraced shadows can drastically increase your render times. The next section goes more deeply into some techniques for optimizing your lighting to try to deal with that. However, if you do want to use raytraced shadows, you should be aware of a few options:

- ✔ **QMC Sampling Types:** You generally have the choice between Adaptive QMC and Constant QMC. QMC stands for Quasi-Monti Carlo, and is an algorithm for taking random samples. Generally speaking, the Adaptive QMC setting should give you faster render times.

- ✔ **Soft Size:** This controls how blurry the edge of your cast shadows are. The higher the value, the blurrier the shadow. However, with only one sample (the next option) the shadows will not blur that much. Blurry shadows require more shadows.

- ✔ **Samples:** This dictates how many samples the raytraced light uses. Increasing this value increases the accuracy of the shadows at the expense of longer render times.

- ✔ **Threshold:** This option is only available when you choose the Adaptive QMC sampling type. It basically helps the renderer decide which samples to use and which ones to ignore. A higher Threshold value shortens your render times, but may decrease the accuracy of your shadows.

✔ **Shadow color:** Left-click this swatch to get a color picker for selecting the color of your cast shadow.

Without getting too deep into all of the crazy mathematical details, understanding QMC requires knowing a little bit more about how raytracing works. In Chapter 7, I give a brief description of raytracing that said it's done by tracing each and every vector of light bouncing from the light source(s) to the camera. This is somewhat over-simplified. Tracing *every single vector* would take an incredibly excessive amount of time. In order to get around that, programmers decided to take a sampling of those vectors and approximate everything in between them. To make the best use of these samples, they first tried just randomly picking them. The problem with this, though, is that raw random selection doesn't give consistent or accurate results. Samples may or may not be where they're most useful. So to accommodate that, they decided that samples could be random, but they should be evenly dispersed. This is basically Constant QMC. Of course, the downside to constant QMC is that you still might be taking samples from parts of the scene that don't need very many. If you can stay random, but have more of the samples taken from busier parts of the scene, you might get better performance. This is the logic behind Adaptive QMC.

Like with materials for objects, you can also apply textures to your lights and apply them to the lamp's color, it's shadow's color, or both. This is a great way to use lighting to enhance the environment of your scene or to fake certain lighting effects that are typically only achievable with raytracing. One specific example are *caustic* effects. If you have some free time, take a glass of water and shine light through it. Due to the refractive nature of the glass and the water, you usually see a strange light pattern on the table near or around the glass. This is an example of caustics and, if you don't need 100% accuracy, you can fake it with a noise texture on a spot light. On a larger scale, caustics are what make the cool moving patterns you can see on the bottom of a swimming pool.

Light-specific options

As you can see in Figure 9-5, the Lamp light type has options that are available on nearly every other light type but doesn't have much in the way of unique controls. The same could actually be said of the Hemi light. In fact, it has fewer controls because Hemis can't cast shadows. However, the remaining three lights have some interesting options that allow you to optimize their usage to meet your needs.

Sun

The Sun lamp, in particular, is a lot more useful in Blender 2.48 because it has the ability to behave more like the real sun. It's the only type of light that Blender has that influences the look of the sky and even provides some atmospheric effects. You control this lamp with the Sky/Atmosphere panel that appears in the Lamp buttons. By default, both the Sky and Atmosphere buttons are disabled, but you can turn them on with a left-click. Figure 9-6 shows the panels and options for the Sun light type.

Figure 9-6:
Lamp
buttons for
the Sun light
type.

When you enable the Sky button, you get the set of buttons that control how the Sun lamp influences the sky background. The first thing you may want to do is make the Sun visible. Doing this requires that you increase the Sun Bright and Sun Size values. Now if you try to render your scene, you may not see the Sun in your sky, even if you've placed the Sun lamp within your camera's view. This is because, if you recall, the position of the Sun lamp is irrelevant to how it lights the scene. Only its orientation is important. So if you want to see your Sun, you may have to angle the camera up and more skyward. You also have to rotate the lamp so it points in the opposite direction that the camera's pointing.

Now, when you look at the sky on a clear day — the real sky outside; you know, in the for-really-real world — you may notice that it's naturally lighter near the horizon and gets darker as it moves farther from the horizon. The Hor Bright and Hor Spread values are what you use to recreate and control this effect in Blender. At the top of the panel is the Turbidity value. Keep this at a low value for clear day skies and increase it for more foggy, overcast skies.

When you enable the Atmosphere button, you get some buttons that control the Sun's influence on how the air in your scene looks from a distance. These options are best suited for cases where you have a wide camera shot that shows off a large portion of your set's environment. There's really no good way to preview the effects of these values other than to do test renders. Here's a quick guideline to help understand what each one does, though:

- ✔ **Sun Intens:** Increasing this value makes objects in the distance bluer, mixing with the natural sky color.

- ✔ **Inscattering:** Increasing this value makes the light appear to scatter more between the camera and the objects it's pointing at. Set this to 1.0 for the most physically accurate results.

- ✔ **Extinction:** Lower numbers for this option reduce the amount of detail the light brings out in your objects. Like inscattering, having this set to 1.0 gives you the most physically accurate results.

- ✔ **Distance:** This setting is similar to Extinction, except it controls how much detail you see as you get closer to the camera. At low values, everything can be seen. As you increase the value, the light becomes yellower and distant objects become more and more like silhouettes.

Spot

When working with Spot lights, you have the option of two different ways to cast shadows: raytraced and buffered. The simplest way to know the difference between the two is to know that, generally speaking, raytraced shadows are more accurate whereas buffered shadows render faster. Regardless of which type of shadows you decide to cast (if you decide to have this lamp cast shadows at all), a couple of settings are always available for Spots:

- ✔ **SpotSi:** Spot Size. This controls the width of the Spot's throw, measured in degrees. So a value of 180 is completely wide, whereas a value of 30 gives you a narrower cone. Unless I'm doing something special, I like to start with my Spots around 60 degrees.

- ✔ **SpotBl:** Spot Blur. This controls the sharpness of the edges at the boundary where the Spot's cone of influence ends. Lower values give you a crisp edge, whereas higher values soften it, making the light appear somewhat more diffuse.

- ✔ **Halo:** Enabling this button allows the renderer to show the full cone of light generated by the Spot. This is called *volumetric* light. You see this effect when you use a flashlight in a dusty room or when you want the "sunbeams from the sky" effect.

- ✔ **HaloInt:** Halo Intensity. This value has no influence unless you enable the Halo button. If you do have Halo enabled, increasing this value increases the intensity, or brightness, of the volumetric halo effect.

- ✔ **Square:** Enable this button if you would prefer the Spot light to come from a square source rather than a round one.

If you decide to use buffered shadows rather than raytraced ones, the options in the Shadow and Spot panel change. All of the raytraced shadow controls — QMC sampling, Soft Size, Samples, and Threshold — are replaced with a somewhat more involved set of options. The reason for this is because buffered shadows are more of an image-based process than the raytracing method. This means that there are more ways to control how the shadows look because you're no longer constrained by the limits of reality. Figure 9-7 shows the Lamp buttons for a Spot lamp with buffered shadows.

Figure 9-7:
Lamp
buttons for
a buffered
Spot lamp.

Trying to sort out all of these controls can be daunting. However, the following values are the most important ones that you should know about:

✔ **ShadowBufferSize:** Buffered shadows is an image-based technique. The Shadow Buffer Size is the resolution of the image used to create the shadows. Lower values work faster, but look more jagged.

✔ **Samples:** If you increase this value, Blender creates multiple versions of the shadow buffer and mixes them together to get smoother shadow edges. This increases render times, but if you want soft shadows with blurry edges, more samples make it look better.

✔ **Halo Step:** This value only has an effect if you have the Halo option enabled. Adjusting it controls your *volumetric shadow*, or how much of the volumetric effect your object blocks. Higher values render faster, but are less accurate. Setting it to one gives you the best, albeit the slowest, results. However, setting it to zero means that there is no volumetric shadow, so you have the volumetric cone, but your object won't block it at all.

✔ **Bias:** Normally you can leave this value at its default setting. It offsets the shadow from where it connects to the shadow-casting object. Occasionally, you may get some weird jaggies or artifacts in your shadows. Increasing the Bias can help get rid of those artifacts. If you do have to adjust the Bias, adjust it only as low as it can go before artifacting. Otherwise, your shadows will begin to look very unnatural.

✔ **Soft:** Increasing this value makes your shadows softer and blurrier. To use this setting effectively, make sure you have a Samples value greater than one. And at the same time, you get the best results by not setting the Soft value higher than double your Samples value. So at the default Samples setting of 3, you should keep your Soft value below 6.

✔ **ClipSta/ClipEnd:** Clip Start and Clip End. Consider these values as a secondary control in addition to the Dist value. Objects that appear within these two values, indicated by a line on the Spot lamp in the 3D View, cast shadows, whereas objects outside of this range do not. Keeping the Clip values as close to your shadow-casting objects as possible gives you the most accurate results. If you don't want to adjust these values manually, left-click the car (*auto*mobile) icon next to either one. Blender automatically sets the clip values to include objects within the Spot's cone.

✔ **SampleBuffers:** It's easy to misunderstand the usefulness of this setting and confuse it with the normal Samples setting. In essence, it basically does the same thing. However, this was added to Blender with the specific purpose of helping render hair and fur more effectively. Higher values give you better results, but at the cost of using more system memory when rendering. Unless you're rendering hair or fine detail, keep this set to one.

Area

Area lamps are very similar to Spots, except unlike Spots, which can use both buffered and raytraced shadows, Area lamps can only use raytracing for creating shadows. This makes the shadows generally smoother and more accurate; however, they can increase your render time dramatically. Figure 9-8 shows the panels and options for Area lights.

Figure 9-8:
The Lamp buttons for Area lights.

The way an area light works is pretty simple. Imagine that at the lamp's location, you don't have a single light, but instead you have a grid of lights and you can control the width and height of this grid as well as the number of lights in it. This means you have even more control over your lamp's throw.

To control the dimensions of your Area lamp, use the Size value in the Lamp panel. This size is measured in Blender units and, by default, controls both the width and the height of the Area lamp. You control the number of lights in the Area lamp by adjusting the Samples value in the Shadow and Spot panel. Because the default shape of the lamp is a square, increasing the number of samples gives you the square of the sample value. So setting Samples to 3 creates 9 lights in the grid, and setting it to 5 creates 25 lights in the grid.

If you would rather have a rectangular Area lamp, left-click the drop-down menu above the Size button and change the shape from Square to Rect. When you do this, the Samples value changes to SampleX and SampleY, giving you control over the number of horizontal and vertical lights you have on your Area light's grid. The total of lights you have in the grid is the value of SampleX multiplied by the value of SampleY. Figure 9-9 shows an illustration of how the lights are arranged in square and rectangular Area lamps.

When working with Area lights, remember that you actually have multiple lights arranged on the lamp's grid. This can make an Area light with an Energy of 1.0 excessively bright. So if you use an Area lamp, try a much lower Energy value. I usually drop it down 0.050 and use that as my starting point.

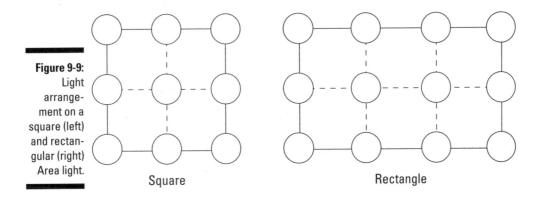

Figure 9-9:
Light
arrange-
ment on a
square (left)
and rectan-
gular (right)
Area light.

Square   Rectangle

Lighting for Speedy Renders

I haven't yet talked about six buttons in the Lamp buttons: I like to refer to
them as my "cheat buttons" because they're incredibly useful for achieving
lighting effects that are difficult or impossible in the real world. The functions
that these buttons control are really what makes lighting in 3D computer
graphics so powerful. More often than not, if you use them effectively, they
can speed up your render times without having a negative effect on the overall
quality of your image. Figure 9-10 highlights these buttons in the Lamp buttons.

Figure 9-10:
The "cheat
buttons" in
the Lamp
panel and
the Shadow
and Spot
panel.

Descriptions of the function of each button are below:

✔ **Layer:** Enabling this button makes the light illuminate only the objects
   that are on the same layer as the light. In real-world lighting, technicians
   do a lot of work to hide or mask out some lights, so they only shine on
   certain parts of the scene. For instance, you may want to brighten up the
   environment without making the lighting on your characters any brighter.
   You don't have to mask anything out: You just enable the Layer button
   and make sure your characters aren't on the same layer as the light.

- ✔ **Negative:** Turning on this button enables what is, in my opinion, one of the coolest capabilities in CG lighting, inverting the light's output. What this means is that you can basically shine *darkness* on your scene! This is impossible to do in meatspace and it opens the door to all sorts of interesting possibilities. If part of your scene is too bright or you want to have deeper shadows, don't play with adjusting the Energy of your lights or increasing the Samples for your shadows. Just shine some darkness on the area with a negative light!

- ✔ **No Diffuse:** Sometimes when you're lighting, you want to have fine control of your highlights, but you don't want to change the basic illumination of the scene. If you turn off shadow casting for the light and enable this button, you basically have a specular highlight that you can move around your subject at will. This is not a commonly used feature, but having it available has certainly made my life easier on more than one occasion.

- ✔ **No Specular:** Earlier in this chapter, I explain that in three-point lighting, you want to reduce the highlights produced by the fill so they don't compete with the key's highlights. Meatspace lighting technicians often attempt to do this by diffusing the fill as much as possible. In Blender, you don't have to go through the trouble. You can just turn off the lamp's specular highlights altogether by left-clicking this button. Pretty sweet, huh?

- ✔ **OnlyShadow/Layer:** Enabling this option allows your lamp to cast shadows without adding any additional light to the scene. The best reason why you'd want to do such a thing is to reduce render times by using buffered Spots for shadows while using other lights without shadows for your main illumination. The Layer button just beneath this works like the Layer button in the Lamp panel, but only relates to shadows.

Any object — even lights — can exist on multiple layers. This dramatically increases the power of layer-only lights and shadows. With the object selected, press M to bring up the layer selection pop-up. To place your object on more than one layer, Shift+left-click the layer buttons you want it on.

I often tell people that when it comes to computer graphics, if you're not cheating or faking something, you're probably doing it wrong. I say this because even though you can get great results by using raytraced shadows everywhere with the highest number of samples, this all comes at the expense of high memory usage and lengthy render times. So your scene may look perfect, but if you're taking 16 hours to render every frame in an animation, you could be rendering for a month and not even have two seconds of it done.

A large part of being a CG artist is doing everything you can to reduce the amount of work that needs to be done by both you *and* the computer while still creating high-quality images. You don't want to be old and gray by the time your first animation is complete. This is why CG artists worry so much about keeping their render times as short as possible and why they use functions like these to cut corners where they can.

Three-point lighting in Blender

As I mentioned at the beginning of the chapter, my preferred lighting rig in Blender usually starts with a three-point lighting setup. This is what I normally start with:

- **Key:** A buffered Spot works well as the key light. Keep all settings at their default values except for the Spot Size and Clip range. Set the Spot Size to 60 and activate the auto icons for the Clip Start and Clip End values.

- **Fill:** Typically, this is a Hemi with an Energy of 0.5 and the No Specular button enabled in the Lamp panel.

- **Back:** Also a Hemi, but the Energy is usually between 0.75 and 1.0 to get a nice rim light. The lamp is behind the subject, so specularity doesn't matter as much, but just to make sure it doesn't complete with the key's spec, I normally enable the No Specular button on this light as well.

Figure 9-11 shows what this three-point rig looks like. This is a good setup for "studio lighting" and it works really well for scenes set indoors or for lighting isolated objects.

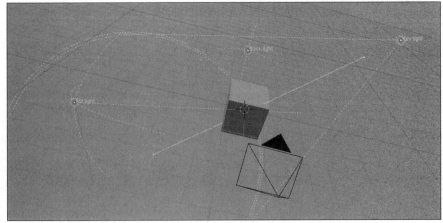

Figure 9-11: A standard three-point lighting rig.

Creating a "fake" Area light with buffered Spots

Using a buffered Spot as your key works nicely, but an Area light can usually give you softer shadows. However, Area lights can only use raytracing for shadows, and you have somewhat limited control of the Area light's shape because it can only be a flat square or rectangle. To get around these limitations, you can actually be creative with buffered Spots and use them to make your own Area light. To do this, start with the three-point rig in the last section and then go through the following steps:

1. **Create a circle mesh (Spacebar⇨Add⇨Mesh⇨Circle).**

   Set the number of vertices to 8, set the radius to 2.0, and enable the Fill button.

2. **Add the Spot to your selection, making it the Active object.**

   Adding the circle should have made it selected by default, so all you should have to do is Shift+right-click the buffered Spot you're using as your key.

3. **Copy the location and rotation of the Spot to the circle object (Ctrl+C⇨Location, Ctrl+C⇨Rotation).**

   This should place the circle in the same place as the Spot with the same orientation.

4. **Make the circle your Active object (Shift+right-click).**

   This keeps both the Spot and the circle selected, but now the circle is active.

5. **Parent the Spot lamp to the circle (Ctrl+P⇨Make Parent).**

   Now if you just have the circle selected and try to move it around, the Spot follows.

6. **Turn on Dupliverts for the circle (F7⇨Anim settings⇨Dupliverts).**

   Dupliverts are a cool part of Blender. When you have an object parented to a mesh, activating Dupliverts on the mesh object places a copy of the child object at every vertex on the parent.

7. **Congratulations! You now have an Area lamp created by buffered Spots arranged on a custom shape.**

   Now you can select your Spot and adjust its settings to taste. I typically use the following settings as my starting point:

   - Energy: 0.200
   - SpotBl: 1.000
   - Samples: 8
   - Soft: 16.00
   - ClipSta/ClipEnd: These values may need to be manually adjusted to make sure the shadow appears properly.

Figure 9-12 shows the basic three-point lighting rig above with a circular Area light created with buffered spots.

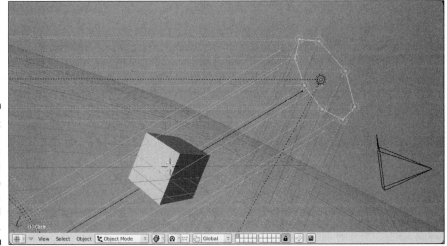

Figure 9-12:
Using
Dupliverted
buffered
Spots to
create a
buffered
Area light.

Outdoor lighting

What if you have a large scene or your scene is set outdoors? The limited lighting cone of a single Spot or Area light makes it difficult to illuminate the whole scene in a believable way. For this, I usually bounce between one of two solutions. Both of them involve the Sun lamp. The easiest solution to implement is to change the buffered Spot into a Sun with raytraced shadows. This is a nice way to go because you get shadows for all objects in your scene and, with the sky and atmosphere settings, you can get a really believable result. That said, lighting your scene this way brings two disadvantages. First, it uses raytracing for your shadows, so that can increase your render times if you're not careful. And second, because the Sun illuminates the same everywhere, you don't have as much control over individual shadows. An alternative situation is to use the Sun for full scene lighting and atmosphere, but leave the shadow creation to the Spot light. To do this, begin with the basic three-point lighting rig above and proceed with the following steps:

1. **Add a Sun lamp (Spacebar⇨Add⇨Lamp⇨Sun).**

   I like to put the Sun at the center of the scene (press Shift+C to put the 3D cursor at the center before adding the Sun).

2. **Add the buffered Spot to your selection (Shift+right-click).**

   The newly added Sun should be selected by default. Shift+right-clicking the Spot also selects it and makes the Spot light the Active object.

3. **Copy the Spot light's rotation (Ctrl+C⇨Copy Rotation).**

   Now light from the Sun is coming from the same direction as the Spot. Location for the Sun is irrelevant.

4. **Make the Spot light a shadow-only light (F5⇨Shadow and Spot⇨ OnlyShadow).**

5. **Disable shadows on the Sun by selecting the Sun (right-click) and then disabling raytraced shadows by left-clicking the Ray Shadow button in the Shadow and Spot panel.**

   Done! If you have other objects in your scene that need shadows, make a linked duplicate (Alt+D) of your shadow-only spot and position the duplicate by Grabbing (G) it to the correct location.

Figure 9-13 shows an outdoor lighting rig with a shadowless Sun and shadow-only buffered Spots.

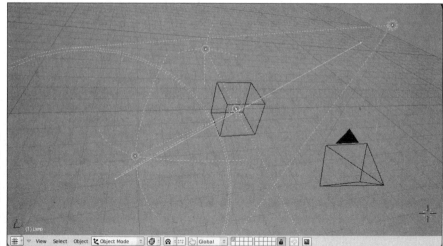

Figure 9-13:
An outdoor lighting rig with the lights all selected.

Setting Up the World

When you set up your scene for rendering, lighting is really only part of the equation. You must also consider your scene's environment. For instance, are you outdoors or indoors? Is it daytime or nighttime? What color is the sky? Are there clouds? What does the background look like? These are considerations you have to make when thinking about the final look of your image. Fortunately, nearly all of the controls for setting up your environment are in the World buttons (F8), shown in Figure 9-14.

Figure 9-14:
The World
buttons.

Changing to something other than bright blue

If you've worked in Blender for a while and gotten a few renders out, you might be pretty tired of that incredibly bright blue background color that the renderer uses by default. Here's where you change that color: Look in the World panel of the World buttons. The left color swatch sets the horizon color. You can adjust it by using the RGB sliders below it or by left-clicking the swatch and using the color picker.

To the right of the horizon color is the *zenith* color. You may notice that trying to change this color doesn't seem to affect the background color at all. This is because, by default, Blender is set to use only the horizon color, so you end up with a solid color as the background. To change this, left-click the Blend button in the Preview panel. When you do this, the Preview should show a linear gradient that transitions from the horizon color at the bottom to the Zenith color at the top. If I'm doing a render where I just want to see a model I've created, I often use this setup with my horizon color around 50% gray and my zenith color nearly black.

Of course, the next question you might have is, "Okay, so what do the other two buttons in the Preview panel do?" I'm glad you asked. You can actually activate any combination of these buttons. Here is a description of what each button does when enabled:

✔ **Blend:** Enables a gradient going from the horizon to the zenith. When enabled by itself, the horizon is always at the bottom of the camera view and the zenith is at the top. This is good for when you want to have a static background that doesn't change based on the camera's orientation.

✔ **Paper:** You typically use the Paper setting with both Blend and Real also enabled. It keeps the horizon at the center of the camera, no matter where it's pointing. It also adjusts the gradient to make sure that the full zenith color is visible as well as the full horizon color.

✔ **Real:** Enabling Real sets the horizon to the XY ground plane and the gradient moves in the opposite direction to the zenith color. A bonus to this is that, because the horizon is locked to the XY ground plane, the gradient rotates with the camera, giving a much more realistic feeling to the background. I'm very fond of this setting, especially if I'm using a texture in the background.

Figure 9-15 shows a simple scene rendered with the various combinations of the Blend button enabled with the other two buttons so you can get a better idea of what they do.

Figure 9-15:
Ways to
control the
Blend gradi-
ent and the
horizon.

Blend   Blend + Real   Blend+Real+Paper

Understanding ambient occlusion

Take a look outside. Now, hopefully it's daytime or this isn't going to work, but notice how much everything seems to be illuminated. Even on a bright sunny day, the deepest shadows aren't completely black. The reason for this is that light from the sun is basically bouncing off of every surface many times, exposing nearly all objects to at least *some* amount of light. In computer graphics, this phenomenon is often referred to as *global illumination*, or GI, and it's pretty difficult to recreate efficiently. As you may have guessed, the biggest reason for this is the "light only bounces once" rule that I talked about at the beginning of Chapter 7.

Another reason, which goes hand-in-hand with this one, is that all this bounced light also actually makes subtle details, creases, cracks, and wrinkles more apparent. At first, this may seem like a paradox. After all, if light is bouncing off of everything, intuitively, it would make sense that everything should end up even brighter and seem flatter. However, remember that not only is the light bouncing off of everything, but it is also casting small shadows from all the weird angles that it bounces from. This is what brings out those minor textural details.

The GI effect is most apparent outdoors on overcast days where the light is evenly diffused by cloud cover. However, you can even see it happening in well-lit rooms with a high number of light sources (think about an office building with rows and rows of fluorescent lights lining the ceiling). Now, you can somewhat fake this effect by using a Hemi lamp, but the problem with Hemis is that they don't cast shadows, so you don't get that nice added detail that you GI gives you.

The bad news is that Blender's internal renderer doesn't actually have a "true" global illumination capability. You can use radiosity to do it, but it's a bit slow, unwieldy, and it's not really designed for that purpose. The good news, however, is that Blender does have a great way of approximating the GI effect. It's done with a feature called *ambient occlusion* or AO. Often called "dirty GI" or "dirt shader," AO basically looks for the cracks, creases, and small details in your object and makes them more apparent by making the rest of the model brighter, making the details darker, or a combination of the two. To enable AO, go to the Amb Occ panel in the World buttons (F8). Blender gives you two ways of calculating AO: as an approximation or with raytracing. Figure 9-16 shows the Ambient Occlusion panel with the options for approximate AO and raytraced AO.

Figure 9-16:
The Ambient Occlusion panel in the World buttons with raytraced AO options (left) and approximate AO options (right).

If you're going to use raytraced AO, make sure you have the Ray button enabled in the Render panel of the Render buttons (F10).

As Figure 9-16 shows, most of the controls in raytraced and approximate AO are the same. Below is a description of the options available for both types of AO:

- **Use Falloff:** This option controls the size of the extra shadows that the AO creates. When you enable it, a value field appears below the button. Setting this value to higher numbers makes the shadows more subtle. Note that for this option to work, you must have the Plain button enabled.

- **Add/Sub/Both:** With these buttons, you can control how the AO creates the shadows. Enabling the Add button brightens the rest of the object, making the details apparent by simply staying their own color. Enabling the Sub button darkens the detailed areas while keeping the object's original shading. If you enable both, the details tend to really pop out, but occasionally they pop too much. However, if you increase the Falloff value, that can help mitigate the situation.

✔ **Plain/Sky Color:** These buttons control the source color for the diffuse energy used by AO. Setting it to Plain means the diffuse energy is just white light. Setting it to Sky Color uses the horizon and zenith colors to provide the diffuse energy. Also, if you're using raytraced AO, there is an additional option to use the sky texture for AO's diffuse energy.

✔ **Energy:** This the energy for the AO effect. The effect created by the Add and Sub buttons is multiplied by this value. Usually it's a good idea to keep this at 1.0.

Another setting that you may want to adjust is the Ambient color value in the World panel. You can change it by adjusting its RGB sliders or by left-clicking the swatch and using the color picker. The Ambient color adds itself to the overall color of the scene. I don't normally advocate setting the Ambient color to anything other than black because it has a tendency to wash out the shading in the scene under most circumstances. However, when you use the Ambient color with ambient occlusion enabled, the shading isn't washed out as much and you actually end up with a more believable image.

The other values for raytraced and approximate AO are there for refining and optimizing how they work. If you read about raytraced lights earlier in this chapter, the settings for raytraced AO should be pretty familiar. I recommend using Adaptive QMC for raytraced AO because it typically yields faster results at good quality. Using the other sampling types usually gives you a *noisier*, or more speckled, result.

When choosing between raytraced and approximate AO, there are a set of trade-offs to keep in mind. As you might expect, raytraced AO gives you more accurate results, but it usually takes longer to process. Approximate AO works very fast and doesn't suffer the noise problem that you get with raytraced AO. Of course, some people actually prefer that noisy grain that raytraced AO gives, and approximate AO is a bit more error-prone in creating its shadows, especially where things touch. So it may take some additional time to set things up so that they look believable. Both techniques offer advantages and disadvantages. You have to weigh them for yourself and see which works best for your projects. I personally prefer approximate AO for the short render times. Figure 9-17 shows the same scene rendered with both types of AO, as well as without any AO at all.

Figure 9-17:
From left to right, with their render times: no AO, raytraced AO, and approximate AO.

Mist, stars, and sky textures

The other tab next to the Ambient Occlusion panel is the Mist/Stars/Physics panel. These settings are somewhat primitive in terms of what they actually do, but they can be pretty handy in a pinch for creating nice atmospheric effects and quick backgrounds. Figure 9-18 shows the Mist/Stars/Physics panel.

Figure 9-18:
The Mist/ Stars/ Physics panel.

Mist

Blender's Mist works by taking objects as they go into the distance and decreasing their opacity so that they mix more with whatever the background image or color is. To use it, left-click the Mist button in the Mist/ Stars/Physics panel. From here, you can adjust the Start and Dist values. Start defines how far away from the camera the mist starts to take effect. Dist is the distance from the Start value that the mist effect is at 100%. Anything farther away from the camera than this now shows up in the render.

These values are in Blender units, but it can be difficult to know intuitively where they actually fall in the scene, relative to your camera. Fortunately, there's a way to see this visually. Select (right-click) the camera and switch to the Editing buttons (F9). On the right side of the Camera panel are four buttons under the label of Show. Left-click the Mist button. When you do this, a line should appear extending from your camera. If you switch back to the World buttons (F8) and adjust the Start and Dist values, you can now see exactly where the mist region of influence is. Figure 9-19 shows a scene in the 3D view with a camera that has its mist limits visible.

Figure 9-19: A camera in the 3D view with its mist limits visible. To the right is a render of that scene.

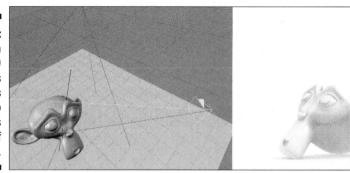

The Quad, Lin, and Sqr buttons control how the mist gets thicker from start to finish. Quad tends to be a more subtle effect, whereas Sqr tends to make the mist thicker faster. If you want to limit the mist to a certain height, like when you see an early morning mist in a field, adjust the Height value. Like the other values, this is set in Blender units and works relative to the XY ground plane. The Mist value increases the mist's intensity. Be careful with this setting. Putting it too high hides your entire scene from you.

Stars

Blender's Stars feature is a quick way of adding star-like halos to your scene. You enable it by left-clicking the Stars button in the Mist/Stars/Physics panel. There aren't very many controls for stars, but they can definitely have an effect on how the stars appear. One thing to bear in mind is that Blender creates these stars in 3D space. They actually have a physical location and they aren't just a randomly generated speckled background. Descriptions of each option are as follows:

✔ **StarDist:** This is the average distance between stars. Stars are randomly placed in the background, but this controls how dense the star field is.

✔ **MinDist:** This value controls the minimum distance that stars can be from the camera. Unless you want stars to show up in front of some objects in your scene, this value should be larger than the distance between the camera and the farthest object away from it.

- ✔ **Size:** Size controls the size of the stars. Like StarDist, this is an average value. For realistic stars, use a relatively small Size value.

- ✔ **Colnoise:** Increasing this value colors the stars randomly. Setting this to its maximum value makes your scene look a bit like a piñata exploded in space. However, putting this at a lower value like 0.050 gives some subtle variety to your stars.

Figure 9-20 shows a simple scene rendered with the Stars feature enabled.

Figure 9-20: Monkeee-eeeeeyyyyy-ssssss-innnnnn Spaaa-aaaace!

When using stars, enable the Real button in the Preview panel of the World buttons (F8). This way, if you animate your camera moving in the scene, the stars actually behave realistically.

Sky Textures

Flat colors, gradients, and stars are nice, but there are definitely cases where you would rather have an image as your background. Doing this is pretty straightforward. The World for your scene, like materials and lights, can have a texture applied to it. You do this with the Texture and Input panel and the Map To panel in the World buttons as shown in Figure 9-21.

The Texture and Input panel has the familiar texture channels like the ones used by materials and lights. The Map To panel gives you the ability to map the color of the texture to the Blend, horizon color, and the upper and lower zenith colors. To use an image as your Sky texture, use the following steps:

Figure 9-21:
The Texture and Input panel and the Map To panel in the World buttons, used for adding textures to your sky.

1. **Left-click the Add New button in the Texture and Input panel (F8⇨Texture and Input⇨Add New).**

   This creates a new texture and places it in the first texture channel.

2. **Switch to the Texture buttons and change the Texture Type to Image (F6⇨Texture⇨Texture Type⇨Image).**

3. **In the Image panel, left-click the Load button and use the File Browser to find the image you want to use.**

   If you would like to use Blender's Image Browser, Ctrl+left-click the Load button.

4. **Switch back to the World buttons and map the texture to the horizon color (F8⇨Map To⇨Hori).**

   You can leave Blend enabled if you'd like, but it's not necessary.

5. **In the Preview panel, enable the Real button (F8⇨Preview⇨Real).**

   This ensures that the sky moves properly as you move your camera in the scene.

6. **Tweak the mapping and input settings to taste.**

   In the Texture and Input buttons, you may have to adjust the input as well as the texture size and offset. I tend to get best results with the Global input setting, but it may be different for you. In the Map To panel, you can control how the Sky texture interacts with the horizon and zenith colors. It's worth it to play around with these settings a bit to land on the look you want. When you're finished, you may have something that looks like Figure 9-22.

Figure 9-22:
A simple
scene
with a Sky
texture as
well as the
World but-
tons that set
it up.

Part III
Get Animated!

The 5th Wave · By Rich Tennant

"You know, I've asked you a dozen times _not_ to animate the torches on our Web page!"

In this part . . .

There's just *something* about making things move. Your work can take on a life of its own and communicate to an audience in a way that a single still image could never do. It has to do with how the visuals you create work in coordination with time. This part goes into the steps you need to go through to give your creations the illusion of life. Not only is there technical information on the details of Blender's tools for rigging characters and creating animations, but the chapters in this part also cover some of the essential principles of animation that are applicable to all forms of animation.

The last chapter in this part goes into how to make Blender do the heavy lifting in animation. Integrated simulation tools allow you to do complex, physically accurate animations more quickly than you could by hand. Blender gives you this power.

Chapter 10

Animating Objects

I have to make a small admission: Animation is not easy. It's time-consuming, frustrating, tedious work where you often spend days, sometimes even weeks, working on what ends up to be a few seconds of finished animation. An enormous amount of work goes into it. However, there's something incredible about making an otherwise inanimate object move, tell a story, and communicate to an audience. Getting those moments when you have beautifully believable motion – life, in some ways – is a positively indescribable sensation. The process of animation truly has my heart more than any other aspect of computer graphics. It's simply my favorite thing to do. It's like playing with a sock puppet, except better because you don't have to worry about wondering whether or not it's been washed.

This chapter, as well as the following three chapters, go pretty heavily into the technical details of creating animations using Blender. It's a great tool for the job. Beyond what this book can provide you with, though, animation is about seeing, understanding, and recreating motion. I highly recommend that you make it a point to get out and watch things. And not just animations: Go to a park and study how people move. Try to move like other people move so you can understand how the weight shifts and how gravity and inertia compete with and accentuate that movement. Watch lots of movies and television and pay close attention to how people's facial expressions can convey what they're trying to say. If you get a chance, go to a theater and watch a play. Understanding how and why stage actors exaggerate their body language is incredibly useful information for an animator.

While you're doing that, think about how you can use the technical information in these chapters to recreate those feelings and that motion with your objects in Blender.

Working with Animation Curves

In Blender, the fundamental way for controlling and creating animation is with animation curves called *Ipos*. Ipo is short for *interpolation*. To understand interpolation better, flash back to your grade school math class for a second. Remember when you had to do graphing, or take the equation for some sort of line or curve and draw it out on paper? By drawing that line, you were interpolating between points. Don't worry though; I'm not going to make you do any of that. That's what we have Blender for. In fact, the following example should help explain things more clearly:

1. **Start with Blender's default scene (Ctrl+X⇨Erase All).**

2. **Select the default cube object and switch to the camera view (right-click, Numpad 0).**

3. **Split the 3D View window vertically and change one of the new windows to the Ipo Curve Editor window (right-click⇨Split Area, Shift+F6).**

4. **In the right column of the Ipo Curve Editor, left-click LocZ.**

   This selects the control for the cube's position in the global Z-axis.

5. **Ctrl+left-click in the graph area of the Ipo Curve Editor.**

   This creates a single control point and a colored line in the Ipo Curve Editor. You should also see the default cube jump up or down along the Z-axis, depending on where you clicked. This colored line is the Ipo curve.

6. **Create more control points for this curve by Ctrl+left-clicking in other parts of the Ipo Curve Editor.**

   Your Blender screen should look something like the one in Figure 10-1.

Congratulations! You've just created your first animation in Blender. Here's what you've done: The largest part of the Ipo Curve Editor is a graph. Moving from left to right on this graph – its X-axis – is moving forward in time. Moving up and down on this graph changes the value of whatever channel you've selected from the list along the right side of the Ipo Curve Editor. So the curve that you created describes and controls the change in the cube's Z-axis location as you move forward in time. Blender creates the curve by interpolating between the control points you've created. You can see the result for yourself by playing back the animation. Keeping your mouse cursor in the Ipo Curve Editor window, press Alt+A. This makes a green vertical line move from left to right in the graph. As it does this, you should basically see your cube bouncing up and down in the 3D View. Press Esc to stop the playback. You can watch the animation in a more controlled way by left-clicking in the graph area of the Ipo Curve Editor and dragging your mouse cursor left and right. The vertical green line, called the *timeline cursor*, follows your mouse cursor, and you can watch the change happening in the 3D View. This is called *scrubbing*.

There's actually a screen layout in Blender specifically set up for animation. You can choose it from the Screen Layout button at the top of the Blender window or by using the Ctrl+left arrow hotkey combination. When you do this, you should have a screen layout that looks like the one in Figure 10-2.

This screen layout is pretty similar to the one you created in the earlier example, except that you also have an Outliner window and a Timeline window. The Outliner is helpful for selecting objects in complex scenes that have many, many objects to work with. The Timeline gives you a central place to control the playback of your overall animation. This way, you can use the Ipo Curve Editor to focus on specific detailed animations. Like the Ipo Curve Editor, you can scrub the Timeline by left-clicking in it and dragging your mouse cursor left and right.

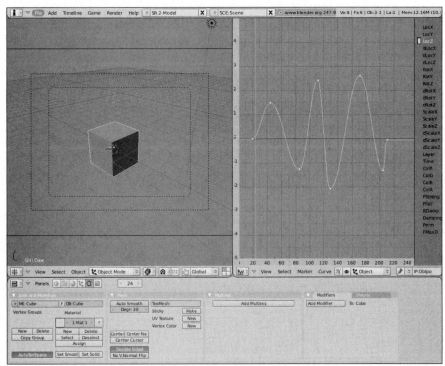

Figure 10-1:
Animating the Z-axis location of the default cube object.

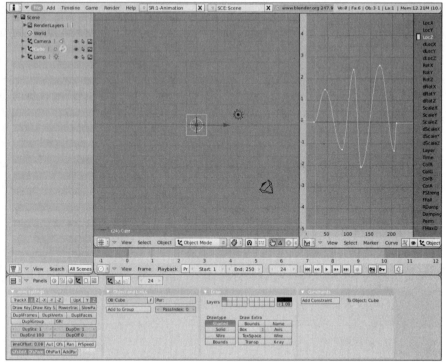

Figure 10-2:
The
Animation
screen
layout in
Blender.

One change I usually like to make to this layout is the addition of another 3D View window split from the Outliner. I set this window to a shaded or textured camera view and remove its header. I do this so that I can use any perspective in the main 3D View window but still retain an idea of what the camera sees. That way, I don't end up animating something that will never be on camera. In this camera-view window, I also disable the Transform Manipulator (Ctrl+Spacebar⇨Enable/Disable). In the main 3D View, I swap out the Translate manipulator for the Rotate manipulator (Ctrl+Spacebar⇨Rotate) and change its coordinate space to Normal (Alt+Spacebar⇨Normal). I do this because normally I can Grab and Scale with the G and S hotkeys pretty quickly, but, often, precise rotation when animating is faster and easier with the Rotate manipulator. Plus, this manipulator doesn't obstruct my view as much as the other ones do. Figure 10-3 shows my modified Animation screen layout.

Working in the Ipo Curve Editor is very similar to working in the 3D View. Middle-clicking moves around your view of the graph and Ctrl+middle-clicking allows you to interactively scale your view of the curve horizontally and vertically at the same time. If you prefer using your scroll wheel, you can navigate the entire graph that way. Plain scrolling zooms in and out, whereas Shift+scrolling moves the graph vertically and Ctrl+scrolling moves it vertically. You can select individual Ipo curves by right-clicking on them or toggle selecting all or no curves by pressing A. Even Border Select works by pressing B and using your mouse to draw a box around the curves you want to select.

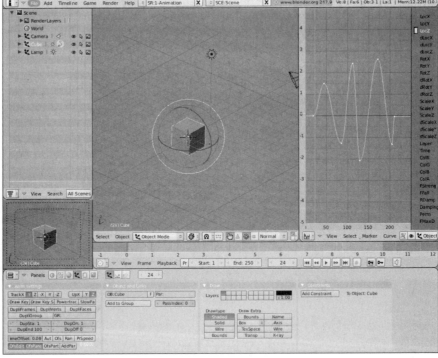

Figure 10-3:
The
Animation
screen lay-
out with a
modification
to allow a
referential
camera
view.

Inserting keys

You might be thinking, "Well, that was pretty neat, but there's got to be a more controlled way of adding control points than Ctrl+left-clicking in the Ipo Curve Editor. It seems awfully imprecise." And if you were thinking that, you'd be completely correct. Although it's possible to work like this, Blender uses a workflow that's a lot more like traditional hand-drawn animation. In traditional animation, a whole animated sequence is planned out ahead of time. Then an animator goes through and draws the primary poses of the character. These drawings are referred to as *keyframes* or *keys*. They're the poses that the character must make in order to most effectively convey the intended motion to the viewer. With the keys drawn, they are handed off to a second set of animators called the *inbetweeners*. These animators are responsible for drawing all of the frames between each of the keys in order to get smooth motion.

Translating this to how work is done in Blender, you should consider yourself the keyframe artist and Blender the inbetweener. Using the example at the beginning of this chapter, every time you Ctrl+left-clicked in the Ipo Curve Editor, you created a keyframe. By interpolating the curve between those keys, Blender creates the in-between frames. Some animation programs refer to this as *tweening*.

To have a workflow that's even more similar to traditional animation, you would prefer to be able to define your keyframes in the 3D View. Then you could use the Ipo Curve Editor to tweak the change from one keyframe to the next. And this is exactly what you can do. In the 3D View, press I to bring up the Insert Key menu, as shown in Figure 10-4.

Figure 10-4:
The Insert
Key menu.

Through this menu, you can create keyframes for the main animatable channels for an object. They are described in more detail here:

- **Loc:** Insert a key for the object's X, Y, and Z location.

- **Rot:** Insert a key for the object's rotation in the X, Y, and Z axes.

- **Scale:** Insert a key for the object's scale in the X, Y, and Z axes.

- **LocRot/LocScale/LocRotScale/RotScale:** Inserts keyframes for various combinations of the previous three values.

- **VisualLoc/VisualRot/VisualLocRot:** Inserts keyframes for location, rotation, or both, but based on where the object is visually located in the scene. These options are explicitly made for use with constraints, which are covered later in this chapter.

- **Layer:** Inserts a keyframe for the layers that the object exists on. Keyframing this channel is a great way to make objects disappear from view. Note that because layers are discrete elements and Blender can't smoothly transition from one to another, the curve for this channel jumps from one value to the next with no smooth interpolation.

- **Available:** If you have already inserted keys for some of your object's channels, choosing this option adds a key for each of those already-existing curves in the Ipo Curve Editor. If there are no curves already created, no keyframes are inserted.

- **Mesh:** This inserts a key for the mesh itself. This is important for shape keys, a topic covered in more detail in Chapter 11.

When Blender sets keyframes for location, rotation, and scale, you should bear in mind which coordinate system the Ipo Curve Editor is using. Location is stored in global coordinates, whereas rotation and scale are stored in the object's local coordinate system.

So to see the basic workflow for animating in Blender, bring up the default scene (Ctrl+X) and use the following steps:

1. **Switch to the Animation screen layout (Ctrl+left arrow).**

2. **Insert an initial location keyframe (I⇨Loc).**

   This creates a keyframe at frame one in your animation. If you look at the Ipo Curve Editor, notice that LocX, LocY, and LocZ are highlighted and have colored blocks next to them.

3. **Move forward ten frames (up arrow).**

   This puts you at frame eleven. The up arrow and down arrow hotkeys move you ten frames forward or backward in time, regardless of the window your mouse cursor is in. To move forward or back one frame at a time, use the left and right arrow keys. Of course, you could also use the Timeline or Ipo Curve Editor to change what frame you are in.

4. **Grab your cube and move it to a different location in 3D space (G).**

5. **Insert a new location keyframe (I⇨Loc).**

   Now you should have curves in the Ipo Curve Editor that describe the motion of the cube.

There is another way to insert keys, and it's actually a little bit easier. It's a feature called Autokey, and like its name indicates, it automatically creates keys when you move, resize, and scale your object. To enable the Autokey feature, look in the Timeline window. Next to the VCR-like controls for controlling animation playback is a button with a red circle on it, like the Record button on a VCR. Figure 10-5 shows this button. Left-click it to activate Autokey. Now you can simply use the Grab (G), Rotate (R), and Scale (S) tools as you move forward in time and keyframes are automatically inserted for you. Pretty sweet, huh?

Figure 10-5:
The Autokey
button in
the Timeline
window.

Some of the other Blender window types allow you to set keys for other attributes as well. For instance, if you bring up the Material buttons and press I with your mouse cursor in that window, a menu with a set of materials-related keyable channels appears. Figure 10-6 shows the different Insert Key menus that appear for the various Buttons windows.

Figure 10-6:
From L to R: Insert Key menus for Lamp, Material, Texture, World, and Physics, and the menu for Editing when a camera is selected.

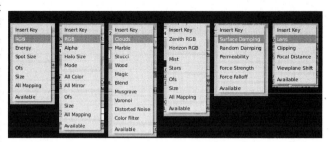

You may notice that if you insert a key using these menus, many times, their curves don't seem to appear in the Ipo Curve Editor. This is because the types of keyable channels have been broken down and organized into seven different possible categories: Object, Material, World, Texture, Shape, Constraint, and Sequence. To show the curves and keyable channels in these categories, look in the Ipo Curve Editor's header. By default, you're looking at the Object curves, so there's a button in the header next to the Ipo datablock button that says Object. Left-click that button to see and choose from the other available Ipo types. Figure 10-7 shows what this menu looks like.

Figure 10-7:
The Ipo Types menu in the header of the Ipo Curve Editor.

Editing motion curves

After you know how to add keyframes to your scene, the next logical thing to do is tweak, edit, and modify those keyframes as well as the interpolation between them. This, too, happens in the Ipo Curve Editor. Earlier in this chapter, I said the Ipo Curves Editor is similar to the 3D View and that individual motion curves could be selected by right-clicking or by using the B key for border selecting. Well, it goes further than that. Not only can you select motion curves in the Ipo Curve Editor, but you can Tab into Edit mode with them and edit them like a 2D Bézier curve object in the 3D View. The only constraint on this is that Ipo Curves cannot cross themselves. Having a curve that describes motion in time do a loopty-loop doesn't logically make any sense.

For more detailed descriptions of the hotkeys and controls for editing Bézier curves in Blender, have a look at Chapter 6. Selecting and moving control point handles, as well as the hotkeys for Free/Aligned (H), Auto (Shift+H), and Vector (V) handles all work as expected. However, because these curves are specially purposed for animation, you have a few additional controls over them. For instance, you can control the type of interpolation between control points on a selected curve by pressing T or going to Curve⟲Interpolation Mode in the Ipo Curve Editor's header. Doing so gives you the following options, as shown in Figure 10-8:

- ✔ **Constant:** This is sometimes called a *step function* because a series of them look like stair steps. Basically, this interpolation type keeps the value of one control point until it gets to the next one, where it instantly changes.

- ✔ **Linear:** The interpolation from one control point to the next is a completely straight line. This is similar to changing both control points to have Vector handles.

- ✔ **Bézier:** The default interpolation type. This uses Auto handles on the control points to smoothly transition from one to the next. In traditional animation, this is referred to *easing in* and *easing out* of a keyframe.

Figure 10-8:
Changing the inter-polation type on a selected Ipo curve.

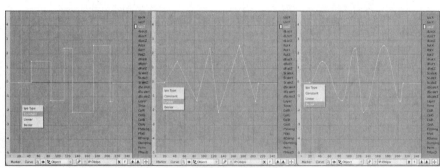

You can also change what a selected Ipo curve does before and after its first and last keyframes. This is called the curve's *Extend Mode* and you can change it by pressing E or navigating to Curve⇨Extend Mode in the Ipo Curve Editor's header. When you do this, notice that there are four possible choices:

- ✔ **Constant:** This is the default setting. The values of the first and last control points are maintained into infinity beyond those points.

- ✔ **Extrapolation:** Rather than maintaining the same value in perpetuity before and after the first and last control points, this extend mode takes the direction of the curve in those control points and extends the curve that way.

- ✔ **Cyclic:** A Cyclic extend mode takes the entire shape of the curve from the first control point to the last one and repeats it before and after those "control points so that the same motion loops over and over forever.

- ✔ **Cyclic Extrapolation:** This option combines the previous two extend modes. So the same motion loops before and after the first and last keyframes, but it loops in the direction that the Ipo curve is going when it gets to those points.

Figure 10-9 shows the menu for the different type of extend modes, as well as what each one looks like with a simple Ipo curve.

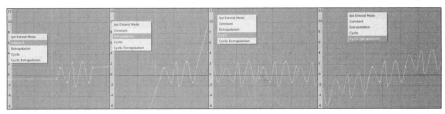

Figure 10-9:
The four different extend modes you can have on Ipo curves.

If you have an object with a high number of animation curves, it may be help-ful to hide extraneous curves from view so you can focus on the ones you truly want to edit. To toggle a curve's visibility, Shift+left-click its name in the keyable channel list along the right side of the Ipo Curve Editor. Doing so shows its name in either white text or black text. Black text means the curve is hidden, whereas white text means it's visible. Also, if the channel has a color swatch to the left of it, then you know it's been keyed. That color swatch is useful for selecting the curve (left-click the swatch) as well as visu-ally distinguishing one curve from another because the color in the swatch is the color of the curve in the graph of the Ipo Curve Editor.

If you need explicit control over the placement of a curve or a control point, the Ipo Curve Editor has a floating panel like the 3D View has. You bring it up the same way too: either press N or choose View⇨Channel Properties. With this floating panel, you can enter the exact value that you would like to set your selected curve, control point, or keyframe to. Figure 10-10 shows the Channel Properties floating panel in the Ipo Curve Editor. Note that the panel has a heading that says "Transform Properties". It's a little user-interface inconsistency in Blender. Just know that they're the same thing.

Figure 10-10:
The Channel
Properties
floating
panel (N)
in the Ipo
Curve
Editor.

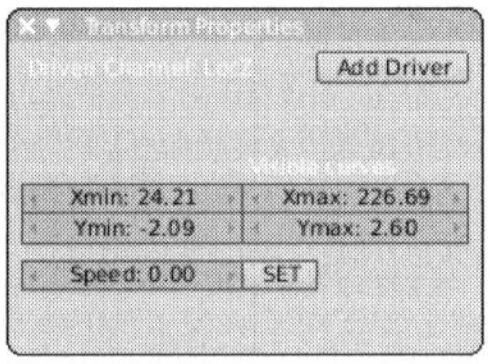

There's another really helpful feature for editing curves in the Ipo Curve Editor. Often, you may run into the occasion where you need to edit all of the control points in a single keyframe to change the overall timing of your animation. It may be tempting to select all curves with the A key, Tab into Edit mode, and use Border Select (B) to select the strip of control points you want to move around. However, there's an cleaner and easier way to do this. Rather than go through that process, press K in the Ipo Curve Editor or choose View⇨Show Keys. This shows your keys in the graph as a series of yellow vertical lines. These keys can be selected (right-click) and moved around in the graph by pressing G. You can even duplicate keys by pressing Shift+D.

When you're moving around keys or even control points in the Ipo Curve Editor, you should hold down Ctrl. This ensures that you've moving them around in frame-length increments. It's a good practice to make sure your keyframes actually happen on the frame, rather than between frames. If you're ever unsure as to whether a key is on the frame, select it (right-click) in the Ipo Curve Editor and press Shift+S⇨To Frame. This snaps the selected keys to their nearest frame.

The Show Keys functionality also has one more trick up its sleeve. Move your mouse cursor into the 3D View and press K. Doing this actually shows ghosted wireframes of your object's keyframes. This is kind of a 3D version of something called _onionskinning_ in traditional animation. This can give you a very clear picture of your entire animation at a glance. But wait, it gets better! Note that if you right-click one of the yellow key lines in the Ipo Curve Editor, the corresponding key is also highlighted in the 3D View. Now you can use your Grab (G), Rotate (R), and Scale (S) hotkeys to interactively edit and adjust that keyframe while the other keyframes are in view. How's that for totally awesome? Figure 10-11 shows the Show Keys feature in action.

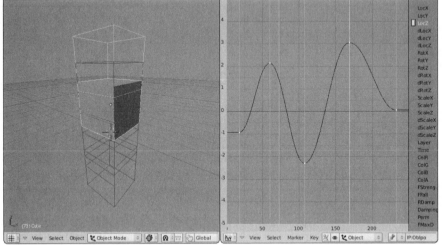

Figure 10-11:
"Press K in the 3D View to show your object's keyframes and make them directly editable.

Table 10-1 covers some of the most common hotkeys and mouse actions used to control animation in the Ipo Curve Editor.

Table 10-1	Commonly Used Hotkeys and Mouse Actions for the Ipo Curve Editor		
Mouse Action	**Description**	**Hotkey**	**Description**
Left-click graph	Move time cursor	Alt+A	Playback animation
Left-click channel	Hide/Reveal channel (Shift+left-click for multiple)	E	Extend Mode
Left-click swatch	Select channel	K	Show keys
Right-click	Select channel	O	Clean Ipo curves
Middle-click	Pan graph	Shift+O	Smooth Ipo curves
Ctrl+middle-click	Scale graph	N	Channel Properties
Scroll	Zoom graph	Shift+S	Snap Menu
Shift+scroll	Pan graph vertically	T	Ipo Type
Ctrl+scroll	Pan graph horizontally	Home	Fit curves to graph

Using Constraints Effectively

Occasionally I get into conversations with people who assume that because there's a computer involved, doing good CG animation takes less time than traditional animation techniques. In most cases, this is not true. High quality work takes roughly the same amount of time, regardless of the technique. The time is just spent in different places. Whereas in traditional animation, a very large portion of the time is spent drawing the inbetween frames, CG animation lets the computer handle that. However, traditional animators don't have to worry as much about optimizing for render times, tweaking and re-tweaking simulated effects, or modeling, texturing, and rigging characters.

That said, computer animation does give you the opportunity to cut corners in places and make your life as an animator much simpler. One of the features that fits this description perfectly are constraints. Literally speaking, a *constraint* is a limitation put on one object by another, allowing the unconstrained object to control the behavior of the constrained one. The simplest example of a type of constraint is parenting. This is covered in more detail in Chapter 4, but as a quick example, bring up the default scene in Blender (Ctrl+X). Now Shift+right-click the Lamp so both it and the cube are selected and the Lamp is the active object. Press Ctrl+P⇨Make Parent. After this, select just the Lamp (right-click) and Rotate (R) it. The cube now rotates around the Lamp because it's the child object. If you insert keyframes for the Lamp's rotation, you'd automatically be animating the cube without really doing any extra work! This parent-child relationship is the very simplest form of constraint in Blender. With constraints like this one, and ones that are even more powerful, you can do quite a lot without doing much at all. Animation is hard work; it's worth it to be lazy whenever you can.

Although parenting with the Ctrl+P hotkey combination is a constraint in the literal since of the word, it's used in Blender for doing more things than simply binding the location, orientation, and size of one object to another. For that reason, it's not a constraint like the ones discussed later in this chapter. In fact, to see the actual constraints that you do have available to you, go to the Object buttons (F7) and left-click the Add Constraint button in the Constraints panel. When you do this, you see the menu that looks like the one in Figure 10-12.

Because of limitations to this book's page count, I can't cover the function of each and every constraint in full detail. However, the end of this chapter gives some usage examples for some of the more frequently used constraints.

Figure 10-12:
The types of constraints available by default within Blender.

The all-powerful Empty!

Of all the different types of objects available to you in Blender, none of them are as useful or versatile in animation as the humble Empty. It's not much: just a little set of axes that indicate a position, orientation, and size in 3D space. It doesn't even show up when you render. However, this means that it's an ideal choice for use as control object and it's a phenomenal way to take advantage of constraints. To illustrate this, allow me to use simple parenting as an example again.

One of the things that 3D modelers like to have is a *turnaround* render of the model they create. Basically, it's like taking the model, placing it on a turntable, and spinning it in front of the camera. It's a great way to show off all sides of the model. Now, for simple models, you can just select the model, rotate it in the global Z-axis, and you're done. However, what if the model consists of many objects, or for some reason everything is at a strange angle that looks odd when spun around the Z-axis? Selecting and rotating all of those little objects can get time-consuming and annoying. A better way of handling it is with the following rig:

1. **Add an Empty (spacebar⇨Add⇨Empty).**

2. **Grab the Empty and move it to somewhere at the center of the model (G).**

3. **Select the camera and position it so the model is in the center of view (right-click, G).**

   It would be wise to aim the camera roughly at the location of the Empty.

4. **Add the Empty to your selection (Shift+right-click).**

   This makes the Empty the Active object in the selection.

5. **Make the Empty the camera's parent (Ctrl+P⇨Make Parent).**

6. **Select the Empty and insert a rotation keyframe (right-click, I⇨Rot).**

7. **Move forward in time 50 frames.**

8. **Rotate the Empty 90 degrees in the Z-axis and insert a new rotation keyframe (R⇨Z⇨90, I⇨Rot).**

    In doing this, you should notice that the camera obediently matches the Empty's rotation.

9. **Bring up the Ipo Curve Editor and set the Extend Mode for the RotZ channel to Extrapolate (Shift+F6, right-click, E⇨Extrapolate).**

10. **Switch to the camera view and playback the animation (Numpad 0, Alt+A).**

    In the 3D View, you should be seeing what appears to be your model spinning in front of your camera. Congratulations, you've made a turnaround.

In this setup, the Empty behaves as the control for the camera. Imagine that there's a beam extending from the Empty's center to the camera's center and that rotating the Empty is the way to move that beam. And you can add to this. Suppose you wanted the Lamp to stay with the camera, rather than remaining static throughout the turnaround. You could solve this by parenting (Ctrl+P) the lamp to either the Empty or the Camera. Either way gets you the results you're looking for.

Copying the movement of another object

Using simple parenting is helpful in quite a few instances, but it's often not as flexible as you need it to be. You can't control or animate the parenting influence or just use the parent object's rotation without inheriting the location and scale as well. And you can't have movement of the parent object in the global X-axis influence the child's local X-axis location. More often than not, you need these sorts of refined controls rather than the somewhat ham-fisted Ctrl+P parenting.

Copy location, scale, and rotation

To this end, there are a set of constraints that provide you with just this sort of control. They are the Copy Location, Copy Rotation, and Copy Scale constraints. Figure 10-13 shows what each of these constraints look like when added in the Constraints panel.

You can mix and match multiple constraints on a single object in a way that's very similar to the way you can add multiple modifiers to an object. So if you need both a Copy Location and a Copy Rotation constraint, just add both. After you add them, you can change which order they come in the stack to make sure they suit your needs.

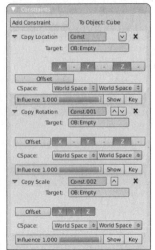

Figure 10-13:
The Copy
Location,
Copy
Rotation,
and Copy
Scale
constraint
controls.

Words and picture aren't always the best way of explaining how constraints work. It's often more to your benefit to see them in action. To that end, CD-ROM that accompanies this book has a few example files that illustrate how these constraints work. It's worth it to load them up in Blender and play with them to really get a good sense for how these very powerful tools work.

Probably the most apparent thing about these constraints is how similar their options are to one another. The most critical setting, however, is the object that you name in the Target field. If you're using an Empty as your control object, this is where you type that Empty's name. Unless you do so, the Constraint Name field at the top of the constraint block remains bright red and the constraint simply won't work.

Next up is the Offset button. This is useful if you've already adjusted your object's location, rotation, or scale prior to adding the constraint. By default, this feature is off, so the constrained object mirrors the target object's behavior completely and exactly. With it enabled, though, the object adds the target object's transformation to the constrained object's already set location, rotation, or scale values. The best way to see this is to create a Copy Location constraint with the following steps:

1. **Start with the default scene (Ctrl+X).**

2. **Grab the default cube to a different location (G).**

3. **Add an Empty (spacebar⇨Add⇨Empty).**

4. **Select the cube and put a Copy Location constraint on it (right-click, F7⇨Constraints⇨Add Constraint⇨Copy Location).**

   When you do this, the cube automatically snaps directly to the Empty's location.

5. Left-click the Offset button in the Constraints panel.

The cube goes back to its original position. Grabbing (G) the Empty influences the cube's location from there.

To the right of the Offset button are a series of six buttons, with the X, Y, and Z buttons already enabled, separated by disabled buttons with minus signs on them. These buttons control which axis or axes the target object influences. If the axis button is enabled and the minus button next to it is also enabled, the target object has an inverted influence on the constrained object in that axis. Using the previous Copy Location example, if you left-click the X button and then Grab the Empty and move it in the X-axis (G⇨X), the cube remains perfectly still. However, left-clicking the X button as well as the minus button next to it causes the cube to translate in an opposite X direction when you move the target Empty.

Beyond these options, one of the most useful settings that's available to all constraints is at the bottom of each constraint block. I'm talking about the Influence slider. This slider works on a scale from zero to one, with zero being the least amount of influence and one being the largest amount. With this, you have the capability of just partially copying the target object's attributes. There's more to it, though. Notice the Show and Key buttons to the right of the slider. With the Key button, you can animate the influence of the constraint. The show button makes the constraint curves visible in an Ipo Curve Editor window if you have one open. Say you're working on an animation that involves a character with telekinetic powers using his ability to make a ball fly to his hand. You can do that by animating the influence of a Copy Location constraint on the ball. The character's hand is the target and you start with zero influence. Then, when you want the ball to fly to his hand, you increase the influence to one and set a new keyframe. BAM! Telekinetic character!

When setting keys for constraints, the Ipo curves for the influence doesn't show up in the default Ipo Curve Editor. To see these curves, either press the Show button next to the Influence slider or use the Ipo Type menu in the Ipo Curve Editor's header.

It's in your best interest to use the Show button to see the constraint Ipo. The reason for this is that if there are multiple animated constraints on the same object, left-clicking Show insures that you're looking at the right one.

The CSpace buttons in these constraints are pretty interesting, although they have a somewhat specialized use. Specifically speaking, they only really have any effect if the constrained object is also parented to an object that is not the target object. Consider the previous offset Copy Location example, but make a few changes:

1. Rotate the target Empty an arbitrary amount in the Z-axis (R⇨Z).

Somewhere around 30 degrees should be fine — just enough so that it's different from the global coordinate system.

2. **Add a new Empty to the scene (spacebar⊅Add⊅Empty).**

3. **Grab the new Empty and move it so that it's not near the origin (G).**

   If you want some specific numbers, bring up the Transform Properties floating panel and set LocX to -2, LocY to 2, and LocZ to 7.

4. **Rotate the new Empty some arbitrary amount in the Z-axis (R⊅).**

   Again, no specific number is necessary — just something that offsets it from the global coordinate space.

5. **Parent the cube to the new Empty (right-click the cube, Shift+right-click the new Empty, Ctrl+P⊅Make Parent).**

Now with the above set up, you can play with the CSpace options. The left button controls the coordinate space in which the constraint evaluates the target and the right button controls the coordinate space in which the constraint evaluates the constrained, or owner, object. With both of these values set to World Space, the constraint behaves as you would expect. Move the target Empty and the cube obediently follows along. However, left-click the right button and change the Owner Space to Local (Without Parent) Space. Now, select the target Empty and move it in the global X-axis (right-click, G⊅X). Notice that the cube moves, but not quite like you'd expect. Rather than move along the global X-axis with the target Empty, the cube actually moves along its local X-axis. That, in a nutshell, is what you can do by changing the CSpace buttons. This gets used quite a bit more when creating animation rigs using Blender's armatures. There's more information on that in Chapter 11.

The Child Of constraint

Okay, so I lied a little bit when I said you couldn't control or animate the influence of a parent-child relationship in Blender. That was a half-truth. It's true that if you use Ctrl+P to make one object the parent of another, no additional controls are available to you. *However*, if you add a Child Of constraint, the situation changes a bit. Figure 10-14 shows that if you create a parent-child relationship between objects using this constraint, you have quite a few controls available to you.

Figure 10-14: Options for the Child Of constraint.

After you type in the name of the object you wish to use as the parent, you can choose any combination of location, rotation, and scale channels in the X, Y, and Z axes for the parent relationship. You can even take advantage of having an offset from where the standard parent-child relationship would put your object. And, like the other constraints, you can control and animate how much this constraint has an effect on your object by using the Influence slider and keying its values over time.

Another unique feature of this constraint is the VG field that shows up after you type in a valid object in the OB field. In the VG field, you can type the name of a vertex group in the parent mesh. When you do this, the constrained child object is the child of those specific vertices. To create a vertex group, tab into Edit mode on the parent object and select a couple of vertices. Then switch to the Editing buttons (F9) and left-click the New button under Vertex Groups in the Link and Materials button. This creates a new vertex group called Group. To make the vertices you've selected part of the group, left-click the Assign button. This is covered in more detail in Chapter 11. Figure 10-15 shows a Suzanne head parented to a vertex group consisting of a single vertex on a circle mesh.

In many ways, this constraint is a much more flexible and powerful way of parenting than using Ctrl+P. Of course, regular parenting can do some things that this constraint can't, like Dupliverts. Perhaps, however, future versions of Blender will merge the functions of these two features.

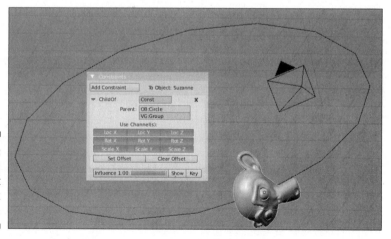

Figure 10-15:
Parenting an object to a vertex group.

Putting limits on an object

Often when animating objects, it's helpful to prevent objects from being moved, rotated, or scaled beyond a certain extent. Say you're animating a character trapped inside a glass dome. It would be helpful to you as an animator if Blender forced you to keep that character within that space. Sure you *could* just pay attention to where your character is and visually make sure he doesn't accidentally go farther than he should be allowed, but why do the extra work if you can have Blender do it for you? Figure 10-16 shows the constraint options for most of the limiting constraints Blender offers you.

Figure 10-16:
The options
for the
limiting
constraints
that Blender
offers you.

Descriptions of what each of these constraints does are below:

✓ **Limit Location/Rotation/Scale:** Unlike most of the other constraints, these three constraints don't have a target object that they're constrained to. They're just limitations on what the object can do within its own space. For any of them, you can define minimum and maximum limits in the X, Y, and Z axes. After you've defined the limit, you enable it by left-clicking the button for that limit next to it. The For Transform button that's in each of these constraints can be pretty helpful. To better understand what it does, enable the Transform Properties floating panel in the 3D View. If you have limits and For Transform is not enabled, the values in the Transform Properties panel change even after you reach the limits defined by the constraint. However, if you enable For Transform, the value in the Transform Properties panel is clipped to the limitations you defined with the constraint.

✓ **Limit Distance:** This constraint is similar to the previous ones except it relates to the distance from the centerpoint of a target object. The Clamp Region menu gives you three ways to use this distance:

• **Inside:** The constrained object can only move in the sphere of space defined by the Distance value.

• **Outside:** The constrained object can never enter the sphere of space defined by the Distance value.

• **Surface:** The constrained object is always the same distance from the target object, no more and no less.

✓ **Floor:** The Floor constraint uses the centerpoint of a target object to define a plane that the centerpoint of the constrained object can't move beyond. So, technically, you can use this constraint to define more than a floor; you can also use it to define walls and a ceiling as well. One thing to keep in mind is that this constraint defines a plane. If your target object is an uneven surface, it will not use that object's geometry to define the limit of the constrained object, just it's centerpoint. Despite this limitation, this constraint is actually quite useful. This is especially true if you enable the Use Rot button. Doing that allows the constrained object to recognize the rotation of the target object, so you can have an inclined floor if you like.

When animating while using constraints, particularly limiting constraints, it's in your best interest to insert keyframes using the VisualLoc and VisualRot. This sets the keyframe to where the object is located visually, within the limits of the constraint, rather than how you actually transformed the object. For instance, assume you have a Floor constraint on an object that you're animating to fall from some height and land on a floor plane that's even with the XY grid. For the landing, you Grab (G) object and move your mouse cursor 4 Blender units below the XY grid. Of course, because of the constraint, your object stops following the mouse when it hits the floor. Now, if you insert a regular Loc keyframe here, the Z-axis location of the object is set to -4.0 even though the object can't go below zero. However, if you insert a VisualLoc key, the object's Z-axis location is set to what you see it as, zero.

Tracking the motion of another object

Another set of constraints that are helpful for animation are tracking constraints. Their basic purpose is to make the constrained object point either directly at or in the general direction of the target object. They're useful for things like controlling the eye movement of characters or building mechanical rigs like pistons. Figure 10-17 shows the options for three of Blender's tracking constraints.

Figure 10-17: Control options for Blender's tracking constraints.

Descriptions of each of these constraints are below:

✔ **Track To:** Of these constraints, this one is the most straightforward. In other programs, this constraint may be referred to as the Look At constraint, and that's what it does. It forces the constrained object to point at the target object. The best way to see this would be to load the default scene (Ctrl+X) and add a Track To constraint to the camera with the target object being the cube. Now, no matter where you move the camera to, it always points at the cube's centerpoint. By left-clicking the X, Y, and Z buttons next to the To and Up labels, you can control how the constrained object points to the target.

✔ **Locked Track:** The Locked Track constraint is similar to the Track To constraint, with one large exception: It only allows the constrained object to rotate on a single axis. This means that the constrained object points in the general direction of the target, but not necessarily directly at it. A good way to think about this is to imagine you're wearing a neck brace. With the brace on, you can't look up or down; you can only rotate your head left and right. So if a bird flies overhead, you can't look up to see it pass. All you can do is turn around and hope to see the bird flying away.

✔ **Stretch To:** This constraint isn't exactly a tracking constraint like Track To and Locked Track, but it's behavior is similar. It makes the constrained object point toward the target object like the Track To constraint. However, it also changes the constrained objects scale relative to the distance that the target is away from it, stretching that object toward the target. And it can even try to preserve the volume of the constrained object to make it seem like it's really stretching. This is a great constraint for cartoony effects as well as controlling organic deformations such as rubber balls and the human tongue. On a complex character rig, you can use the Stretch To constraint to help simulate muscle bulging.

Chapter 11

Rigging: The Art of Building an Animatable Puppet

. . . .

In This Chapter

▶ Making shape keys

▶ Taking advantage of hooks

▶ Working with armatures to control characters

▶ Building a simple character rig

. . . .

*W*hen it comes to character animation, a character is often a single seamless mesh. This makes it virtually impossible to animate that character with any detailed movement using the object animation techniques in Chapter 10. I mean, you can move the whole character mesh at once from one location to another, but you can't make the character smile or wriggle her toes or even bend her arms. You could break the mesh apart and use a complex set of parenting and constraints, but then you lose the nice seamless nature of the mesh.

What you really want to do is find ways to animate specific parts of the mesh in a controlled way without tearing the mesh apart. To do that, you need to create a rig for your character. A *rig* is an underlying structure for your mesh that allows you to control how it moves. It's an integral part of modern computer animation and, if it's done well, it makes the life of an animator monumentally easier. Think about it like turning your 3D mesh into a remote control puppet. This chapter explains the various tools and techniques used to create rigs. Then you can create a rig for nearly any object in Blender and have a blast animating it.

Creating Shape Keys

If your mesh, whether it's a character or a tree or a basketball, is to be animated in a detailed way, it has to deform from its original shape to a new and different shape. If you know what this new shape looks like, you can model it ahead of time. As an example, say you have a cartoony character, maybe the head of a certain monkey. You know that you're going to need her eyes to bulge out because all cartoon characters' eyes do this. To do this in Blender, you create a *shape key*, sometimes called a *morph target* in other programs. A rough outline of the process goes something like this (the next section in this chapter goes into more detail):

1. **Start with your original mesh.**

2. **Edit the vertices of the original mesh *without creating new geometry* to the new pose you want to use.**

   In our example, you would model the character's eyes all bulgy. (Yes, *bulgy* is a real word. I think.)

3. **Record this new arrangement of your vertices as a shape key to be used later when you animate.**

Creating new shapes

So that's the general example, but where are the actual controls? They're in the Editing buttons (F9) in the Shapes panel. Figure 11-1 shows three different states for the Shapes panel. By default, it looks pretty innocent and empty with just the one Add Shape Key button. However, when you left-click that button, you get buttons to control the Basis shape, or the original shape that other shape keys relate to. Left-clicking the Add Shape Key button a second time gives you another set of controls that controls the change from the Basis shape to this one, named Key 1.

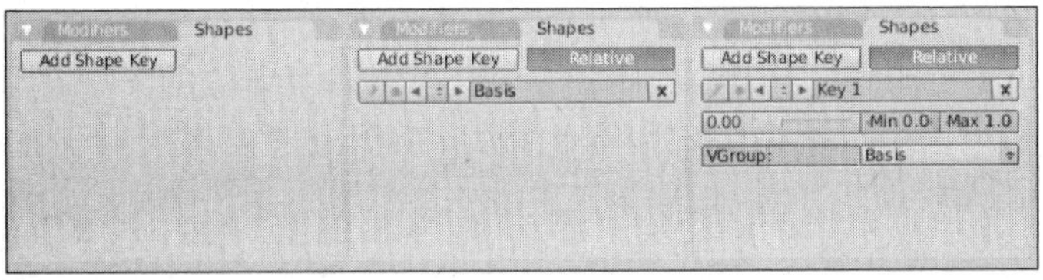

Figure 11-1:
The three different sets of options that the Shapes panel can provide you.

The best way to see how all of this works is to go through a practical example. Staying with the "bug-eyed monkey" theme, use Suzanne as your test subject, and go through the following steps:

1. **Start with the default scene and delete the cube (Ctrl+X, right-click the cube, X).**

2. **Add Suzanne, give her a Subsurf modifier, set her smooth, and rotate her 90 degrees around the X-axis (spacebar⇨Add⇨Mesh⇨Monkey, Ctrl+1, Tab⇨W⇨Set Smooth⇨Tab, R⇨X⇨90).**

3. **Change to the front view (Numpad 1).**

4. **Add a shape key (F9⇨Shapes⇨Add Shape Key).**

   For quicker access, you can use the I⇨Mesh hotkey sequence. This creates your Basis shape. The other shapes that you create will be relative to this one.

5. **Tab into Edit mode and change the mesh to have bulged eyes.**

   Be sure that as you do this, you *do not add any extra vertices* to the mesh. The shape should be defined by moving around the vertices you already have. A quick way to get make Suzanne's eyes bulge is to move your mouse cursor over each eye and press L to select just the vertices there. Then, with the Proportional Edit Tool (O) turned on, Scale (S) the eyes.

6. **While still in Edit mode, add a new shape key (I⇨Mesh).**

   Now the Shapes panel should look like the last one in Figure 11-1. You've created Key 1. If you want, you can rename it in the Shapes panel by left-clicking its name field. I named mine "Eye Bulge."

7. **Tab back to Object mode.**

   Figure 11-2 illustrates this process.

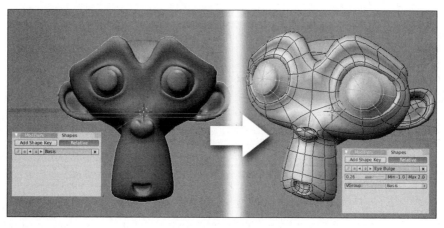

Figure 11-2: Creating a bug-eyed shape key for Suzanne.

This process creates two shape keys, the Basis and Eye Bulge. Using the slider in the Shapes panel, you can smoothly transition from the Basis shape to the Eye Bulge shape. A value of zero means that Eye Bulge has no influence and you just have the Basis, whereas a value of one means that you're fully at the Eye Bulge shape. But here's where things get really cool. Notice the Min and Max values to the left of the slider. The Min is set to 0.0 and the Max is set to 1.0. Just for kicks, change the Max value to 2.0 and pull the slider all the way to the right. Doing this pushes your bulged eyes larger than your actual shape key made them. Now change the Min value to -1.0 and pull the slider to the left. Now Suzanne's eyes pinch in to a point smaller than the Basis pose. Figure 11-3 shows the results of these changes. This is a great way to provide even more extreme shapes for your characters without having to do any additional shape key modeling. How's that for cool?

Figure 11-3:
Suzanne with excessively bulged and pinched eyes, just by changing the minimum and maximum values for a single shape key.

Mixing shapes

From this point, you can create additional shape keys for the mesh. Say you want to have a shape key of Suzanne's mouth getting bigger, like she's screaming because her eyes have gotten so huge. If that's the case, the first thing you want to do is switch back to the Basis key. To do this, use the left/right arrows next to the key's name in the Shapes panel. You can also left-click the up/down arrow button and choose Basis from the list. The reason for doing this is because unless you're doing something special, it's a good idea to have most of your shapes based on the Basis. Otherwise, you may end up accidentally over-amplifying a shape key or nullifying it. When you're back at the Basis key, the process is about the same as before:

1. **Tab into Edit mode and model the mouth open with the existing vertices.**

   One thing to note here is that you're not really touching Suzanne's eyes. You're just editing the mouth to get bigger.

2. **While still in Edit mode, add a new shape key (I⇨Mesh).**

   Feel free to name this key whatever you want. I called mine "Scream."

3. **Tab back into Object mode.**

   Figure 11-4 shows the results of this process.

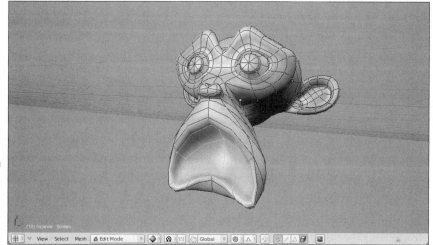

Now that you have the Scream shape key, you can freely mix it with the Eye Bulge shape key or you can have Suzanne screaming with her regular, bulge-free eyes. The choice is yours. You have the flexibility here to mix and match your shape keys as it pleases you. And animating the mesh to use these keys is really easy. Split off an Ipo Curve Editor window from your 3D view and change the Ipo Type to Shape by left-clicking the drop-down button in the Ipo Curve Editor's header that says Object. You should notice that you have two animation channels here with the names you gave your shape keys. Scrub the timeline cursor forward in time and adjust the sliders in the Shapes panel. When you do this, new keys are added to the curves in the Ipo Curve Editor. Now you can freely scrub the timeline and watch Suzanne bulge and scream to your complete delight. Figure 11-5 shows a screenshot of me having exactly this kind of fun.

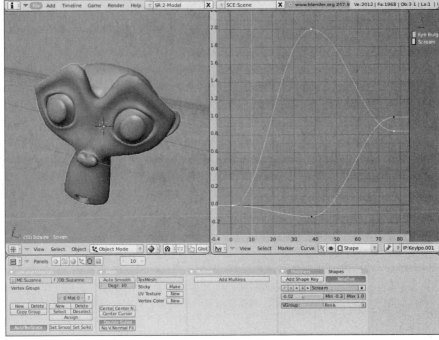

Figure 11-5:
Animating
shape keys
with the
Shapes
panel
and the
Ipo Curve
Editor.

Knowing where shape keys are helpful

Now, you *could* do an entire animation using shape keys. But do I recommend doing that? No. There are other ways to control your meshes that may give you more natural movement for things like animating arms and legs. That said, shape keys are the perfect choice for things that can't be done with these other means (or, at least, that are very difficult). One big one is facial animation. The way parts of the face wrinkle up and move around is pretty difficult to re-create without modeling those deformations in. Furrowed brows, squinty eyes, natural-looking smiles, and *phonemes*, or mouth shapes for lip-syncing, are where shape keys shine. You can also team them up with other controls discussed later in this chapter to achieve cool effects like cartoon stretchiness, muscle bulges, and morphing objects from one shape to another.

Adding Hooks

Shapes work well for getting specific pre-defined deformations, but they can be pretty limiting if you want to have a little bit looser control over your mesh. It's also not as easy to use them on curve and surface objects. For these sorts of situations, we have another control mechanism: hooks. *Hooks* are a special kind of modifier that takes a set of vertices or control points and binds them to be controlled by another object, usually an Empty.

Creating new hooks

The workflow for adding a hook is pretty straightforward. You Tab into Edit mode and select one or more vertices or control points. Then you press Ctrl+H⟹Add, To New Empty. When you do this, an empty is created at a location that's the middle point of all your selected vertices or control points. You get a new modifier added to the Modifiers panel in the Editing buttons (F9), as shown in Figure 11-6.

Figure 11-6:
Control
options for
the Hook
modifier.

You may try to find the Hook modifier as a selectable option in the list of available modifiers in the Modifiers panel. Don't look too hard; you won't find it. Because it requires you to actively select vertices or control points for the hook to control, the Hook modifier can only be added using Ctrl+H in the 3D View.

Tab back into object mode and transform the hook. When you do, all the vertices or control points that you assigned to the hook move with it. And with the options in the Hook modifier, you can control how much influence the hook has over these vertices or control points. The following example should give you a clearer understanding of this:

1. **Start with the default scene in Blender (Ctrl+X).**

2. **Select the cube and Tab into Edit mode.**

   All of the cube's vertices should be selected by default. If they are not, press A until they are.

3. **Do a multi-subdivide with four cuts (W⟹Subdivide Multi⟹Number of Cuts: 4).**

4. **Select one of the cube's corner vertices (right-click).**

5. **Press Numpad+ a few times to increase the vertex selection.**

6. **Add a new hook (Ctrl+H⟹Add, To New Empty).**

7. **Tab back into Object mode.**

   At this point, behavior is as expected. If you select and move the Empty, all of the vertices that you assigned to the hook move with it, like they were parented to the Empty.

8. **Increase the Falloff value in the Hook modifier to 2.0 (F9⇨Modifiers⇨Hook-Empty⇨Falloff: 2.0).**

   Now when you select and transform the Empty, the way the vertices follow it is much smoother, kind of like when you're modeling with the Proportional Edit Tool enabled. For additional kicks, do the next step.

9. **Add a Subsurf modifier to the cube and have it drawn smooth (Ctrl+1, F9⇨Link and Materials⇨Set Smooth).**

   Now the transition is even smoother, as shown in Figure 11-7.

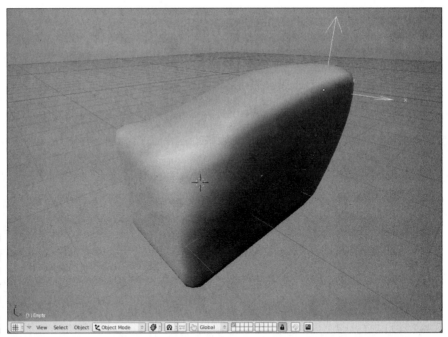

Figure 11-7:
A cube smoothly deformed by a hook.

 Does it bug you a bit that Blender placed the hook in the middle of your mesh? It would be easier to select if it were closer to the corner. Fortunately, the hook menu and modifier give you the option to do just that. There are two things that you can do. First, you can simply reposition the empty at a more acceptable location. And second, you can actually move the center of influence for the hook itself. The next example uses your smooth cube from before and does both of these things.

1. **Select the cube and Tab into Edit mode.**

2. **Select the corner vertex of the cube that you selected in the last example.**

3. **Snap the 3D cursor to this vertex (Shift+S⇨Cursor⇨Selection).**

4. **Tab back into Object mode and select the Empty.**

5. **Snap the Empty to the location of the 3D cursor (Shift+S⇨Selection⇨Cursor).**

   This deforms the cube, but don't worry about that.

6. **Select the cube again and Tab into Edit mode.**

7. **Clear the hook offset (Ctrl+H⇨Clear Offset⇨Hook-Empty).**

8. **Tab back into Object mode.**

   Now the hook performs like before, but with the Empty sitting outside of the mesh, making it easier to select and visualize.

9. **Select the cube and left-click the Recenter button in its modifier options (F9⇨Modifiers⇨Hook-Empty⇨Recenter).**

   This sets the hook center to the same location as the Empty. Now when you transform the Empty, you have a slightly different sort of deformation that points directly at the Empty's center and looks quite a bit nicer, in my opinion. Figure 11-8 shows these steps visually.

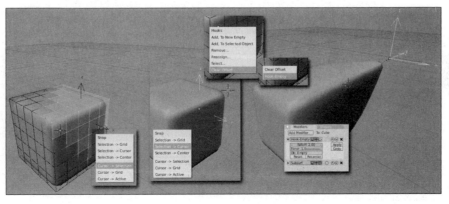

Figure 11-8:
Moving the hook Empty and recentering the hook's location.

Knowing where hooks are helpful

The best use for hooks is for large organic deformations. Like shape keys, they're nice for creating muscle bulges and cartoony stretching. You can even use them along with shape keys. Because shape keys always use the same shape as the basis for deformation, adding a hook can give it a little bit more variety. For example, in the bug-eyed Suzanne example that you did for shape keys, you could add a hook for one of the eyes so it bulges more than the other one. It's touches like these that can give more *character* to your 3D characters.

The other great use for hooks is in animating curves. All of the things in the previous examples work for curves and surfaces as well as meshes. If you have a curve that you're using as a character's tail, you can add a hook at each control point and then you can animate that tail moving around.

Using Armatures: Skeletons in the Mesh

Shape keys and hooks are great ways to deform a mesh, but the problem with them is that both are lacking a good underlying structure. They're great for big, cartoony stretching and deformation, but for a more structured deformation, like an arm bending at the elbow joint, the motion that they produce is pretty unnatural-looking. To solve this, 3D computer animation took a page from one of its meatspace contemporaries, stop-motion animation. *Stop-motion animation* involves small sculptures with a metal skeleton underneath them, referred to as an *armature*. The armature gives the model both structure and a mechanism for making and holding poses. Blender has the same thing and it too is called an armature.

To add an armature to your scene, go to the 3D View window and press spacebar⇨Add⇨Armature. The result initially appears to be rather unspectacular. As Figure 11-9 shows, it creates a single object with a weird shape called an *octahedron*. Continuing to use the skeleton analogy, this is referred to as a *bone* in the armature. The wide end of the bone is referred to as the bone's *head* or *root* and its narrow end is referred to as the bone's *tail*. Typically, a bone pivots at the head. This becomes more important as you work your way through this chapter.

Editing armatures

Now it's time to take that rather inauspicious single bone armature and do something more interesting with it. Like nearly every other object in Blender, you can edit it in more detail by selecting it (right-click) and Tabbing into Edit mode. In Edit mode, there are three things you can select: the sphere at the bone's head, the sphere at the bone's tail, and the bone itself. Selecting the bone body actually also selects both the head and tail spheres as well.

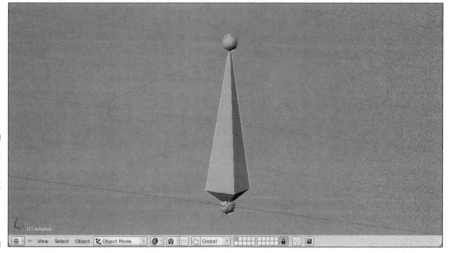

Figure 11-9:
An arma-
ture object
with a
single bone.
Woohoo!

There are four ways to add a new bone to the armature:

- ✔ **Extrude:** Select either the head or tail of the bone and press E to extrude a new bone from that point. This is the most common way to add new bones to an armature. If you add a bone by extruding from the tail, you get the additional benefit of having an instant parent-child relationship. The new bone is the child of the one you extruded it from. These bones are linked together, tail to head, and referred to as a bone *chain*. The Ctrl+left-click extrude shortcut for meshes and curves also works for bones as well.

- ✔ **Duplicate:** Select the body of the bone you want and press Shift+D to duplicate it and create a new bone with the same dimensions, parent relationships, and constraints.

- ✔ **Subdivide:** Select the body of the bone you want and press W⇨Subdivide. This gives you two bones in the space that the one you selected used to occupy. The cool thing about this option is that it keeps the new bone in the correct parent-child relationship of the bone chain.

- ✔ **Use the toolbox:** Press spacebar⇨Add⇨Bone while still in Edit mode. This creates a new bone with its head at the location of the 3D cursor.

Armatures can get very complex very quickly, so you should name your bones as you add them. Let me say that again: *name your bones as you add them*. The fastest way to name your bones is to use the Transform Properties floating panel in the 3D View (N), shown in Figure 11-10. Left-click the name in the Bone field in the right column of this panel and type a name for the bone that makes sense. For example, if you have a two-bone chain to control a character's arm, you may name one bone "arm_upper" and the other "arm_lower."

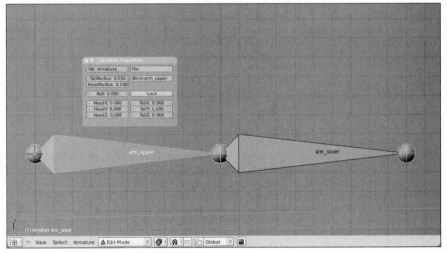

Figure 11-10:
Using the
Transform
Properties
floating
panel to
name your
bones.

Blender has a pretty cool way of understanding *symmetric rigs*, or rigs that have a left side that's identical to the right. For cases like this, it's best to use a ".L" and ".R" suffix on your bone names. So in the previous example, if you are rigging a character with two arms, the bones in the left arm would be named "arm_upper.L" and "arm_lower.L". The right arm bones would be named "arm_upper.R" and "arm_lower.R". This gives you a couple of advantages, but the one that's most apparent when modeling is the X-Axis Mirror feature.

To understand this better, create a new armature at the origin (Shift+C⇨C) and follow these steps:

1. **Tab into Edit mode on your new armature and change to the front view (Numpad 1).**

2. **Select the tail of the bone for this armature and extrude a new bone to the right (E).**

3. **Name this bone "Bone.R".**

4. **Select the tail of the main, or *root*, bone again and extrude another new bone, but this time to the left (E).**

5. **Name this bone "Bone.L."**

6. **In the Armature panel of the Editing buttons, enable the X-Axis Mirror button (F9⇨Armature⇨X-Axis Mirror).**

7. **Select the tail of Bone.R and Grab it to move it around (G).**

   Now, wherever you move the tail of this bone, the tail of Bone.L matches that movement on the other side of the X-axis. In fact, you can even extrude (E) a new bone, and a new bone is extruded on both sides of the axis. As you might guess, this can speed up the rigging process immensely.

As you continue to build your armature, another pretty useful set of tools is in the Specials menu. You access it by pressing W in the 3D View. Two of the options in this menu are the Subdivide function and the Switch Direction function. As you may guess about the former, it takes the selected bones and creates more bones in their place, based on the number of subdivisions you would like to have. This is good if you've done something like make a character's spine a single bone and then later want to change that to two or three bones. The Switch Direction function is also pretty helpful. It prevents you from trying to do the same thing with an imprecise rotation.

When editing bones, it's a good idea to have the mesh you're rigging for visible. This way, you get your proportions correct. A good rule of thumb for placing bones is to think about where the character's real anatomical bones would be located. Then use that as your guideline to where to place the bones in the character's armature.

Parenting bones

One of the important things that make armatures helpful is the notion of how its bones relate to one another. The most important of these relationships is the parent-child relationships between bones. The same hotkeys for parenting and unparenting objects also work with bones, but there are a couple additional features. To illustrate this, start a new scene (Ctrl+X), delete the default cube (X), add a new armature object (spacebar⇨Add⇨Armature), and then tab into Edit mode. After you've done that, go through the following steps:

1. **Duplicate the single bone created and place it somewhere in space (Shift+D).**

   After you confirm placement (left-click), this new bone should be selected.

2. **Add the original bone to your selection (Shift+right-click).**

3. **Press Ctrl+P to make the original bone the parent of the duplicate. When you do this, you are given two options:**

   - **Connected:** Choosing this option moves the head of the child bone to the same location as the tail of the parent. This creates a bone chain as if you'd created the second bone by extruding it from the first.

   - **Keep Offset:** Choosing this option leaves the child bone in place and draws a dashed relationship line between the two bones. They're not connected, but one still has an influence on the other.

4. **After you've created the parent relationship, select the child bone.**

5. **Clear the parent relationship by pressing Alt+P**.

   When you do this, you have another pair of options:

   • **Clear Parent:** Choosing this option removes any sort of parent-child relationship this bone has. This also means that if it was connected to the parent bone, it is now disconnected and can be moved around freely.

   • **Disconnect Bone:** This option doesn't actually clear the parent relationship. Instead, if you have bones that are connected, choosing this option maintains the parent-child relationship, but you can move the child bone independently of the parent. It would behave as if you made the parent by using the Keep Offset option.

   Figure 11-11 shows two bones that are unparented, parented with an offset, and parented as a connected bone.

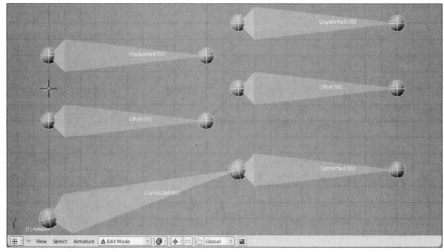

Figure 11-11:
Bones that are unparented, with an offset parent, and parented with a connection.

You may notice that even with bones parented – connected or otherwise – if you rotate the parent bone, the child does not rotate with it as you might expect in a typical parent-child relationship. This is because you are still in Edit mode, which is designed mostly for building and modifying the armature's structure. The parent-child relationship actually works in a special mode for armatures called Pose mode. You access this mode by pressing Ctrl+Tab. When you're in pose mode, if you select individual bones and rotate them, their children rotate with them, as you might expect. From there, you can swap back out to Object mode by pressing Ctrl+Tab again, or you can jump back into Edit mode by just pressing Tab.

Armature panels in the Editing buttons

When working with armatures, the Editing buttons (F9) have some panels with options that are incredibly helpful. Select all the bones in your armature (A) and have a look at the Editing buttons. What you see should look like Figure 11-12.

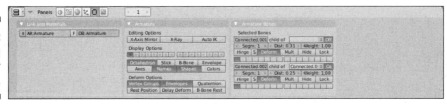

Figure 11-12: Editing buttons for armatures.

Because the Armature Bones panel can display options for up to five bones at the same time, it may be a good idea to change your screen layout and put your Buttons window along the left or right side of the screen and display them vertically.

As you may have guessed, the Armature panel provides options for the Armature overall while the Armature Bones panel provides options for the currently selected bone or bones. Looking at the Armature Bones panel first, there are some options and controls that are immediately helpful. The first row of buttons lets you name your bone and define its parent. Rename the bone by left-clicking in the BO field and typing a new name. The drop-down menu to the right of the name field displays the selected bone's current parent, if it has one, and allows you to choose another existing bone as its parent. If you have a parent defined here, the Co button to the right of it allows you to tell Blender whether it's connected to its parent. These options change a bit between Edit mode (Tab) and Pose mode (Ctrl+Tab), so keep that in mind.

There are two other really important sets of buttons in the Armature Bones panel. The first is the Deform button. It's a simple toggle that tells Blender whether this bone will be used to directly deform geometry. A quick way of explaining it is that you can have bones that actually deform your mesh and bones whose purpose are to control the location of these deformer bones. Disabling the Deform button for those controller bones is how you prevent them from directly controlling your mesh's geometry.

The other really important buttons in the Armature Bones panel are those on the last row. These are *bone layers*. Just as you can place objects on layers in Object mode, Blender's armatures have a special set of layers to themselves. The reason for this is that character rigs with armatures can get pretty involved. Using bone layers is a good way to keep the rig logical and organized. Left-click on a layer button to assign the bone to it. If you would like the bone to live on more than one layer, you can Shift+left-click the layer button.

Notice that there's a corresponding row of layer buttons in the Armature panel. These buttons control which layers the armature is actually displaying. One thing to note is that unlike Blender's regular layers, these layers do not indicate whether they have anything in them, so you just have to keep track of where you place things.

Below the layer buttons in the Armature panel are a set of buttons for controlling how bones in the armature are displayed. A description of each bone follows:

- **Bone types:** Only one of these four buttons can be enabled at any point in time. Note, however, that even though the bone type may not be drawn in the 3D View, the things it influences are still valid. That is, even if you're displaying Stick bones, they still control the same vertices within the range of the Envelope bones. Figure 11-13 shows examples of each of these bone types.

  - **Octahedron:** The default bone type. These bones are great for building a rig because they show which way the bone points and if it's rotated.

  - **Stick:** Draws the bones as a thin stick. I like to animate with my bones in this draw type so they stay out of my way while I work.

  - **B-Bone:** Bones are drawn as boxes and can be treated as simple Bézier curves. To make them deform more smoothly, increase the individual bones' Segm, or segment value in the Armature Bones panel. One thing to note is that even if you don't use the B-Bone drawtype, Blender still pays attention to the Segm value. So if your character deforms in an expected way, this may be why.

  - **Envelope:** Draw the bones with a scalable sphere at each end and a tube for the bone. Vertices within the influence area of these bones will be affected by them. Alt+S increases the bone's range.

- **Extra display options:** All, one, or none of these controls can be enabled in any combination you desire.

  - **Axes:** Display the center axes of the bones. This is helpful for understanding their true position and orientation.

  - **Names:** Display the name of each bone in the 3D view. This can make selection and defining constraints much easier.

- **Shapes:** To help communicate a bone's purpose to the animator, any bone in Blender can be replaced with any object in your scene. While in Pose mode, for a selected bone in the Armature Bones panel, you define the object you want by typing its name in the OB field. Enabling the Shapes button allows the replaced object to be seen in Pose mode.

- **Colors:** To help organize bones in an armature for an animator, you can actually define custom colors for bones by using bone groups (explained later in this chapter in the section entitled "Making the rig more user-friendly"). Set all facial controls to blue, or the left side of the armature in red. Use whatever convention you care to and enable this button so you can make use of it.

Two other buttons I like to enable in this panel are X-Ray and Quaternion. The X-Ray button does the same thing that the X-Ray button in the Object buttons (F7) does. It allows you to see the bone in the 3D View, even if it's technically inside or behind another object. This makes your bones much easier to select when animating. The Quaternion button is more relevant after you begin animating with your rig, but enabling it makes the armature deform the mesh a lot more cleanly than if it's disabled.

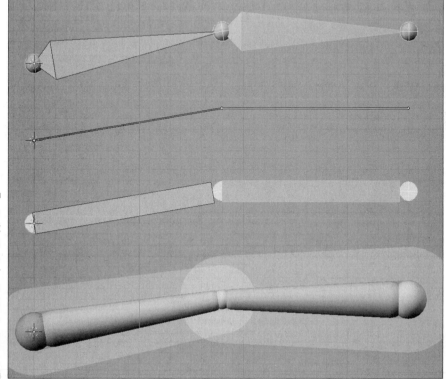

Figure 11-13:
The different drawtypes for bones in Blender from top to bottom: Octahedron, Stick, B-Bone, and Envelope.

Putting skin on your skeleton

Armatures and bones are pretty interesting, but they do you no good if they don't actually deform your mesh. If you've been using the last section as a guide for the tools to create your own rig, you might notice that when you Ctrl+Tab to Pose mode, you can Grab, Rotate, and Scale bones, but the moving bones have no influence whatsoever on your mesh. What you need to do is bind the vertices of the mesh to specific bones in your mesh. This binding process is commonly referred to as *skinning*. Blender has two primary ways of going about this: Envelopes and Vertex Groups.

Quick and dirty skinning with envelopes

Envelopes are the quickest way to get the mesh's vertices to be controlled by the armature. Nothing extra has to be created: It's just a simple parenting operation that seals the deal. To use envelopes to control your mesh, use the following steps:

1. **In Object mode or Pose mode, select the mesh by right-clicking it and then add the armature to your selection by Shift+right-clicking.**

2. **Press Ctrl+P to make the armature the parent of the mesh.**

   A set of options appears: You want to choose Armature. Immediately after you select the type of armature, you are prompted with a question about whether to make vertex groups. For this example, choose Don't Create Groups.

3. **After you do this, when you Ctrl+Tab into Pose mode, the mesh should be under the influence of your armature.**

   To see this better, go to the Armature panel in the Editing buttons and enable the Envelope drawtype for the bones. This lets you see exactly where the influence of your envelopes really lie. And if some part of your mesh is not under the influence of an envelope, you can Tab into Edit mode and edit its size and influence.

That's the basic workflow for envelopes. Figure 11-14 illustrates this in action.

Now, envelopes are great for quickly roughing out a rig and testing it on your mesh, but for detailed deformations, they aren't ideal. Where the influence of multiple envelopes overlap can be particularly problematic, and there's a good tendency for envelope-based rigs to have characters pinch a bit at their joints. For these cases, a more detailed approach is necessary.

That said, using envelopes in your armature does give you one distinct control that you can't have with armatures otherwise. You can actually use an armature with envelopes to control the deformation of curves and surfaces. So long as a control point is within the influence space of a bone's envelope, it can be modified and therefore be animated with the armature.

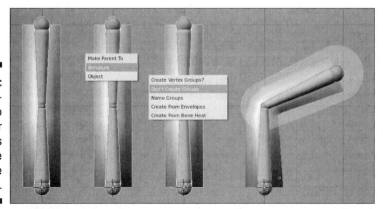

Figure 11-14:
Using enve-
lopes to
control your
armature's
influence
over the
mesh.

Assigning weights to vertices

So if envelopes are the imprecise way of controlling your mesh, what's the precise way? The answer is vertex groups. Chapter 10 briefly touches on vertex groups in reference to the use of the Child Of constraint. A *vertex group* is basically what it sounds like: a set of vertices that have been assigned to a named group. In many ways, it's a lot like a material index, as discussed in Chapter 7. Besides the fact that vertex groups don't deal with materials, there are a couple of distinctions between them and material indices. First of all, vertex groups are not mutually exclusive. Any vertex may belong to any number of vertex groups that you define. The other distinction is that a vertices can be given a *weight*, or a numerical value that indicates how much that particular vertex is influenced or dedicated to the vertex group. A weight of 1.0 means that the vertex is fully dedicated to that group, whereas a weight of zero means that the vertex may as well not even be part of the group.

To use vertex groups with armatures, you need to do two things first. First of all, like with envelopes, it's best that the mesh object is a child of the armature object.

Secondly, vertex groups need to have the exact name of the bones that control them. So if you have a bone called "pelvis," there should be a corresponding vertex group with the same name. The vertices assigned to that group then have their position influenced by the location, rotation, and scale of the pelvic bone. That influence is tempered by the vertices' weights.

To adjust the assignments and weights of vertices in their respective vertex groups, you can use the Link and Materials panel in the Editing buttons (F9). All of the vertex group controls are on the left side of the panel, as shown in Figure 11-15. You create a new group with the New button and select the vertices that you wish to assign to the group. With the vertices selected, you can adjust the value in the Weight field and then assign them by left-clicking the Assign button.

Figure 11-15:
The Link and
Materials
panel gives
you control
over vertex
groups.

Something to note about vertex weights is that they are *normalized* to 1.0. That is, a vertex can be a member of two vertex groups and have a weight of 1.0 for both. In cases like this, Blender adjusts the weights internally so they add up to 1.0. So in my example, that double-grouped vertex behaves like it has a weight of 0.5 on both groups.

Of course, on a complex armature, this process of creating vertex groups and painstakingly assigning weights to each vertex can get excessively tedious. Fortunately, Blender has a couple tools to make things less painful. First of all, you don't have to create all of the vertex groups by yourself. Recall the process of skinning with envelopes. You have to parent the mesh to the armature there and, in doing so, you're presented with a few options, as shown in Figure 11-16. For using envelopes only, you choose Ctrl+P⇨Armature⇨ Don't Create Groups. However, the other options give you a lot of power:

Figure 11-16:
The ver-
tex group
options you
get when
parenting a
mesh to an
armature.

- ✔ **Don't Create Groups:** As the name says, this option does not create any vertex groups, thereby ensuring that the mesh is only influenced by the bone envelopes.

- ✔ **Name Groups:** This option creates vertex groups for you using all of the bones that have the Deform button enabled in the Armature Bones panel. However, it doesn't automatically assign any vertices to any of the groups. Use this option if you want to handle assigning weights on your own. Without assigning any weights, the default behavior is to be controlled just by bone envelopes.

✔ **Create from Envelopes:** This option is a bit of a compromise. It first creates the vertex groups based on the bones with their Deform option turned on. Then it looks at the influence area of the bone envelope and uses that to assign vertices to the group, with their weights varied accordingly. The advantage of this option is that it gets you weighted vertices. The downside, though, is that if the influence area of your envelopes isn't set up well, the weight assignment can look messy.

✔ **Create from Bone Heat:** This is my favorite option to use. It works like the Create from Envelopes option, but instead of using the influence area of the bone envelopes to determine weights, it uses a more complex process that generally results in better vertex assignments and weights.

Regardless of which option you choose, you'll likely have to go in and manually tweak the weights of the vertices. And as you've noticed, trying to do that just from the Link and Materials panel can be pretty painful. Fortunately, there's a solution for that as well called Weight Paint mode. This mode is almost exactly like Vertex Paint mode, as described in Chapter 7, except that rather than painting color on the mesh, you're painting the weight assignment to a vertex group. To access Weight Paint mode, select the mesh (right-click) and press Ctrl+Tab. Even if you don't intend to paint weights, this is a great way to see how the weights were assigned by Blender if you used the Create from Envelopes or Create from Bone Heat options.

The way that weights are visualized is kind of like a thermal map where red is the hottest value and blue is the coldest value. Extending this logic to work with bone weights, vertices that are painted red have a weight of 1.0, whereas vertices painted blue are either not assigned to the vertex group or have a weight of zero. The 50% weight color is bright green.

After you're in Weight Paint mode, you get a new Paint panel in the Editing buttons (F9), as shown in Figure 11-17. Also like with Vertex Paint, if you have the Transform Properties floating panel visible in the 3D View (N), it changes to a Weight Paint Properties floating panel. This panel shares the same content as the Paint panel in the Editing buttons.

Figure 11-17:
The Paint panel in the Editing buttons when Weight Paint mode is activated.

Some buttons in this panel are more interesting and helpful than others. The first of the useful buttons is the Wire button. Enabling this button overlays the mesh's wireframe on it. This is actually really helpful when weight painting because it helps you see where the actual vertices on the mesh are. That way, you're not just painting in empty space where no vertices exist.

The next button that's pretty helpful is the Vgroup button. This limits your paintable vertices to the ones that are already part of the vertex group you're working on. This way, you don't accidentally add a set of vertices on the other side of the mesh to the group you're working on while you try to tweak their weights. This is especially useful if you're trying to paint weights with a mouse, which can be a bit harder to control for painting than a drawing tablet.

I also love the X-Mirror button. It can literally cut your weight painting time in half. When you enable this button, Blender takes advantage of the left/right naming convention discussed earlier in this chapter and allows you to paint symmetrically. So if you're tweaking the vertex weights on the left leg, Blender automatically updates the weights for the corresponding bone on the right leg so that they match. If that ain't cool, I don't know what is.

The actual process of weight painting is nearly identical to painting colors with vertex paint. However, there is one other thing with weight painting, and that's the need to tell Blender which vertex group you're painting. There are two ways to do this. The slow way, you already know: Select the group from the Vertex Groups menu in the Link and Materials panel in the Editing buttons (F9). Of course, though, there's a faster way. That is to simply right-click the bone that you want to paint weights for. Doing that selects the bone and automatically switches to the corresponding vertex group in the mesh and allows you to paint it. Figure 11-18 shows a mesh in Weight Paint mode with some painting done on it. Because weight paint relies so much on color, I highly recommend you look at the corresponding full-color version of this image in this book's color insert.

If you choose to use vertex groups, you have something else to decide. Refer back to the Armature panel in Figure 11-12. At the bottom of the panel is a block of buttons under the heading of Deform Options. With both of the first two buttons, Vertex Groups and Envelopes, enabled, the mesh is influenced by both vertex groups as well as the bone envelopes. This can be useful in some instances, but I tend to prefer to work with just one or the other. And if I've created vertex groups and assigned weights to vertices, I generally disable the Envelopes button. Your rigging needs may be different, but this works for me because this way I know that the only reason a vertex is deforming improperly is that I didn't assign its weight properly. I don't have to concern myself with the influence of the bone's envelope.

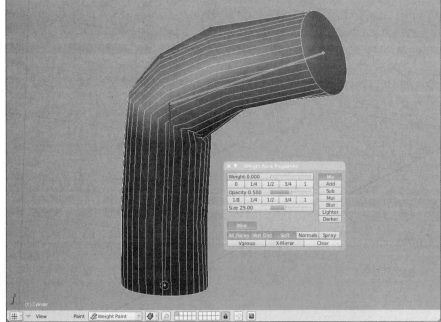

Figure 11-18:
Painting
vertex
weights.

Bringing It All Together in a Single Rig

As you may have guessed, rigging is a pretty intensive process. You need to be technically-minded and creative at the same time. The best riggers I've ever met are the sort of people who fit this description and have an eye for the big picture. These are the sort of people who enjoy playing Minesweeper, finding pleasure in solving the integrated relationships in each part of that game.

Well, regardless of whether you're one of these people, the best way to understand the full process of rigging is to actually create a rig of your own. The examples throughout the rest of this section are done with a simple stick figure character that I like to use for creating quick animations that test body language and timing. I love animating with stick figures, even in 3D. Ninety percent of an animated character's personality comes through in his body language. Animating with stick figures allows you to focus on that essential part of the process and keeps you from getting distracted with secondary details.

This stick figure, in both rigged and unrigged versions, is included with the CD-ROM that accompanies this book, so that you have a finished reference as well as a file to practice with. So you can have an idea of what you're looking for, Figure 11-19 shows the stick figure in a pose in the 3D View. Of course, if you have a character already modeled and want to rig it, that's great. You should be able use the techniques here for nearly anything you want to build a rig for.

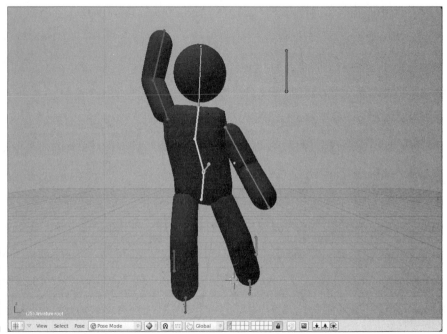

Figure 11-19: Say hello to Stickman! Hi, Stickman!

If you load the stickman.blend file from the DVD, the first thing you might notice is his pose. He's standing up with his arms out to his sides. This is referred to as a *T pose* because the character looks like the letter T. This is probably the most common pose that modelers use when they create their characters and it's the most preferred pose for riggers. Some modelers may also model with the arms at the sides or somewhere halfway between the T pose and having arms at the side. There are valid reasons people give for any of these poses, but ultimately it really comes down to personal preference. I find that the T pose is easier for me to rig, so I have little bias for that one.

Now, time to get an armature in this mesh. Probably the best way to handle this is to create the centerline bones first. These would be the body bones, the head, and the hip bone. To do this, use the following steps:

1. **Add your armature and start with the first body bone (spacebar⇨Add⇨Armature).**

2. **Enable X-Ray viewing for the armature (F9⇨Armature⇨X-Ray).**

   Doing this ensures that you can see the bones of your armature, even if you're in the Shaded draw mode and the bones are inside your character's mesh.

3. **Tab into Edit mode and move this bone up in the Z-axis until it's around Stickman's waistline (G⇨Z).**

4. **Select the tail of this bone and move it up in the Z-axis until it's at the top of the torso (right-click, G⇨Z).**

5. **Subdivide this bone into two bones (W⇨Subdivide).**

   Name the bottom bone "body.1" and the top bone "body.2."

6. **Select the joint between the two bones and move it back in the Y-axis a little bit (right-click, G⇨Y).**

   This helps the bones match the natural curvature of the spine a little bit better.

7. **Select the tail of body.2 and extrude it up in the Z-axis to the top of Stickman's head (right-click, E⇨Z).**

   Name this bone "head."

8. **Select the head of body.1 and extrude it down in the Z-axis to the bottom of Stickman's pelvis (right-click, E⇨Z).**

   Name this bone "hip." If you enable the Names and X-Ray buttons in the Armature panel of the Editing buttons (F9), you should now have something that looks like Figure 11-20.

The next step is to create bones for the arms and the legs. The way to do this is to create bones for half of the rig and then let Blender do the rest of the work for you by mirroring the bones. First things first, though — you have to create one half of the rig:

1. **Switch to the front view and select the head bone and duplicate it, putting its root at Stickman's left shoulder joint (Numpad 1, right-click, Shift⇨D).**

   Note that by doing it this way, the new bone is an offset child of the body.2 bone. Name this new bone "arm_upper.L."

2. **Select the tail of arm_upper.L and move it to Stickman's elbow. It may help to press Ctrl to guarantee that the bone is perfectly horizontal (right-click, G⇨Ctrl).**

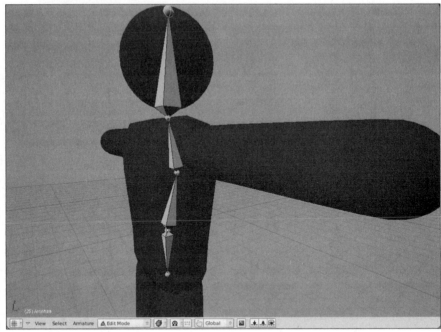

3. **Extrude this tail to create a new bone along the X-axis that extends to Stickman's hand (E⇨X).**

   Name this new bone "arm_lower.L."

4. **From the front view, select the hip bone and duplicate it, placing the new bone's head at the top of Stickman's left leg (Numpad 1, right-click, Shift+D).**

5. **Select this new bone's tail and move it along the Z-axis to Stickman's feet (right-click, G⇨Z).**

6. **Select this bone and subdivide it into two bones (right-click, W⇨Subdivide).**

   Name the top bone "leg_upper.L" and the bottom bone "leg_lower.L."

7. **Select the joint between these bones and move it forward in the Y-axis a little bit (right-click, G⇨Y).**

   This gives the knee a little bit of bend, which helps deformation later on.

8. **Parent leg_upper.L to hip (right-click leg_upper.L, Shift+right-click hip, Ctrl+P⇨Keep Offset).**

   You should now have something that looks like Figure 11-21.

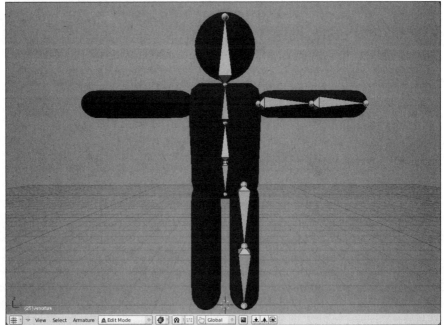

Figure 11-21:
A half-
skeleton
Stickman!

Now for the really cool part of letting Blender do the work for you. You want to select all of the bones that aren't on the centerline, duplicate them, and mirror them along the X-axis. The specific hotkeys and steps to do this are below:

1. **Select both arm bones and both leg bones (B).**

2. **Duplicate the selected bones and immediately press Esc (Shift+D, Esc).**

   This places the newly created bones in the exact same location as their originators.

3. **Switch to using the 3D cursor as your pivot (period [.]).**

   You should be building your armature around the Z-axis, so it would probably be a good idea to make sure your 3D cursor is at the origin (Shift+C).

4. **Mirror these new bones along the X-axis (Ctrl+M⇨X).**

5. **Switch back to using the median point as your pivot (Shift+comma [,]).**

6. **Have Blender automatically give these new bones the .R suffix to indicate that they're on the right side (W⇨Flip Left-Right Names).**

   Pow! All of your bones should be properly named now and your rig should now look like what's in Figure 11-22.

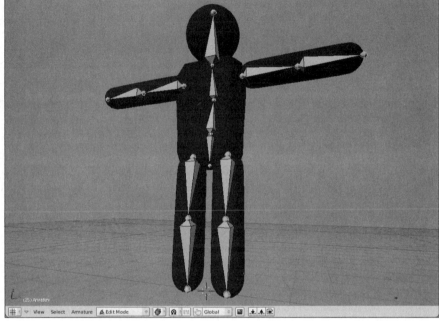

Figure 11-22:
Stickman
with a skel-
eton in him.
He's almost
rigged,
but he still
needs some
controls.

Taking advantage of parenting and constraints

What you currently have in place is the basic structure of the rig's armature. The primary function of these bones is to deform the character mesh.
Technically, you *could* animate with just these bones after you skin them
to the mesh. However, there are some additional bones that you can (and
should) add to the armature to make it easier to animate. They work by
taking advantage of the parenting set up by the bone chains and combining
them with some reasonable constraints.

For example, you currently have a structured skeleton in place, but what
happens if you Ctrl+Tab into Pose mode and Grab the body.1 bone and
move it (G)? Because the entire upper body is directly or indirectly a child
of this bone, the upper torso, arms, and head move with the body.1 bone.
Unfortunately, the lower half of the body doesn't share this relationship, so
as Figure 11-23 shows, you end up tearing Stickman's skeleton in half. Ouch!

To compensate for this, you need a bone that both the hip and body.1 relate
to, binding the upper half of the body to the lower half. This is what you call
the *root bone*. Moving this bone should move the entire armature. Adding this
bone to the rig is pretty simple:

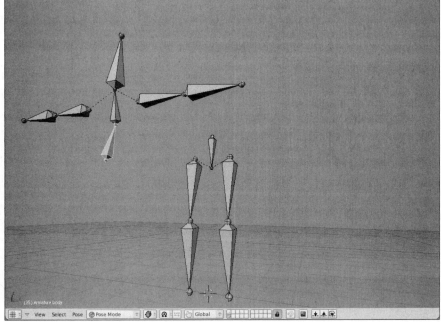

Figure 11-23:
There's nothing relating the upper body to the lower body, so you can accidentally tear Stickman in half.

1. **Tab into Edit mode on the armature and switch to the side view (Numpad 3).**

2. **Select the head of either the body.1 or hip bones (right-click).**

   Both heads are located in the same place, so it doesn't really matter which one you select.

3. **Extrude a new bone in the Y-axis (E⇨Y).**

   You should move in the positive Y direction, towards the back of Stickman. Name this bone "root."

4. **Select the body.1 and hip bones and then select the root bone (right-click, Shift+right-click, Shift+right-click).**

5. **Make root the parent of both body.1 and hip (Ctrl+P⇨Keep Offset).**

   This parent relationship means that you can move the entire armature by just selecting and moving the root bone. Before doing this, some people may choose to switch the direction of the root bone (W⇨Switch Direction) so that they can have the root bone actually connected to body.1 and hip. It's all a matter of taste, but I prefer not to do that. Because bones naturally rotate around their head, it's more useful to me to keep the head of the root bone in the center of the character. In my opinion, it helps make bending at the waist look more natural.

6. **Select the root bone and disable the Deform button in the Armature Bones panel (right-click, F9⇨Armature Bones⇨Deform).**

This bone is intended purely to control the other bones. You don't want any of the mesh's vertices assigned to it. Your Stickman rig should now look something like Figure 11-24.

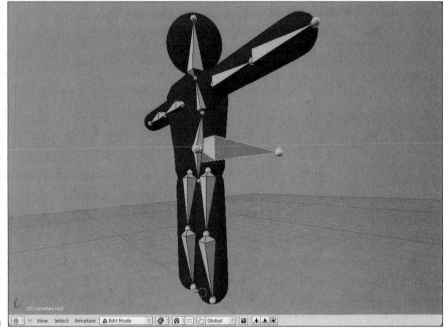

Figure 11-24:
Adding a root bone to the rig prevents the top of the body from unnecessarily leaving the bottom.

Another convenient control bone that you may want to add is a head control. Sure, you can rotate the head bone as you wish, but often it's easier to use a bone as the head's (or eyes') target. That way, when you want the character to look at something, you just move the target bone to that something's location. An added benefit of this is that by doing it this way, you can successfully create complex moves, such as keeping the character looking at an object as he walks by it. Again, you could do this by animating the rotation of the head bone by itself, but this control certainly simplifies things for the animator. To do this, you just use a Track To constraint:

1. **Tab into Edit mode and select the head bone (Tab, right-click).**

2. **Duplicate the head bone and move it in the Y-axis (Shift+D⇨Y).**

   The idea here is that you want the control bone to be far enough in front of the face so you can have some control without getting in the way of the rest of the rig. I moved mine about 3 Blender units out. Name this bone "head_target."

3. **Clear the parent relationship on the head_target bone (Alt+P⇨Clear Parent).**

Because the head_target bone came into being by duplicating the head bone, it inherited the parent relationship with the body.2 bone. You don't want that because you want to be able to move the head target independently of the rest of the rig.

4. **Ctrl+Tab into Pose mode, select the head_target bone, and then also select the head bone (right-click, Shift+right-click).**

5. **Add a Track To constraint to this bone (Ctrl+Alt+C⇨Track To).**

   This should automatically add a Track To constraint to the Constraints panel in the Editing buttons (F9). Chances are good that it also made the head bone rotate toward head_target and point directly at it. This is certainly not the behavior you want. To fix this, you need to change the alignment axes that the constraint works on.

6. **In the Track To constraint, change the To axis to X and the Up axis to Y.**

   This should fix the head bone so it points in the proper direction. Now when you Grab (G) the head_target bone and move it around, the head bone always points at it.

7. **Select the head_target bone and disable the Deform button in the Armature Bones panel (right-click, F9⇨Armature Bones⇨Deform).**

   Like the root bone, this bone is not intended to deform the mesh, so disabling the Deform button ensures this. Figure 11-25 shows what your rig should look like now.

Figure 11-25:
The Stickman rig, now with head control!

Your Stickman is mostly functional now. However, there's another constraint that is a staple of nearly all character rigs and is monumentally helpful to animators. It's called an *inverse kinematics*, or IK, constraint. The next section goes into what this constraint does, how it works, and how to give your rig its benefits.

Understanding the difference between inverse kinematics and forward kinematics

When it comes to animating characters in 3D with an armature, you have two ways to move limbs around: inverse kinematics and forward kinematics, or IK and FK. *Kinematic* is just a fancy way of saying motion. By default, your rig is set up to use FK. Say you have a bone chain and you want to place the tip of the last bone to a specific location in 3D space. In order to achieve this, you have to rotate the first bone in the chain, and then the next, and then the next, and so on until you can get that last bone's tip properly placed. You're working your way *forward* down the bone chain. Because of the parenting relationships between the bones, you can currently do this with your Stickman rig right now.

That's FK. It gets the job done, but it can be awfully difficult and tedious to try and get the tip of that last bone exactly where you want it. It would be nice if you could just grab that tip, put it in place, and let the computer figure out how all the other bones have to bend to compensate for that. This, basically, is the essence of IK. You move the tip of the last bone and Blender works *backwards* up the chain to get the other bones properly placed.

To see what this is like, select your Stickman armature and Ctrl+Tab into Pose mode. Now, select the body.2 bone and press G to Grab and move it. Notice that all it does is rotate. It doesn't actually change its location. Now go to the Armature panel of the Editing buttons (F9) and left-click the button that says Auto IK. This isn't a real IK constraint, but it will help you understand how IK works. Now Grab and move the body.2 bone. Notice that now, it moves around, and the body.1 bone rotates to compensate for the locations that you try to put body.2. Selecting the head bone or one of the arm_lower bones results in similar behavior. Click around and play with it. It's pretty cool. When you're done, disable the Auto IK button.

IK is really awesome stuff and it's very powerful, but it's not the ultimate solution for animating. See, one of the core principles of animation is movement that happens in arcs. Generally speaking, arcing movement is move believable and natural-looking. Things that move in a straight line tend to look stiff and robotic. Think about how a person's arms swing when they walk. It doesn't necessarily matter exactly where the hand is. The entire arm rotates and swings back and forth. That is FK movement. If you're animating, you can recreate that motion by keying the upper arm bone at the extreme ends of the rotation.

In contrast, IK movement tends to happen in a straight line. You're just keying the tip of the chain, so that tip moves directly from one location to the next. To recreate a swinging arm in IK, you'd need *at least* three keyframes: one at each extreme and one in the middle to keep the hand from going in a straight line. And even then you might need even more intermediary keys to try to get that smooth arc that you get automatically with FK.

Where IK shines is when the tip of the bone chain needs to be precisely positioned. A perfect example of this are feet. When a person walks, the feet must touch the ground. Trying to achieve this with just FK usually ends up with feet that look "floaty" and not locked into place as the character moves. Another example is if the character is holding on to something and doesn't want to let go of it. You want to keep the hand in place and let the elbow bend naturally. In instances like these, IK is really helpful. The biggest use, though, is for foot/leg rigs on characters. And to that end, you're going to use the following steps to add IK controls to the Stickman rig:

1. **Tab into Edit mode on the armature and select the tip of the leg_lower.L bone.**

    You can actually select either the left or right bone. Because you have X-Axis Mirror enabled, whatever you do on one side also happens on the other.

2. **Extrude a new bone in the Z-axis (E⇨Z).**

    You don't have to extrude the new bone very far. Just enough to know it's there. Name this bone "leg_IK.L," and make sure that the mirrored bone is named "leg_IK.R."

3. **Disconnect leg_IK.L from leg_lower.L (Alt+P⇨Disconnect Bone).**

4. **Ctrl+Tab into Pose mode, select leg_IK.L, and add leg_lower.L to the selection (right-click, Shift+right-click).**

5. **Add an IK constraint (Shift+I⇨To Active Bone).**

    This adds an IK constraint in the Constraints panel. Go to this panel and change the ChainLen value to 2. By default, the IK bone chain goes all the way back to the head of the hip bone. You actually only want it to have an influence to the head of the upper leg bone. Setting the chain length to 2 confirms this.

6. **Perform steps 4 and 5 on leg_IK.R and leg_lower.L.**

    Sadly, X-Axis Mirror only works in Edit mode, so you have to add your IK constraints on both sides on your own.

7. **Select the leg_IK.L and leg_IK.R bones and disable the Deform button for each of them in the Armature Bones panel (F9⇨Armature Bones⇨Deform).**

    Like the root and head_target bones, these are control bones and should not be used for skinning. At this point, you have a basic IK rig on your character's feet. It should look something like Figure 11-26.

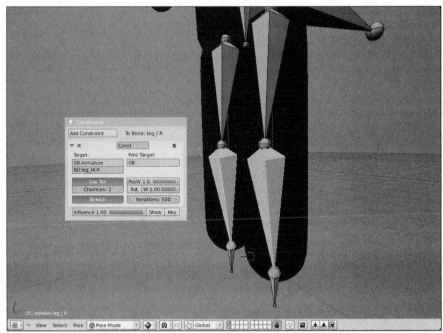

Figure 11-26:
A basic
IK rig for
the legs of
Stickman.

Test your rig out by selecting the root and moving it around, particularly up and down the Z-axis. The leg bones in your Stickman rig should bend all by themselves to compensate for the location of the root bone relative to the IK bones. You can also select each of the leg_IK bones and move them around to control the bending of each leg independent of the other.

In doing this, however, you may notice that there are occasions where the legs don't quite know how to bend. They may randomly flip backward or roll out in odd angles. This is because, aside from slightly bending the rig at the knees when you created the leg bones, you haven't provided the legs with much of a clue as to *how* exactly they should bend. Fortunately, the solution to this is pretty simple. It's called a *pole target*. To define it, you need to create two more bones, one for each leg:

1. **Tab into Edit mode on Stickman's armature and select leg_IK.L.**

   Again, because X-Axis Mirror is enabled and you're in Edit mode, choosing either leg_IK bone works fine.

2. **Switch to side view, duplicate the bone, and move the new bone to somewhere in front of the knee (Numpad 3, Shift+D).**

   Name this bone "knee.L" and make sure the mirrored bone is named "knee.R."

3. **Rotate knee.L 180 degrees in the X-axis (R⇨X⇨180).**

   This step isn't essential. I just like to have my floating bones pointing up.

4. **Parent knee.L to leg_IK.L (right-click knee.L, right-click leg_IK.L, Ctrl+P⇨Keep Offset).**

5. **Ctrl+Tab into Pose mode.**

6. **Select leg_lower.L and, in the IK constraint panel, enter** Armature **under the Pole Target field for OB. Enter knee.L in the BO field that appears after that.**

   Doing this defines knee.L as the pole target for the left leg's IK chain. When you do this, however, the knee joint for the left leg may instantly pop to the side, bending the leg in all kinds of weird ways. The next step compensates for that.

7. **Still in leg_lower.L's IK constraint panel, adjust the Pole Offset value to -90.**

   This should cause the leg's knee joint to properly point at the knee.L bone. If it doesn't, try adjusting this until it looks correct. Usually this value is 0, 90, -90, or 180. The reason for this is because the default behavior is to point leg_lower.L's local X-axis toward the pole. If the local X-axis isn't forward, adjusting the offset accounts for this.

8. **Perform steps 6 and 7 on leg_lower.R.**

   At this point, you have a fully configured IK rig for both of Stickman's legs. You're nearly ready to animate him. For reference, your rig should look like the one in Figure 11-27.

Figure 11-27:
A completely working Stickman rig.

At this point, it should be pretty safe to skin the Stickman mesh to your armature. Using the bone heat method should give you the best results, so select the mesh (right-click), select the armature (Shift+right-click) and press Ctrl+P➪Armature➪Create from Bone Heat. Now when you move around and pose your rig, the Stickman mesh should obediently follow in kind. To ensure that your deformations look good, go to the Armature panel and look at the Deform Options. Disable Envelopes and enable Quaternion. This should keep the mesh from pinching unnaturally at Stickman's joints.

Making the rig more user-friendly

At this point, you've got a great basic rig that you can start animating with immediately. However, you can make a few tweaks that make it even more usable. The first thing you can do is change the way the bones display in the 3D View. Now that you're done with the bulk of rigging, knowing which end of a bone is the head or the tail is a bit less important. Go to the Armature panel in the Editing buttons (F9) and change from Octahedron to Stick. Stick bones are the least obtrusive bones that are immediately available to you. Now you can see more of your mesh while you're animating and there's not as much clutter and geometry in the way. Figure 11-28 shows the Stickman rig with stick bones.

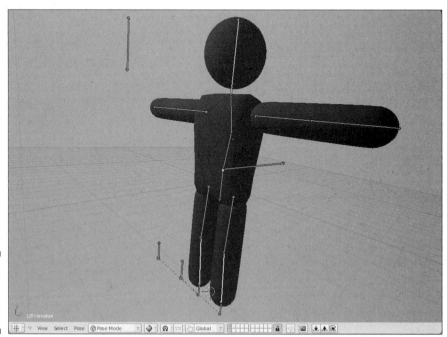

Figure 11-28:
Stickman . . .
rigged with
sticks!

Another relatively new feature to Blender that is quite helpful for organizing your rigs is the ability to create bone groups. To do this, select the bones you would like to group together and press Ctrl+G. When you do this, you get four options:

> ✔ **Add Selected to Active Group:** If you already have a group created and it's the one visible in the Link and Materials panel, choosing this option adds the selected bones to that group.
>
> ✔ **Add Selected to Group:** Choosing this option gives you a second pop-up that gives you a list of your existing groups, as well as the ability to add a new group. Whichever you pick, the selected bones are added to it.
>
> ✔ **Remove Selected from Groups:** If the bones you have selected are part of any groups, choosing this option removes them.
>
> ✔ **Remove Active Group:** Choosing this option removes the group that is currently visible in the Link and Materials panel. Note that this does not remove the bones, just the group that they're associated with.

I used the bone groups feature to create groups for my main bone chains: left arm, right arm, left leg, right leg, and body. I left root, head, and head_target groupless. Create your own groups as you see fit.

Beyond organization, there's an additional benefit to using bone groups. You can define custom bone colors based on the bone groups you have. The control for this is in the Editing buttons. First, in the Armature panel, enable the Colors button under display options. Then, in the Link and Materials panel, left-click the button that says Default Colors and choose a Theme Color Set from the menu that pops up. I used this feature to make all of my left-side bones green and my right-side bones red. It's a good visual trick to let you or another animator quickly identify which bones are being used. Figure 11-29 shows what the bone groups and bone colors options look like in the Link and Materials panel.

Figure 11-29:
The Link and Materials panel with controls for bone groups and bone colors for those groups.

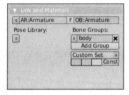

Besides groups, another organizational tool for making your rig more usable are bone layers. Bone groups make it easy to visualize bones and even select them. However, bone layers are a faster, more reasonable way of showing and hiding the bones in your rig. As an example, have a look at Stickman's legs. They're entirely controlled by the IK and knee bones. Because you can see the Stickman mesh, you really don't need to see these leg bones. In some ways, they just get in the way of seeing your character's acting. In that case, it makes plenty of sense to move them to a different layer and hide that layer. To do this, use Shift+right-click, Border Select (B), or press L with your mouse over the leg bones to select the entire leg chain and then press M to move them to a different layer. I moved the bones to the first layer in the second block of layers. Now, if you ever want to see those bones, just go to the Armature panel and enable the layer there. In the meantime, though, as Figure 11-30 shows, your Stickman rig is much cleaner and now you're *really* ready to start animating.

Figure 11-30:
Stickman,
reporting
for duty!

Chapter 12

Animating Object Deformations

- -

In This Chapter

▶ Becoming familiar with the Action Editor

▶ Animating shape keys

▶ Using armatures for animations

▶ Animating quickly with the Non-Linear Animation window

- -

L ooking at the title of this chapter, you may find yourself wondering how this chapter is different from Chapter 10. Both chapters cover animation, but this chapter covers the cool things you can do in Blender if you're animating with a fully rigged mesh. Chapter 10 covers what is often referred to as *object animation:* that is, animating the attributes of a single object. You can actually squeeze quite a bit of personality out of object animation. However, the level of control and detail that you can get when your object has an animation rig is exponentially greater. There are simply way more possibilities for expression and communication. And at the same time, the process of animating is a little bit more complex. With an animation rig, there are more bits and pieces to manage, keep track of, and control.

Trying to manage all of that additional complexity can be daunting if all you have to work with is the Outliner and the Ipo Curve Editor. Fortunately, Blender offers a few more features that help make rigged *character animation* easier to wrap your head around.

Of course, this doesn't change anything that's covered in Chapter 10. In fact, if you're not familiar with the Ipo Curve Editor and the process of setting keyframes in Blender, you probably ought to go back and review that chapter.

Working with the Action Editor

So you have a rigged character that you want to animate. Awesome! Change your screen layout to the Animation layout (Ctrl+left arrow). After that, the first thing that you're probably going to want to do is change the 3D View to the Shaded draw type (Z), change the Translate widget to the Rotate widget (Ctrl+spacebar⇨Rotate), and set it to Normal orientation

(Alt+spacebar⇨Normal). You should switch to Normal orientation because when you're animating with an armature, most of the time, you're animating bone rotations. By setting the rotation widget to the Normal coordinate space, you can have quick, controlled manipulation of bone rotations without having the widget get in your way too much.

The next thing you need to do is go to the Ipo Curve Editor and change the Ipo Type to Pose. This gives you the channels necessary for animating bones. Of course, as nice as seeing those channels may be, the Ipo Curve Editor only shows the keyframes for a single selected object or bone. The Timeline window shows multiple keys, but you don't have a good way to see which key belongs to which object, and the Timeline provides no tools for actually editing these keyframes, aside from inserting and deleting them. You need a different window: one that lets you see the keyframes for multiple bones and edit their timing individually. What you're looking for is the Action Editor window (Shift+F12), shown in Figure 12-1.

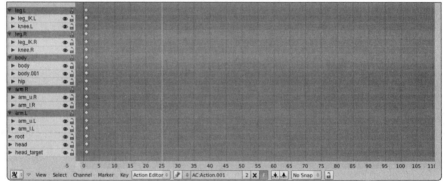

Figure 12-1:
The Action
Editor.

As Figure 12-1 shows, when you have an armature selected, the Action Editor shows a channel for each of the keyed bones in the rig. Furthermore, if you've got a rig that has bone groups, the Action Editor actually breaks up the channels according to those bone groups.

The Action Editor's ability to understand bone groups really makes it easy to see if any bone in a group gets animated. Now, the Action Editor doesn't give you full control over the Ipo curves for each animatable channel in a single bone. You do have the ability to "drill down" to the individual location, rotation, and scale keys per axis on each channel by left-clicking the triangle icon to the left of each one. But to edit curves, you still need the Ipo Curve Editor. The Action Editor shows a diamond-shaped dot to indicate that a key has been created. This way, you can get a sense for the "big picture" in your character animation. When it comes to editing the overall timing of a character's performance, the Action Editor is really the tool for the job.

Like other parts of Blender, you can select individual keyframes by right-clicking the diamond-shaped keyframe indicator. Multiple keyframes can be selected in a variety of ways. You can use the familiar Shift+right-click or Border Select (B) functions. However, there's another way to select that's incredibly helpful. If you have an Action Editor open and a few keyframes set, right-click any keyframe to select it. Now, with that key selected, press K. Doing this selects any other key in the armature that's on the same frame as your selected key. This is called a *column key selection*. You can get similar functionality with the time cursor. If you place your time cursor on a column of keys and press Ctrl+K, that column of keys is selected, rather than the column with your original selected keys.

Initially, you might not think that column key selection would be all that useful. However, if you think about the process used for animating – especially cartoon-style animation – it starts making more sense. The workflow for animation is usually to go from pose to pose. This means that at each pose that you key, multiple bones are all keyed at the same time, forming a column in the Action Editor. In fact, unless you're doing some kind of frantic, shaky animations, it's a pretty good practice to make sure you have nice columns in your Action Editor. Uneven columns tend to indicate that your timing may be off on a specific part of the rig. Of course, this is a guideline more than a hard-and-fast rule.

After they're selected, keys can be manipulated with Grabbing (G) and Scaling (S). When performing these actions, there are two things to pay attention to. First of all, when you scale selected keyframes, the scale is relative to the position of the time cursor in the Action Editor window. So if you want to increase the length of your animation by stretching out the keyframes, put your time cursor at frame 1 before scaling. If you place it in the middle or at the end, the keys at the beginning of your animation are arranged so that they take place before your animation starts. This is typically exactly what you don't want, so be careful.

The other thing to take into account is that even though the time cursor snaps to frames, the individual keyframes do not. When Grabbing (G), you can get around this by holding down Ctrl while you're moving the keys around. This snaps the keys to even increments of 1 frame length. When Scaling keyframes, however, the same trick doesn't work. Instead, you need to use snapping. With your mouse in the Action Editor window press Shift+S. You should get a menu that looks like the one in Figure 12-2.

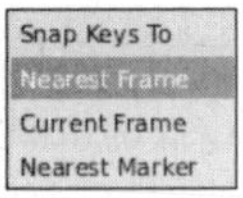

Figure 12-2:
The Snap menu in the Action Editor.

Snap Keys To
Nearest Frame
Current Frame
Nearest Marker

You have three options in this menu:

- **Nearest Frame:** Choosing this option takes the selected keys and shifts them to the even frame number that's closest to them.
- **Current Frame:** This option snaps selected keys to the location of the time cursor in the Action Editor.
- **Nearest Marker:** Blender's Action Editor allows you to place reminders on the timeline referred to as *markers*. You can add a new marker at the location of the timeline cursor by pressing M in the Action Editor window. If you have one or more of these markers on you timeline, choosing this option snaps selected keyframes to the marker that's nearest to it.

Alternatively, you can use Blender's autosnapping feature. Enable it by left-clicking the button in the Action Editor's header that says "No Snap." That's the default snapping type. It has almost all the same options mentioned above. The only difference is the Frame Step option, which behaves like pressing Ctrl while moving keys.

If you're familiar with other animation software or traditional hand-drawn animation, you might recognize Blender's Action Editor as being similar to a dope sheet. In traditional animation, the *dope sheet* was the entire animation planned out, frame by frame, on paper prior to a single pencil line being drawn by the animator. In computer animation, it's taken on a slightly different meaning and purpose. Some software has a dope sheet editor that allows the animator to see the keyframes and timing for all of the animatable channels in a character, and in some packages, a whole scene. Blender doesn't quite have that right now as the Action Editor is limited to showing multiple bones in the same armature at the same time, but not other animatable channels or objects. Hopefully, however, this will change in the future and Blender will have an even more powerful Action Editor. In the meantime, what Blender does have certainly isn't anything to turn your nose up to.

Animating Shape Keys

Although the Action Editor is optimized to be used with armature objects, it still has some other tricks up its sleeves. You can use it as a more intuitive way of animating shape keys. Take a gander back at Figure 12-1 and notice that the header of the window has a drop-down menu that says Action Editor. This button controls the editing modes that the Action Editor can take on. If you left-click the button, you see that there are three modes to choose from:

- **Action Editor:** This is the default mode described in the last section. It can handle objects, but it's optimized for working with armatures.
- **ShapeKey Editor:** An Action Editor mode for tweaking shape keys. For a refresher on shape keys, have a look at Chapter 11.

✔ **Grease Pencil:** This is for a very new feature in Blender that allows you to draw and write notes on the 3D View. The cool thing about this feature is that it actually allows you to animate those drawings. This Action Editor mode is how you can edit the timing of those drawn animations.

If you have a mesh with shape keys, each shape has a channel on the left of the Action Editor. Figure 12-3 shows the shape key Action Editor for the bugeyed screaming Suzanne example from Chapter 11.

Although it's nice to be able to tweak the Ipo curves for the transition from one shape to the next, the simpler Action Editor interface is certainly a lot better and less cluttered for characters that have many, many shape keys. But you get another really sweet bonus by using the Action Editor. Notice the word *Sliders* above the shape channels. If you left-click the triangle icon to the right of that, Blender makes the shape key sliders from the Shapes panel available to you. Now you can animate multiple shape keys without having to cycle through them in that panel. And what's more, if you left-click on one of the channel names, a little box pops up that allows you to set the custom minimum and maximum values for the sliders. You can even rename the shape key through this box.

To make a long story short, the ability to use sliders to edit your shape keys in the Action Editor is pretty sweet and an extremely powerful feature.

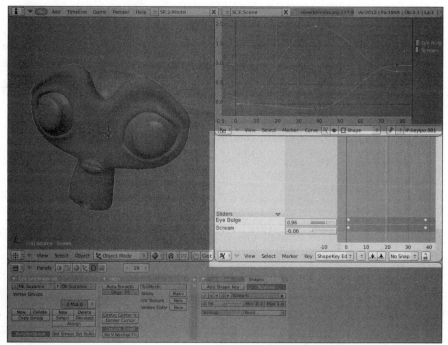

Figure 12-3: Using the Action Editor for animating shape keys.

Animating with Armatures

Alright, so now it's time to get to animating. If you're already used to object animation, using armatures to animate using the Action Editor extends naturally from that base. When I animate, I like to use the following process:

1. **Pre-plan the animation.**

   This can't be emphasized enough: There's nothing worse than sitting down to animate without a plan. You end up doing two or three times the amount of work you would've done if you'd just done a little planning, and the results are usually worse for the effort. Know what you're going to animate and have an idea about the timing of the motion. If you can, sketch out a few quick thumbnail drawings of the sequence. Even if the drawings are stick figures, they can be really helpful for determining poses and figuring out how things are going to look.

2. **Set your timeline at frame 1 and create the starting pose for your character by manipulating its rig.**

3. **Select all visible bones (A) and Insert a LocRot keyframe for *everything* (I⇨LocRot).**

   Granted, there's a good chance that most of the bones can't be Grabbed, so setting a location keyframe for them is kind of moot. However, setting a keyframe for all the bones is faster than going through and figuring out which bones can be keyed for just rotation and which bones can be keyed for both rotation and location.

4. **Move the timeline cursor forward to roughly when you think the next major pose should happen.**

5. **Create your character's second pose.**

   If the next pose is a *hold*, or a pose where the character doesn't change position, you can duplicate the keys of the previous pose by selecting them and pressing Shift+D.

6. **Select all visible bones (A) and Insert an Available keyframe (I⇨Available).**

7. **Continue with steps 4-6 until you complete the last major pose for your character.**

8. **Using the Action Editor, play back the animation, paying close attention to timing.**

   In fact, pay even *more* attention to timing than the accuracy of the poses.

9. **Go through the keys set in the Action Editor and tweak the timing of the poses so they look natural.**

10. **Continuing to tweak, go back and start adding secondary poses and keyframes for secondary motion between your major poses.**

11. **Continue on this course, refining the timing and detail more and more with each pass.**

You should notice that in the last set of steps, a pattern is beginning to emerge. One of the luxuries we have in computer animation is the ability to continually go back and tweak things, make changes, and improve the animation. You can take advantage of this process by training yourself to work in passes. Animate your character's biggest, most pronounced motion first. Make sure you have the timing for that down right. Then move to the next pass, working on slightly more detailed parts of the performance. The biggest reason to work this way is time. It's much easier to go in and fix the timing on a big action if you do it earlier. Otherwise, you run into situations where you find yourself shuffling around a bunch of detail keys after you find out that your character doesn't get from Point A to Point B in the right amount of time.

Don't be afraid to break out a stopwatch and act out the action to find out exactly how long it takes to perform and what the action feels like. If you're fortunate enough to have friends, have them act out the action for you while you time it. Animation is all about timing. One of the things that I like to tell people is, "If you can tell a joke that people genuinely laugh at, you can animate." This is because both animating and telling jokes both rely almost entirely on good timing. You can tell a bad joke, or even speak a completely unfunny sentence and make people laugh if you do it with the right timing. Animation is the same way. It may be the most mundane of actions, but if you nail the timing on it, naturally it becomes a lot more interesting.

Principles of animation worth remembering

As you create your animations, draw on a variety of sources to really capture the essence of some action, motion, or character expression. My first and most emphatic recommendation is to keep your eyes open. Watch everything around you that moves. Study it and try to get an idea of how its structure facilitates motion. Then think about how you would recreate that.

Of course, merely gawking at everything in the world isn't the only thing you should do (and you should be prepared for the fact that people might look at you funny). Studying early animation is also a good idea. Most of the principles that those wonderfully talented pioneers developed for animation are still relevant and applicable to computer animation. In fact, you should remember the classic 12 basic principles of animation that were established by some of the original Disney animators. This is a bit of divergence, but if your aim is to create good animation, you should know about these principles and try to use them in even the most simple of animations:

- **Squash and stretch:** This is all about deformation. Because of weight, anything that moves gets deformed somehow. A tennis ball squashes to an oval shape when it's hit. Rope under tension gets stretched. Cartoon characters hit all believable and unbelievable ranges of this when they're animated, but it's valuable, albeit toned-down, even in realistic animation.

- **Anticipation:** The basic idea here is that before every action in one direction, there's a build-up in the opposite direction first. A character that's going to jump bends her knees and moves down first to build up the energy to jump up.

- **Staging:** The idea of staging is to keep the frame simple. The purpose of animation is to communicate an idea or a movement or an emotion with moving images. You want to convey this as clearly as possible with the way you arrange your shots and the characters in those shots.

- **Straight-ahead action versus pose-to-pose action:** These are the two primary methods of animating. The process that I discussed near the beginning of this chapter is more of a pose-to-pose technique. Pose-to-pose can be more clear, but it may be a bit cartoony. Straight-ahead action is generally more fluid and realistic, but the action may be less clear.

- **Follow through and overlapping action:** The idea here is to make sure your animations adhere – or seem to adhere – to the laws of physics. If there is movement in one direction, the inertia of that motion requires you to animate the follow-through even if you're changing direction.

- **Ease in and ease out:** Ease in and ease out, sometimes known as "slow in, slow out" means that natural movement does not stop and start abruptly. It flows smoothly, accelerating and decelerating. By using Bézier curves in the Ipo Curve Editor, you actually get this principle for free.

- **Arcs:** Along the same lines as the previous two principles, most natural movement happens in arcs. So if your character is changing direction or moving something, you typically want that to happen in some sort of curved, arc motion. Straight lines are generally stiff and robotic.

- **Secondary action:** These actions are those additional touches that make characters more real to the audience. Clothing that shifts with character movement, jiggling fat or loose skin, and blinking eyes are just a few actions that can breathe life into an otherwise stiff robot.

- **Timing:** This is, in my opinion, one of the most important of the 12 principles. Everything happens according to time. If the timing is off, it throws off the effect for the whole animation. This doesn't just mean controlling the timing of actions to appear believable. It also means story-based timing: knowing exactly the right time to make a character give a sad facial expression that impacts the audience the most.

✔ **Exaggeration:** Exaggeration is one of the things that makes animation fun. You can do anything with animation and you're nearly duty-bound to take advantage of that fact. Otherwise, you may as well just work in video or film with for-real people.

✔ **Solid drawing:** Solid drawing refers to the actual skill of being able to draw. Computer animators *can* get away with not being experts at drawing, but it's to your benefit to make the effort. This is because drawing is an extension of seeing. When you draw, you turn on a part of your brain that studies how things look relative to each another. Being able to see the world with these eyes can make all the difference in recreating believable motion.

✔ **Appeal:** This one is easy. Make things that are awesome. If you're going to animate something that is boring, what's the point? It needs to be interesting for you to make and it's nice if it's also interesting for other people to watch.

Those are the basic principles of animation, but not a single one of them is carved in stone. You can effectively break every one of them and still pull off some incredible animation. That said, more often than not, it's in the best interest of your work and your sanity that you at least start within these principles and then find ways where you can break them in the best way possible.

Making sense of quaternions (or, "Why are there four rotation curves?!")

Even though the bulk of your time animating with armature is spent working with the Action Editor, you still may frequently need to tweak things in the Ipo Curve Editor. If you do go to the Ipo Curve Editor and view the Pose Ipo type with the intention of tweaking rotation, you may run into a particularly jarring shock. The RotX, RotY, and RotZ channels that you would expect for rotation aren't there: They've been replaced with *four* channels to control rotation, called quaternions. Figure 12-4 shows a set of quaternions in the Ipo Curve Editor, describing the rotation of some bone.

Quaternions are a different way of defining rotations in 3D space and they're quite a bit different from the standard X, Y, and Z or *Euler* (pronounced "oiler") rotations. They're used in the rotation of bones because Euler rotations can get into a nasty situation referred to as *gimbal lock*, which involves being mathematically unable to compensate for or adjust a rotation because you only have three axes to define it. Having that happen in an armature is unacceptable. Fortunately, quaternions don't suffer from gimbal lock. However, they do suffer from another affliction: They have virtually no intuitive relationship to rotation that non-mathematicians can understand.

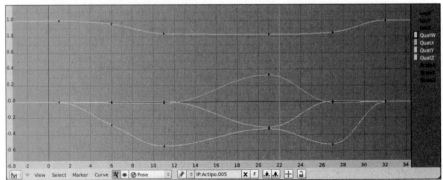

Figure 12-4:
Quaternions
in action!
They're
nearly
incompre-
hensible!

To make a long story short, it may be easier for you to tweak a rotation by adding additional keyframes to the rotation. If you're not fond of mathematics, you may very well go crazy trying to figure out how they relate to your bone's rotation.

Copying mirrored poses

One of the beauties of working in computer animation is the ability to take advantage of the computer's ability to calculate and process things so that we don't have to. In the animation world, we love to find ways that the computer can do more work. Granted, we can (and should) always temper the computer's work with our own artistic eye, but there's nothing wrong with doing half the work and letting the computer do the other half. To that end, let me introduce three incredible little buttons to you in Figure 12-5.

Figure 12-5:
Pose copy
and paste
buttons
in the 3D
View's
header.

These three buttons are located at the far right end of the 3D View's header and are only visible when you have an armature in Pose mode. "What do they do," you ask? Why, these buttons are designed for copying and pasting poses from the armature. From left to right, the buttons are Pose Copy, Pose Paste, and Pose Mirror Paste. Here's how to use them:

1. **Select all bones (A).**

   You can actually get away with just selecting a few bones, but this actually illustrates my point a little better.

2. **Left-click the Copy Pose button.**

   Doing this loads the armature's pose into the computer's memory.

3. **Move to a different location in the timeline where you would like your character to resume this pose.**

4. **Paste the pose back to the character.**

   In pasting, you have two options:

   - **Paste Pose:** This takes the coordinates of all the bones you selected when copying the pose and applies those poses back to your character exactly as you copied them.

   - **Mirror Paste:** This option does the same thing as the regular Paste Pose, except it takes advantage of Blender's built-in left/right naming convention (see Chapter 11 for more details) and pastes the mirrored version of the pose to your character. This is really handy if you're doing something like creating a walk cycle. You can create a left-foot-forward pose and then use Mirror Paste to instantly create a right-food-forward pose. Figure 12-6 shows a character posed one way and then mirror pasted to pose the other.

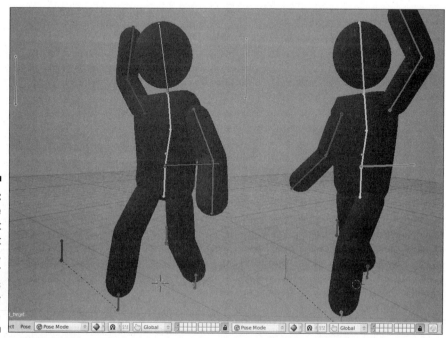

Figure 12-6: All you have to do is put one foot forward, and Blender handles the other for you.

Note that after you paste the pose, you need to insert a keyframe for that pose at that location. Otherwise, the next time you scrub the timeline, the pose won't be there and you'll have to copy and paste it all over again.

Seeing the big picture with ghosting

Traditional animation has a process called *onionskinning*, which consists of drawing on relatively thin paper and working on a table with a light in it. With this setup, the animator can stack his drawings on top of each other and get an overall sense of the motion in the animation. In Chapter 10, I introduce the Show Keys feature (press K while doing object animation) to display the object's keyframes in the 3D View. Unfortunately, when working with armatures, the Show Keys feature doesn't work in the 3D View. However, another feature works in a similar way and is, in some ways, even nicer than the Show Keys feature. It's for your rig, and it's called *Ghosting*. The controls for it are in the Editing buttons (F9) on the left side of the Visualizations panel, as shown in Figure 12-7.

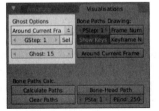

Figure 12-7:
The Visual-
izations
panel for
armatures
has options
for showing
ghosts of
your rigs.

To get the best sense of what the Ghost feature does, increase the Ghost value in this panel to its maximum value of 30 ghosts. Now, for short animations or non-complicated movement, having this enabled might not be all that useful. However, it's great for the more common forms of animation that are a bit longer and more complex. Having Ghost turned on is a great way to get a sense of where your character's coming from and where she's going. Granted, it's not like the Show Key feature of object animation, where you can actually select and edit the real keyframe from the 3D View, but as a way of having three-dimensional onionskinning, it's certainly useful. Figure 12-8 shows a character jumping up and down, visualized with armature ghosting.

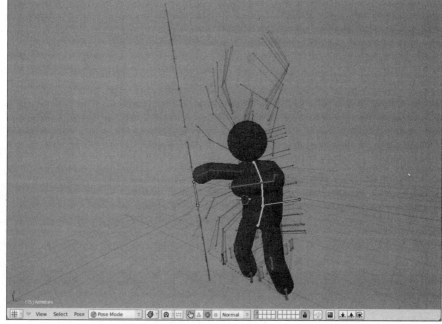

Figure 12-8:
Turning
on ghosts
in the
Visualization
panel allows
you to see
a 3D onion-
skin of your
rig's motion.

Visualizing motion with bone paths

One of the fundamental principles of animation is having arcs for movement.
Smooth arcs are favorable for believable, natural-looking animated movement. To that end, Blender has a nice feature that makes it easier to analyze
your animation and figure out if you have acceptable arcs in your character's
movement. This feature is called Bone Paths and it's also available from the
Visualizations panel in the Editing buttons, highlighted in Figure 12-9.

Figure 12-9:
The controls
for display-
ing Bone
Paths in the
3D View.

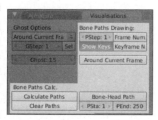

This feature isn't like Ghosts, where you just turn them on and they display instantly. They may take a second to generate. In order to generate them, first select the bone or bones that you want to visualize, and then left-click the Calculate Path button on the bottom left side of the Visualizations panel. This uses the settings along the right side of the panel to create the Bone Path visualization. An added bonus to this feature is the ability to show the location of the keys along the path as a bright dot by left-clicking the Show Keys button in the Visualizations panel. If you want, you can also show the numerical frame numbers along the curves by enabling the Frame Nums feature in the same panel. Figure 12-10 shows the same jump animation as before, but this time with Bone Paths enabled.

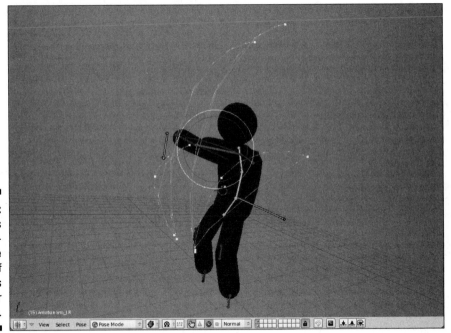

Figure 12-10:
Bone Paths help visu-alize the motion of bones in your armature.

One thing to note is that, although it might be nice, you can't actually change or edit the Bone Path directly. It can only reflect the motion created by your keyframes. So if you notice that the curve isn't as smooth as you might like, you need to go back into the Action Editor and Ipo Curve Editor and tweak the motion a bit there. Then when you re-calculate the Bone Paths, hopefully you should have a cleaner result.

Doing Non-Linear Animation

Animation is hard work, really hard work. So any time you can cut down the amount of work you have to do without detracting from the quality of the final animation, it's a good thing. Computer animation has given us another cool way to effectively and efficiently cut corners: *non-linear animation.* Non-linear animation, or NLA, is a way of animating that can only really be done with computers. In the previous section of this chapter, the process of animating is very linear and straightforward. You may animate in passes, but you're still generally working forward in time with the full start-to-finish of your animation already planned out.

What if you didn't have to work this way? What if you could animate little chunks of your character's motion and then mix and match as you like? Like mixing a simple hand-waving motion with a jumping animation so your character is sometimes just jumping and sometimes jumping and waving his arms? This is the basic concept behind non-linear animation. It's applying many of the same principles used in non-linear video editing and applying them to 3D computer animation.

The idea is that you create a library of simple motions or poses and then combine them any way you like to create much more complex animated sequences. This is useful for background characters in larger productions and it's also very handy for video game developers. Instead of trying to pull a specific set of frames from a single unified timeline, they can now just make a call to one or more of these library animations and let the computer do the rest of the work. In Blender, the basic building blocks for this library are Actions. Earlier in this chapter, I explained that Actions are really cool for visualizing the complete animation of an armature. Well, it turns out that they're even cooler than that. You can create multiple actions within a single .blend file.

To create a new action, use the Action datablock in the header of the Action Editor window, as highlighted in Figure 12-11. This datablock widget is just like the one used for materials, textures, Ipos, and even objects in other parts of Blender's interface. Create a new action by left-clicking the up/down arrow on the left side of the datablock and choosing Add New. And you can give your Action a custom name by left-clicking on the name field and typing in its new name.

Figure 12-11:
Using the
Action
datablock in
the Action
Editor to
create a
new action
for your
armature.

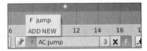

With the new action created, you can create another core animation and start building up your character's Action library. Animate waving each arm, a walk cycle, various facial expressions, a standing idle animation, and any other simple action that comes to mind. Ultimately, your library will be populated enough that you'll want to start mixing and matching them together. To do this, you're going to want to use the NLA Editor (Ctrl+Shift+F12) window. Add the NLA Editor to the Animation screen layout with the following steps:

1. **Left-click the seam at the top of the Timeline window and drag it up, making more room for that window.**

   Because the NLA Editor is covering the entire animation, it makes sense to forsake the timeline and use the NLA Editor exclusively. But if you still would like to use the Timeline, you can split if off of another window.

2. **Change the Timeline window to the NLA Editor (Ctrl+Shift+F12).**

   In doing this, you should have a screen layout that looks something like Figure 12-12.

The NLA is a very cool feature of Blender, but don't rely on it too much for animation. Blender has had the NLA Editor for a long time, but it could still use some refinement to be a truly effective tool. There was some heavy discussion about it at the last Blender Conference and hopefully there will be improvements to it in future versions of Blender. The good news is that most of what I explain here should still apply.

Mixing actions to create complex animation

To add one of your actions to the NLA Editor, bring your mouse into the NLA Editor window and press Shift+A. This brings up a menu of all the Actions you've created so you can choose one to add to the NLA Editor. After you choose the Action you would like to add, it's placed in the NLA Editor as a *strip* and is positioned wherever the time cursor is located. And now you can continue to keep adding Actions to the NLA. Of course, unless you make the last frame of one Action strip match the pose at the head of the next frame, the animation looks pretty erratic.

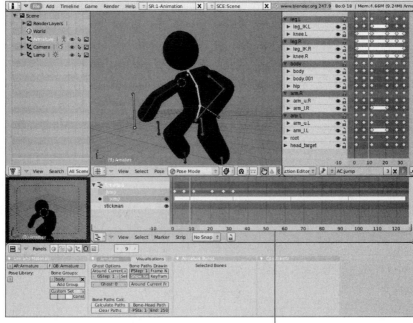

Figure 12-12: An animation screen layout with the NLA Editor added to it.

The NLA editor

The way to smooth things out is to bring up the Transform Properties floating panel in the NLA Editor. Figure 12-13 shows a full-screen NLA Editor window with the Transform Properties floating panel visible. To make the transition from one strip to the next smoother, either enable the Auto-Blending button for each strip and let them overlap a bit, or manually set the blend-in and blend-out values in this panel. This is how you create complex animations from a library of simple Actions.

Figure 12-13: Using the Transform Properties floating panel in the NLA Editor.

Taking advantage of looped animation

Another benefit of using the NLA is the ability to easily loop any Action strip and rescale its timing. This is done also in the NLA Editor with the Transform Properties floating panel. On the right side of the panel are some buttons under the heading of Options. The very first of these options is Repeat. By default, this is set to 1.0. However, you can increase this value as much as you like. As you do, you should see the strip increase in length proportional to the increase of the Repeat value. Now, to have an effective looping animation, it's definitely in your best interest to make the first pose in the action and the last pose in the action identical. The easiest way to do this is to use the copy and paste pose buttons in the 3D View:

1. **In the NLA Editor, select the Action strip you want to loop (right-click).**

2. **In the Action Editor, move the time cursor to the first pose in the Action (left-click and drag).**

3. **In the 3D View, select all bones (A) and left-click the Copy Pose button in the header.**

4. **Back in the Action Editor, move the time cursor to some place after the last keyframe.**

5. **In the 3D View, left-click the Paste Pose button in the header.**

6. **Insert a new keyframe (I⇨Available).**

   When you get to this step, all of the bones should still be selected, so there's no need to reselect anything.

7. **Now when you return to the NLA Editor, the Action strip should automatically be longer to account for the addition frame at the end.**

   Additionally, it should also loop seamlessly upon playback (Alt+A).

The Transform Properties floating panel also gives you the opportunity to rescale Actions. If you want an action to play faster or slower, you can adjust the Scale value in this panel. Values greater than 1.0 increase the length of the strip, slowing down the action, and values lower than 1.0 decrease the length of the strip, speeding up the action. Figure 12-14 shows the NLA Editor with looped strips that have varied scales.

Be careful when changing the scale of Action strips. More often than not, changing the scale results in a keyframe being placed at what's called a *fractional frame*, or a spot on the timeline that isn't a nicely rounded frame number. This isn't necessarily a bad thing, but animations do tend to look a little bit better if the keyframes fall on full frames so the audience has the chance to "read" the pose.

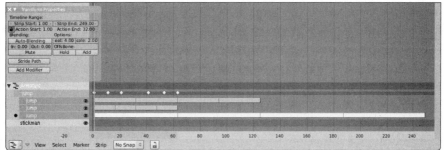

Figure 12-14:
Action strips in the NLA Editor, looped and rescaled.

Many of these animation concepts, especially ones involving the NLA, are much easier to grasp if you can see them in motion. After all, this is animation, the art of motion. Have a look at the .blend files that accompany this book to get a stronger notion of how these things work together.

Chapter 13

Letting Blender Do the Work for You

*W*hen animating, some actions are difficult or very time-consuming to get right, such as explosions, fire, hair, cloth, and physics-related actions like moving fluids and bouncing objects. In order to get these things to look right, one solution is to let the computer do the work and create a simulation of that action taking place. You use variables like gravity and mass to define the environment and the computer calculates how the objects in the scene behave based on the values you set. It's a great way to get nearly accurate motion without the need to key everything by hand. That said, don't make the mistake of thinking simulations give you a huge time savings in animation. This isn't necessarily true, as some highly detailed simulations can take hours, or even days, to complete. Instead, think of it as a way to more reliably animate detailed, physically accurate motion better than you might be able to do by hand alone.

This chapter only scratches the surface of what can be done with the simulation tools in Blender, so you should certainly look at additional resources, such as Blender's official online documentation, as well as Tony Mullen's *Bounce, Tumble, and Splash!* (published by Wiley) book on physics simulation in Blender to get a full understanding of how each feature works. But hopefully, this chapter gives you an idea of the possibilities you have at hand.

Using Particles in Blender

Blender has had an integrated particle system from its early beginnings. Over the years, though, it has grown and matured into a much more powerful system for creating particle-based effects like hair, flocks, and explosions. And the particle system gets more and more powerful with every release.

The controls for Blender's particle systems live in the Object buttons (F7). Figure 13-1 shows the header for the Object buttons window. You can get to the Particle buttons by left-clicking the button in the header that looks like a small explosion. Alternatively, you can keep pressing F7 until the particle panels appear. Initially, this buttons window looks pretty barren, with just a single panel that says Particle System. However, if you have a Mesh object selected and press Add New in this panel, five more panels for controlling particle behavior appear in the window.

Figure 13-1:
Left-click the Particle buttons icon to bring up the particle control panels.

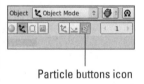

Particle buttons icon

Knowing what particle systems are good for

Particle systems have a handful of good uses. Each of these uses involves large numbers of individual objects that share some general behavior. This means that particle systems are ideal for groups of objects that move according to physics, such as fireworks or tennis balls being continuously shot at a wall. It also makes particle systems good for simulating hair and fur. If the path that an individual particle travels along were to be considered a strand, you could use groups of these particle strands to make hair. This is exactly what Blender does. There's also one other use for particle systems, and that is simple flocking or crowd simulation. Say you want to have a swarm of gnats constantly buzzing around your character's head. A particle system is a great way to pull off that effect. Figure 13-2 shows the panels you have available when you add a new particle system.

Figure 13-2:
The panels in
the Particle
buttons.

The Particle System panel offers you three types of particle systems to choose from: Emitter, Reactor, and Hair. In most instances, you will probably use the Emitter type. Reactor particle systems create particles based on the behavior of another particle system. And Hair particle systems are the way to create manageable hair and fur in Blender.

If you choose Emitter, the five values on the lower left of the Particle System panel are important for controlling how many particles you have and how long they exist in your scene. Here is a brief explanation for each value:

✔ **Amount:** As the name implies, this is the total number of particles created by the mesh. After the mesh generates this number of particles, it stops. There are a couple ways to get more particles, but the most straightforward way is to increase this number.

✔ **Sta:** Short for "Start," this is the frame where particles start being emitted from the source object. By default, this is set to frame 1, but if you don't want to have your particles start until later in your animation, you can increase the value in this field.

✔ **End:** This is the frame where Blender stops emitting particles from the source object. By default, this is set to frame 100. This means that with the default values for Amount and Sta (1000 and 1.0, respectively), Blender creates ten particles in each new frame in the animation up to frame 100.

✔ **Life:** The Life value controls how long an individual particle exists in your scene. With the default value of 50.0, this means that a particle born on frame 7 disappears from the scene when you reach frame 57. If you find that your particles aren't lasting as long as you need them to, increase this value.

✔ **Rand:** This is a value that pertains specifically to the Life of the particle. At its default of 0.0, it doesn't change anything. However, if you increase this value, it introduces a random variation to the life of your particles. This way, not all of the particles born on one frame disappear at the same time, so you end up with a more natural effect.

Any of these types can be associated with one of four varieties of physics simulation models: None, Newtonian, Keyed, and Boids. Very rarely do you have a need to use None as an option, but it's good to have. Typically, the default Newtonian setting is the most useful option because it tends to simulate real-world physical attributes such as gravity, mass, and velocity. Occasionally, though, you may want to have more explicit control over your particles, such as when you are shaping the hair on a character. This is where Keyed physics come to play. You can use the *Emitter object* of one particle system to control the angle and direction of another one.

To create a basic particle system, use the following steps:

1. **Add a mesh to work as your particle Emitter (spacebar⇨Add⇨Mesh⇨Grid⇨OK).**

   In this example, I'm using a simple grid, but really any mesh works. In fact, depending on what you're trying to do, different mesh types work better than others. The key thing to remember is that particles tend to be emitted from the faces of your mesh. They move away from the face in the direction of that face's normal.

2. **Navigate to the Particle Buttons (F7⇨F7⇨F7) and add a new particle system.**

   After you press the Add New button, all of the options available to particles become visible. Of course, trying to play back the animation now won't be all that interesting. You need to set a few options first.

3. **Choose the type of particle system you wish to use from the Particle System panel.**

   In this example, I'm choosing the default setting of Emitter. Feel free to try using one of the other types, but be aware that Reactor particle systems require that you have more than one particle system set up. Also, a button I usually click in this panel is the Random button that appears under Emit From.

   Left-clicking this button changes the timing on the birth of your particles, making it look more natural and less mechanical.

4. **Decide what type of physics you would like to have controlling your particles.**

   As I mentioned before, Newtonian physics are usually the most common type of particle system used, but I'm also pretty fond of Boids physics for Emitter particle systems. It just looks cool, and they're a lot of fun!

5. **Adjust the physics settings to control particle behavior.**

   For Newtonian physics, you have to give your particles some sort of initial velocity. I tend to adjust the Normal velocity first because it gives the most immediate results. Values above zero go along each face's normals, whereas values below zero go in the opposite direction. Boid particles don't require an initial velocity, but the settings do adjust how each Boid particle interacts with its neighboring particles.

6. **Play back the animation to watch the particles move (Alt+A).**

   When you playback, it would be a good idea to make sure you're at frame 1 when you start. Otherwise, you might not see the proper particle simulation. Watch how your particles move and behave. If you don't like how they're working, press Esc to stop the playback and go adjust your settings. Then play the animation again. This back-and-forth tweaking is how you refine your particle system's behavior.

Figure 13-3 shows the above process being done. Bear in mind that this is a very basic particle system setup and you're just barely scratching the surface of what's possible. I definitely recommend that you take some time to play with each of the settings and figure out what they do, as well as read some of the more in-depth documentation on particles in Blender's online documentation.

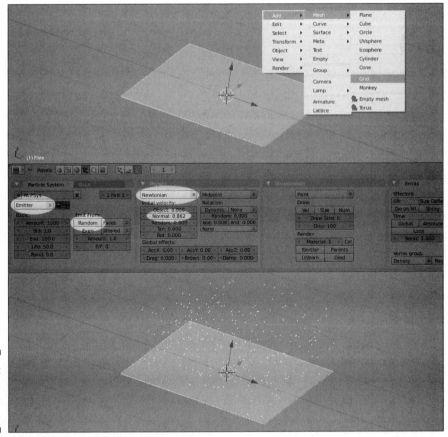

Figure 13-3:
Creating a basic particle system.

Using forces and deflectors

After you've created a basic particle system, you can have a little bit of fun with it, controlling the behavior of your particles. You control this by using forces and deflectors. A *force* is a controlling influence on the overall behavior of the particles, such as wind, vortices, and magnetism. In contrast, in Blender terms a *deflector* is basically something that a particle collides with and impedes its progress. Generally speaking, forces are defined using Empties, whereas deflectors are created with Meshes.

All of the controls for forces and deflectors live in the Physics buttons. Referring back to Figure 13-1, the Physics buttons are accessed by left-clicking the button to the left of the Particle buttons icon. You can also reveal these buttons by pressing F7 repeatedly, cycling through the Object buttons until they appear. For particle forces, use the Fields panel on the far left. In a separate tab on that panel are the Collision settings. This is specifically for particle collisions, or deflectors.

Now, I could go through each and every option available here exhaustively, but things usually make more sense if you have an example to work with. That being the case, use the following steps to create a particle system that creates particles that are influenced by a wind force that causes them to collide with a wall and then bounce off of it:

1. **Create a simple particle system.**

   If you need a refresher, use the steps in the last section to create a basic Emitter particle system with Newtonian physics.

2. **Add an Empty (spacebar⇨Add⇨Empty).**

   This Empty is the source of your wind force. The wind moves along the Empty's local Z-axis, so keep that in mind as you position and orient it in space.

3. **Make the Empty a Wind force.**

   Navigate to the Physics buttons (F7⇨F7) and, in the Fields panel, choose Wind from the menu. When you do this, notice that the Empty now has circles arranged along its local Z-axis. This is a visual cue to let you know that you've got a wind force. Increasing the Strength value in the Fields panel spaces out four circles to help show how much wind you're creating. Scrub back to frame 1 and you can play back the animation (Alt+A) to see how your wind is affecting the movements of the particles.

4. **Add a Plane (spacebar⇨Add⇨Mesh⇨Plane).**

   This Plane is your deflector. Grab the plane (G) and move it so that it's in the path of the wind that is pushing your particles. Rotate (R) the plane to make sure the particles actually run into it head-on.

5. Make the Plane a Collision object.

In the Physics buttons, left-click the Collision tab in the Field panel and left-click the Collision button in this panel. Whammo! You've made a deflector! If you set your time at frame 1 and play back the animation (Alt+A), your particles should be blown by your wind force into your plane, which they should bounce off of rather than shoot straight through.

Figure 13-4 shows this results of this step-by-step process. And like the section before this one, you're just seeing the tip of the iceberg in terms of what's possible with forces and deflectors. There are all sorts of cool forces and settings that you can use to get some very unique behavior out of your particle systems.

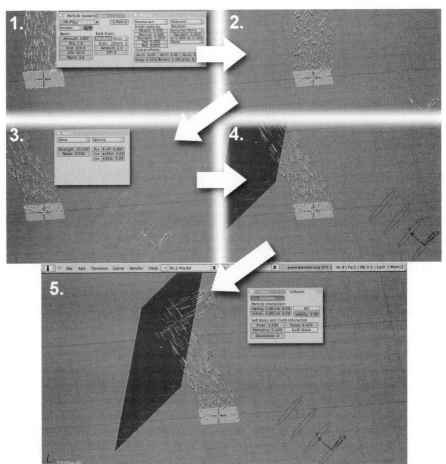

Figure 13-4:
Creating a wind force that blows your particles into a plane, which they bounce off of.

Using particles for hair and fur

It would be remiss of me to cover particles and not say anything about Blender's hair and fur system. Blender uses particles to create hair and fur for your characters. As you may have guessed, this is done when you choose Hair as the type of particle system you want from the Particle System panel in the Particle buttons. From there, the setup is roughly the same as using a regular Emitter system with Newtonian physics, but there are two notable differences. The first difference is the Set Editable button that appears to the right of the particle system type menu. By left-clicking this button, you freeze the particle settings that you've already set and, by doing so, you make it so you can specially customize the hair in Blender's Particle Edit mode. Figure 13-5 shows a screenshot of an object with particle hair being combed in Particle Edit mode.

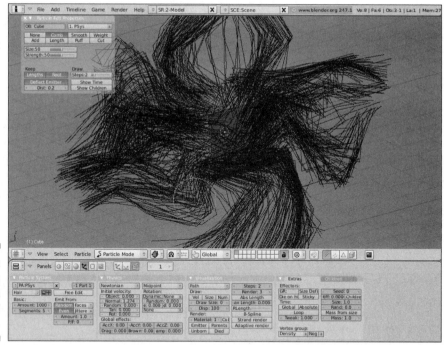

Figure 13-5: Combing hair in Particle mode.

You switch to Particle mode using the Mode menu in the 3D View window's header. With your Emitter object selected, left-click the menu and choose Particle Mode. When you're in Particle mode, you have the ability to directly edit particle hair, including combing, cutting, growing, and smoothing it out. To see these controls, enable the Particle Edit Properties floating window by pressing N or choosing Particles⇨Particle Edit Properties from the 3D View's header. Particle Mode gives you a circular brush like the one used in sculpting and vertex paint modes. You can adjust its size and strength using the sliders in the Particle Edit Properties window or by pressing F and Shift+F, respectively.

The other thing that differs in the setup of hair particles is the use of *child particles*. Creating and displaying hair particles can take up a lot of computing power, and when animating, you don't necessarily want to be waiting on Blender to draw your character's fur in the 3D window. To deal with this, there are two solutions, and the results are best when they're used together. The first thing is to reduce the number of viewable particles in the 3D view. This is done with the Disp value in the Visualization panel of the Particle buttons. Disp changes the percentage of particles being displayed in the 3D view. When you make this change, fewer particles show up in the 3D View, but all of them appear when you render. That gives you the best of both worlds.

Of course, for characters with a lot of hair, just reducing the displayable particles might not be enough. This is where child particles are useful. In the last panel of the Particle buttons, left-click the Children tab and choose Faces from the menu in this panel. This causes additional particle strands to grow from the faces of your emitter, with their locations determined by the particles around them. The Children panel has two Amount settings on the left column. The first Amount dictates how many particles are seen in the 3D View. For speed while animating, I often set this value to zero. The second value is the Render Amount. This is the number of child particles that each parent particle has at render time.

With the particle system properly generating your hairs, the only thing you have to worry about now is controlling how Blender renders this hair. Here's a quick-and-dirty rundown of the steps I go through to get the hair to render nicely (a reference file for this is included on the CD-ROM that comes with this book):

1. **Enable Strand render in the Visualization panel of the Particle buttons.**

   This tells Blender's rendering engine to render the particles as strands. Another helpful option in this panel is the Emitter button on the left side under the Render label. Enabling this option makes the emitter visible, which is helpful if you're using your actual character mesh to generate the hair.

2. **In the Material buttons (F5), turn on ZTransp in the Links and Pipeline panel and set your Alpha value to zero in the Material panel.**

   If you're using the Hair strands preview type in the Preview panel (I recommend doing this), you may notice that your hair is virtually nonexistent because of the zero Alpha value. Don't worry: This will all make sense in the next couple of steps.

3. **In the Texture buttons (F6), add a new Blend texture and use the Colorband in the Colors panel to control the color and transparency along the length of the hair.**

   The most important thing here is that the right hand side of the colorband should be completely transparent. All other color positions in it should be opaque.

4. **Back in the Material buttons (F5), under the Map Input panel, enable the Strand button. In the Map To panel, enable Col and Alpha.**

   Now the Preview panel should show hair strands that use your colorband gradient along the length each strand, feathered out to semi-transparent tips.

5. **Still in the Material buttons, go to the Links and Pipeline panel and left-click the Strands button near the bottom of the panel.**

   There are a couple fields here worth mentioning:

   - Make sure Use Tangent Shading is enabled. This gives the hair a nice shiny effect.

   - Enable the Use Blender Units button. By default, Blender's hair strands are measured in pixels. This works fine except in situations where you have a hairy object move toward or away from the camera. Enabling this button makes the hair size relative to your scene rather than the size of your final render.

   - Because you're using Blender Units for hair size, you need to reduce the sizes for the Start and End of the hair strands. I usually use something like 0.02 and 0.01, respectively. You may need a few test renders to get it just right for your object.

   - The other sliders control the shape of the strands; you can adjust these to taste with a few test renders.

Giving Objects Some Jiggle and Bounce

Have you ever sat and watched what happens when a beach ball gets hit or bounces off of the ground? Or seen what happens when someone places a plate of Jell-O on a table? Or observed how a person's hair moves when they shake their head? When these things move and collide with other objects, they have a bit of internal jiggle that can be difficult to reproduce correctly with regular animation tools. This is the basis for what we refer to as *soft body dynamics*. That effect can be simulated in Blender using the second set of panels in the Physics buttons (F7⇨F7). What follows is a simple step-by-step process for creating a simple soft body simulation with the default cube object:

1. **Select the cube with a right-click and grab it up in the Z-axis so it floats above the 3D grid (G⇨Z).**

   You want to give the cube some height to fall from. It doesn't have to be very high; 3 to 5 Blender units should be enough.

2. **Create a Plane mesh as a ground plane (Spacebar⇨Add⇨Mesh⇨Plane) and Scale it larger so that you have something for the Cube to hit (S).**

   This is the surface for your jiggly cube to bounce off of. It may be helpful to put your 3D cursor at the origin (Shift+C) before adding the plane.

3. **In the first Collision panel of the Physics buttons (F7⇨F7), left-click the Collision button.**

   Doing so makes Blender understand that the plane is an obstacle for our falling cube.

4. **Right-click the cube to select it and then left-click the Soft Body button in the Soft Body panel.**

   That's all you really have to do to enable soft body physics on your 3D objects. However, in order to get the cube to properly act according to gravity, there's one more step.

5. **Left-click the Use Goal button in the Soft Body panel.**

   This disables the default Use Goal behavior of soft bodies. This means that when Use Goal is enabled, you can define a group of vertices in the object to be unaffected by the soft body simulation. A scenario where you may want to do this would be a character with loose skin, like the jowls of a large dog. You may want the dog's snout to be completely controlled by your armature animation, but have the jowls that hang off to be influenced by soft body simulation. Because in this case we want the entire object to be affected by the simulation, it's best just to turn it off.

6. **Play back the animation (Alt+A) to watch the cube fall, hit the ground plane, and jiggle as it lands again.**

   Pretty cool, huh? Figure 13-6 shows this process being completed. As with particles, it's a good practice to make sure you're at frame 1 before playing back your simulation.

Now, I have to admit that I cheated a bit in the example above by using a cube. If you were to try those steps with another type of mesh, like a UV Sphere or Suzanne, the mesh would collapse and look like it instantly deflated when it hit the ground plane. In order to get around this, you need to adjust one more setting. In the Soft Body panel on the last row of buttons is a button that says Be: with a default value of 0.00. This value sets the Bending Stiffness of your object. With a setting of zero, there is no stiffness, so the mesh collapses. However, if you set this to a higher value such as 3.0 or 5.0, the falling mesh retains its shape better when it collides with the ground plane.

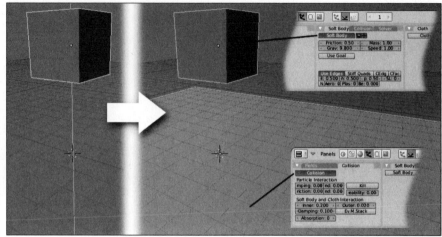

Figure 13-6:
Dropping a
jiggly cube
into the
scene.

Dropping Objects in a Scene with Rigid Body Dynamics

Not everything that reacts to physics has the internal jiggle and bounce that soft bodies have. Say, for example, you have to animate a stack of heavy steel girders falling down at a construction site. For that, you don't want to have a soft body simulation. You'd much prefer to have what's called *rigid body dynamics*. As their name implies, rigid bodies don't get warped by collisions the way that soft bodies do. They either hold their form when they collide, or they break.

Unlike the other physical simulation, the controls for rigid bodies are not in the Physics buttons. Not yet, at least; there are plans to integrate the rigid body simulation tools with the other physics tools in a future release of Blender. In the meantime, however, the way to get rigid body dynamics in Blender is to use the integrated game engine. Use the following steps to get a simple rigid body simulation with the default cube:

1. **Select the cube by right-clicking and Grab it up in the Z-axis by a few Blender units (G⇨Z).**

   Like the soft body simulation, 3 to 5 Blender units should be fine.

2. **Create a mesh Plane to act as the ground (spacebar⇨Add⇨Mesh⇨Plane) and Scale it larger so that you have something for the Cube to hit (S).**

3. **In the World buttons (F8), make sure the physics engine is set to Bullet and the gravity is set at 9.80.**

You can find these settings at the top of the Mist/Stars/Physics panel. Bullet is the name for the main physics suite built into Blender's game engine.

4. **Right-click the cube to select it and bring up the Logic buttons (F4).**

   The Logic buttons house the controls for Blender's integrated game engine. There's a lot that goes on here, but you're really only interested in the left-most column.

5. **Left-click the Actor button and enable the Dynamic and Rigid Body buttons.**

   Left-clicking the Actor button makes the cube recognized as a moving object in the game engine. By turning on the Dynamic and Rigid Body attributes, you tell the game engine that the cube is going to have simulated movement, and that motion will be controlled by the rigid body dynamics simulator.

6. **Left-click the Bounds button.**

   Activating the Bounds button enables the game engine to understand that the cube has boundaries that need to be recognized for collisions. Because you're using a cube, the default setting of Box will work fine in this example. For more complex meshes, you may prefer to use the Convex Hull or Triangle Mesh settings.

7. **Test the simulation by pressing P to start the game engine.**

   At this point, you have a valid rigid body simulation. You can stop the game engine at any time by pressing Esc. If you'd like, you can rotate (R) the cube to an odd angle and rerun the simulation to see how that affects the cube's motion. However, even though you have a valid simulation now, at this point, you can't see the simulation when you play back using Alt+A. This is because the simulation is only happening in the game engine. To get it to play back in regular Blender, you have to feed the simulation data to Blender's animation system. That is done with the next steps, called *baking* the simulation.

8. **Enable recording game physics to Blender's animation system.**

   To do this, go to the main header and enable the Record Game Physics to IPO option (Game⇨Record Game Physics to IPO).

9. **Start the game engine (P) to run the simulation.**

   When the simulation is complete, press Esc to get back into the regular interface.

10. **The simulation is now baked to Ipo curves.**

    You can see this by selecting the cube (right-click) and bringing up an Ipo Curve Editor window (Shift+F6). Now when you play back the animation (Alt+A), the results of the simulation should appear just fine. Figure 13-7 shows a breakdown of these steps.

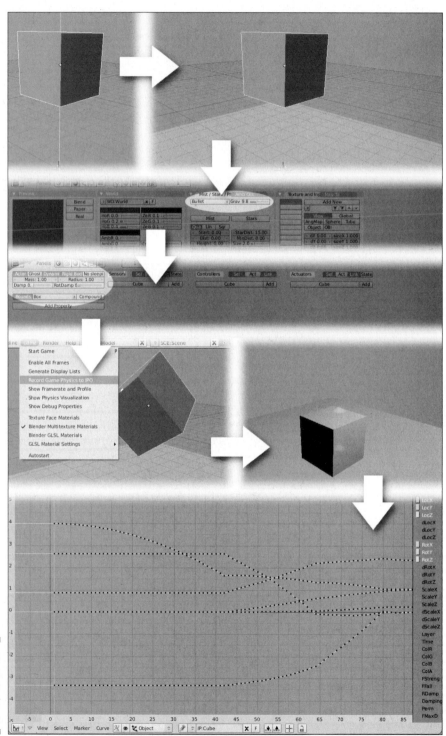

Figure 13-7:
Creating
a simple
rigid body
simulation.

Simulating Cloth

Cloth simulation and soft body simulation are very similar in Blender. There are a few key differences, though. Both soft bodies and cloth work on open as well as closed meshes. (That is, the mesh could be flat like a plane or more of a shell like a cube or sphere.) However, soft bodies tend to work better on closed meshes, whereas cloth is better suited for open ones. Also, the cloth simulator tends to work better with *self collisions*. Think about the fabric of a flowing dress. In the real world, if you bunch up part of a dress, it's technically colliding with itself. In computer simulations, you want to re-create that effect; otherwise, the fold of one part of the dress breaks through the fold of another part, giving you a completely unrealistic result. The cloth simulator handles situations like this much better than the soft body simulator.

Revisiting the simple default cube, here's a quick walk-through on getting some cloth to drape across it:

1. **Create a mesh Grid (Spacebar⇨Add⇨Mesh⇨Grid⇨OK) and Grab it along the Z-axis (G⇨Z) so that it's above the default cube. Scale the Grid so it's larger than the Cube (S).**

   It doesn't have to be too high over the cube; just a couple of Blender units should be plenty.

   It would also probably be a good idea to Set Smooth these vertices (Tab⇨W⇨Set Smooth⇨Tab).

2. **Apply a Subdivision Surfaces modifier to the plane (Ctrl+1).**

   This just gives the simulator even more vertices to work with. Of course, adding too many vertices causes the simulation to take a long amount of time, but this should be fine for this example.

3. **In the Cloth panel of the Physics buttons (F7⇨F7), left-click the Cloth button to enable the cloth simulator.**

   The default material preset for the cloth simulator is Cotton. That should work fine here, but feel free to play with the values and change them to something else.

4. **In the Collision tab of this same panel, left-click the Enable Self-Collisions button.**

   This ensures that the simulator does everything it can to prevent the cloth from intersecting with itself. At this point, your cloth simulation is all set up for the plane. However, if you were to play the animation with Alt+A right now, the plane would drop right through the cube. You want the cube to behave as an obstacle, so follow the next steps.

5. **Select the cube object (right-click) and navigate to the Collision tab on the left-most panel in the Physics buttons and left-click the Collision button.**

This is where things can be a little confusing. You may have noticed that there are actually three different Collision panels in the Physics buttons. Well, think of the left-most Collision panel as the controls for general collisions, whereas the other panels are specific to soft body and cloth objects, respectively. Because the cube is not a cloth or soft body object, you use this panel to control how those other objects collide with it.

6. **Your simulation is set up. Press Alt+A to watch the cloth simulate.**

Figure 13-8 shows what the results of this process should look like. Make sure that you're at frame 1 before playing back the simulation.

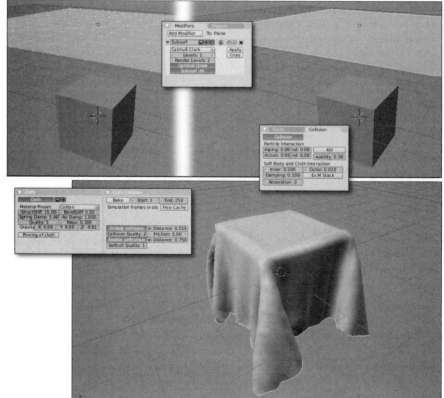

Figure 13-8:
Creating a simple cloth simulation.

Splashing Fluids in Your Scene

In my opinion, one of the most remarkable features in Blender is its integrated fluid simulator. This thing is just really cool and a ton of fun to play with, to boot. Before running head-long into fluid simulation-land, however, you should know a few things that are different about the fluid simulator. Like most of the other physics simulation controls, the main controls for the fluid simulator are in the Physics buttons (F7⇔F7). However, unlike the other simulations, which can technically work in an infinite amount of space, the fluid simulator requires a *domain*, or world, for the simulation to take place. Otherwise, the numbers get to be incredibly large, making the simulation slow to solve.

Another difference is that the fluid simulator actually creates a separate mesh for each and every frame of animation that it simulates. Because of the detail involved in a fluid, these meshes can get to be quite large and take up a lot of memory. To account for that, the fluid simulator actually saves these meshes to your hard drive in .bobj.gz files. The other simulation systems also save data to your hard drive, but because fluid simulation data can take up an enormous amount of hard drive space, you need to tell Blender where to save these files. And because these files can get pretty large, it's a good idea to make sure you have plenty of hard drive space available for storing your simulation meshes.

The fluid simulator has all of the other features of the other physics simulators. It recognizes gravity, understands static and animated collisions, and has a wide array of available controls. Use the steps below to create a simple fluid simulation:

1. **Right-click the default cube and Scale (S) it larger.**

   This cube serves as your simulation's domain. The domain can actually be any size, but I definitely recommend that you use a cube or box shape as the domain. Other meshes are turned into a box shape just based on their width and height. In this example, I scaled the default cube by 5 units.

2. **In the Fluid panel of the Physics button, left-click the Enable button and choose Domain from the block of buttons to the right.**

   Now the fluid simulator recognizes your cube as the domain for the simulation. Figure 13-9 shows the Fluid panel with the Domain button enabled.

Figure 13-9:
The Fluid panel with options for a domain object.

3. **Set the location where simulation meshes are saved.**

   This is in the bottom input box of the panel. By default, Blender sends the .bobj.gz files to the /tmp directory, but I recommend you create your own folder somewhere else on your hard drive, especially if you're on Windows and don't have a /tmp directory. Left-click the folder icon to navigate to that location with the File Browser window.

4. **Decide at which resolution you would like to bake the simulation.**

   These values are set in the same panel as Resolution and Preview-Res. The Resolution setting is the value that is used when you render. Typically, it's a higher number than the Preview-Res, which is usually used in the 3D view, so you want a smaller number for this so you can get your timing correct. The defaults should work fine for this example, although higher values would look better. Be careful, though, depending on the type of machine you're using: Values greater than 150 may try to use more RAM than your computer has, bringing the simulation time to a crawl.

5. **Determine the time that you want to simulate the fluid's behavior.**

   The Start Time and End Time values in the Fluid panel are the time of the simulation, measured in seconds. By default, the simulator starts at 0.0 and runs until 0.3 seconds. An important thing to realize here is that this time is scaled across the full number of frames in your animation, as noted in the Anim panel of the Render buttons. This means that if you're using Blender's default frame rate of 25 fps and length of 250 frames, you're simulation will be in slow motion, showing three-tenths of a second of fluid simulation over a span of 10 seconds. For this test, I set the End time in the Fluid simulator to 3.0 seconds and the duration of the animation to be 75 frames long.

6. **Create a mesh to act as the fluid in your simulation (spacebar⇨Add⇨Mesh⇨Icosphere).**

   For this, I typically like to use an Icosphere, but any mesh will work. To give yourself some more room, you may also want to move this mesh up the Z-axis (G⇨Z) to somewhere near the top of the domain cube, so you have some room for the fluid to fall.

7. **In the Fluid panel of the Physics button, left-click the Enable button and choose Inflow from the block of buttons to the right.**

   This sets your source mesh as the source for the fluids entering the domain. Choosing Inflow means that the mesh constantly produces more and more fluid as the simulation goes on. If you would prefer to have a single fluid object with a fixed volume, choose Fluid instead of Inflow. Figure 13-10 shows the Fluid panel with the Inflow fluid type chosen.

Figure 13-10:
The Fluid
panel with
options for
an inflow
object.

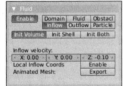

8. **Give the Inflow object an initial velocity in the negative Z direction.**

   This value doesn't have to be large: –0.10 should work just fine. You want to make this value negative so that it pushes the fluid down. This initial velocity is added to the force already set by gravity. At this point, your simulation is configured.

9. **Select the domain cube (right-click) and bake the simulation.**

   Do this by clicking the large Bake button in the Fluid panel. I know that this sounds odd — "Baking fluids? Really?" — but that's the terminology used. You are running the simulation for each frame and "baking" that frame's simulation result to a mesh that's saved on your hard drive. If you look at it like that, it *kind* of makes sense.

10. **Watch the progress of the fluid simulation.**

    Depending on how powerful your computer is, this baking process can be pretty time-consuming. I once had a four-second fluid simulation that took 36 hours to bake. (Granted, it was at a high resolution and I had a lot of crazy Inflow objects and complex moving obstacles, so it was entirely my own fault.) Just know that the more complexity you add to your simulation and the higher the resolution, the more time it's going to take. Along with watching the actual simulation, you can keep an eye on a progress bar at the top of the screen that shows which frames the simulator is processing.

11. **Play back the finished simulation with Alt+A.**

    One thing to note here is that your mesh looks faceted. This is easily fixed by pressing the Set Smooth button in the Link and Materials panel of the Editing buttons (F9).

And, *POW:* You have water pouring into your scene! Using these same basic steps, you can add obstacles to the scene that can move the water around as you see fit. Check out the color insert for an awesome still image created with the fluid simulator by Blender artist, Mike Pan.

Part IV
Sharing Your Work with the World

In this part . . .

So you've created something awesome. Well, as great as that is, it's always more fun to show it to other people. You can get feedback and critiques for improvement and you can get accolades and awards for your excellent work. In order to do that, you want to get your scenes out as still images and your animations out as video files. The chapters in this part don't just focus on rendering your 3D scene: They also cover the integrated Node Compositor and video sequencer. These tools are fantastic for quick fixes, adjustments, and visual effects such as mixing your animation with live video.

Chapter 14

Exporting and Rendering Scenes

In This Chapter
- ▶ Exporting to other programs
- ▶ Rendering still images and animations

Working in Blender is great, but, eventually, you'll want to make the things you create viewable in programs other than Blender. You may want to have a still image of a scene, or a movie of your character falling down a flight of stairs, or you may want to export the geometry and textures of a model to use in a video game. In these situations, you want to export or render. The best way to remember the difference between the two is that *exporting* takes your 3D data from Blender and restructures it so that other 3D programs can understand it, whereas *rendering* is the process of taking your 3D data and creating a 2D picture from the perspective of a camera. That 2D image can then be seen in image editors like The GIMP and Photoshop or movie players like QuickTime and VLC.

Exporting to External Formats

There are two primary reasons why you'd want to export to a different 3D file format than Blender's .blend format. The most common is to do additional editing in another program. For instance, if you're working as a modeler on a large project and you decide to use Blender, chances are good that whomever hired you unfortunately is not using Blender, so you're probably going to have to save it in a format that their program understands.

The other reason for exporting is for video games. Many video games have a public specification for the file format they use for the 3D information in them. Blender can export in many of these formats, allowing you to create custom characters and sets for the games that support them.

All of Blender's exporters are scripts written in the Python programming language. This means that if you have the knowledge (or know someone who does), you can customize pretty quickly an exporter for your needs. It also means that if you there's a format that Blender doesn't currently export to, it's pretty easy to write a script to add that support.

Although all of the export scripts that ship with Blender support the basic specifications in their respective formats, they may not support all of the features. For instance, many of the exporters have difficulty getting armature or animation information out of them. So keep this in mind and, as many open source programmers like to say, "Your mileage may vary."

In order to export to a different format, choose File➪Export and choose the format that you would like to use. Some of these exporters immediately pop up a second box so you can choose some options that are specific to that exporter. After you make your choices there, you get the File Browser window, where you can tell Blender where to save your new file. Figure 14-1 shows the Export menu with a list of the available file types.

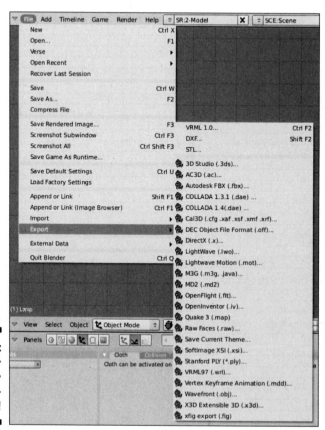

Figure 14-1:
File➪
Export➪
Wheee-
eeee!

Rendering a Scene

More often than exporting, though, you probably want to render your scenes. Rendering creates an image or animation that nearly anyone can view, even if they don't have Blender. You can upload your renders to a Web site for others to see and comment on, or you take your renders into an image editing program or video editor for additional processing

 When you render an image, you're creating a two-dimensional image from your three-dimensional scene, using the perspective of your camera object. This is very much like taking a photograph or a movie in the real world. If you don't have a camera, you can't take a picture. Likewise in Blender, if there's no camera in your scene, Blender doesn't know what to render, so make sure you have a camera in there.

Creating a still image

Rendering single images, or *stills*, in Blender is remarkably easy. Blender actually offers three different ways to do it. The fastest way is to simply press F12. Alternatively, you can click the large Render button in the Render buttons (F10) or choose Render⟶Render Current Frame from the top header. Any way you decide to do it, by default, Blender pops up a new window where the render output shows up while it's being created. However, I'm not particularly fond of Blender popping up a new window. I prefer to have just one window to work within. Fortunately, there are options available to allow you (and me!) to do just that. The control for where the render is displayed is in the Output panel of the Render buttons. It's the menu button at the bottom of the panel. By default, it's set to Render window. The grid of buttons to the left is used to tell Blender where to place the Render window. The default setting places it in the upper right corner of your screen. Click any of these buttons to place the window there. If you have more than one button depressed at the same time, Blender places the Render window approximately between those two points on your screen.

Figure 14-2 shows the Output panel and the three different options you have for where to send your renders. I like to use Image Editor or Full Screen. When you choose one of these options, rather than open a new window for the render, Blender uses its integrated Image Editor window to display the rendered output. If you choose Image Editor, Blender takes the largest window in your screen layout and changes it to the UV/Image Editor window to display your image. Choosing Full Screen does the same thing, except it also maximizes that window to the entire Blender work area. For any of these render options, you can quickly toggle between your regular Blender screen and the render screen by pressing F11.

Figure 14-2:
To view
your
renders,
choose to
use Full
Screen,
Image
Editor, or
Render
Window.

Another cool feature that works regardless of which way you like to see your renders is the render buffer swap. When you have your render output onscreen and press J with your mouse cursor in that window, Blender switches to a different image buffer. The first time you do this, it may seem odd because it will just give you a blank window. However, make a small change to your scene and render again (F12). Now when you press J on your render, you can quickly compare the differences between the two renders. This is a great way to see whether you like the changes you've made.

Now, you have your image rendered, but you still haven't saved it anywhere on your hard drive, so that you can share it with other people. This, too, is easy, but before you save, you may want to change the file format you save to. This is done in the Format panel of the Render buttons, as shown in Figure 14-3.

Figure 14-3:
Format
panel in
Render
buttons.

You choose your format in the bottom block of buttons on this panel. By default, Blender renders to JPEG images. If you wish to render to a different image format, such as PNG, Targa, TIFF, or OpenEXR, left-click on the first button in this block and choose your desired format. Below the format selection button are a couple of options that relate to how the image is output. For instance, the Q button is a quality setting. It controls the level of compression in the image. Higher numbers give higher quality renders with low compression (and therefore larger file sizes), whereas smaller numbers give lower quality renders with heavy compression. The FPS buttons are more relevant for animation, so I cover those in the next section.

The BW/RGB/RGBA buttons are pretty important for both animations and stills. They control whether Blender renders a black and white (grayscale) image, a full color image, or a color image with an alpha channel for transparency. Typically, you use one of the latter two. RGB is the most common and is supported by all formats, creating a full color image. There are occasions, however, when you want to render with transparency. As an example, say you've made a really cool building model and you want to add your building to a photo of some city skyline. For this, you need everything that's not your building, including the background of your image, to be rendered as transparent. That transparency is defined by an alpha channel. The *alpha channel* is basically a grayscale image that defines what is and is not transparent. Totally white pixels are opaque and totally black pixels are transparent. Gray pixels are semi-transparent.

Not all image formats support an alpha channel. For instance, the JPEG and BMP formats don't recognize alpha, so if you have RGBA set, Blender just omits the alpha information when saving to either of these. If you want to make sure your alpha channel is preserved, though, choose one of the following formats: PNG, Targa, TIFF, or OpenEXR.

The Format panel also gives you control over the size of your final render with the buttons at the top of the panel. The SizeX and SizeY values set the width and height of your image in pixels. The AspX and AspY values are for determining the horizontal and vertical aspect ratio of your image. This is for certain circumstances where you want to render your image with rectangular pixels rather than square ones. Typically, this is done only for television formats, so unless you know exactly what you're doing or if you're using a preset, I'd recommend setting these to the same value. I use 1.0 most of the time.

Speaking of presets, Blender offers a number of format presets for you to render to. These are listed down the right side of the panel, and left-clicking any one of them changes settings throughout the Render buttons to get the render to properly match that format. This is a great timesaver when you know, for instance, that you have to render to high definition video specifications, but for some reason cannot remember all of the right resolution and frame rate information.

Whenever you change the size or aspect settings in the Format panel, you need to render your scene again (F12) to get it to appear in the right size. Re-rendering is not necessary, however, for setting your output file format.

After you've adjusted all your settings, rendered, and chosen your output file format, there's just one thing left to do: save your still. Saving is quick and painless. Press F3 (File➪Save Rendered Image) and Blender brings up a File Browser window, where you can dictate where on your computer you want to save your render. That's it!

Remember, if you're rendering a still image, it's *not* saved anywhere on your hard drive unless you explicitly save it by pressing F3 or navigating to File➪Save Rendered Image. I can't tell you how much time I spent re-rendering images that I forgot to save when I first started using Blender. Hopefully, you can learn from my mistake.

Creating a finished animation

For rendering animations, the steps are similar to rendering stills, but you have a few more considerations. The largest consideration deals with the format you choose. If, for instance, you choose a still image format like JPEG, PNG, or OpenEXR, Blender creates an individual image for each frame in your animation. However, if you choose the AVI, QuickTime, or FFMPEG options, Blender creates a single movie file that contains all the frames in the animation, as well as any sound you use for the animation. Note that Macintosh and most Windows users have the QuickTime option available, but Linux users are able to use only FFMPEG or AVI.

In the case of QuickTime and FFMPEG, you have a second set of choices that enables you to pick the *codec*, or compression format, you want to use. QuickTime has its own dialog box that pops up, whereas FFMPEG reveals tabs for two more panels in the Render buttons: Video and Audio. Figure 14-4 shows these two new panels.

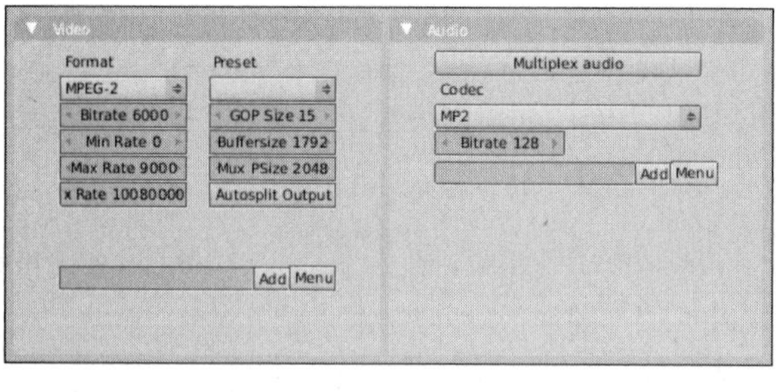

Figure 14-4:
The Video and Audio panels in the Render buttons.

A note about formats and codecs

When it comes to video files, you'll often hear people refer to formats, containers, codecs, and compression formats. Trying to figure out what each thing is can get to be pretty confusing. To start at the beginning, codecs are compression formats. They are the *algorithms*, or methods, by which all the frames in a video are compressed, in an effort to make the size of the movie file small. When one codec has a better *compression ratio* than another, it means that for the small file size created with that codec, there's a higher quality image when it's played back. Some examples of video codecs are MPEG-4, h.264, Sorenson, MPEG2, and DV. Common audio codecs are MP3, FLAC, and Vorbis.

Some codecs can live on their own as files, often called *raw files*, but more often, they are wrapped in *container format* like QuickTime or AVI. QuickTime and AVI don't actually do any compression on their own. Instead, they serve as a home for the codecs to live in. The benefit of a container format is that it can contain both audio and video data, and it supports a bunch of different codecs. Theoretically, a player that can read QuickTime files can be

made to understand anything that's wrapped in a QuickTime container. The other benefit of container formats is something called *metadata*. Basically, metadata is information about the file, packed alongside the codecs in it. This includes functional information like knowing the codecs used in the container, as well as supplemental information like knowing who made the file, when, and for which project.

The relationship between codecs and containers does get a bit hairy because a few codecs *also* can be containers, such as MP4. MP4 is the type of file for an MPEG-4 video, and therefore the raw format for that type of codec. However, MP4 can act as a container for not only MPEG-4 video (and all the nuanced ways you can create MPEG-4 videos), but also any other MPEG video codec and audio codec. These kinds of scenarios can drive an artist crazy (okay, crazier than normal). If you have the time, it's worth learning more about it. If you don't, I'd recommend simply sticking with QuickTime or AVI for your delivery format and then pick your favorite compression codecs from there.

The Video panel lets you choose which codec you would like to use, and it also offers you the ability to tweak how the actual video gets compressed. More often than not, though, the default settings tend to work pretty well. The button at the top of the right column in this panel is a preset selector. Using this menu automatically enables the proper settings to render for these outputs, such as DV, DVD, and VCD. The Audio panel gives you similar control to the sound that Blender renders, but arguably the most important button in this panel is the Multiplex audio button. Left-clicking this button ensures that the movie file has both the video and audio information embedded in it.

 Make sure you test your files if you want other people to be able to read them. I can't tell you how many times I've rendered a movie file that plays just fine on my Linux machine, but won't even open on a Windows or Macintosh machine. It's kind of ugly and makes everyone look bad. So make sure you try to view the file on as many machines as possible before sharing it with the world.

The other consideration to make when saving an animation is where on your hard drive you intend to store it. Enter this information on the first text box on the Output panel. By default, Blender saves your animations to the /tmp directory on your computer. However, you might not have a /tmp directory, or you explicitly may want to save the animation to a different folder on your hard drive. Left-click the file folder icon to the left of this text box and navigate to where you want to save your animation.

I would highly recommend that if you choose to save a sequence of still images, you should create a specific folder just for these render files. You're going to create a *lot* of files. If the animation is 250 frames long and you render to still images, you're going to get 250 individual images saved to your hard drive.

So, to render animation, the steps are pretty similar to rendering a still:

1. **Set up your resolution and output format in the Format panel.**

   Now, if you've been working on your animation, hopefully you've set all this up already. Although changing the output resolution (the width and height) of the image after you animate generally is not too bad, changing to other frame rates after the fact can get to be a pain. The frame rate is set with the FPS button in the second block of buttons.

2. **Confirm the start and end frames for your animation in the Anim panel.**

   This is another setting that you probably already made while animating, but it's worth it to double-check these start and end frames to make sure that they're correct.

3. **Verify where you want to save your file in the Output panel.**

4. **Animate by pressing Ctrl+F12.**

   Also you can press the large Anim button in the Render buttons or choose Render➪Render Animation. Your animation immediately starts being created. Now go get a cup of coffee. This might take quite some time.

Unlike the Render button, which does not save anything to your hard drive, clicking the Anim button automatically saves your renders wherever you stipulate in the Output panel.

Creating a sequence of still images for editing or compositing

In reading the last section, you may have found yourself wondering, "He keeps talking about rendering out a sequence of still images rather than a single movie file. Why would I ever want to do that?" There are actually a couple of situations where this makes sense. One of the biggest reasons for rendering still is for *compositing*, or combining multiple images together. When you do compositing, you often rely on having an alpha channel that makes everything transparent except for your rendered subject. Most video formats simply don't support an alpha channel, so to accommodate this, you render out a sequence of still images in a format that does support alpha, such as PNG.

Another reason that you may want to have a still images sequence instead of a movie file is for *editing*, or sequencing multiple video and animation clips. To get smaller file sizes, many video codecs throw out large chunks of image data from one frame to the next. The result is a small file that plays well, but is pretty difficult to edit because in editing, you may want to cut on a frame that doesn't have very much image data at all. Using a sequence of still images guarantees that all image data for each and every frame is completely there for smooth editing.

The third reason you may want to render a sequence of still images is largely practical. When rendering to a movie format, what happens if you decide to stop the render and change a small part of it? Or what happens if Blender crashes in the middle of rendering? Well, you have to restart the whole render process from the start frame. This, of course, is painful. If you render using a sequence of still images, those images are saved the second that they're created. This means that if your render gets stopped for any reason, you don't have to start rendering again from the beginning. You can adjust the Sta (short for *Start*) value in the Anim panel of the Render buttons (F10) to pick up where you left off and resume the render process.

Chapter 15

Compositing and Editing

....

In This Chapter

▶ Editing video and animations with Blender's Video Sequence Editor

▶ Compositing images, video, and un-rendered scenes

....

In live-action film and video, the term *post-production* usually includes nearly anything associated with animation. Nearly every animator or effects specialist has groaned upon hearing a director or producer say the line, "We'll fix it in post." Fortunately, in animation, post-production is more specific, focusing on editing and compositing.

Editing is the process of taking rendered footage – animation, film, or video – and adjusting how various shots appear in sequence. This is typically done using a *non-linear editor* (NLE). An NLE, like Apple's Final Cut Pro or Adobe Premiere, differs from older *linear* tape-to-tape editing systems that required editors to work more sequentially. With an NLE, you can easily edit the beginning of a sequence without worrying too much about it messing up the timing at the end. Blender has very basic NLE functions built into its integrated Video Sequence Editor.

Compositing is the process of mixing animations, videos, and still images into a single image or video. It's the way that credits show up over footage at the beginning of a movie, or how an animated character is made to appear like she is interacting with a real world environment. Blender has an integrated compositor that can be used to do these sorts of effects, as well as simply enhance your scene with effects such as blur, glow, and color correction.

This chapter is a quick guide to editing and compositing using Blender's Video Sequence Editor and Node Compositor. Understand that these topics are large enough for a book of their own, so the content of this chapter isn't comprehensive. That said, you can find enough solid information here and in Blender's online documentation (wiki.blender.org) to figure it out. I've tried to explain not only Blender's interface for these tools, but also some fundamental concepts such as non-linear editing and working with nodes. With this understanding, these tools can help turn your work from "Hey, that's cool" to "Whoa!"

Working with the Video Sequence Editor

Figure 15-1 shows the default Sequence screen in Blender, accessible through the Screens menu in the header or by pressing Ctrl+Right Arrow twice from the default Modeling screen. The large window in the middle of the screen is a Video Sequence Editor (VSE) window in Sequence mode. In this mode, you can add and modify sequences, called *strips*, in time. The numbers across the bottom of the Sequencer correspond to time in the VSE in seconds. The numbers to the left label the tracks, or *channels*, that the strips live in. The upper left window is an Ipo Curve Editor in its Sequence view, used for tweaking the influence or timing of individual strips. To the right of that is a VSE window in Image Preview mode. When you're editing, the footage under the time cursor appears in this window. At the bottom is a Timeline window and a Buttons window.

Ipo Curve Editor
(Sequence view)

VSE
(Image Preview mode)

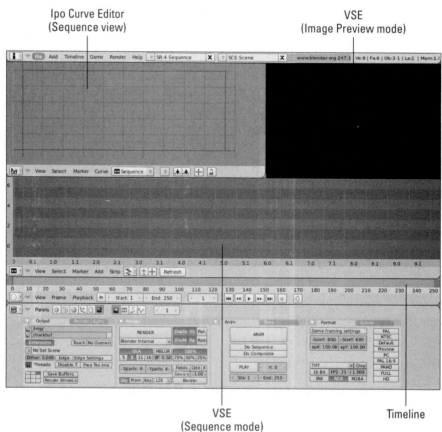

Figure 15-1:
The
Sequence
screen in
Blender.

VSE
(Sequence mode)

Timeline

The settings in the Format panel amid the Render buttons (F10) are important for editing in Blender because that's where you set the frame rate, measured in frames per second (fps), and resolution for the project. If you are editing footage that runs at a different frame rate or resolution than the one that is set here, that footage is adjusted to fit. This means that if your project is at standard HD settings (24 fps and 1920x1080 pixels in size), but you import an animation rendered at 50 fps and at a size of 640x480 pixels, the footage appears stretched and in slow motion.

Besides the Render buttons, other Scene buttons are relevant to sequences. Notice the second set of buttons in the header, as seen in Figure 15-2. By default, the first button is depressed, giving you the Render buttons. However, you also have Sequencer buttons, Animation/Playback buttons, and Sound Block buttons.

Figure 15-2: From left to right: Render buttons, Sequencer buttons, Animation/ Playback buttons, and Sound Block buttons.

As you might guess, the most relevant set of buttons for working in the VSE are the Sequencer buttons. Five panels are available in the Sequencer buttons: Edit, Input, Filter, Proxy, and Effect. Depending on the type of strip you select, all panels may not be visible. For instance, audio strips can't have proxies, so that panel doesn't show up when you select one of those strips. Figure 15-3 shows the default panels in the Sequencer buttons for an image strip.

Figure 15-3: The Sequencer buttons.

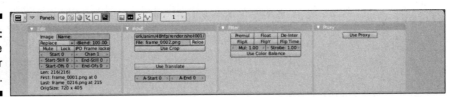

Following are descriptions for the most commonly used panels:

- ✔ **Edit:** The buttons in this panel pertain to where a selected strip appears in the VSE and how it interacts with other strips. You can name individual strips for easy identification, control how a strip blends with strips beneath it, mute or lock a strip, set the frame that the strip starts at, and adjust which channel the strip lives in.

- ✔ **Input:** The buttons in this panel allow you to crop and move the strip around the frame, as well as control which portion of the strip shows up in the Sequencer.

  The Reload button is also quite helpful. Assume you've added an image to the Sequencer, but decide that you would like to modify it in another program before continuing to edit. After you make your changes, you need to make Blender aware that the file has been updated. Left-clicking Reload in this panel does that for you.

- ✔ **Effect:** This panel only appears for certain effect strips that have editable attributes. More detail on some effects that use this panel are given later in this chapter in the section "Adding effects."

The Animation/Playback buttons, as shown in Figure 15-4, control how Blender plays and renders scenes. With this panel, you can change pretty quickly the project frame rate, the start and end frames for playback, and how many frames Blender steps forward or back when you press the up/down arrow keys. However, the most relevant button for the VSE is the Sync button. Clicking this button ensures that your audio plays back in sync with your video while editing. Nothing is worse than doing a ton of work to get something edited only to find out that none of the audio lines up with the visuals after you render.

Figure 15-4:
The
Animation/
Playback
buttons.

The Sound Block buttons can be used to modify both individual audio clips as well as the sound for the overall project. Figure 15-5 shows the available panels in the Sound Block buttons context: Sound, Listener, and Sequencer. As you may have guessed, the most relevant panel for the VSE is the Sequencer panel. In it, some of the functions of the Animation/Playback buttons are duplicated with the Sync button. However, this panel has a few other helpful buttons too.

Figure 15-5:
The Sound
Block
buttons.

Enabling the Scrub button plays a small bit of audio at each frame change while you're editing. This is a great way to know where you're at in your audio, and it's also quite helpful to confirm that your audio and video are actually in sync. The next set of buttons controls the overall volume for the project. The Main mix slider adjusts the volume in decibels (dB). This means that setting the slider to zero actually keeps the sound as it is in the VSE. Values above zero make the sound louder, and negative values soften it. You also have the option of muting all sound outright.

The Mixdown button is like the Anim button in the Render buttons, except instead of creating an animation, it mixes all of the audio in the VSE into a single WAV file and saves it on your hard drive. You may want this sort of feature if you're animating to some dialogue and you have the timing right, but you want to add effects and tweak the sound in an external program. Doing a mixdown gives you a single properly-timed audio file that you can add to.

Before I get heavily into using the VSE, let me first say that Blender's VSE is *not* a complete replacement for a traditional NLE. Although it is a very powerful tool, the VSE is best suited for animators who want to create a quick edit of their work. Professional video editors may have trouble because VSE is missing a number of expected features, such as a listing of available footage, sometimes called a *clip library* or *bin*. That said, Blender's VSE was used successfully to edit both of the open movie projects, *Elephants Dream* and *Big Buck Bunny*, and I've found it more than sufficient for quite a few of my own projects, so you'll ultimately have to decide for yourself.

Adding and editing strips

So you want to use the VSE to edit some footage you have. The first thing you have to do is bring that footage into Blender. You do this by clicking in the Sequencer window and pressing Spacebar. Figure 15-6 shows the menu of options that appears when you do this.

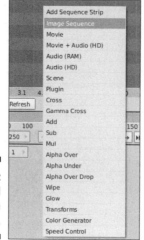

Figure 15-6:
The Add
Sequence
Strip menu.

Generally speaking, there are four primary kinds of strips that you can import: still images, movies, audio, and scenes. These are represented by the following options in the menu:

- ✔ **Image Sequence:** Selecting this option brings up a File Browser window that allows you to select one or more images in any of the formats that Blender recognizes. If you select just one image, the VSE displays a strip for that one image that can be resized in time arbitrarily. If you select multiple images, the Sequencer interprets them as a sequence of images and places them all in the same strip with a fixed length that matches the number of images you selected.

- ✔ **Movie/Movie + Audio (HD):** When you select these options, the File Browser that comes up allows you to select a video file in one of the many formats Blender supports. Note that when you use the Movie option, no audio is imported. However the Move+Audio (HD) option loads the audio along with the video file as separate strips in the sequencer.

- ✔ **Audio (RAM)/Audio (HD):** These options give you a File Browser window for loading an audio file into the VSE. For Audio (RAM), Blender takes your selected file and plays it from your computer's RAM. This option is nice because the sequence strip shows the audio waveform, making editing easier. However, sound quality tends to be worse, with periodic pops and hisses. Audio (HD) reads the sound directly from the hard drive. There's no waveform on the strip and it may perform a bit slower than the Audio (RAM) option, but it tends to give more accurate results with fewer pops and less hissing. When importing audio, you definitely want to import sound files in WAV format. It gives you the best quality sound, when other compressed sound formats like MP3 won't work.

✔ **Scene:** Scene strips are an extremely cool feature that is unique to Blender. When you select this option, a secondary menu pops up that allows you to select a scene from the .blend file you are working in. This means that if you use a single .blend file with multiple scenes in it, you can edit those scenes together to a final output sequence without ever rendering out those scenes first! This is a very handy feature that allows you to create a complete and complex animation entirely within a single file. It's also a great way to use Blender to create overlaying graphics, like titles, on video that you are editing.

The other options in the menu are strips used mostly for effects and transitions. They are covered more in-depth in the next section.

When you load a sequence strip, it is brought into the VSE under your mouse cursor. Left-clicking your mouse or pressing Enter confirms the placement of the strip. Table 15-1 shows helpful mouse actions for working efficiently in the VSE.

Table 15-1	Helpful Mouse Actions in the VSE
Mouse Action	*Description*
Right-click	Select strip to modify. Right-clicking on the arrow at either end of the strip selects that end of the strip and allows you to trim or extend the strip from that point.
Shift+Right-click	Select multiple strips.
Middle-click	Pan the VSE workspace.
Ctrl+Middle-click	Zoom height and width of the VSE workspace.
Scroll wheel	Zoom the width in and out of the VSE workspace.
Left-click	Move the time cursor in the VSE window. Left-clicking and dragging scrubs the time cursor, allowing you to view and hear the contents of the Sequencer as fast or slow as you move your mouse.

One thing you might notice is that quite a few of the controls are very similar to those present in other parts of Blender, such as the 3D View and Ipo Curve Editor. This is very true also when it comes to the hotkeys that the VSE recognizes, although there are a few differences that are worth mentioning. Table 15-2 is a list of some the most common hotkeys used for editing.

Table 15-2	Common Features/Hotkeys in the VSE	
Hotkey	**Menu Access**	**Description**
G	Strip⇨Grab/Move	Grabs a selection to move elsewhere in the VSE.
E	Strip⇨Grab/Extend from frame	Grabs a selection and extends one end of it relative to the position of the time cursor.
B	Select⇨Border Select	Border select, for selecting multiple strips.
Shift+D	Strip⇨Duplicate	Duplicates the selected strip(s).
X	Strip⇨Delete	Deletes the selected strip(s).
K	Strip⇨Cut (hard) at Current Frame	Splits a strip at the location of the time cursor. Similar to the razor tool in other NLEs.
M	Strip⇨Make Meta Strip	Combines selected strips into a single "meta" strip.
Alt+M	Strip⇨Separate Meta Strip	Splits a selected meta strip back to its original individual strips.
Tab	Strip⇨Enter/Exit Meta Strip	Tabs into a meta strip to allow modification of the strips within it.
H	Strip⇨Mute Strips	Hides a strip from being played.
Alt+H	Strip⇨Unmute Strips	Unhides a strip.
Shift+L	Strip⇨Lock Strips	Prevents selected strips from being moved or edited.
Alt+Shift+L	Strip⇨Unlock Strips	Allows editing on selected strips.
Alt+A	View⇨Play Back Animation	Plays the animation starting from the location of the time cursor.

Editing in the Sequencer is pretty straightforward. If you have two strips stacked one above the other, when the timeline cursor gets to them, the strip that's in the higher channel takes priority. By default, that strip simply replaces any of the strips below it. You can, however, change this behavior in the Edit panel of the Sequencer buttons. The first drop-down list button on the left of the panel controls the Blend mode of the selected strip. You can see that the default setting is Replace, but if you left-click this button, you get a short list of modes similar to the layer blending options you would see in a program like Photoshop or The GIMP. Besides Replace, the ones I use the most are Alpha Over and Add.

The Ipo Curve Editor is useful for animating all kinds of values in Blender, and it has a specific mode for the Sequencer. You might notice that no matter what kind of strip you select, there's only one animatable value on the right side: Fac. This controls the influence factor that the strip has on the rest of the sequence. For instance, on a sound strip, you can use the Ipo Curve Editor to animate the loudness of the audio in that strip. A value of 1.0 is the original volume of the strip; values less than 1.0 make the audio softer, and values greater than 1.0 make the audio louder. The same works for image and movie strips. These strips are completely visible at a value of 1.0 and gradually fade away the lower you get. There are a couple of differences when you use Ipo curves on effects strips. I go over a couple of these in the next section.

Chapter 10 has more detail on using the Ipo Curve Editor, but one key difference between the Ipo Curve Editor when used for Sequences is that the Fac value has a defined range, shown by a solid black line. For most strips, that range is from zero to one on the Y-axis and zero to one hundred on the X-axis. The X-axis value represents a percentage of the length of the selected strip. So no matter how long your strip is or where in time it's located, the Ipo curve sticks with it and scales to whatever its length is. Of course, this makes it difficult to create frame-accurate Ipo curves relative to the actual time in the Sequencer. To allow for that kind of accuracy, click the IPO Frame Locked button in the Edit panel of the Sequencer buttons. When you do that, the X-axis values in the Ipo Curve Editor match the time values in the Sequencer.

By combining the Ipo Curve Editor with Blending modes, you can create some very cool results. Say you have a logo graphic with an alpha channel defining the background as transparent and you want to make the logo flicker as if it's being seen through poor television reception. To do this, follow these steps:

1. **Add a your logo image to the Sequencer (Spacebar➪Image Sequence).**

2. **Make sure the logo's strip is selected (right-click) and, in the Edit panel, change the strip's Blend mode to Alpha Over.**

3. **In the Ipo Curve Editor, create a curve that randomly bounces many times between the values of 1.0 and 0.0.**

4. **After tweaking the curve to your taste, you should now have your flickering logo effect.**

Adding effects

As noted in the previous section, pressing Spacebar provides you with quite a few options other than importing audio and video elements. A large portion of these options are effects, and many typically require that you select two strips that are stacked on top of each other in the VSE. When necessary, I point out which ones these are.

Pay close attention to the order in which you select your strips because this often has a dramatic influence on how the effect is applied. A general rule of thumb is that the second strip you select is the primary controller of the effect.

Here is a list of the available options:

- **Cross/Gamma Cross:** These effects are *crossfades* or *dissolves* between overlapping strips. To use them, select the strip you want to start with and then Shift+right-click the strip you want to transition to. Next press Spacebar⇨Cross. A new red strip is created that's the length of the overlap between your two selected strips. On playback (Alt+A), one clip fades away as the other appears. This effect also works in audio to smoothly transition from one sound to another. Gamma Cross works the same Cross, but takes the additional step of correcting the color in the transition for a smoother dissolve.

- **Add/Sub/Mul:** These effects are the same as the Blend mode settings in the Edit panel of the Sequencer buttons. Unless you really need some special control, I'd recommend using those Blend modes rather than adding these as effects sequences. It works just as well and keeps your Sequencer from getting too cluttered. Using these effects requires that you select two strips before pressing spacebar and adding any of them.

- **Alpha Over/Under/Over Drop:** These effects strips control how one strip's alpha channel relates to another. These are also available as Blending modes and I'd also suggest you apply these effects that way in most cases. One example of a time where it makes sense to use these as strips would be if you needed to stack more than one of these effects together or if you needed to use an Ipo curve to individually control the effect. Otherwise, stick with the Blend mode.

- **Wipe:** Wipe is a transition effect like Cross and Gamma Cross. It transitions from one strip to another like a sliding door, a la the *Star Wars* movies. This effect also uses the Effect panel in the Sequencer buttons to let you choose the type of wipe you want, including single, double, iris, and clock wipe. Also you can adjust the blurriness of the wiping edge and the direction the wipe moves.

- **Glow:** The Glow effect works on a single strip. It takes a given image and makes the bright points in it glow a bit brighter. Ever wonder how some 3D renders get that glowing, almost ethereal quality? This is one way to do it. The Effect panel in the Sequencer buttons lets you adjust the amount of glow you have and the quality of that glow.

- **Transforms:** This effect provides very basic animation controls for the location, scale, and rotation of a strip. The effect works on a single strip and the controls for it can be found on the Effect panel of the Sequencer buttons. Each attribute has a start and end value, giving you limited animation controls. For more control, you can use an Ipo curve on this effect strip.

✓ **Speed Control:** With the Speed Control effect, you can adjust the playback speed of individual strips. In the Effect panel of the Sequencer buttons, you can choose to influence the Global Speed (1.0 is "regular speed"; setting it to 0.50 makes the strip play half as fast; setting it to 2.0 makes it play twice as fast). You can also have more custom control using the Ipo Curve Editor.

Rendering from the Video Sequence Editor

To render your complete edited sequence from the VSE, the steps are largely identical to the ones outlined for creating a finished animation in the previous chapter. Actually, there's only one additional thing that you must do. In the Render buttons, on the Anim panel, you need to press the Do Sequence button. Activating this button lets Blender know that you want to use the strips in the Sequencer rather than anything that's in front of the 3D camera for your final output. If you don't press this button, Blender just renders whatever the camera sees, which may be just the default cube that starts with Blender, or whatever else you might place in front of the 3D camera.

Working with the Node-Based Compositor

As I mentioned at the start of this chapter, compositing is the process of mixing multiple visual assets to create a single image or sequence of images. By this definition, you might notice that *technically* Blender's Video Sequence Editor qualifies as a sort of compositor because you can stack strips over each other in channels and blend them together with effects and transitions. Although this is true, the VSE is nowhere near as powerful as the Node Compositor is for mixing videos, images, and other graphics together.

What makes the Node Compositor so powerful? Well, it's in the name: *nodes*. One of the best ways to understand this is to imagine an assembly line. In an assembly line, each step in the process depends on the step immediately preceding it and feeds directly into the following step. This is similar to the layer-based approach used in many image manipulation programs like Photoshop and The GIMP. Each layer has exactly one input from the previous layer and one output to the following one. Figure 15-7 illustrates this idea.

That works well, but let's enhance the assembly line a bit. Say some steps produce parts that can go to more than one subsequent step, and that other steps can take parts from two or more earlier steps and make something new. And take it a bit further by saying that groups of these steps could be duplicated and integrated easily to other parts of the line. We would then have an assembly *network* like that depicted in Figure 15-8. This is what you can do with nodes.

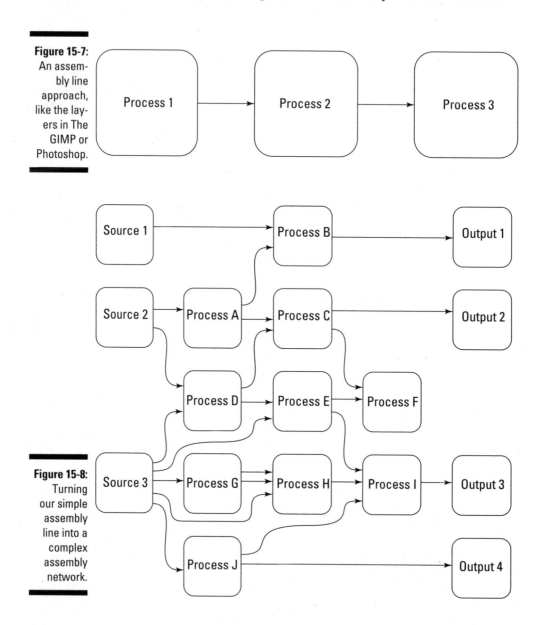

Figure 15-7:
An assembly line approach, like the layers in The GIMP or Photoshop.

Figure 15-8:
Turning our simple assembly line into a complex assembly network.

Understanding the benefits of rendering in passes

Before taking full advantages of nodes, it's worthwhile to take a quick moment and understand what it means to render *in passes*. Assume for a moment that you've animated a character walking into a room and falling down. Even though the camera doesn't move, the room is pretty detailed, so it takes a fairly long time for your computer to render each frame. However, you notice that because the camera doesn't move, you can really render the room just once. Then if you render your character with an alpha channel, you can superimpose the character on just the still image of the room, effectively cutting your render time in half (or less)!

That's the basics of rendering in passes. In the previous example, there were two passes, one for the background and one for the character. However, you can have many more passes with more detailed content. For instance, if you wanted to, you could have a render pass that consists of just the shadows in the image. Then you can take that pass and adjust it to give all the shadows a slightly bluish hue. Or you could tint a character red to isolate her while she's walking through a gray, blurry environment.

Another thing to understand for compositing 3D scenes is the concept of Z-depth. Basically, *Z-depth* is the representation of the distance that an object is from the camera, along the camera's local Z-axis. Z-depth is used quite often in compositing. If you were to describe Z-depth in terms of a black and white image, objects that are nearly white would be the closest to the camera and objects that are nearly black would be almost out of the camera's viewable range. The compositor can use this scale to make an object look like it fits in a scene even though it was never rendered with it.

To do render passes in Blender, you use *render layers*. It's important to make a distinction here between Blender's regular layer system and render layers. They are separate things, although render layers do use Blender's layer system. Basically, you can decide arbitrarily which Blender layers you would like to include or exclude from any of the render layers you create. All of the controls for this are in the Render Layers panel in the Render buttons. It's usually a tab combined with the Output panel. Figure 15-9 shows the Render Layers panel.

Figure 15-9: The Render Layers panel.

The first block of Blender layers shows which ones are going to be sent actively to the renderer. Beneath the layers block is a drop-down list for the Render layer you are currently working in. The first button enables or disables whether this render layer is rendered. From this part on, this block of buttons works just like any of the datablock buttons in other parts of Blender, giving you the ability to rename, select, add or delete render layers. The only difference is the Single button next to the layer name. It gives you the option of rendering just that layer. This is good for spot-checking a layer and making quick adjustments without having to render all of the other layers.

The blocks below this strip are where all the power of render layers lives. These buttons offer a lot of control, so it's worthwhile to understand what each one does. The first set is another block of Blender layer buttons. These buttons determine which Blender layers actually belong in this render layer. For example, if you're creating a render layer for background characters and you have all of your background characters on layers 3 and 4, you would Shift+left-click those layers in this block.

Below this block of layer buttons is another block of buttons that specify which *pipeline products* to deliver to the renderer. This refers to major renderable elements of this render layer that are seen by the renderer. If you disable Halo, for instance, no halo materials are sent to the renderer. Basically, they are omitted. You can use these buttons in complex scenes to turn off pipeline features you don't need in an effort to shorten your render times. Here is a brief description of some of the more useful pipeline features:

- **Solid:** This is for solid faces. Basically, if you disable this option, the only things that render are lights, halo materials, and particles. Any solid-surfaced object doesn't appear.

- **Z-tra:** This is short for *Z-transparency*. If you have an object that has a Z-transparent material, enabling this button ensures that that material gets rendered.

- **Strand:** *Strands* are static particles rendered in place. They're often used to approximate the look of hair or grass. Keeping this option enabled ensures that your characters aren't bald and that their front lawns aren't lifeless deserts.

- **AllZ:** The simplest way to explain this option is with an example. Say you have a scene with a wall between your character and the camera. The character is on one render layer and the wall is on another. If you're on the character's render layer and you enable this option, the character is masked from the render layer and doesn't appear. With AllZ off, the character shows up on its render layer.

- **Mat:** In this text entry field, you can enter the name of any available material in the .blend file. This was originally designed to aid in creating preview renders. However, you could also use this feature to make all objects in this layer behave as a mask or have some other special material.

Underneath the pipeline products button block are the buttons that control which passes are included in the render layer. These passes are most useful when used in the Node Compositor because essentially they make compositing so interesting and fun. Here are some of the most useful passes:

- ✔ **Combined:** The Combined pass is the fully mixed, rendered image as it comes from the renderer before getting any processing.

- ✔ **Z:** This pass is a mapping of the Z-depth information for each object in front of the camera. It is useful for masking as well as effects like *depth of field*, where a short range of the viewable range is in focus and everything else is blurry.

- ✔ **Vec:** Short for *vector*, this pass includes speed information for objects moving before the camera. This data is particularly useful for the Vector Blur node, which gives animations a nice motion blur effect.

- ✔ **Nor:** An abbreviation for normal, the information in this pass relates to the angle that the geometry in the scene has, relative to the camera. This can be used for additional bump mapping as well as completely altering the lighting in the scene without re-rendering.

- ✔ **UV:** The UV pass is pretty clever because it sends the UV mapping data from the 3D objects to the compositor. Basically, this allows the ability to completely change the textures on an object or character without the need to re-render any part of the scene.

  This is often used along with the Index pass to specify on which object you want to change the texture.

- ✔ **Index:** This pass carries index numbers for individual objects, if you set them. This allows very fine control over which nodes get applied to which objects. This is similar to plain masking, but somewhat more powerful because it makes isolating a single object or group of objects so much easier.

- ✔ **Col:** The color pass delivers the colors from the render, completely shadeless, without highlights or shadows. This can be helpful for amplifying or subduing colors in a shot.

- ✔ **Spec:** The specularity pass. This pass delivers an image with the specular highlights that appear in the render.

- ✔ **Shad:** This pass contains all of the cast shadows in the render, both from raytraced shadows as well as buffered shadows. This is the pass you would use in my previous example about taking the shadows from the render and adjusting them (such as giving them a bluish hue).

✔ **AO:** This pass includes any ambient occlusion data generated by the renderer. If you use this pass, it's a good idea to double check and see if you're using Approximate or Raytraced AO in the Amb Occ panel of the World Buttons. If you're using Raytraced AO, verify that raytracing is turned on in your Scene buttons (F10).

Working with nodes

After you set up your render layers the way you like, you're ready to work in the Node Compositor. Unlike the VSE, Blender does not ship with a default screen layout for compositing. Fortunately, the model screen layout serves the purpose quite nicely. Change the 3D View window to Node Editor by pressing Shift+F3, or by choosing Node Editor from the Window Type menu at the left of the 3D view's header. By default, Blender puts you in the Node Editor for materials. This is not where you want to be. Look in the header for the button that looks like a human face. Left-click that icon to enable the Composite node editor. This won't appear to change much. However, click the Use Nodes button that appears just to the right in the header. This should present you with a screen layout that looks similar to the one shown in Figure 15-10.

As shown in Figure 15-10, Blender starts by presenting you with two nodes, one input and one output. You can quickly tell which is which by looking at the location of the connection points on each node. The left node labeled Render Layer has connection points on the right side of it. This means that it can only serve as an input to other nodes and cannot receive any additional data, so it's an input node. It adds information to the node network. In contrast, the node on the right, labeled Composite, is an output node because it has no connection points on its right edge, meaning it cannot feed information to other nodes. Essentially, it's the end of the line, the result. In fact, when you render using the Node Compositor, the Composite node is the final output that gets displayed in Blender's render window.

I personally prefer to see the progress of my node network as I'm working, without having to constantly refer back to another window for the results of my work. Fortunately, Blender can facilitate this with another sort of output node: the Viewer node. To add a new node, position your mouse cursor in the Node Editor window and press Spacebar. This presents you with a variety of options that I go into detail on in a bit. For now, navigate to Add⇨Output⇨Viewer. This creates a new output node labeled Viewer. If the Render Layer input node was selected when you added the Viewer node, you'll notice that it automatically creates a connection, also called a *noodle,* between the two nodes. Noodles are drawn between the circular connection points, or *sockets* on each node. If the noodle was not created for you, you can add it by clicking the yellow Image socket on the Render Layer node and dragging your mouse cursor to the corresponding yellow socket on the Viewer node.

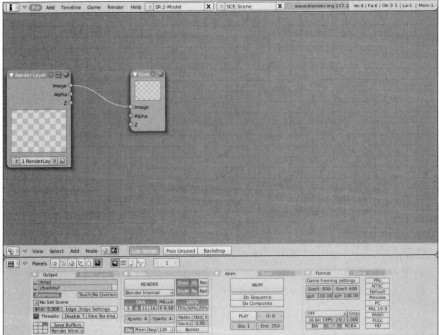

Figure 15-10:
Starting
with nodes
in the
Composite
Node Editor.

However, making this connection doesn't seem to do much. You need to take three more steps:

1. **Left-click the Backdrop button in the Node Editor's header.**

   This loads a black box in the background of the compositor window. (Don't worry, this is supposed to happen, I promise.)

2. **Go to the Anim panel in your Scene buttons (F10) and left-click the Do Composite button.**

3. **Render the scene by left-clicking Render or pressing F12.**

   When the render is complete and you return to the Blender interface by pressing F11, you should notice that the empty black box has been magically replaced with the results of your render. Now anything that feeds into this Viewer node is instantly displayed in the background of the composite window.

This is the way I typically like to work when compositing. In fact, I often take it one step further and press Shift+Spacebar to maximize the Node Editor to the full window size.

If you find that the backdrop gets in your way, you can disable it by clicking on the Backdrop button in the Node Editor's header, or you can move it around in the compositor window by Shift+middle-clicking in the window and dragging the image around. Also you can get more space by middle-clicking in the compositor window and dragging the entire node network around, or by using your scroll wheel to zoom in and out on the nodes. Table 15-3 shows most of the frequently used mouse actions in the Node Editor.

Table 15-3   Commonly Used Mouse Actions in the Node Editor

Mouse Action	Description
Right-click	Select a node.
Shift+Right-click	Select multiple nodes.
Middle-click	Pan compositor work area.
Shift+Middle-click	Move backdrop image.
Ctrl+Middle-click	Zoom compositor work area.
Scroll wheel	Zoom compositor work area.
Left-click (on a node)	Select a node. Click and drag to move the node around.
Left-click (on a socket)	Attach or detach a noodle to/from the socket you click on. Click and drag to the socket you want to connect to.
Left-click+drag the bottom right corner of a node	Resize the node.
Left-click+drag in the compositor workspace	Create a box. Any noodles in the box's area are deleted, leaving just nodes. Think of it as "cutting noodles."
Ctrl+Left-click	Lasso select.

Another thing to notice are the controls at the top of each node, as seen in Figure 15-11. Specifically speaking, there are four buttons, the triangle on the left and the plus, equal, and sphere buttons on the right. Below is a description of what each button does:

- ✔ **Triangle:** Expands and collapses the node, essentially hiding the information in it from view.

- ✔ **Plus:** Hides and shows sockets that have no connections. This button is useful for simplifying the display of your node network. However, a word of warning: It's pretty easy to forget that you have hidden sockets on your node and go a little crazy wondering where they ran off to.

- ✔ **Equal:** Menu expand/collapse. Press this button to hide or show editable values in the selected node. Any values that you set manually are hidden from view.

✔ **Sphere:** View window expand/collapse. This icon is available only on nodes that have an image window, like a render layer node, any output node, or texture node.

Figure 15-11:
Each node has buttons at the top that control how you see it in the compositor window.

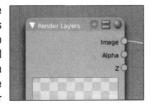

For the most part, editing nodes in Blender conforms to the same user interface behavior that's in the rest of the program. Nodes are selected with right-click, you can grab and move nodes by pressing G, and you can Border Select multiple nodes by pressing B. Of course, there are a few differences that pertain specifically to the Node Editor. Table 15-4 shows some of the most common hotkeys used in Node Editor.

Table 15-4	Commonly Used Hotkeys in the Node Editor	
Hotkey	*Menu Access*	*Description*
Spacebar	N/A	Open toolbox menu
G	Node⇨Grab/Move	Grab a node and move it
B	Select⇨Border Select	Border select
X	Node⇨Delete	Delete node(s)
Shift+D	Node⇨Duplicate	Duplicate node(s)
E	Node⇨Execute Composite	Pushes input data through the node network, refreshing the outputs without re-rendering
Ctrl+G	Node⇨Make Group	Creates a group out of the selected nodes
Alt+G	Node⇨Ungroup	Ungroups the selected group
Tab	Node⇨Edit Group	Expands the node group so you can edit individual nodes within it
H	Node⇨Hide/Unhide	Toggles the selected nodes between expanded and collapsed views
Ctrl+R	Node⇨Rename	Pops up an input box that lets you rename the node

When connecting nodes, pay attention to the colors of the sockets. The sockets on each node come in one of three different colors and each one has a specific meaning for the type of information that is either sent or expected from the node. The colors and their meanings are as follows:

- **Yellow:** Color information. Specifically, this socket relates to color in the output image, across the entire red/green/blue/alpha (RGBA) scale. This is the primary type of data that should go to output nodes.

- **Gray:** Numeric values. Whereas the yellow sockets technically get four values for each pixel in the image – one for each red, green, blue, and alpha – this socket gets or receives a single value for each pixel. You can visualize this as a grayscale image. These sockets are used mostly for masks. For instance, the level of transparency in an image, or its alpha channel, can be represented by a grayscale image, with white for opaque and black for transparent (and gray for semi-transparent).

- **Blue:** Geometry data. These sockets are pretty special. They send and receive information that pertains to the 3D data in the scene, such as speed, UV coordinates, and normals. It's pretty difficult to visualize these values in a two-dimensional image; it usually ends up looking like something seen through the eyes of the alien in *Predator*.

As Table 15-4 shows, nodes can also be grouped together. This is actually one of the really powerful features of the Node Editor. You can border select a complex section of your node network and press Ctrl+G to create quickly a group out of it. There are a few really nice benefits to this. First of all, it can simplify the look of your node network so it's not a huge mess of noodles (spaghetti!). More than simplification, though, it's a great organizational tool. Because you can name groups like any other node, you can group sections of your network that serve a specific purpose. For example, you could have a blurry background group and a color-corrected character group.

But wait, there's more! (Do I sound like a car salesman yet?) When you create a group, it's added automatically to the Group menu when you go to add a new node (spacebar⇨Add⇨Group). To understand the benefit of this, imagine you've created a really cool network that gives foreground elements a totally sweet glow effect. If you make a group out of that network, you can now instantly apply that glow to other parts of your scene or scenes in other .blend files. Go ahead: Try it and tell me that's not cool – you can't do it!

When working with nodes, it's a good idea to have the network flow from the left to the right. Wherever possible, you want to avoid creating situations where you feed a node's output back to one of the nodes that gives it input. This is called a *cyclic* connection. If you've ever heard the painfully loud feedback noise that happens when you place a microphone too close to a speaker, you have an idea of why this is a bad idea.

The best way to get a solid idea of all of the compositing information I've shared so far in this section is to run through a quick example. To make things easier, I've set up a small scene with Suzanne and a cube and included it on the CD-ROM that comes with this book. It's a file called simplecomp-start.blend. It's a very simple scene. Suzanne and a cube are sitting on a plane. Suzanne is on layer 1 and the cube is on layer 2. All the other objects, including the camera and light, are on both layers. Now it's playtime:

1. **In the Render Layers panel of the Render buttons, change the name of the current render layer to** Monkey, **and in the layer block beneath it enable only layer 1.**

   Doing this means that the only Blender layer that the Monkey render layer recognizes is layer 1 (where Suzanne lives).

2. **Add a new Render Layer and name it** Cube. **Enable only layer 2 in the layer block below this render layer's name.**

   Like the previous step, this means that the Cube render layer deals only with Blender layer 2, where the cube lives.

3. **Enable Do Composite in the Anim panel, and change the 3D view into a Composite Node Editor with a backdrop(Shift+F3⇨Composite Nodes⇨Use Nodes⇨Backdrop).**

   Go ahead and render the scene by pressing F12. Notice that in the final result you see only Suzanne and the cube's shadow, but not the cube. To see the cube, proceed to the next steps.

4. **Add a Viewer node (Spacebar⇨Add⇨Output⇨Viewer) and wire it to the Monkey render layer node's image output.**

   Now you should see the render of the Monkey render layer as your backdrop.

5. **Select the Monkey render layer node and duplicate it (right-click⇨ Shift+D) and use the menu at the bottom of the node to choose the cube render layer.**

   If you wire this node to your viewer node, you'll see the render of the Cube render layer. Now you can use any of the various effects nodes that Blender has to modify Suzanne or the cube independently. Maybe you want to blur the cube or tweak Suzanne's color. These are just some of the things that you can do from this point. However, what if you want to recombine the two render layers? That's the next step.

6. **Add a Z Combine node (Spacebar⇨Add⇨Color⇨Z Combine).**

   There's more detailed information on this node in the node descriptions later in this chapter, but Z Combine uses Z-depth data to tell which parts of one render layer belong in front of parts in another.

7. **Wire the Image and Z sockets of the Monkey render layer node to one pair of corresponding sockets on the Z Combine node and the Image and Z sockets of the Cube render layer to the other pair.**

   Now if you make a noodle between the Z Combines Image output and your Viewer node, you can see the finished image, with Suzanne properly placed in front of the cube. Wire this same output to your Composite node and now you can save a still image of this scene.

For reference, I've included a finished version of this scene on the CD-ROM as well, called simplecomp-end.blend.

Blender has quite an extensive list of nodes that you can add to your network. In fact, it seems like with every release of Blender, there are more and more incredible node types added to the compositor. One thing to notice is that many nodes have a *Fac*, or factor, value that you can usually either set with a value from another node or explicitly set by typing. Values less than one make the node have less influence and values greater than one make the node have more influence than usual over the image.

Input

The input nodes are one of the two most important node types in the Node Compositor. If your node network doesn't have any inputs, you don't have a composite. Figure 15-12 shows each of these nodes side-by-side.

Figure 15-12:
Input nodes:
Render
Layer,
Image,
Texture, and
Time.

- ✔ **Render Layer:** This node feeds input from a scene into the compositor. The drop-down menu at the bottom of the node allows you to pick any of the render layers you've created in any scene. Notice also the button to the right of this menu. Press this button to render just this layer. This is a handy feature that allows you to update a portion of your node network without needing to re-render all the layers in the network.

- ✔ **Image:** The name for this node is a bit over-simplistic because it can actually load more than just a single still image. The Image node allows you to bring any sort of image data into the compositor, including sequences of images and movie files, and allows you to control when the sequence starts, how long it is, and whether to loop it continuously.

One thing to notice about the Image node in Figure 15-12 is the node's header. Rather than saying *Image,* it actually gives the name of the image that's loaded. In the case of Figure 15-12, the filename is frame_0001.png

- ✔ **Texture:** The Texture node is unique as an input node in that it's the only one that can actually receive input data as well. Through this node, you can take any texture that you've built in Blender and add it to your node network. This node is particularly useful with UV data because it can actually let you change the textures on objects in your image without re-rendering.

- ✔ **Time:** This is probably one of the most powerful, yet misunderstood nodes in Blender. Unlike the VSE, the Node Compositor is not tied to the Ipo Curve Editor, so it can be difficult to animate attributes of individual nodes. The Time node is a way around this. You might notice that there are no numbers for the X and Y values in this node's graph. Well, the X values still represent time, varying from the start and end frames you stipulate in the buttons at the bottom of the node. The Y values work on a range from zero to one. You can customize this with the orange Clipping Options button. Because this node isn't designed for heavy editing like the Ipo Curve Editor, the controls are simplified. Left-click on the curve to create a new control point and left-click+drag that point to move it around. Multiple points can be selected with Shift+left-click.

Output

In the previous section, I said that Input nodes are one of the two most important node types in Blender. As you may have guessed, the Output nodes are the other important node types, for a similar reason. If you don't have an output node, Blender doesn't know what to save when it renders. Blender recognizes the *Composite* node as the final output from the Node Compositor. When you set up your output files for animation in the Render Buttons, or when you press F3 to save a render, it's the information that comes to this node that Blender saves out. The Viewer node is similar, but it's not for final output. Viewer nodes are great for spot-checking sections of your node network and making sure things are going the way you want them to. Also, output from these nodes is seen in the compositor window's backdrop, if you enable it.

Color

The Color nodes have an enormous influence over the look of the final output. As their name implies, they directly affect how colors appear, mix, and balance in your render. And because an image is basically just a bunch of colors arranged in a specific pattern, you can understand why these nodes have so much control. Figure 15-13 shows some of the most commonly used Color nodes. A description of each follows.

- ✔ **RGB Curves:** This is arguably one of the most powerful color nodes. It takes image data and allows you to use curves to adjust the combined

color, or any of the red, green, or blue channels in the image individually. You edit these curves the same way you edit the curve in the Time
node. Left-clicking the C, R, G, and B buttons on the upper left changes
between combined, red, green, and blue color channels, respectively.
With the RGB Curves, you can actually do anything that the Hue
Saturation Value, Bright/Contrast, and Invert nodes can do, but with
even more control.

- **Mix:** I personally use this node quite a bit. The Mix node has 16 different blending modes to allow you to control how to combine two input
  images. If you've used image editing software like Photoshop or The
  GIMP, they should be pretty familiar to you. One thing to remember in
  this node – and it's something I used to constantly get backwards – is
  that the upper image input socket is the background image, whereas the
  lower image input socket is the foreground image.

- **AlphaOver:** This node is very similar to the Mix node, except it deals
  exclusively with combining images using their alpha channels. Again,
  remember that the lower socket is the foreground and the upper socket
  is the background image. The other thing to note with this node is the
  ConvertPremul button. Basically, if you see weird white or black edges
  around parts of your foreground elements, left-clicking this button
  should fix those nasty edges.

- **Z Combine:** Like the Mix and AlphaOver nodes, the Z Combine node
  mixes two sets of image data together. However, rather than using
  straight color information or alpha channels, this node can use Z-depth
  information. As the example above shows, this is a great way to get an
  object to look like it properly fits in a scene.

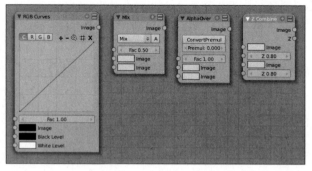

Figure 15-13:
Color
nodes: RGB
Curves, Mix,
AlphaOver,
and Z
Combine.

Vector

Vector nodes are the way that 3D data from your scene can be used to influence the look of your final 2D image. The usage of these nodes tends to be
a bit advanced, but they allow you to do things like change the lighting in
a scene or even change the speed that objects move through the scene . . .
all without re-rendering! If you render to an image format that understands

render passes, like the very cool OpenEXR format (more on this in the next section), and you include vector and normal passes, these nodes can be a huge timesaver.

Filter

Filter nodes can *drastically* change the look of an image and are probably the number one way to fake any effect in an image. These nodes actually process the pixels in an image and can do things like put thick black lines around an object, give the image a variety of customized blurs, or make bright parts of the image glow. Figure 15-14 shows some of the most useful Filter nodes.

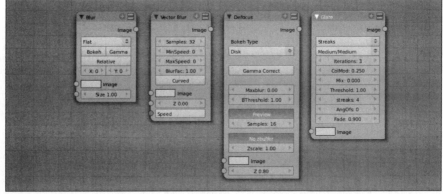

Figure 15-14: Blur, Vector Blur, Defocus, and Glare nodes.

✔ **Blur:** As its name implies, this node applies a uniform blur across the entire input image. The first button gives you a drop-down menu to select the type of blur you want to use. I typically like to use Gauss for most of my effects. When you first apply this node, it might not seem like anything is happening. Change the values in the X and Y buttons to adjust the blur size on a scale from 0 to 256, or 0.0 to 1.0, depending on whether you press the Relative button.

✔ **Vector Blur:** This node is the fastest way to get motion blur out of Blender. The Vector Blur node takes speed information from the Vector pass (enable Vec in the Render Layer panel of the Render buttons) and uses it to fake the motion blur effect. One button I recommend you enable in this node, especially if you're doing character animation, is the Curved button. This gives objects that are moving in an arc a more natural, curved motion blur. Note that this node is specifically for use with 3D data coming from Blender. It can't add motion blur to any arbitrary footage.

✔ **Defocus:** Blender's Defocus node is the way to fake the *depth of field*, or DOF, effect you get with a real camera. If you've seen a photo where something in the middle of the picture is in focus, but objects in the foreground and background are blurry, this is called a *shallow DOF* and it looks pretty sweet. You can get an idea where the camera's focal point is by selecting the camera in your scene and turning on Limits in the Editing buttons. Then when you adjust the DOF Dist value, you can see the focal point as a yellow cross.

- ✔ **Glare:** This node is a really quick way to give the bright parts in your render just a little extra bit of kick. The Fog Glow and Streaks options in the first drop-down menu are what I tend to use the most. Of all the other buttons this node gives you to play with, probably the most influential one is the Threshold button. Setting the threshold to values between 0.0 and 1.0 tends to work best for me, but results vary from image to the next.

Converter

These handy little utility nodes have a variety of purposes, including converting one set of data to another and ripping apart or recombining elements from a rendered image. The Color Ramp and ID Mask nodes in particular get used quite a bit. The Color Ramp node is great for helping visualizing or re-visualizing numerical values on a scale. For instance, the only way to get a good sense of what the Z-depth of an image looks like is to map Z values along a manageable scale and then feed that to a white-to-black color ramp, as shown in Figure 15-15.

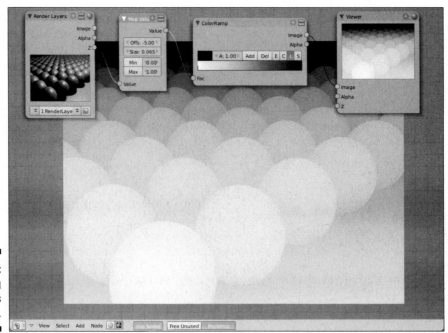

Figure 15-15: Visualizing a scene's Z-depth.

The ID Mask node is handy because it allows you to isolate an object even more specifically than with layers and render layers. Assume you want to apply the Glare node to a ball that your character is holding. If the scene is complex enough, it doesn't really make a lot of sense to give that ball a layer all by itself. So you can give the object a PassIndex value in the Object and Links panel of the Objects buttons. Then, by using the ID Mask node, you can isolate just that ball and make it all shiny.

Matte

The matte nodes are specifically tailored for using color information from an image as a way of isolating certain parts of it. This is referred to as keying because you pick the main color, or key color, to represent transparency. This is the fundamental basis for those cool *bluescreen* effects that they use in movies. The filmmaker shoots the action over a blue or green screen (blue is used for analog film, whereas green is typically used for digital footage), and when he gives the footage to a compositor, the green or blue parts are removed and replaced with other footage or something built in 3D.

Distort

The Distort nodes typically do general-purpose image manipulation operations like Translate, Rotate, Scale, Flip, or Crop It. Want to do that spinning newspaper effect you see in old movies? Wire an image of a newspaper and the Time node to the Rotate and Flip nodes and you've got it! There are three somewhat special nodes in the Distort nodes worth talking more about: Displace, Map UV, and Lens Distortion. Figure 15-16 shows each of these nodes.

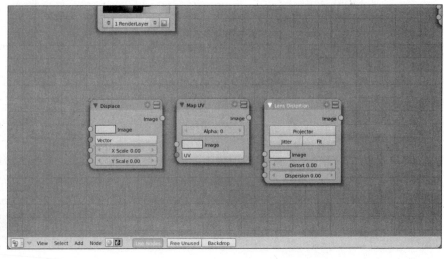

Figure 15-16: Distort nodes: Displace, Map UV, and Lens Distortion.

- **Displace:** This is a great node for doing quick and dirty image distortions such as heat waves in the desert, fake refraction, or making an object appear to push through the image on the screen. The key to this is the Vector input socket. If you feed a grayscale image to it, it uses those values to shift pixels in the image. Connecting a color image, normals, or vectors shifts the image around with a more three-dimensional effect, thereby giving you things like the heat wave effect.

- **Map UV:** In this entire chapter I've been talking about how one of the cool things that the Node Compositor can do is change textures on objects after you've already rendered them. Well, this is the node that lets you do just that. To use it, you'll want to enable the UV pass on your render layer. Feed that pass to this node, along with the new texture you want to use, and BAM! Your new texture is ready to be mixed back with the image. To make sure you're changing the texture on the right object, combine this with the ID Mask node before mixing. Cool, huh?

- **Lens Distortion:** Sometimes it's desirable to introduce the effects that some special (or, in some cases, poor) lenses have on the final image. The Lens Distortion node does that. You can get everything from a wide fisheye lens look to that strange effect when an old projector isn't calibrated properly and the colors don't quite line up right.

Group

When you press Ctrl+G to create a node group, that group is placed in this menu. This means that when you group a set of nodes, you instantly have the ability to apply that network to other parts of your composition. Also, as I mentioned before, grouping gives you the ability to share node networks between .blend files. When you append or link a node group from another file, it shows up in this menu.

Whenever you have the opportunity, name *everything* you create. This is especially important for groups because they're automatically added to the Group menu. Using names that make sense makes choosing the right node group a lot easier. You can always rename node groups by selecting them and pressing Ctrl+R.

Dynamic

Another common name for Dynamic nodes are *PyNodes*, or python nodes. Blender has an integrated scripting engine that uses the Python programming language. By using Python for compositing, this means that you (or someone you know with more programming background) could write a custom compositor node that does exactly what you want. After you have that script loaded in Blender, the custom node you've written appears in this menu.

Rendering from the Node Compositor

If you're using the Node Compositor, you already know all of the basic steps for getting a rendered image out of it. Of course, if you've skipped straight to this section, here's the quick version: Press the Do Composite button on the Anim panel in the Render buttons.

That said, there's one other thing to know about rendering from the compositor. Say you're working on a larger production and want to save your render passes to an external file format so either you or another compositor can work on it later without re-rendering the whole scene. You would have to save your renders to a file format that understands render layers and render passes. That format is the venerable OpenEXR file format, developed and gifted to the world by the cool people at Industrial Light & Magic. Now I know what you're thinking, "Using this format is as easy as setting up my render layers and then choosing OpenEXR from the menu in the Format panel of the Render Buttons." That's actually two-thirds correct. You do set up your render layers and you do go to the Format panel. *However*, choosing OpenEXR only saves the final composite output in an OpenEXR file (extension .exr), but none of the layers or passes. In order to get that information, you should instead choose MultiLayer. With this format, you get an OpenEXR file that has all of the layer and pass information stored with it.

Pay close attention to your hard drive space when you choose to render like this. Keeping all of your render layers and passes is a great way to tweak and make adjustments after rendering; however, the file size for each individual .exr file can be *huge*. Whereas an HD frame in PNG format may only be a couple hundred kilobytes, an OpenEXR file on the same frame with all the passes enabled could be well over 100 *megabytes*. Yes, megabytes. So make sure you do test saves to get a good benchmark for the file size and see that you have enough hard drive space to store all those frames.

Part V
The Part of Tens

The 5th Wave   By Rich Tennant

"I found these two in the multimedia lab morphing faculty members into farm animals."

In this part . . .

This is the (more) fun part of the book. These chapters are quick lists to help make you a better Blender user. Blender is a dense program, stuffed full of features. And it's constantly changing and having new features and enhancements added to it. Because of this, it's not difficult to forget things or get stumped with strange issues. The chapters here give you ways to deal with these issues. It's an incredible world, and it's great to have you as a part of it!

Chapter 16

Ten Problems for New Users in Blender (and Ways around Them)

••

*T*he community forums and web pages for Blender are brimming with questions from new users. Many of them are the same question, or derivatives of the same question. The purpose of this section is to identify some of the most common ones and give you solutions to them so you don't have to dig through these Web sites (unless you really, really want to).

Auto Saves and Session Recovery Don't Work

This problem is mostly unique to users of Microsoft Windows, but even if you're on another operating system, it's worth it to double-check on this. It happens because your Temp directory is improperly set to a folder that does not exist on your computer. If this path is not set properly, your auto saves and Blender's session recovery (File⇨Recover Last Session) don't work. The Recover Last Session feature is particularly important to have for those cases where you close Blender without saving your project. It's amazing how many people have lost hours of work because Blender crashed (it happens sometimes!) or they accidentally closed Blender without saving. Don't be that person!

By default, Blender sets the Temp path at /tmp, a directory that doesn't exist in Windows. There are two solutions to this problem:

✔ Create the /tmp directory. In Windows, you would create "C:\tmp". After you do that, all auto saves and recoverable sessions are stored there.

✔ Change the Temp path in the File Paths Section of the User Preferences window to a directory of your choice that already exists. Many people like to use C:\Windows\Temp.

✔ Get into the habit of quitting Blender by pressing Ctrl+Q or navigating to File⇨Quit Blender rather than clicking the window's close button (the X in the corner). In Windows, closing by pressing the X doesn't get you a quit.blend.

Blender's Interface Is Weird or Glitchy

Blender uses OpenGL, an accelerated 3D programming library, for its entire interface. Because of this, it often uses parts of the library that might never get touched by other programs. On some machines, Blender might run very slow or you may see weird screen glitches around the mouse pointer or menus. The first thing to check is the drivers for your video card. Go to the Web site for the manufacturer of your video card and see if they have any updates for it. You may want to try turning off any fancy effects that your operating system adds, such as transparent windows, shadows on the mouse cursor, or 3D desktop effects. Because all of these little bits of eye candy tend to be hardware-accelerated, they might be conflicting with Blender a bit. At the very least, turning them off usually makes your computer use fewer resources like processor power and memory, thereby making more of those resources available to Blender. If you're using an nVidia video card, make sure the Flipping checkbox in your OpenGL settings is not enabled.

A Notorious "Black Stripe" Appears on Models

Often when modeling, you might run into a situation where there is a strange black crease that goes along some edges. It's usually most apparent when modeling with the Subsurf modifier turned on. What's happening here is that the *normals* for one of the faces adjoining this edge are facing the wrong direction. Usually the quickest way to fix this is to have Blender recalculate the normals for the model and attempt to have them all face outside. To do this, go into Edit mode, select all, and press Ctrl+N. This typically alleviates all issues. If it doesn't, however, you may have to go in and manually flip the normals yourself. This is easiest to do from Face Select mode with Draw Normals turned on in the Editing buttons (F9⇨Mesh Tools More). With that set, you can see which normals are facing the wrong way. From there, select the offending faces and press W⇨Flip Normals. If that still doesn't solve your problem, it could mean that you have multiple vertices in the same place or you have faces inside your mesh. Multiple vertices can be fixed by pressing W⇨Remove Doubles. Internal faces are harder to auto-detect, but if you view your mesh in Wireframe, it may be more apparent.

Objects Go Missing

Occasionally you might run into a problem where not everything shows up in your 3D View, even though you're positive you didn't delete anything. The first thing to do is make sure nothing is hidden. Pressing H in Blender hides whatever you have selected and it's easy to accidentally hit it when you're actually trying to press G and grab an object. Fortunately, you can unhide all hidden objects pretty quickly by pressing Alt+H.

If you're sure nothing is hidden, next try to make all layers visible and check to be sure you didn't inadvertently move your object to a different layer. You do this by pressing the tilde (~) key. You may also want to press Home to bring all objects into view.

One last thing to check is to see if you are in Local View, the view that isolates all objects except for a few that you select. The hotkey that toggles this view is Numpad-slash (/) and it can be pretty easy to accidentally hit it when using the numeric keypad to change views. One quick way to tell if you're in Local View is to look at the header for the 3D View. If there are no layer buttons where they're supposed to be, you are in Local View.

If none of these things worked, there actually *is* the chance that you deleted your object on accident. Fortunately, if you haven't closed your file, you can recover from this as well. I'm going write the next few steps under the assumption that your object was a Mesh, but the same technique works for curves, text, and other types of objects. See, when you delete an object in Blender, it doesn't actually get completely deleted until you close the file, so it still exists in Blender's internal database for this file. To recover a deleted object, use the following steps:

1. **Create a dummy object that's the same type as the one you're trying to recover.**

    For meshes, using Spacebar➪Add➪Mesh➪Empty mesh is particularly handy.

2. **Bring up the Editing buttons (F9) and look in the Links and Materials panel. Press the up/down arrow to the left of the first field in this panel.**

    When you do this, a list of all of the objects in the scene that share this type pops up. Anything you've deleted has an empty circle next to it. Figure 16-1 shows what this might look like.

3. **If your deleted object is in this list, select it and the dummy object you added in the first step is instantly replaced with the mesh for your deleted object. Neat, huh?**

Figure 16-1:
Deleted
objects in
the Link and
Materials
panel of
the Editing
buttons.

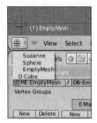

Python Not Found

If you run Blender from a terminal window (or you're a Windows user), you might see something like this show up in there:

```
Checking for installed Python... No installed Python
          found.
Only built-in modules are available. Some scripts may not
          run.
Continuing happily.
```

Although this *is* an error, it's not a huge worry. This is basically saying that Blender can't find the Python language anywhere on your computer. For most cases, this isn't a big deal. Blender has part of the Python language built into it and all of the Python scripts that ship with Blender work just fine even if you don't have Python already on your machine. It only becomes an issue if you download a Blender script that requires the full Python language. In that case, you need to download and install Python from its Web site (www. python.org/download/).

Also, *do not close the terminal window.* This immediately ends your Blender session. The Blender developers are working to make it so that this terminal window doesn't appear, but until they do, we just have to deal with it.

Edge Loop Select Doesn't Work

This happens the most on Linux machines that use the Gnome desktop environment. The Blender hotkey for doing a loop selection is Alt+right-click. Unfortunately, in Gnome and a few other window managers, this key sequence pops up a menu for controlling the window. There are two possible fixes for this. The easiest one is to use Shift+Alt+right-click. This is the combination typically used to select multiple loops, but if nothing is selected, it works exactly the same as the Alt+right-click combination.

Of course, that's a bit of a kludge. A better solution would be to modify the window manager and bind the function that it ties to the Alt key to another key, like the infamous "super" or Windows key that most modern keyboards have. Fortunately, this is a very simple process. From the Gnome taskbar, go to System⇨Preferences⇨Windows. This brings up a dialog box that allows you to change the movement key from Alt to Ctrl or Super. I would recommend you change it to super because Blender also makes extensive use of the Ctrl key as well.

A Background Image Disappears

When using a photographic or drawn reference to base your models on, it's a common practice to load the reference image in the background of the 3D View (see Chapter 5 for more on this). However, when working this way, you may orbit your view to do a spot-check and then when you return to side (or front or top) view, the background image may disappear, even though the Background Image floating panel says it's still there.

The answer here is that you are viewing the scene through Perspective view rather than the Orthographic one. Blender doesn't show the background reference image in perspective. Switch back to Orthographic by pressing Numpad 5. It makes sense to do this because a Perspective view introduces distortion and scaling to the way the scene is viewed, so it's not a good idea to model from reference in this type of view. The Orthographic view is much more effective at getting a model to match a reference image.

There's a Limit to Zooming

When working in Perspective view, you may notice that occasionally you can't zoom in on your scene as much as you would like. This is because there's a center point that you're zooming toward and you are very near it. There are three workarounds for this. The first is to place the 3D cursor at the location you would like to zoom to and press C. This centers the view on the 3D cursor and gives you a clearer target to zoom in on. The other option that may help is to select the object that you want to zoom in on and press Numpad-dot (.). This centers the view on that object's center point so you can now use that as your zoom target. Alternatively, you can try popping quickly into Orthographic view by pressing Numpad 5. Because there is no perspective distortion in the Orthographic view, the way it zooms is somewhat different and it might give you a better angle that you couldn't get before.

Lost Simulation Data

As mentioned in Chapter 13, Blender saves some simulation data to your hard drive. This is especially true for fluid simulations, where simulation data can take up gigabytes and gigabytes of hard drive space. If that simulation data isn't where Blender expects it to be, your simulation doesn't show up in your .blend file. Generally this happens for one of three reasons:

✔ **You work on more than one computer.** If you work in Blender on more than one machine and only copy the .blend file between the two, the simulation data isn't where it needs to be on the second computer. You need to copy that simulation data to the same place on the second computer for it to show up properly.

✔ **You accidentally changed or deleted the path to the simulation data.** This isn't common, but it does happen. Fortunately, the fix is simple. Select the domain object for your fluid simulation and go to your Physics buttons (F7⇨F7). In the Fluid panel, the path to your simulation data is the last field. Enter the proper path here or left-click the folder icon to the left of the field and find the proper directory with the File Browser.

✔ **You are using the /tmp directory for your simulations.** Initially, this doesn't seem like that big of a deal. However, on some operating systems, the /tmp directory is periodically purged, deleting everything in it. If this happens, your simulation won't show up and your only option is to re-bake it. Using /tmp all the time also has another nasty side effect: Different .blend files overwrite the simulation data that's in there. So you might run into a situation where you open one .blend with a fluid simulation only to see the simulation results from another file. Again, the only solution in case is to re-bake your simulation. This time, however, set the path somewhere else so this doesn't happen again.

Blender Doesn't Create Faces as Expected

So you're modeling along and having a good old time creating your next awesome creature. At some point along the line, though, you select four vertices with the intent of creating a quad, or four-side face, between them. Only instead of creating your nice quad when pressing F, Blender gives you two triangles, and they look all twisted. This is because the vertices are not *coplanar*, or all in the same plane in 3D space. Or Blender might give you an error that says "The selected vertices form a concave quad." A *concave face* is when a vertex is placed within the triangular shape formed by the other three vertices, as seen in Figure 16-2.

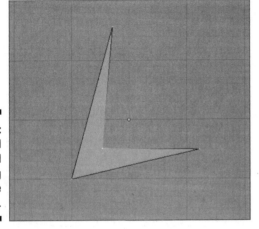

Figure 16-2:
You should
avoid
creating
concave
faces.

In either case, the solution is to move the offending vertex until the quad you want to form is convex and roughly coplanar. You can do this by manually moving the vertices around, or you can repeatedly use the Smooth operation (Editing buttons⇨Mesh Tools⇨Smooth or W⇨Smooth). This is a pretty common practice in Blender. In fact, the very cool Bassam Kurdali, director of *Elephants Dream,* found himself pressing the Smooth button so often, he actually made his own custom version of Blender that binds the T key to the Smooth operation so he wouldn't have to move his mouse as much! You don't necessarily have to go to those lengths, but it's great to know that the option is available.

Chapter 17

Ten Tips for Working More Effectively in Blender

Working in Blender is a ton of fun in any case, but you can get into a few good work habits to make the experience even more enjoyable. These good habits let you work faster without sacrificing the quality of your work. In this chapter, I detail ten of my best suggestions for working more efficiently and effectively in Blender.

Use Blender's Tooltips

Blender is a dense program. It's not uncommon for users to forget what a button does or come across a menu that they've never used before. This is especially true if don't use Blender for a while. If you don't know what a button in Blender does, hover your mouse pointer over it. More often than not, a helpful tooltip pops up that concisely describes what the button does. And even if it isn't completely clear, you have a better idea of what to search for to get help.

Constantly Check Models from Different Views

If you work in a single window environment, modeling and animating using just one 3D View window, you should definitely make it a point to periodically orbit around your scene and look at it from a bunch of different angles. This is particularly important when modeling because it's very easy to get a model that looks perfect from the front, but really distorted and goofy-shaped from one side. Split off another 3D View window if you need it, or use the numeric keypad hotkeys to quickly do spot-checks from different angles.

I also recommend taking advantage of the Smooth View option in the Views & Controls section of the user preferences. This option may seem like just simple eye candy at first, but it's actually quite helpful at helping you figure out which orientation you're viewing your scene from. See Chapter 2 to see how to modify this option.

Lock a Camera to an Animated Character

When animating a character, you may often run into a case where you're trying to animate a secondary detail on the character as he's moving. For situations like this, I like to create a new camera and parent it to the character. This way, the camera goes anywhere the character does. I find this very helpful for facial animation on a moving character. To do this, use the following steps:

1. **Add a new camera (spacebar⇨Add Camera) and put it in front of your character's face.**

2. **With the camera still selected, Shift+right-click the head bone of your character to add it to the selection.**

3. **Press Ctrl+P⇨Bone to parent the camera to the bone.**

    Now, wherever the head goes and whichever direction it turns, the camera is always looking at your character's face.

4. **Whenever you want to work on the facial animation for your character, select this camera and switch to its view by pressing Ctrl+Numpad 0.**

Also, you can bring up the View Properties floating panel (View⇨View Properties) and type in the name of the object you want to look at in the Object field under the View Locking label. This gives you a similar effect, but the view is locked on that object's centerpoint. I like using the camera method described above because it gives me a bit more control over what I'm looking at.

Occlude Background Geometry in Edit Mode

This tip leans a bit toward personal taste, but on complex models, Blender's default way of handling Edit mode can get to be a bit unwieldy. When you are using the Shaded, Solid, or Textured draw type, Blender makes all vertices, edges, and faces of an object visible, even if they are on the back of your model. This can make it difficult to right-click parts of the object that you really want to select. You might be trying to select a vertex on your character's face, but mistakenly pick one on the back of his head. Turning on the Occlude Background Geometry button (the second-to-last button in the 3D View's header with the cube icon) hides these vertices, edges, and faces on the back side of your object. If you need to select one of them, you can orbit around the scene to the other side and select it there. Or you can briefly switch to the Wireframe draw type by pressing Z and then selecting the back side geometry you want.

Name EVERYTHING (Organize Your Projects)

Each and every time you add something to your scene in Blender, make it a point to give it a name that makes sense. Trust me, it's a very disorienting feeling when you open a .blend file that you haven't worked on in a while and you see that your characters are Cube.001, Cube.012, and Sphere.007, and that really cool skin material you made is called Material.015. On small, one-shot projects it might not be so bad, but imagine a situation where you are working on putting materials on a totally sweet killer robot model. You remember that you'd made a model of a metal toolshed a few weeks back that has the perfect brushed aluminum look that you need. If you properly named that material, it's much easier to find.

And on larger projects, good organization is even more valuable. Not only is it smart to name everything in your .blend file, but it's also a good idea to have a good structure for your projects. For most of my projects, I have a separate directory for the project. Within that directory, I create sub-directories for my libraries of models, materials, textures, and finished renders. For animations, my renders directory is broken down even further into each shot. Of course, anyone who's seen my desk might never believe I'm that organized in my projects, but it's true! I promise!

Use Layers Effectively

Although there are only 20 available layers, Blender's layering system is very versatile and used for a variety of purposes. Objects can live on more than one layer, lights can be made to only illuminate the layers they are on, and you can use layers to animate the visibility of objects in your scene. As such, it's in your best interest to keep some form of organization in mind.

One of the things I like to do is place all of my models on the top row of layers (layers 1-10) and all other objects like lights, cameras, and armatures on the bottom row (layers 11-20). Another thing I like to do is keep "high priority" objects such as characters and animated things on the left-most layers, while keeping static objects like backgrounds on the right-most layers. Also, specifically for character animation, when I put my character in one layer, I place his rig in the layer directly below it. It's a little convention I like to stick to and it certainly is a help for me when I want to quickly make sense of a .blend file that I haven't opened in a long time.

Of course, this organizational style might not work for you, but you should definitely make it a point to create *some* conventions that you can remember and reuse.

Do Low-Resolution Test Renders

When you're finalizing the look of a model, you often have to make a quick change to the model and press F12 to see what it will look like when rendered. It's often a case of "hurry up and wait." If you're not careful, you could spend more time waiting for those little test renders than you do actually working on your model. When just doing test previews, here are a couple of tips for reducing the render time:

- ✔ **Turn off OSA.** OSA is *oversampling* and it's used to reduce *aliasing*, or that jaggy stair-stepping that happens around some edges in your renders. The way it works in Blender is by actually rendering the same section multiple times and averaging out the results to make those edges smoother. This is great for final renders, but can really eat up time when you just want to do a quick test. Disable OSA by left-clicking its button in the Render panel of the Scene buttons (F10).

- ✔ **Render at 50% or 25% size.** Most of the time, when you're doing a test, you don't really have to see what the full-sized final image will look like. This is especially true if the final render is for print or film, where the final resolution can be greater than 4000 pixels wide. Now, you could manually enter a smaller size in the Format panel of the Scene buttons, but Blender offers a faster way. If you look in the Render panel, you see a button that says 100% with buttons below it that say 75%, 50%, and 25%. Left-clicking any of these buttons makes Blender render your image at that percentage of the final size, thereby reducing the render time for your test preview.

- ✔ **Turn off computationally intensive features if you don't need them.** Features like ambient occlusion (AO), raytracing, and radiosity look great in a final render, but if you're just looking at the form of a model, they aren't necessarily needed for a test. You can turn off raytracing and radiosity in the Render panel of the Scene buttons. Turning off AO requires you to go to the World buttons (F8) and disable it in the Amb Occ tab.

✔ **Render just the layers you need.** If you're working on just one model in a scene and only want to do a test render for that model, disable the layers for other objects in the scene. As long as you have the object and lights in the scene, your test render will be helpful, accurate, and most importantly, speedy.

✔ **Use the Border Render feature.** If you're only interested in doing a test render on a particular part of your scene, switch to the camera view (Numpad 0) and use Border Render by pressing Shift+B and using your mouse to draw a box around the part of the shot you're interested in. When you finish doing tests, you can take this border off by left-clicking the Border button in the Render panel of the Scene buttons.

Mind Your Mouse

When you're using Blender's hotkeys to transform objects, where you place your mouse cursor before performing the operation is pretty important. This is particularly true for rotating and scaling. For rotating, it's a good practice to keep your mouse distant from the object's center point. Doing so gives you more control over how you rotate. With your mouse cursor too close to the center, you can have your object spinning in all kinds of unpredictable ways. The same is true for scaling, but it's more dependent on whether you are scaling up or down. If you are scaling up, it makes sense to bring your mouse cursor a bit closer to the selection's center point so you don't hit the edge of your screen before you get the object to the size you want. If you're scaling down, start with your mouse cursor farther away from the selection's center point and, as with rotation, you have more control of how small your object can get. For grabbing, it's a bit less important, but I generally like to have my mouse somewhere near my object's center point.

Turn on Passepartout for Your Camera

In the non-Blender world, a *passepartout* has a few definitions, including "master key" and a reference to a character in *Around the World in 80 Days*. The main definition that's used in Blender is a kind of ornamental mat that's used to frame a picture. In Blender, it's used in much the same way for camera objects. By default, cameras have this option turned off, but I find it to be very useful. To enable it, select your camera by right-clicking on it and switch to the camera's view (Numpad 0). In the Editing buttons (F9) within the Camera panel is a Passepartout button on the right-hand side, as seen in Figure 17-1. Left-clicking this button enables it and you should notice that the area in your 3D View that is out of the camera's viewable area is darkened. You can adjust just how much it's darkened to match your tastes by modifying the Alpha slider beneath the Passepartout button. I usually set mine to around 0.700.

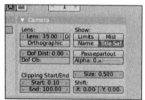

Figure 17-1:
The Passe-
partout
button is on
the right of
the Camera
panel.

Have Fun, but Take Breaks

Don't be afraid to just play with Blender. If you ever find yourself wondering "What does this button do?" just press it and find out. Now, if you're working on something important, you should probably save first, but definitely make it a point to experiment and try things out. By this kind of playing, not only can you figure out how to use new parts of Blender, but you can also find new ways of using existing features in cool ways that might not have been intended.

Working in 3D can be incredibly serious fun, but it can also be a bit addictive. I certainly have had days in the past where I would sit down to work in Blender in the morning, and, the next time I looked away from the monitor, the sky would be dark and I'd realize that I missed lunch and was on my way to missing dinner, too. Not only is this unhealthy, but, ultimately, it can hurt the quality of your work. Now, I'm obviously the last person who would ever tell you to stop working when you're "in the zone," but try to step away from the computer for a bit to rest your eyes, get some food, stretch your legs, or even talk to another human being. (Chatting on IRC doesn't count! Remember, *away* from the computer.) If you do this for just ten minutes every few hours, you come back to the computer refreshed, more productive, and you might even have a solution for getting rid of that nasty triangle in your mesh.

Appendix

About the CD

*W*hat would any Blender book be without a disk full of goodies on it? Well, hopefully the world will never know. The CD that comes with this book is packed not only with copies of Blender for Linux, Windows, and Macintosh platforms, but also with example files for each chapter and a copy of the movie *Big Buck Bunny* in high resolution . . . you know, for creative inspiration. I wanted to make sure that every megabyte of the CD had something worthwhile on it. This chapter goes though the content of the disk and explains how to get at it.

System Requirements

Make sure that your computer meets the minimum system requirements shown in the following list. If your computer doesn't match up to most of these requirements, you may have problems using the software and files on the CD. For the latest and greatest information, please refer to the ReadMe file located at the root of the CD-ROM.

- ✔ A PC running Microsoft Windows or Linux with kernel 2.4 or later.
- ✔ A Macintosh running Mac OS X or later.
- ✔ A video card that supports accelerated OpenGL graphics. Most modern cards support this, but you should double-check yours.
- ✔ A CD-ROM drive.

If you need more information on the basics, check out these books published by Wiley Publishing, Inc.: *PCs For Dummies* by Dan Gookin; *Macs For Dummies* by Edward C. Baig; *iMacs For Dummies* by Mark L. Chambers; *Windows XP For Dummies* and *Windows Vista For Dummies,* both by Andy Rathbone.

Using the CD

To install the items from the CD to your hard drive, follow these steps.

1. **Insert the CD into your computer's CD-ROM drive.**

   The license agreement appears.

   Note to Windows users: The interface won't launch if you have autorun disabled. In that case, choose Start⇨Run. (For Windows Vista, choose Start⇨All Programs⇨Accessories⇨Run.) In the dialog box that appears, type *D:\Start.exe*. (Replace *D* with the proper letter if your CD drive uses a different letter. If you don't know the letter, see how your CD drive is listed under My Computer.) Click OK.

   Note for Mac Users: When the CD icon appears on your desktop, double-click the icon to open the CD and double-click the Start icon.

   Note for Linux Users: The specifics of mounting and using CDs vary greatly between different versions of Linux. Please see the manual or help information for your specific system if you experience trouble using this CD. In most cases, the CD should be automatically mounted and an icon for it appears on your desktop. Double-click this icon to browse the contents of the CD.

2. **Read through the license agreement and then click the Accept button if you want to use the CD.**

   The CD interface appears. The interface allows you to browse the contents and install Blender with just a click of a button (or two).

What You'll Find on the CD

The following sections are arranged by category and provide a summary of the software and other goodies you'll find on the CD. If you need help with installing the items provided on the CD, refer to the installation instructions in the preceding section.

For each program listed, I provide the program platform (Linux, Windows, or Mac) plus the type of software. The programs fall into one of the following categories:

- ✔ *Shareware programs* are fully functional, free, trial versions of copy-righted programs. If you like particular programs, register with their authors for a nominal fee and receive licenses, enhanced versions, and technical support.

- ✔ *Freeware programs* are free, copyrighted games, applications, and utilities. You can copy them to as many computers as you like — for free — but they offer no technical support.

- ✔ *GNU software* is governed by its own license, which is included inside the folder of the GNU software. There are no restrictions on distribution of GNU software. See the GNU license at the root of the CD for more details.

- ✔ *Trial, demo,* or *evaluation* versions of software are usually limited either by time or functionality (such as not letting you save a project after you create it).

Author-created material

For all operating systems. All the examples provided in this book are located in the Author directory on the CD and work on any machine that can run Blender. These are the .blend files that were used to create many of the figures in this book. When you open each file in Blender, you see a Text Editor window that explains the content of the file and usually gives you suggestions or tasks to complete in the file. The structure of the examples directory is

```
Author/Chapter1
Author/Chapter2
```

Also included is a Bonus Chapter that details ten online resources to help you get in touch with the Blender community and stay current on developments in the software.

Big Buck Bunny

Creative Commons Attribution 3.0 License.

For all operating systems. Big Buck Bunny is the second open movie project created by the Blender Foundation. The purpose was to assemble a small team of 3D artists to create a "funny and furry" movie with Blender. Because of this project, Blender gained quite a few features that you can now take full advantage of. You can read more about it and even download the project's .blend files for free at www.bigbuckbunny.org.

Blender

GNU software.

For Linux, Windows, and Mac OS. You can't have a CD accompanying a book on Blender without including a copy of Blender itself. That would just be crazy! On the CD is a copy of the current stable version of Blender, version 2.48a, for each of the major operating systems, including 32-bit Windows, Intel Macintosh, and 32-bit Linux. Everything in this book is tailored to that version of Blender and the provided sample files all work with it. If you're using a 64-bit operating system, Mac OS on a PowerPC computer, or Solaris, head on over to `www.blender.org` to get a copy for those platforms.

VLC

GNU software.

For Linux, Windows, and Mac OS. VLC is short for Video LAN Client, and it's an excellent media player that plays nearly any sound or movie file that you throw at it. I've included it on the CD-ROM because occasionally Windows Media Player or QuickTime have trouble playing some movie formats. If you have problems playing *Big Buck Bunny* in one of those players, give VLC a try. For more information on VLC, check out `www.videolan.org/vlc`.

Troubleshooting

Blender works admirably on most computers with the minimum system requirements. It even runs on my mobile phone! Alas, your computer may differ, and Blender may not work properly for some reason.

The two likeliest problems are that you don't have enough memory (RAM) for the programs you want to use, or you have other programs running that are affecting installation or running of a program. If you get an error message such as `Not enough memory` or `Setup cannot continue`, try one or more of the following suggestions and then try using the software again:

- **Turn off any antivirus software running on your computer.** Installation programs sometimes mimic virus activity and may make your computer incorrectly believe that it's being infected by a virus.

- **Close all running programs.** The more programs you have running, the less memory is available to other programs. Installation programs typically update files and programs; so if you keep other programs running, installation may not work properly.

✔ **Have your local computer store add more RAM to your computer.** This is, admittedly, a drastic and somewhat expensive step. However, adding more memory can really help the speed of your computer and allow more programs to run at the same time.

Customer Care

If you have trouble with the CD-ROM, please call Wiley Product Technical Support at 800-762-2974. Outside the United States, call 317-572-3993. You can also contact Wiley Product Technical Support at `http://support.wiley.com`. Wiley Publishing provides technical support only for installation and other general quality control items. For technical support on the applications themselves, consult the program's vendor or author.

To place additional orders or to request information about other Wiley products, please call 877-762-2974.

Index

GNU GENERAL PUBLIC LICENSE

Version 3, 29 June 2007

Copyright © 2007 Free Software Foundation, Inc. <http://fsf.org/>

Everyone is permitted to copy and distribute verbatim copies of this license document, but changing it is not allowed.

Preamble

The GNU General Public License is a free, copyleft license for software and other kinds of works.

The licenses for most software and other practical works are designed to take away your freedom to share and change the works. By contrast, the GNU General Public License is intended to guarantee your freedom to share and change all versions of a program–to make sure it remains free software for all its users. We, the Free Software Foundation, use the GNU General Public License for most of our software; it applies also to any other work released this way by its authors. You can apply it to your programs, too.

When we speak of free software, we are referring to freedom, not price. Our General Public Licenses are designed to make sure that you have the freedom to distribute copies of free software (and charge for them if you wish), that you receive source code or can get it if you want it, that you can change the software or use pieces of it in new free programs, and that you know you can do these things.

To protect your rights, we need to prevent others from denying you these rights or asking you to surrender the rights. Therefore, you have certain responsibilities if you distribute copies of the software, or if you modify it: responsibilities to respect the freedom of others.

For example, if you distribute copies of such a program, whether gratis or for a fee, you must pass on to the recipients the same freedoms that you received. You must make sure that they, too, receive or can get the source code. And you must show them these terms so they know their rights.

Developers that use the GNU GPL protect your rights with two steps: (1) assert copyright on the software, and (2) offer you this License giving you legal permission to copy, distribute and/or modify it.

For the developers' and authors' protection, the GPL clearly explains that there is no warranty for this free software. For both users' and authors' sake, the GPL requires that modified versions be marked as changed, so that their problems will not be attributed erroneously to authors of previous versions.

Some devices are designed to deny users access to install or run modified versions of the software inside them, although the manufacturer can do so. This is fundamentally incompatible with the aim of protecting users' freedom to change the software. The systematic pattern of such abuse occurs in the area of products for individuals to use, which is precisely where it is most unacceptable. Therefore, we have designed this version of the GPL to prohibit the practice for those products. If such problems arise substantially in other domains, we stand ready to extend this provision to those domains in future versions of the GPL, as needed to protect the freedom of users.

Finally, every program is threatened constantly by software patents. States should not allow patents to restrict development and use of software on general-purpose computers, but in those that do, we wish to avoid the special danger that patents applied to a free program could make it effectively proprietary. To prevent this, the GPL assures that patents cannot be used to render the program non-free.

The precise terms and conditions for copying, distribution and modification follow.

TERMS AND CONDITIONS

0. Definitions. "This License" refers to version 3 of the GNU General Public License. "Copyright" also means copyright-like laws that apply to other kinds of works, such as semiconductor masks. "The Program" refers to any copyrightable work licensed under this License. Each licensee is addressed as "you". "Licensees" and "recipients" may be individuals or organizations. To "modify" a work means to copy from or adapt all or part of the work in a fashion requiring copyright permission, other than the making of an exact copy. The resulting work is called a "modified version" of the earlier work or a work "based on" the earlier work. A "covered work" means either the unmodified Program or a work based on the Program.

    To "propagate" a work means to do anything with it that, without permission, would make you directly or secondarily liable for infringement under applicable copyright law, except executing it on a computer or modifying a private copy. Propagation includes copying, distribution (with or without modification), making available to the public, and in some countries other activities as well.

    To "convey" a work means any kind of propagation that enables other parties to make or receive copies. Mere interaction with a user through a computer network, with no transfer of a copy, is not conveying.

    An interactive user interface displays "Appropriate Legal Notices" to the extent that it includes a convenient and prominently visible feature that (1) displays an appropriate copyright notice, and (2) tells the user that there is no warranty for the work (except to the extent that warranties are provided), that licensees may convey the work under this License, and how to view a copy of this License. If the interface presents a list of user commands or options, such as a menu, a prominent item in the list meets this criterion.

1. Source Code. T he "source code" for a work means the preferred form of the work for making modifications to it. "Object code" means any non-source form of a work. A "Standard Interface" means an interface that either is an official standard defined by a recognized standards body, or, in the case of interfaces specified for a particular programming language, one that is widely used among developers working in that language.

    The "System Libraries" of an executable work include anything, other than the work as a whole, that (a) is included in the normal form of packaging a Major Component, but which is not part of that Major Component, and (b) serves only to enable use of the work with that Major Component, or to implement a Standard Interface for which an implementation is available to the public in source code form. A "Major Component", in this context, means a major essential component (kernel, window system, and so on) of the specific operating system (if any) on which the executable work runs, or a compiler used to produce the work, or an object code interpreter used to run it.

    The "Corresponding Source" for a work in object code form means all the source code needed to generate, install, and (for an executable work) run the object code and to modify the work, including scripts to control those activities. However, it does not include the work's System Libraries, or general-purpose tools or generally available free programs which are used unmodified in performing those activities but which are not part of the work. For example, Corresponding Source includes interface definition files associated with source files for the work, and the source code for shared libraries and dynamically linked subprograms that the work is specifically designed to require, such as by intimate data communication or control flow between those subprograms and other parts of the work.

    The Corresponding Source need not include anything that users can regenerate automatically from other parts of the Corresponding Source.

    The Corresponding Source for a work in source code form is that same work.

2. Basic Permissions. All rights granted under this License are granted for the term of copyright on the Program, and are irrevocable provided the stated conditions are met. This License explicitly affirms your unlimited permission to run the unmodified Program. The output from running a covered work is covered by this License only if the output, given its content, constitutes a covered work. This License acknowledges your rights of fair use or other equivalent, as provided by copyright law.

   You may make, run and propagate covered works that you do not convey, without conditions so long as your license otherwise remains in force. You may convey covered works to others for the sole purpose of having them make modifications exclusively for you, or provide you with facilities for running those works, provided that you comply with the terms of this License in conveying all material for which you do not control copyright. Those thus making or running the covered works for you must do so exclusively on your behalf, under your direction and control, on terms that prohibit them from making any copies of your copyrighted material outside their relationship with you.

   Conveying under any other circumstances is permitted solely under the conditions stated below. Sublicensing is not allowed; section 10 makes it unnecessary.

3. Protecting Users' Legal Rights From Anti-Circumvention Law. No covered work shall be deemed part of an effective technological measure under any applicable law fulfilling obligations under article 11 of the WIPO copyright treaty adopted on 20 December 1996, or similar laws prohibiting or restricting circumvention of such measures.

   When you convey a covered work, you waive any legal power to forbid circumvention of technological measures to the extent such circumvention is effected by exercising rights under this License with respect to the covered work, and you disclaim any intention to limit operation or modification of the work as a means of enforcing, against the work's users, your or third parties' legal rights to forbid circumvention of technological measures.

4. Conveying Verbatim Copies. You may convey verbatim copies of the Program's source code as you receive it, in any medium, provided that you conspicuously and appropriately publish on each copy an appropriate copyright notice; keep intact all notices stating that this License and any non-permissive terms added in accord with section 7 apply to the code; keep intact all notices of the absence of any warranty; and give all recipients a copy of this License along with the Program.

   You may charge any price or no price for each copy that you convey, and you may offer support or warranty protection for a fee.

5. Conveying Modified Source Versions. You may convey a work based on the Program, or the modifications to produce it from the Program, in the form of source code under the terms of section 4, provided that you also meet all of these conditions:

   a) The work must carry prominent notices stating that you modified it, and giving a relevant date.

   b) The work must carry prominent notices stating that it is released under this License and any conditions added under section 7. This requirement modifies the requirement in section 4 to "keep intact all notices".

   c) You must license the entire work, as a whole, under this License to anyone who comes into possession of a copy. This License will therefore apply, along with any applicable section 7 additional terms, to the whole of the work, and all its parts, regardless of how they are packaged. This License gives no permission to license the work in any other way, but it does not invalidate such permission if you have separately received it.

   d) If the work has interactive user interfaces, each must display Appropriate Legal Notices; however, if the Program has interactive interfaces that do not display Appropriate Legal Notices, your work need not make them do so.

A compilation of a covered work with other separate and independent works, which are not by their nature extensions of the covered work, and which are not combined with it such as to form a larger program, in or on a volume of a storage or distribution medium, is called an "aggregate" if the compilation and its resulting copyright are not used to limit the access or legal rights of the compilation's users beyond what the individual works permit. Inclusion of a covered work in an aggregate does not cause this License to apply to the other parts of the aggregate.

6. Conveying Non-Source Forms. You may convey a covered work in object code form under the terms of sections 4 and 5, provided that you also convey the machine-readable Corresponding Source under the terms of this License, in one of these ways:

   a) Convey the object code in, or embodied in, a physical product (including a physical distribution medium), accompanied by the Corresponding Source fixed on a durable physical medium customarily used for software interchange.

   b) Convey the object code in, or embodied in, a physical product (including a physical distribution medium), accompanied by a written offer, valid for at least three years and valid for as long as you offer spare parts or customer support for that product model, to give anyone who possesses the object code either (1) a copy of the Corresponding Source for all the software in the product that is covered by this License, on a durable physical medium customarily used for software interchange, for a price no more than your reasonable cost of physically performing this conveying of source, or (2) access to copy the Corresponding Source from a network server at no charge.

   c) Convey individual copies of the object code with a copy of the written offer to provide the Corresponding Source. This alternative is allowed only occasionally and noncommercially, and only if you received the object code with such an offer, in accord with subsection 6b.

   d) Convey the object code by offering access from a designated place (gratis or for a charge), and offer equivalent access to the Corresponding Source in the same way through the same place at no further charge. You need not require recipients to copy the Corresponding Source along with the object code. If the place to copy the object code is a network server, the Corresponding Source may be on a different server (operated by you or a third party) that supports equivalent copying facilities, provided you maintain clear directions next to the object code saying where to find the Corresponding Source. Regardless of what server hosts the Corresponding Source, you remain obligated to ensure that it is available for as long as needed to satisfy these requirements.

   e) Convey the object code using peer-to-peer transmission, provided you inform other peers where the object code and Corresponding Source of the work are being offered to the general public at no charge under subsection 6d.

A separable portion of the object code, whose source code is excluded from the Corresponding Source as a System Library, need not be included in conveying the object code work.

A "User Product" is either (1) a "consumer product", which means any tangible personal property which is normally used for personal, family, or household purposes, or (2) anything designed or sold for incorporation into a dwelling. In determining whether a product is a consumer product, doubtful cases shall be resolved in favor of coverage. For a particular product received by a particular user, "normally used" refers to a typical or common use of that class of product, regardless of the status of the particular user or of the way in which the particular user actually uses, or expects or is expected to use, the product. A product is a consumer product regardless of whether the product has substantial commercial, industrial or non-consumer uses, unless such uses represent the only significant mode of use of the product.

"Installation Information" for a User Product means any methods, procedures, authorization keys, or other information required to install and execute modified versions of a covered work in that User Product from a modified version of its Corresponding Source. The information must suffice to ensure that the continued functioning of the modified object code is in no case prevented or interfered with solely because modification has been made.

If you convey an object code work under this section in, or with, or specifically for use in, a User Product, and the conveying occurs as part of a transaction in which the right of possession and use of the User Product is transferred to the recipient in perpetuity or for a fixed term (regardless of how the transaction is characterized), the Corresponding Source conveyed under this section must be accompanied by the Installation Information. But this requirement does not apply if neither you nor any third party retains the ability to install modified object code on the User Product (for example, the work has been installed in ROM).

The requirement to provide Installation Information does not include a requirement to continue to provide support service, warranty, or updates for a work that has been modified or installed by the recipient, or for the User Product in which it has been modified or installed. Access to a network may be denied when the modification itself materially and adversely affects the operation of the network or violates the rules and protocols for communication across the network.

Corresponding Source conveyed, and Installation Information provided, in accord with this section must be in a format that is publicly documented (and with an implementation available to the public in source code form), and must require no special password or key for unpacking, reading or copying.

7. Additional Terms. "Additional permissions" are terms that supplement the terms of this License by making exceptions from one or more of its conditions. Additional permissions that are applicable to the entire Program shall be treated as though they were included in this License, to the extent that they are valid under applicable law. If additional permissions apply only to part of the Program, that part may be used separately under those permissions, but the entire Program remains governed by this License without regard to the additional permissions.

When you convey a copy of a covered work, you may at your option remove any additional permissions from that copy, or from any part of it. (Additional permissions may be written to require their own removal in certain cases when you modify the work.) You may place additional permissions on material, added by you to a covered work, for which you have or can give appropriate copyright permission.

Notwithstanding any other provision of this License, for material you add to a covered work, you may (if authorized by the copyright holders of that material) supplement the terms of this License with terms:

a) Disclaiming warranty or limiting liability differently from the terms of sections 15 and 16 of this License; or

b) Requiring preservation of specified reasonable legal notices or author attributions in that material or in the Appropriate Legal Notices displayed by works containing it; or

c) Prohibiting misrepresentation of the origin of that material, or requiring that modified versions of such material be marked in reasonable ways as different from the original version; or

d) Limiting the use for publicity purposes of names of licensors or authors of the material; or

e) Declining to grant rights under trademark law for use of some trade names, trademarks, or service marks; or

f) Requiring indemnification of licensors and authors of that material by anyone who conveys the material (or modified versions of it) with contractual assumptions of liability to the recipient, for any liability that these contractual assumptions directly impose on those licensors and authors.

All other non-permissive additional terms are considered "further restrictions" within the meaning of section 10. If the Program as you received it, or any part of it, contains a notice stating that it is governed by this License along with a term that is a further restriction, you may remove that term. If a license document contains a further restriction but permits relicensing or conveying under this License, you may add to a covered work material governed by the terms of that license document, provided that the further restriction does not survive such relicensing or conveying.

If you add terms to a covered work in accord with this section, you must place, in the relevant source files, a statement of the additional terms that apply to those files, or a notice indicating where to find the applicable terms.

Additional terms, permissive or non-permissive, may be stated in the form of a separately written license, or stated as exceptions; the above requirements apply either way.

8. Termination. You may not propagate or modify a covered work except as expressly provided under this License. Any attempt otherwise to propagate or modify it is void, and will automatically terminate your rights under this License (including any patent licenses granted under the third paragraph of section 11).

However, if you cease all violation of this License, then your license from a particular copyright holder is reinstated (a) provisionally, unless and until the copyright holder explicitly and finally terminates your license, and (b) permanently, if the copyright holder fails to notify you of the violation by some reasonable means prior to 60 days after the cessation.

Moreover, your license from a particular copyright holder is reinstated permanently if the copyright holder notifies you of the violation by some reasonable means, this is the first time you have received notice of violation of this License (for any work) from that copyright holder, and you cure the violation prior to 30 days after your receipt of the notice.

Termination of your rights under this section does not terminate the licenses of parties who have received copies or rights from you under this License. If your rights have been terminated and not permanently reinstated, you do not qualify to receive new licenses for the same material under section 10.

9. Acceptance Not Required for Having Copies. You are not required to accept this License in order to receive or run a copy of the Program. Ancillary propagation of a covered work occurring solely as a consequence of using peer-to-peer transmission to receive a copy likewise does not require acceptance. However, nothing other than this License grants you permission to propagate or modify any covered work. These actions infringe copyright if you do not accept this License. Therefore, by modifying or propagating a covered work, you indicate your acceptance of this License to do so.

10. Automatic Licensing of Downstream Recipients. Each time you convey a covered work, the recipient automatically receives a license from the original licensors, to run, modify and propagate that work, subject to this License. You are not responsible for enforcing compliance by third parties with this License.

An "entity transaction" is a transaction transferring control of an organization, or substantially all assets of one, or subdividing an organization, or merging organizations. If propagation of a covered work results from an entity transaction, each party to that transaction who receives a copy of the work also receives whatever licenses to the work the party's predecessor in interest had or could give under the previous paragraph, plus a right to possession of the Corresponding Source of the work from the predecessor in interest, if the predecessor has it or can get it with reasonable efforts.

You may not impose any further restrictions on the exercise of the rights granted or affirmed under this License. For example, you may not impose a license fee, royalty, or other charge for exercise of rights granted under this License, and you may not initiate litigation (including a cross-claim or counterclaim in a lawsuit) alleging that any patent claim is infringed by making, using, selling, offering for sale, or importing the Program or any portion of it.

11. Patents. A "contributor" is a copyright holder who authorizes use under this License of the Program or a work on which the Program is based. The work thus licensed is called the contributor's "contributor version".

A contributor's "essential patent claims" are all patent claims owned or controlled by the contributor, whether already acquired or hereafter acquired, that would be infringed by some manner, permitted by this License, of making, using, or selling its contributor version, but do not include claims that would be infringed only as a consequence of further modification of the contributor version. For purposes of this definition, "control" includes the right to grant patent sublicenses in a manner consistent with the requirements of this License.

Each contributor grants you a non-exclusive, worldwide, royalty-free patent license under the contributor's essential patent claims, to make, use, sell, offer for sale, import and otherwise run, modify and propagate the contents of its contributor version.

In the following three paragraphs, a "patent license" is any express agreement or commitment, however denominated, not to enforce a patent (such as an express permission to practice a patent or covenant not to sue for patent infringement). To "grant" such a patent license to a party means to make such an agreement or commitment not to enforce a patent against the party.

If you convey a covered work, knowingly relying on a patent license, and the Corresponding Source of the work is not available for anyone to copy, free of charge and under the terms of this License, through a publicly available network server or other readily accessible means, then you must either (1) cause the Corresponding Source to be so available, or (2) arrange to deprive yourself of the benefit of the patent license for this particular work, or (3) arrange, in a manner consistent with the requirements of this License, to extend the patent license to downstream recipients. "Knowingly relying" means you have actual knowledge that, but for the patent license, your conveying the covered work in a country, or your recipient's use of the covered work in a country, would infringe one or more identifiable patents in that country that you have reason to believe are valid.

If, pursuant to or in connection with a single transaction or arrangement, you convey, or propagate by procuring conveyance of, a covered work, and grant a patent license to some of the parties receiving the covered work authorizing them to use, propagate, modify or convey a specific copy of the covered work, then the patent license you grant is automatically extended to all recipients of the covered work and works based on it.

A patent license is "discriminatory" if it does not include within the scope of its coverage, prohibits the exercise of, or is conditioned on the non-exercise of one or more of the rights that are specifically granted under this License. You may not convey a covered work if you are a party to an arrangement with a third party that is in the business of distributing software, under which you make payment to the third party based on the extent of your activity of conveying the work, and under which the third party grants, to any of the parties who would receive the covered work from you, a discriminatory patent license (a) in connection with copies of the covered work conveyed by you (or copies made from those copies), or (b) primarily for and in connection with specific products or compilations that contain the covered work, unless you entered into that arrangement, or that patent license was granted, prior to 28 March 2007.

Nothing in this License shall be construed as excluding or limiting any implied license or other defenses to infringement that may otherwise be available to you under applicable patent law.

12. No Surrender of Others' Freedom. If conditions are imposed on you (whether by court order, agreement or otherwise) that contradict the conditions of this License, they do not excuse you from the conditions of this License. If you cannot convey a covered work so as to satisfy simultaneously your obligations under this License and any other pertinent obligations, then as a consequence you may not convey it at all. For example, if you agree to terms that obligate you to collect a royalty for further conveying from those to whom you convey the Program, the only way you could satisfy both those terms and this License would be to refrain entirely from conveying the Program.

13. Use with the GNU Affero General Public License. Notwithstanding any other provision of this License, you have permission to link or combine any covered work with a work licensed under version 3 of the GNU Affero General Public License into a single combined work, and to convey the resulting work. The terms of this License will continue to apply to the part which is the covered work, but the special requirements of the GNU Affero General Public License, section 13, concerning interaction through a network will apply to the combination as such.

14. Revised Versions of this License. The Free Software Foundation may publish revised and/or new versions of the GNU General Public License from time to time. Such new versions will be similar in spirit to the present version, but may differ in detail to address new problems or concerns.

   Each version is given a distinguishing version number. If the Program specifies that a certain numbered version of the GNU General Public License "or any later version" applies to it, you have the option of following the terms and conditions either of that numbered version or of any later version published by the Free Software Foundation. If the Program does not specify a version number of the GNU General Public License, you may choose any version ever published by the Free Software Foundation.

   If the Program specifies that a proxy can decide which future versions of the GNU General Public License can be used, that proxy's public statement of acceptance of a version permanently authorizes you to choose that version for the Program.

   Later license versions may give you additional or different permissions. However, no additional obligations are imposed on any author or copyright holder as a result of your choosing to follow a later version.

15. Disclaimer of Warranty. THERE IS NO WARRANTY FOR THE PROGRAM, TO THE EXTENT PERMITTED BY APPLICABLE LAW. EXCEPT WHEN OTHERWISE STATED IN WRITING THE COPYRIGHT HOLDERS AND/OR OTHER PARTIES PROVIDE THE PROGRAM "AS IS" WITHOUT WARRANTY OF ANY KIND, EITHER EXPRESSED OR IMPLIED, INCLUDING, BUT NOT LIMITED TO, THE IMPLIED WARRANTIES OF MERCHANTABILITY AND FITNESS FOR A PARTICULAR PURPOSE. THE ENTIRE RISK AS TO THE QUALITY AND PERFORMANCE OF THE PROGRAM IS WITH YOU. SHOULD THE PROGRAM PROVE DEFECTIVE, YOU ASSUME THE COST OF ALL NECESSARY SERVICING, REPAIR OR CORRECTION.

16. Limitation of Liability. IN NO EVENT UNLESS REQUIRED BY APPLICABLE LAW OR AGREED TO IN WRITING WILL ANY COPYRIGHT HOLDER, OR ANY OTHER PARTY WHO MODIFIES AND/OR CONVEYS THE PROGRAM AS PERMITTED ABOVE, BE LIABLE TO YOU FOR DAMAGES, INCLUDING ANY GENERAL, SPECIAL, INCIDENTAL OR CONSEQUENTIAL DAMAGES ARISING OUT OF THE USE OR INABILITY TO USE THE PROGRAM (INCLUDING BUT NOT LIMITED TO LOSS OF DATA OR DATA BEING RENDERED INACCURATE OR LOSSES SUSTAINED BY YOU OR THIRD PARTIES OR A FAILURE OF THE PROGRAM TO OPERATE WITH ANY OTHER PROGRAMS), EVEN IF SUCH HOLDER OR OTHER PARTY HAS BEEN ADVISED OF THE POSSIBILITY OF SUCH DAMAGES.

17. Interpretation of Sections 15 and 16. If the disclaimer of warranty and limitation of liability provided above cannot be given local legal effect according to their terms, reviewing courts shall apply local law that most closely approximates an absolute waiver of all civil liability in connection with the Program, unless a warranty or assumption of liability accompanies a copy of the Program in return for a fee.

END OF TERMS AND CONDITIONS